THE STEPHENS-SARLÓS PROGRAM

Rewiring the Brain Using Sensorimotor Therapy

Elizabeth Stephens-Sarlós

THE STEPHENS-SARLÓS PROGRAM

Rewiring the Brain Using Sensorimotor Therapy

ELIZABETH STEPHENS-SARLÓS

STEPHENS - SARLÓS
SENSORIMOTOR DEVELOPMENT

2023

Translated by the author and Patrick Stephens

First published in 2023

Illustrations & cover design: Zsolt Kecseti
Layout: Péter Hári
Editor: Selena Class

Originally published in Hungarian under the title
A Stephens-Sarlós Program
by Kulcslyuk Kiadó in 2022

ISBN 978-615-01-8409-8

drsarlos.com

CONTENTS

Preface	7
Introduction	9
Help! Something is wrong!	11
A brief history	14
It's all based on movement	25
The infant within us, and the primitive reflexes	30
Theories in sensorimotor development	41
Sensorimotor integration	48
The symphony of sensory perception and sensation	56
The sense of balance in the labyrinth	58
The world of our eyes	65
I hear, I understand, I answer	73
Outside and within	82
Touch	88
Tastes, flavors, smells	93
Move it! ... and more	100
Research, studies, results	104
When, what, how, and for whom?	111
The problem, and clarifying the origin of the problem	113
Age group	117
Performing the exercises: warm-up, intensity, number of repetitions, rest time, correction of errors, cool-down	119
Regression	123
Other questions related to the exercise program	127
What you need to know before doing the exercises	131
ADHD	134
Fecal retention	157
Bedwetting	176
Delayed speech and language development, and other problems related to speech formation	194
Autism spectrum disorder	219
Dyslexia and dysgraphia	256

Clumsiness 286
Anxiety, excitement, sleepless nights 305
"Your tiny little hand fits perfectly in mine" 321
An old man is not an obsolete man 339
About sensory activities 355
Primitive reflexes: symptom checklists and test exercises 364

Acknowledgments 380
Glossary 382
Bibliography 389

PREFACE

Anyone who picks up this book has a reason for doing so. Presumably, they want to get help for themselves or, more likely, for their child. The sooner help arrives, the better. This book was created to help, but I ask the reader not to be impatient. Please read the chapters carefully. Some parts may seem familiar. You might even feel like it's written about your child (or yourself). The theoretical part provides background to help understand the processes behind the problems—those of your child or yourself. Many more people are in similar situations than we think; many children and adults need help, according to their individual issues.

In this book, I discuss the role of primitive (sometimes called infant) reflexes and why it is a problem if they do not disappear in time or do not "merge" into another reflex. I write about the role of movement, how it affects our nervous system, and how it shapes our brain, behavior, and experiences. I provide a glimpse into the history of reflex research and briefly introduce sensorimotor development researchers and their hypotheses. I try to explain how the functioning of primitive reflexes is related to the processing of sensory stimuli, and how our sensory organs process the stimuli from the world around us and our internal environment.

Afterwards, I present some research and results that are related to the topic. I write about whom I recommend the training for, and which problems and symptoms may be caused by neurological immaturity. I will list important things to know about performing the exercises, and then discuss the regression symptoms that may be associated with the training.

I will answer questions such as whether it is possible to do sports while doing the exercises, and for whom the training is not recommended. I will also try to provide answers about why children do not develop equally and how to motivate them. After that, the training exercises follow, which I have put together based on problem types. The exercises in the book are very simple. Many of them are part of a normal physical education lesson plan, and some of them can be found in the repertoire of yoga exercises. While some may be accessible on the internet, nowhere are they completely organized for the purposes of primitive reflex integration.

There are other exercises that can help with reflex integration, but this book is already voluminous, and I have chosen the included exercises because they are the easiest to perform and require no special skills.

Following the exercises, I also recommend sensory development tasks for each sense as a supplement to the training. Everyone can choose from these as they please.

Finally, there are checklists of the symptoms that are the most characteristic of each undeveloped primitive reflex. Together with these checklists, I present simple exercises that can be used to test the reflex profile of the individual.

The meanings and explanations of medical terms can be found in the glossary at the end of the book.

Those who flip quickly through the book will see that I recommend exercises for children of all ages, including very young children, to young adults, older adults, and even those over 80. Why? You will find the answer to this question by reading the book.

I wish you happy reading and above all, success with the exercises and good health!

INTRODUCTION

Why can't my son concentrate, even though he has an exceptional memory? Why isn't my three-year-old speaking yet? Why does my six-year-old son still wet the bed? Why can't I perform as well in competitions as I do in practice? Why can't my daughter follow the sheet music while playing the violin? Why can't my grandchild sit still for even two minutes? Why? Why? Why? I too asked this same question: WHY? Why did I discover that only 50% or less of the five-, six-, and seven-year-old children I studied as part of my doctoral research had the sensory and motor skills necessary for starting school?

Similar results were found in the UK in 2021, where a study of 120 children about to start school found that 73 of them, or 60.8%, still had many primitive reflexes that should have disappeared by the age of two or 2½. Swedish, Spanish, Indian, and American scientists found similar results with slight variations.

When a child's sensorimotor system is immature, they have great difficulty in reaching, or are unable to achieve, the results in school that their innate intelligence should enable them to. The tension that arises in young children due to the difference between their actual and potential performances often manifests in their behavior and social relationships. The problems parents, and I, often ask about stem from the same underlying issue: immaturity of the nervous system.

As the symptoms of an immature nervous system often overlap with symptoms of other diagnoses, a child may not receive the treatment, therapy, or training that leads to a solution. Often, the correct diagnosis—and thus treatment—involves a much longer and winding road to "recovery" than is necessary. Foreign literature suggests, and my own experience agrees, that caution must be exercised in making diagnoses until someone's nervous system reaches the appropriate level of maturity for their age.

I wrote this book to help understand this phenomenon and start with the stance that, although not in every case, reaching the age-appropriate level of nervous system maturity leads to a solution for many problems.

Movement has played a central role in my life, and I can say that it is capable of wonders in the literal sense of the word. Parents whose children have developed through movement or sensory development can attest to this. They have been released from burdens such as bedwetting, stool retention, reading or writing difficulties, hyperactivity, attention-deficit, anxiety, or even autistic symptoms.

Some say that miracles do not exist, but this is only partially true. Unfortunately, there are congenital or acquired anomalies that cannot be remedied with our current knowledge. However, everyone's condition can be improved. If it is only a matter of delayed nervous system maturation, performing enough of the appropriate exercises can work wonders.

For those who do not believe it, read on, and start today!

HELP! SOMETHING IS WRONG!

Four-year-old Jack doesn't speak. He mostly just screams or cries. He eats only four types of food: plain boiled rice, peeled apples, breaded chicken breast, and bread crusts. He doesn't make eye contact, but instead fixates on a point on the wall where the thermostat is located. He wears diapers day and night. He seems oblivious to what's happening around him, but when an ambulance siren passes by, he is startled and covers his ears with his hands. His parents are young, perhaps not even 30 years old. Jack is their first child, and they are tired and desperate to help him, but he lives in his own little world where the rules are different from the world we live in.

Eleven-year-old Emma has two long braids and wears thin, light blue-framed glasses, giving the impression of a typical well-behaved, studious girl. And she is. She is an excellent student, which is remarkable for a child whose parents must read out longer, more complex writing to her. Reading is a struggle for Emma, and her life is getting harder because the lessons are getting more complex, and despite much practice, reading doesn't come easily to her. The little girl is deeply ashamed of this. Her two-year-older sister devours books, and her third-grade brother reads fluently as well.

Nine-year-old Hanna's mother asks to speak to me privately while Hanna waits outside. The mother wrings her hands as she tells me that her daughter still wears a diaper at night. She doesn't go to sleepover camps or pajama parties with her friends because she's afraid her secret will be discovered. The child is anxious, and her mother thinks she feels guilty about wetting the bed at night. Even her cousins aren't allowed to know about the child's "shame."

Michael, who will start school in a year, has a problem that is somewhat similar, but different. He doesn't feel when he needs to poop. Sometimes it takes three or four days before he feels the urge. At these times, the little boy is filled with fear because he knows what's coming and it's going to hurt. His stool is as hard as a rock, and sometimes there is blood. For him, going to the bathroom is not only painful but also terrifying. He is very thin, and his muscles are almost spasming. His father tells me that although

Michael doesn't pick and choose his food, he is only willing to eat very small amounts of anything. The little boy is quiet and afraid.

Tom is 12 years old. He effortlessly solves probability problems assigned by his tenth-grade sister. He loves learning, but he doesn't have any success in school! Not only does he excel in math, but his language ability is excellent too. He watches movies on Netflix in foreign languages. He admits that he sometimes needs subtitles, but less and less often. While I am taking down his information, he is constantly tapping his foot and asking his father questions or wanting to say something. I can't really have a conversation with the dad. Finally, Tom gets up, goes to the toy shelf, takes down half of the toys without asking, then starts bouncing a ball. Or would be bouncing if the ball didn't keep rolling away. With great difficulty, I find out from his dad that Tom will have to leave his second school. On the one hand, his classmates are ostracizing him, and on the other hand, the teachers cannot teach him. The dad says that Tom has only one friend, a similarly aged deaf and mute little boy. How they communicate is unknown. When Tom hears what we're talking about, he chimes in on the conversation, smiles mischievously, and says they have a secret sign language. When Tom leaves us again, his father asks, "He doesn't have to take medication, does he?" I reply, "I hope not."

The complaints are almost endless. The child doesn't draw, even though he's about to start school. She only swallows pureed food or only eats chunky food. He's 14 and still sucks his thumb at night. She has a speech impediment that doesn't improve. He can't handle even the slightest change. She writes unreadably. He can't concentrate, can't stay focused on a task. Even the smallest label on clothing needs to be cut off because it bothers her. He can't fall asleep at night. She has compulsive movements, and if they happen to stop, another one immediately takes its place. He bites his nails. She hates all sports. He can't sit still for two minutes. She is clumsy, unable to coordinate her movements. He falls. She walks on tiptoes. He is lonely.

There are many, many problems—a wide range. A thousand things can be hiding behind the symptoms. Occasionally organic (physical) disorders, genetic problems, metabolic disorders, hormonal reasons, injuries, and traumas. Other times, the child's socio-cultural background, a low-stimulation or overly stimulating environment, and we could go on. Unfortunately, sometimes it is very difficult, and in some cases impossible, to help.

But behind all of the above, a further possible cause may be lurking. Something that many do not think of or have not even heard of, but it still exists. A "something" that is almost tangible, lying in the background, which makes life difficult and bitter for many children and adults, but it can be treated and eliminated. This is nothing else but an IMMATURE NERVOUS SYSTEM.

A BRIEF HISTORY

In this chapter, I will highlight a few moments from the history of neuroscience, specifically from the research into reflexes. Hopefully, no one will get lost in the details of scientists and their discoveries. Listing the facts of the history of science serves a definite purpose. I would like the reader to be aware that it is thanks to many years of work by countless scientists that we know about the negative effects of unintegrated primitive reflexes, which adversely affect smooth sensorimotor developmental processes, learning, movement, behavior, and everyday life.

Since René Descartes, reflex activity has been considered one of the fundamental manifestations of neural function. In his work Passions of the Soul published in 1649, Descartes described the eyelid reflex, and in 1662, he formulated the duality of body and soul. He compared humans to a machine that performs physical activities under the direction of the mind. He believed that the latter is responsible for human decisions and involuntary actions.

Since reflexes were relatively easy to observe, they played a prominent role in the study of the central nervous system (CNS) for a long time, and were studied from anatomical, physiological, and psychological perspectives using scientific methods.

Thomas Willis, who worked as a royal physician in 17th-century England, studied the nervous system intensively. Although his studies did not directly address the functioning of reflexes, his work, which resulted in a book outlining the anatomy of the brain, contributed to the understanding of the mechanism of reflex activity. The book, titled De Motu Musculorum (On the Movement of Muscles), was published in 1684. Willis believed that the "seat of the soul" was in the head, more precisely in the cerebral cortex and subcortical areas. He imagined that the "soul" was released from the nerves and met the "spirit" released from the blood in the brain. He held the gray and white matter of the brain responsible for its functioning.

The word "reflex" was first used by Jean Astruc, a medical professor, in the early 1700s. He illustrated the essence of reflex function with the reflection of light on a mirror. He drew a parallel between the incoming stimulus and the light reflected on the mirror, as well as the response to the stimulus and the reflected light ray.

Albrecht von Haller, a Swiss anatomist, physiologist, naturalist, bibliographer, and poet, who was considered a prodigy in his childhood, described the difference between perception and irritability. He believed that "nerves are intelligent" because they are capable of perceiving events in the outside world. Meanwhile, "muscles are irritable" because the "muscle fiber" shortens measurably when it is irritated by a foreign body. This phenomenon is independent of human perception, so it occurs even if the person does not notice it. In 1752, at the University of Göttingen, Haller published his thesis related to the above findings.

Robert Whytt, a Scottish neurophysiologist, was one of the most successful scientists in the 19th century. Several discoveries are attributed to his name. He experimentally refuted Descartes' theory of "life spirit."[1] He studied the spinal cord of beheaded frogs and proved that if the spinal cord is intact, the frog's legs react to stimulation. Based on this, he established that the spinal cord is a crucial component in terms of the response to stimuli. In addition, he discovered that certain sensory responses are independent of willpower. As an example, he mentioned that just looking at a lemon can cause someone to start salivating.

The first accurate description of the reflex is attributed to Prochaska and Unzer. Unzer established in 1775 that the movement of animals is influenced not only by mechanical and physical laws but also by sensory and motor functions, and emphasized their importance in reflex processes.

Prochaska wrote his dissertation On the Function of the Nervous System in 1784, and emphasized two important principles. The principle of "vis nervosa" states that "nervous force" is transmitted through the nerves, connecting different parts of the nervous system. Its strength depends on the intensity of the stimulus, and it exists even when the nerve is separated from the central structures. The second principle ("sensorium commune") refers to the meeting point of sensory and motor nerves, which can

1 In metaphysics, Descartes stressed the difference between matter and spirit. But in his study of man, he concluded that the mind is intimately connected with the body. The unity of body and mind was explained by the "life spirit" and pineal gland theories.

be found in the brain and spinal cord. Through this phenomenon, he drew attention to the role of sensory and motor functions in reflexes.

In the 1850s, John Hughlings Jackson divided the nervous system into three parts based on the degree of automaticity of the movements controlled by a particular area. He classified the lowest order movements as the automatic functions of the body, which are linked to the spinal cord and brainstem. He considered the cortical motor area as the middle area. He named the prefrontal lobe (the front part of the frontal lobe) as the most developed region, which controls the most complex activities. He believed that the highest level is capable of interpreting and coordinating sensory stimuli through the mediation of the lower and middle areas, as well as enabling the complex, fine control and coordination of motor function. He also proposed that higher-level nervous system structures inhibit the functioning of lower-level areas during development.

In 1870, Jackson hypothesized that if lower-level areas are not inhibited, problems can arise in sensory integration. He supplemented this claim in 1884 with the observation that in pathological mental states, patients exhibit behavioral regression and return to more primitive, automatic activities. For example, they may make involuntary mouth movements or grasp objects so strongly that it is almost impossible to remove them from their hands.

The latter discovery is significant in that similar regression processes are observed during the integration of undeveloped infant reflexes and the presence of primitive reflexes leads to sensory and motor integration problems.[2]

Eduard Pflüger described many of the fundamental phenomena of spinal reflexes in 1853. He emphasized that the spinal cord also has sensory functions.

Rudolph Lotze (1817–1881) preached that the nervous system is more flexible and adaptable than previously thought. Voluntary actions in vertebrates are the result of previous learning that is transferred to the level

2 Jackson called this state "daydreaming," in which primitive functions are not under control.

of the spinal cord. Lotze believed that the spinal cord is entirely under the control of the brain, and reflexes correspond to the first level of integration.

In his book The Principles of Psychology, Herbert Spencer (1820–1903) explained that increasing complexity characterizes the CNS. Tighter functioning occurs at lower levels, while higher levels are independent and capable of more complex functions (today we might say they exhibit much greater plasticity). Psychological functions are in line with this hierarchy. Reflexes operate at the lowest organizational level, while higher levels are responsible for more complex functions.

William T. Preyer was one of the most significant pioneers in child psychology. He was born in England and worked and published in Germany. His historically significant work The Soul of the Child was published in 1882. This was the first document to mention infantile reflexes. Preyer observed and studied infants, and wrote the book based on his experiences. In his later book The Development of Reason, published in 1895, he also discussed the mysteries of sensory and sensorimotor processes.

In the second half of the 1800s, Russian doctor Ivan Sechenov established that reflex processes are not only the consequences of the functioning of lower nerve centers but can also be extended to the operation of the cerebral cortex. He believed that all manifestations of brain function can be traced back to muscle movements. During mental processes, an individual reflex can be suppressed, and in this case, the motor response becomes a mental process. As a result, he interpreted mental phenomena as vital processes.

According to Sechenov, all our movements, whether involuntary or voluntary, are created in response to a previously experienced external stimulus. The nervous system develops its own mental repertoire based on incoming stimuli, and the elements of this repertoire serve to elicit responses to later stimuli. Therefore, all our activities are influenced by a previously experienced external stimulation.

> The infinite diversity of external manifestations of cerebral activity can be reduced ultimately to a single phenomenon – muscular movement. Whether it's the child laughing at the sight of a toy, or Garibaldi smiling when persecuted for

excessive love for his native land, or a girl trembling at the first thought of love, or Newton creating universal laws and inscribing them on paper – the ultimate fact in all cases is muscular movement. To help the reader reconcile himself to this thought I shall remind him of the framework which has been created by the popular mind and includes all the manifestations of cerebral activity; this framework is "word" and "action". Under "action" the popular mind undoubtedly visualises every external mechanical activity of man which can be accomplished exclusively with the aid of muscles, while "word", as the reader will readily appreciate, implies a certain combination of sounds produced in the larynx and in the mouth cavity also by means of muscular movement. (Sechenov, 1965 [1863])

Ivan Petrovich Pavlov became most famous for discovering the phenomena of classical conditioning and the conditioned reflex. He believed that an analyzing "apparatus" (a set of analyzers) develops in the brain in response to incoming sensory stimuli, which allows us to perceive the complexity of the external world. He concluded that there are no spontaneous activities since all actions depend on the stimuli picked up by the sensory organs.

In the 20th century, the neurophysiological mechanisms of reflexes were studied and described much more frequently than other neurological functions.

Sir Charles Sherrington was the first to name the connection between adjacent neurons a synapse. When he was invited to Yale University in the USA in 1904, he began writing his famous book, The Integrative Action of the Nervous System. Published in 1906, its main idea was that the CNS is capable of significant integrative function because many reflexes coordinate the separate activities of various organs. The book was significant in providing a comprehensive functional description of the CNS. In the introduction, he described the functioning of a simple reflex, which he believed to be the functional basis of all complex operations, and from there, he derived the complex system of reflex–muscle units, ultimately controlled by the brain. Starting in 1913, he began to study the functioning of the spinal cord in more detail, during which time he described almost all the cat's spinal reflexes. Sherrington quickly became convinced that sensory information generated in the muscles was essential. He believed that motor neurons receive stimulating and inhibitory information from various sources at the same time. The cell measures the conflicting information and responds accordingly.

Sherrington insisted that cortical activity influences spinal cord activities, and he maintained that the CNS's activity depends on perception and is not centrally generated.

Those scientists who precisely described an individual infant reflex deserve special mention regarding this book's topic.

Among them, the first is Louis Robinson. In 1891, he described how a newborn human baby can hold its own weight when its palm touches a stick and grabs onto it. He tested more than 60 infants younger than one month and found that they could hang on to the stick for at least 10 seconds. Interestingly, he noted that one baby was able to hang for two minutes and thirty-five seconds. The reflex he discovered is the grasping reflex, which can also be elicited in the foot.

Joseph Jules François Félix Babinski, the Polish-born French neurologist, described the Babinski reflex named after him in 1896. He observed that if a pointed object is drawn from the heel to the little toe on the outer sole of a baby's foot, the big toe will bend backward, and the other toes will spread fan-like. This reflex integrates with walking and cannot be elicited in a healthy, developed nervous system.

In his doctoral dissertation in 1917, the Russian neurologist Johann Susmann Galant described the hip–lumbar reflex, which is also known as the Galant reflex. He mentioned that this reflex is present at birth and its absence or atypical functioning may indicate damage to the spinal cord or brain. He also noted that the reflex gradually integrates after six months of age and its later elicitation always indicates pathological processes.

The Moro reflex was documented by the Austrian pediatrician Ernst Moro in 1918. He observed that when a baby is dropped, exposed to bright light, sudden noise, heat, or cold, they first extend their arms backward, then, after taking a deep breath, they bring their arms forward and clasp them. Moro described the reflex as important for diagnostic purposes, as its absence, weakness, or asymmetry after birth may indicate brain damage.

Arnold Landau discovered a reflex in 1923, later named the Landau reflex or reaction, which appears in infants around the third month when they are held horizontally in a prone position. He observed that they lift their head slightly and bend their arms and legs.

Rudolf Magnus, a pharmacist and physiologist, published his famous book Körperstellung (Body Position) in 1924. The book dealt with reflexes that regulate posture. Magnus and his research partner, Adriaan de Kleijn, were nominated for the Nobel Prize; however, Magnus passed away unexpectedly shortly thereafter. They were credited with describing, among other things, the tonic labyrinthine reflexes. de Kleijn linked the functioning of the neck reflexes to eye movements and the operation of the vestibular (balance) organ located in the inner ear.

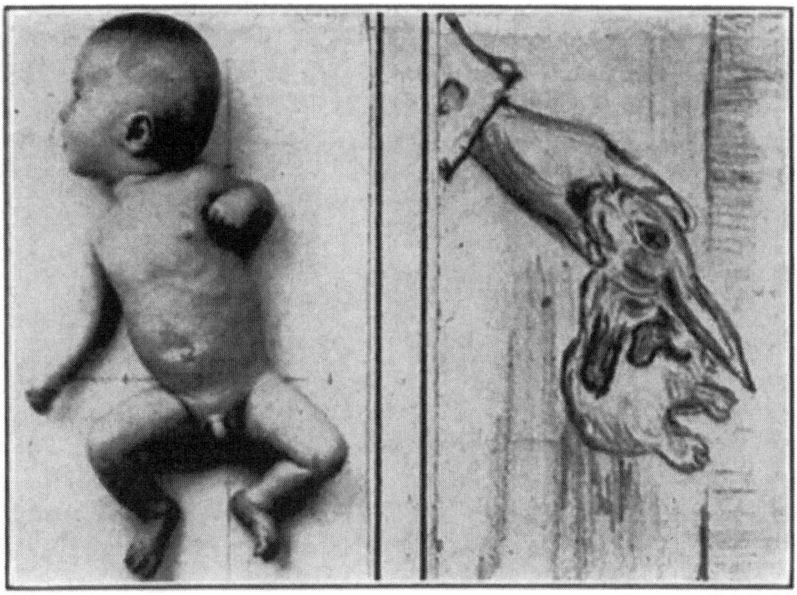

Detection of asymmetrical tonic neck reflex by head rotation in a rabbit and an eight-week-old infant (Source unknown)

Based on Magnus's observations, Arnold Gesell described the asymmetrical tonic neck reflex in a pediatric journal in 1938. He illustrated his detailed observations with diagrams and images. The stimulus was turning the head to the side, and the response was stretching the arm on the same side and bending the opposite arm. According to his observations, the reflex is already present at birth, and Gesell found that it could be elicited in premature infants born in the 34th week of pregnancy. It is most active in the third month and gradually integrates after six months of age.

Around this time, Boris Babkin found an interesting connection between two reflexes. He discovered that if an infant's palm is stimulated with pressure, the mouth opens. He initially called it the hand–mouth reflex. In 1958, the phenomenon was named the Babkin reflex after its discoverer. The reflex is significant in torso development, and its early establishment is typical of individual development, as it appears as early as the 14th week after conception.

Mary R. Fiorentino presented the testing of infant reflexes in 1963. She also described how primitive reflexes, if not inhibited in time, can cause various nervous system symptoms. Fiorentino later published several books, including her 1981 work A Basis for Sensorimotor Development – Normal and Abnormal: The Influence of Primitive, Postural Reflexes on the Development and Distribution of Tone. This book discusses "critical developmental periods" and behavioral patterns, and draws attention to the infant reflexes that underlie abnormal posture and muscle tone. She warns that the persistence of these primitive reflexes has diagnostic significance.

Meanwhile, in 1946, David Lloyd described the myotatic reflex, i.e., that each muscle is controlled by a motor unit that triggers muscle contraction. Meanwhile, a parallel structure makes contact with the muscle spindles via gamma motor neurons, thus sensing muscle tension. In the 1940s, Berlin-born pediatrician Karel Bobath formulated that normal posture requires a sufficiently mature balance-sensing system and the integration of earlier (infant) reflexes. This is how the ability to regulate all our muscles against gravity is created.

In the 1970s, psychologist Peter Blythe suggested that there might be a link between the lack of integration of primitive reflexes, delayed motor development, and learning difficulties.

By the 1980s, about 70 brainstem reflexes had been mapped in infants. By this time, it was certain that some of these primitive reflexes were closely linked to the vestibular system, the precise functioning of which is essential for perfect perception.

Illingworth said in 1987 that brainstem reflexes are easily triggered and can be seen as a "survival kit" for the infant.

A 1991 study by Capute and Accardo found that early reflexes become less and less activated as the nervous system matures during the first year of life. These early reflexes are called "primitive reflexes," given that they are only typical for a few months after birth, do not persist throughout life, and are related to the functioning of the "immature" infant brain.

Andermann in 1997 and Jacyna in 2011 independently confirmed that Jackson's 19th-century findings were correct and are still valid today. In the complex processes that facilitate the development of the nervous system, ontogenetically higher levels can inhibit the function of lower regions. In other words, if development is smooth, the higher-level neural formations inhibit primitive functions.

This claim that Jackson was right 150 years ago has been confirmed by Franz and Gillett (2011), who add that if infant reflexes are not inhibited, they impede the operation and coordinated functioning of the CNS, leading to various dysfunctions.

Ellenberger in 1970 and Meares in 1999 formulated that if inhibition does not occur during an individual's development, or if primitive areas of inhibition are released again, primitive reflexes may persist or reappear, which can be the cause of psychological and cognitive dysfunction. This may occur as a result of post-traumatic stress or in the post-operative phase (Nicolson et al., 2011). Sensorimotor integration cannot take place. Automatic, involuntary movements, disorganization, and disturbances of higher neural functions may occur.

Teicher, Tomoda, and Andersen in 2006, Fagiolini, Jensen, and Champagne in 2009, and Kolb and Gibb in 2011 have published essential studies on the topic. The three groups agreed that the developing nervous system is highly vulnerable. Maturation can be hindered by injury, toxic effects, and even psychological stress. One of the problems underlying deficits in higher motor and cognitive function, and for this book the most relevant, is the persistence of primitive reflexes.

Since the 2000s, a growing number of researchers have sought a link between unintegrated infant reflexes and learning and behavioral disorders, attention-deficit hyperactivity disorder (ADHD), dyslexia, dysgraphia, and other symptom complexes.

Taylor, Houghton, and Chapman in 2004, followed by Konicarova and Bob in 2013, described a strong association between ADHD and the presence of primitive reflexes.

McPhillips, Hepper, and Mulhern published a study in The Lancet in 2000, and McPhillips and Jordan-Black in 2007, on the association between persistent infantile reflexes and dyslexia.

In 2009, Buderath et al., and in 2011 Ghanizadeh found that ADHD is associated with a disturbance in balance perception and impaired higher motor coordination and executive functions.

In a study published in 2013, Jana Konicarova and Petr Bob summarized the associations between ADHD symptom clustering and persistent reflexes. They point out possible causes of the disturbances in the maturational processes in the CNS and emphasize the importance of the different stages of individual development and their temporal sequence.[3]

In 2012, Mats Niklasson published a paper presenting the results of a study which concluded that when children are involved in a development training program that includes primitive reflex inhibition, integration, vestibular stimulation, maturation, sensorimotor development (auditory, tactile development), fine motor development, large motor development, and playful exercises, they achieve significantly better results in reading, writing, and mathematics than those in control groups who did not partake in such activities.

As can be seen from the above, our knowledge of infant reflexes results from centuries of dedicated work by pediatricians, neurologists, psychologists, pharmacists, psychiatrists, and researchers.

The research has not stopped. It continues. New research results are emerging, contributing to the development of ever more effective therapies.

3 In 2013, Konicarova and Bob specifically looked at Moro and Galant reflexes in children with ADHD. Their research found that the persistence of these reflexes was significantly higher among children with ADHD than in the control group.

IT'S ALL BASED ON MOVEMENT

The development of the nervous system begins as early as the third week after conception. By the tenth week of fetal development, the skin around the mouth is capable of sensing. Hearing and balance perception also begin to develop early on, followed by taste and then vision. The fetus begins to move around the sixth week after conception and prior to birth already possesses the full range of movements needed by a newborn baby. These movements are self-initiated and not in response to external stimuli. Genetically programmed primitive sensation and movement have a developmental effect on the nervous system, allowing for more precise perception and execution of movements with a more advanced nervous system. When the baby is born, its nervous system already contains nearly all the neurons it will use throughout its life. However, the weight of a newborn's brain is only one-quarter that of an adult's brain. The first 5–6 years are the most dynamic period of nervous system development, during which time the weight of a child's brain reaches 90% of that of an adult's brain.

The growth of a baby's brain is not primarily due to the multiplication of nerve cells, but rather to the development of connections between nerve cells, as well as myelination. Myelination is the formation of an insulating layer around the long projections of nerve cells, called axons, which allows for faster and more targeted nerve impulses. This process facilitates the formation of connections between different areas of the brain. These transformations refine the functioning of the brain area responsible for higher-level coordination of the centers in the brain.

Part of the genetic program of the nervous system's development involves genes that become activated after birth, while others are suppressed. The number of patterns under the control of genes is far less than the number of synapses (connections between nerve cells) that are formed in the infant's brain through the process of gaining experience. Every event that the baby encounters from the outside world and from within their own body leaves an imprint on their brain. Vision, hearing, smell, taste, touch, and gravity perception all contribute to the gathering of information, the discovery of the world, and the reaction to external events. It is observable that the baby's movement changes in response to light, sound, and touch already in the first few days following birth. Continuous reinforcement is the basis of learning in genetically determined sensory processing and motor development programs.

During development, the enormous number of synapses formed between nerve cells is far greater than the organism requires. The important connections are selected via "natural selection" and a genetic program that induces cell death. Therefore, new connections are formed between nerve cells from birth, and different regions of the brain are constantly restructuring themselves depending on the stimuli the infant receives and the experiences they gain from the outside world and from within their own body.

Reinforcement, trial and error, and experience of pain and pleasure all play important roles in the establishment and dismantling of neural networks. Essentially, this is learning, which occurs through the process of gaining experience.

What experiences does a baby collect? For example, when the mother's breast touches the baby's mouth, the baby turns its head towards the stimulus. When the mother's nipple touches the child's tongue, sucking movements begin. The search for the nipple and the sucking movements are caused by the same reflexes in every baby. The taste, temperature, and texture of the milk create a pleasant sensation for the baby, as well as eliminating hunger and promoting relaxation. The networks necessary for this process are strengthened, as they not only create a pleasant feeling in the baby but are also essential for survival. Later, when sucking is no longer necessary because the baby can feed in other ways, the network responsible for sucking is dismantled. The baby may still be able to suck unintentionally but touching its lips will no longer induce sucking movements.

Let's take another example. During birth, a network begins to activate which, by the age of 3–4 months, allows the baby to bend their arms and legs by tilting their head forward. Shortly after, the baby will be able to sit up with the help of this reflex. Once the baby has successfully sat up and repeated this process enough times, the network responsible for this movement sequence will disappear. Tilting the head forward will no longer trigger bending of the arms and legs.

It is very important to know that our experiences of the world are due to movement from the beginning of our lives. We need to open our eyes to see. If we are interested in events that are not happening just in front of our eyes, we need to turn our heads. If there is too much light, our pupils constrict, which is also a consequence of muscle movement. If there is a lot of noise, the tiny bone in the middle ear, the stirrup, regulates the amount of noise entering the ear through the tension of muscles. To touch something, we need to reach out for it. To taste something, we need to put it in our mouth or lick it, like ice cream. To liquefy our food, which makes taste sensation possible and more precise, we need the functioning of salivary glands. Muscle movement is necessary to secrete saliva.

The question arises: What is the reason for the movement of a newborn or an infant? After all, they are not yet able to consciously control their arms, legs, head, or lips. They just wave, kick, make faces, and smack their lips.

The movement of newborns and infants is genetically programmed. Within their movements, three major groups can be distinguished.

First, let's look at the group of elementary movement patterns. These are already triggerable reactions in newborn infants, which work according to the genetic program of human motor development. Their stimulus is gravity. They are specific and stereotypical, since the same movement can always be triggered by specific stimuli, and the movements have a regular pattern. They do not occur spontaneously and do not play a role in the survival of the newborn or infant. These patterns project the movements that will determine later human activities. For example, the position of the head and torso against gravity, balance, and walking. They are precursors to the movements that will appear during later development.

The postural reactions and locomotor movements are present in the elementary movement patterns. The harmony between the two prepares the body for the development of locomotion, the movement that relies on a stable posture for changing the body position.

The primitive reflexes and postural reactions must be distinguished from the elementary movement patterns. While the latter are very much like the fully matured human movements and develop according to the appropriate age and maturity level, primitive reflexes disappear during the child's development. The primitive reflexes form the second large group. Each primitive reflex has a specific stimulus to which the response occurs only once. This is different from the elementary movement patterns, where the movement repeats regularly as long as the stimulus persists.

For example, one primitive reflex (the Moro reflex) is triggered by a strong or sudden external stimulus, which can be practically anything: loud noise, bright light, cool or hot bathwater in which the baby is placed, or pain. The response in every case is the spreading of the child's arms, followed by bringing them together in front of the body, accompanied by taking a big breath. The described response occurs only once to a given stimulus.

Primitive reflexes are automatic movement sequences that begin to appear around the 25–26th week of pregnancy. Their maturation is complete either around birth or in the first few months after birth, and they start to become inhibited from around six months of age. They protect the body from irreparable damage, so they play an essential role in survival, being indispensable in the period around birth and in the first 6–10 months of a baby's life. During the stages of growth and development, if primitive reflexes do not integrate at the appropriate time and extent, they can result in immature behavioral patterns.

The third group is postural reflexes. These require an appropriate coordinated level of functioning of the nervous system and are not present in newborns. They develop postnatally, that is, after birth. They have an essential role in the development of normal muscle tone and the appearance of mature body posture. This is extremely important because, without them, we would not be able to hold up our bodies against the force of gravity. These reflexes form the basis of motor behavior.

Postural reactions work independently of the will. They provide a complex motor response to various types of sensory stimuli. Their appearance is quite varied. Depending on the point of stimulation, the response occurs in the joints, tendons, or muscles. Due to coordinated, unified functioning, the posture of the head, torso, and limbs automatically adjusts against gravity. Postural reactions are necessary for higher-level motor learning and behavior, responding to complex stimuli such as sound, balance, light, body position, touch, and pressure.

From around the 25–26th week of pregnancy until the baby is about six months old, nearly 100 reflexes are known to exist. In the following section, I will present those primitive reflexes and postural reactions that, if not integrated in time, can lead to learning and behavioral disorders, as well as other problems.

THE INFANT WITHIN US, AND THE PRIMITIVE REFLEXES

In this section, I will list the primitive reflexes that, in my experience, are the most commonly retained and cause problems not only in learning and behavior but also in many areas of everyday life. When not integrated, these reflexes can produce a variety of symptoms, ranging from attention-deficit to speech problems or delayed speech development, and even bedwetting. The nature of the symptoms depends on which reflex has been retained and how it combines with other reflexes, and can also be influenced by the different levels of maturity in the two hemispheres of the brain.

Parents and educators who were not previously aware of retained primitive reflexes may be amazed to discover that the problems they regularly encounter during the upbringing and development of children can often have relatively simple explanations. As parents, caregivers, and educators, we should adopt an attitude that before we label a child's "illness," or learning or behavioral problem, we should consider that these may be related to the non-optimal development of the nervous system, especially due to the negative effects of certain reflexes or sensorimotor immaturity. Sensorimotor development is nothing more than our experiences gained through the effects of external and internal stimuli on our body and the coordination of our movements, as well as the development of the harmonious functioning of our sensory and motor systems.

Later, we will also discuss how first parents, and secondly educators and therapists, can do a lot to solve these problems.

How and why are primitive reflexes inhibited?

Primitive reflexes serve multiple purposes. They promote the development of sensory perception and awareness, contributing to the refinement of both gross and fine motor skills.

They play a significant role in speech development and also serve protective functions. All primitive reflexes have in common that they elicit a motor response to a stimulus. This motor response is not only manifested in physical movement but also impacts various areas of the cerebral cortex.

Primitive reflexes stimulate the cortex to help it mature. The maturation process is reflected, among other things, in the production of neurotransmitters by nerve cells. These neurotransmitters can be either excitatory or inhibitory.

In the context of primitive reflexes, inhibitory neurotransmitters are of particular importance. One such inhibitory neurotransmitter is gamma-aminobutyric acid (GABA). Nerve cells produce this substance. In infants, when produced in sufficient quantities, it will inhibit primitive reflexes. The persistence of primitive reflexes after three years of age is a sign of immaturity because it shows that a specific cortical area still requires the presence of these reflexes. The movement triggered in response to a primitive reflex prompts the cortical cells to produce GABA, inhibiting the reflex.

This is a wonderfully organized process. We can be thankful that reflexes persist because they act as warning signs indicating that the primitive reflexes still need to be present to stimulate the production of GABA by cortical cells, which will then inhibit those reflexes.

The Moro reflex

The Moro reflex is present from the seventh month of pregnancy. Any sudden stimulus can trigger it, whether it be light, sound, touch, cold, warmth, or a rapid change in head position. The baby responds to the stimulus by spreading its arms, followed by a quick inhalation, and then swinging their arms in front of their body. This latter movement supports exhalation.

The Moro reflex helps with survival in the first months of life by eliciting a sympathetic response in the autonomic nervous system. This is known as the "startle response." In this state, the body responds to an event that threatens its functioning. For example, when a baby's breathing weakens, the Moro reflex is triggered due to the increased concentration of carbon dioxide in the blood, which releases adrenaline into the bloodstream. Adrenaline is a hormone that, among other things, increases respiration rate, pulse, and blood pressure. It can restart a baby's system, preventing cessation of breathing.

This reflex should be inhibited in the 4–6th month following birth (Fiorentino, 1981). If the reflex remains elicitable, many sensory channels may become hypersensitive, causing the child to react more intensely to various sensory stimuli. Because the Moro reflex elicits sympathetic responses and the nervous system "overreacts" to sensory information, the child may become constantly tense, irritable, and insecure.

If the Moro reflex is still elicitable after six months of age, various long-term problems may arise. The researchers Goddard, Melillo, and Rentschler all mention hypersensitivity to visual, auditory, balance, touch, smell, and taste stimuli. Psychological symptoms such as continuous anxiety, worry, and emotional fluctuations may also develop. The child may have difficulty adjusting to change and may not like it when events deviate from what they are used to. They may also experience indecisiveness, low self-esteem, alternating periods of hyperactivity, and strong feelings of fatigue.

The most common long-term effects of the unintegrated Moro reflex are:

- Sleep disorders, difficulty falling asleep
- Easily triggered intense emotional reactions
- Shyness
- Poor sense of balance and weak motor coordination
- Poor stamina
- Susceptibility to musculoskeletal disorders
- Digestive problems, a tendency towards hypoglycemia (excessively low blood sugar levels)
- Weak immune system; asthma, allergies, and susceptibility to infections
- Oversensitivity to light, movement, sound, touch, and smells
- Difficulty with reading and writing
- Difficulty adapting to change
- Alternating between hyperactivity and extreme fatigue
- Easily distracted
- Difficulty with tasks involving balls (especially catching)
- Difficulty with auditory and visual perception
- Increased fatigue and sensitivity to vibrating light (e.g., neon tubes)
- Lack of self-confidence, low self-esteem
- Increased "pre-race jitters" or "apathy" in competitive situations or during exams
- Difficulty learning to swim backstroke

The rooting, sucking, and grasping reflexes

The pressure exerted on the baby's skull during birth contributes to the full maturation of the rooting and sucking reflexes. After birth, the rooting reflex can be triggered in newborns by stimulating their face or the edge of their mouth. The baby's head then turns towards the stimulus. When the mother's breast touches the baby's face, the child turns towards the stimulus and starts to suckle contentedly.

The sucking reflex is triggered by touching the lips. The baby's tongue then moves forward and backward, performing a sucking motion.

The primary goal of these reflexes is to facilitate the infant's feeding and to allow them to taste their first flavors. The sucking reflex also has another important function. The intense sucking movement exercises the tongue and facial muscles, contributing to smooth speech development.

The grasping reflex occurs when the palm is stimulated, causing the fingers to close. Initially, the thumb is inactive and rests under the first three fingers. It can be observed that the grasping reflex follows the Moro reflex when it appears. When the arms are thrown forward, the grasping reflex helps close the fingers. Interestingly, in adulthood, it is often observed that when someone is frightened or in a crisis situation, they clench their fist. It is possible that in this case, the Moro and grasping reflexes are released from cortical inhibition and activated.

The grasping reflex closely cooperates with the sucking reflex. When the infant sucks, the fingers rhythmically "pump." This connection between the grasping and sucking reflexes is called the Babkin response (Babkin, 1960). The Babkin response is normally triggered from birth to the fourth month (Fiorentino, 1981).

When the grasping and sucking reflexes integrate 4–6 months after birth, the "pincer grip" develops. The thumb is now able to face the index finger, allowing the infant to grasp and release smaller objects. Due to the Babkin response, the connection between the grasping and sucking reflexes plays an extremely important role not only in the child's hand-eye coordination but also in speech perception, comprehension, and production.

If the grasping and sucking reflexes do not integrate in time, the child may have difficulty gripping a pencil, articulation (mouth movement) problems may arise, and there may be difficulties with speech perception and comprehension, and speech production. It is often observed that the child's tongue moves or protrudes from their mouth when writing, drawing, or manipulating objects with their fingers. In addition, speech therapy problems such as "tongue thrust swallowing" may develop.

Persistence of the rooting reflex leads to sensitivity around the mouth area, and swallowing becomes obstructed, leading to drooling and eating difficulties.

According to Montagu (1986), the lips, tongue, smell, sight, and hearing are closely connected with each other and with the experience of sucking. During sucking, both hands perform grasping movements. This relationship (which has the corresponding representation within the brain) prepares children for articulated speech, reading, and writing.

The most common long-term effects of the unintegrated sucking, rooting and grasping reflexes are:

- Delayed speech development
- Speech perception disorders
- Speech formation disorders
- Swallowing problems
- Issues related to eating and mealtimes
- Difficulties in social situations
- Drooling
- Poor hand dexterity
- Poor pencil grip
- Difficulties with writing, messy handwriting
- Difficulty expressing thoughts in writing
- Addictions (e.g., smoking, chewing gum, constant snacking)
- Need tactile stimuli for the hands, constant fidgeting

The asymmetrical tonic neck reflex

The asymmetrical tonic neck reflex (ATNR) is present in the fetus before birth. When the baby turns its head, the arm and leg on that side stretch out, while the opposite arm and leg bend. It assists with movement in the womb and during birth. It appears together with the spinal Galant reflex and supports the birth process. Birth strengthens the ATNR, which later helps the child reach for objects and thus participates in establishing hand-eye coordination. This reflex is also the basis for the segmental rolling reflex (the baby's ability to roll over onto their belly and back) and crawling.

The ATNR is related to the vestibular (balance) system, head movement, vision, and regulation of muscle tone.

If the ATNR does not integrate by 6–7 months of age, the child may have difficulties when trying to transfer something from one hand to the other. In addition, a persistent ATNR adversely affects learning to walk.

In the long term, if not integrated the ATNR can have many unwanted effects. The most commonly occurring ones are as follows. Poor execution of fine motor movements, resulting in poor handwriting. The child's hand may cramp during writing. They may mix up letters and numbers. There may be problems with eye movement and eye–hand coordination. When reading, the child may jump letters and words, and may not be able to follow the lines. The reading space may narrow because when the ATNR is active, not only the limbs but also the eyes do not "feel comfortable" crossing the body's midline. It may be difficult for the left eye to look to the right, and the right eye to look left. Thus, the eyes are not parallel at the beginning and end of the line, and the child doesn't read the full lines. Practically, they often guess what is written at either end. This is especially true at the end of the line.

Impatience and impulsivity may characterize such children and crossed or mixed dominance (e.g., ambidexterity, or confusing left and right) may be common. Their drawing skills are usually below the expected level for their age, and they may have difficulty learning certain sports. For example, they may struggle with breathing every three strokes when swimming front crawl, making a lay-up shot in basketball, or achieving a coordinated running style.

The most common long-term effects of a persistent ATNR are:

- Symptoms of dyslexia, dysgraphia, and dyscalculia
- Difficulties in reading, text comprehension, handwriting, and spelling
- Difficulty in mathematics (word problems, tasks requiring sequencing, etc.)

- Poor spatial orientation and sense of direction
- Mixed dominance
- Weak focus (especially at the beginning and end of lines when reading)
- Balance difficulties
- Fine motor problems
- Difficulty executing tasks that require eye–hand coordination
- Difficulty distinguishing between objects and background, and distinguishing parts from the whole
- Cannot learn to breathe every three strokes when swimming front crawl

The spinal Galant reflex

The spinal Galant reflex can be triggered in the uterus and is fully present after birth. During the birth process, when the infant's hip–lumbar area presses against the wall of the birth canal, this reflex results in a slight extension of the hip, which, along with the ATNR, helps in the process of delivery. If the area near the spine in the lumbar region is stimulated in the infant, the back muscles on the same side contract, resulting in the hip moving toward the stimulus.

The spinal Galant reflex should begin to integrate in the infant at around four months of age. If integration does not occur or is incomplete, problems with toilet training often occur. It is not uncommon for bedwetting to persist until five or six years of age, and sometimes even later. The presence of the Galant reflex is also common in children with fecal retention problems.

Weak short-term memory and attention-deficit can be observed. Children with a persistent Galant reflex typically have a posture where they push their hips to the side when standing still. The development of scoliosis and an increased need for movement are common. This manifests not only in a desire for sports but also in constant fidgeting and rocking in chairs. It is not uncommon for them to tap their feet or make noise in some way. They often trip or fall, and their movements are clumsy, even though they generally enjoy sports. It is characteristic that they do not like tight-fitting clothes around their waist, and when they wear them, they squirm and move, making it difficult for them to concentrate for long periods during class.

Long-term consequences of the spinal Galant reflex:

- Hypersensitivity, especially in the back
- Bedwetting
- Fatigue
- Poor attention span
- Hip rotation while standing and walking
- Poor concentration
- Poor coordination
- Poor posture
- Poor short-term memory
- Overactivity/hyperactivity
- Inability to sit still
- Irritable bowel syndrome (in adulthood)
- Scoliosis (lordosis, kyphosis, scoliosis)
- Difficulty with bowel movements

The tonic labyrinthine reflex

The tonic labyrinthine reflex (TLR) begins to activate during the birth process. The reflex is triggered by changes in head position. Depending on whether the head is raised from the back to the front or from the front to the back, we talk about forward or backward TLR. The forward reflex integrates around four months of age, while the backward reflex integrates around two and a half years of age. The forward inclination of the head triggers flexion (bending) of the torso and limbs, while the backward inclination triggers extension of the torso and limbs. Whether flexion or extension is involved, the stimulus is followed by a change in muscle tone.

After birth, the child must contend with the effects of gravity. The TLR helps the infant's body straighten up from the position it had in the womb. Since the TLR sets muscle tone based on head position, it is important for the nervous system to receive information about the head's spatial position. This is made possible by the vestibular organ located in the inner ear. The maturation of the vestibular system is greatly influenced by reflexes like the TLR and ATNR.

The TLR has not only an impact on the child's motor development, from lifting the head to the process of walking, but also strongly affects sensory integration.[4]

Different problems arise depending on whether the forward or backward TLR is retained. If the forward reflex can be triggered after the fourth month following birth, the child's muscles will have hypotonia (weak muscle tone), which leads to postural problems and curvature. Problems related to balance and often travel sickness are common. Due to inadequate muscle tone, the child does not usually enjoy sports. Problems can arise in the areas of auditory and visual perception, proprioception, visceroception, and spatial perception. A poor sense of time and weak seriality (handling sequential tasks) are also characteristic.

In my experience, children in whom the forward neck-tonic response is not inhibited have weak sustained attention and short-term memory. It is common for them to be easily distracted.

For children who are slow in achieving control over their bladders or who continue to have bedwetting problems after the age of five or six, not only can the Galant reflex be triggered, but also the forward TLR. Since the TLR persists, it results in weak muscle tone, which may affect not only skeletal muscles but also sphincter muscles, such as the bladder sphincter. If the forward TLR integrates and the Galant reflex can no longer be triggered in a child who previously had difficulties regulating urination, the problem disappears.

The presence of the backward TLR also causes balance problems, weak motor coordination, travel sickness, poor ability to follow sequences (time, information, etc.), and visual and auditory perceptual disorders. Unlike in the forward TLR, the muscles are tight (hypertonic) due to increased muscle tone. Walking on tiptoe is very common, even up to the age of 10–12.

The long-term consequences of the unintegrated TLR include:

- Problems with balance and coordination
- Crouched, forward-leaning, or overly tight posture

4 Sensory integration is a neurological process that makes stimuli from the body and the environment perceptible and interpretable in a unified manner, thereby ensuring the body's efficient response to stimuli. During integration, incoming signals are not only added together, but the nervous system also selects and differentiates them (Katona, 2001).

- Fatigues easily
- Hypotonic (loose) or hypertonic (overly tight) muscle tone
- Difficulty in judging distance, depth, space, and speed
- Excessive fear of height or depth
- Sitting on the floor in a "W" position, knees out front with feet either side of the hips
- Increased tendency to musculoskeletal problems
- Visual and auditory perception problems
- Speech problems
- Prone to fidgeting when tired
- Stiff jerky movements
- Toe walking
- Difficulty in navigating stairs
- Inability to follow movement-related instructions (such as gymnastics exercises)
- Acid reflux
- Problems with bowel and bladder control

Symmetrical tonic neck reflex

According to Fiorentino, the symmetrical tonic neck reflex (STNR) develops as part of the integration of labyrinthine reflexes. This reflex appears around the 6–8th months and is inhibited around 9–10 months of age. When the child is on all fours and tilts their head down, their arms bend and their legs straighten out. If they lift their head up, their arms extend and their legs bend at the knees. An interesting thing about this reflex is that it may also be temporarily triggered soon after birth, presumably to help support the newborn "crawl" on their mother's belly to find the breasts. O'Connor Leppert and her colleagues believe that the STNR is a connecting element between the prone position and crawling. If the reflex does not integrate in time, it complicates the coordination of gross motor movements. When it persists, "clumsy child" syndrome develops. This includes children who frequently trip or fall, drop things, cannot button up their shirts, and bump into tables and chairs.

The long-term consequences of the persistent STNR are:

- Frequent shivering or anxiety
- Poor posture, "hunched over"
- Headaches

- Reading and writing difficulties
- Inability to sit normally (either leaning on the table or slouching under it)
- Difficulty in copying from the board
- Monkey-like gait
- Vision problems
- Difficulty with independent tasks
- General clumsiness
- Difficulty with gross motor skills
- Messy eating, chewing loudly
- Inability to learn the breaststroke swimming technique

Note: The fear paralytic reflex (FPR) and core tendon guard reflex (CTGR) are not specifically infant reflexes. The FPR normally integrates in the womb and it is not present after birth. The CTGR reflex persists throughout life, but depends on what kind of stimulus triggers it. These reflexes and their effects will be discussed in the chapter on anxiety.

THEORIES IN SENSORIMOTOR DEVELOPMENT

The importance of sensorimotor development cannot be questioned. Different concepts and understandings have emerged in the literature regarding the nature and causes of this process.

The following chapter aims to give the reader an idea of how the perception of sensorimotor development has changed from the 1920s/30s to the present day. The purpose is not to introduce every researcher who published on this topic. The scientists I have chosen to write about created something unique, and, very importantly, they examined sensorimotor development in a complex way during their observations and research.

Let us look at the views and theories of Jean Piaget, Margaret Rood, Jane Ayres, and Rhonda Douglas Brown on sensorimotor development.

Jean Piaget (1896–1980) was a biologist and philosopher who taught at several universities and was a professor of child psychology at the Sorbonne University from 1952 to 1963. He drew conclusions mostly from the precise and systematic observation of his own children and from this developed his theories.

He stated that children cannot be seen as small adults; they should be allowed to play and ask questions. Piaget himself used questioning as a research technique with his own children. He recorded the children's questions and using them drew conclusions about their cognitive, psychological, and social development.

As an interesting example, here is an excerpt from the recorded conversations:

> The 3-year, 2-month-old L. is lying in bed at night, but it is still light outside:
> – Please turn off the light!
> – But it is not on, look! *(To demonstrate, I turn it on and then off.)*
> – But, it's not night. Look outside, it's daytime. Turn it off!

– I can't turn off the outside light.
– But you can make it nighttime.
– How?
– By turning it off very strongly.
(Mérei, 1978, p. 415)

Piaget believed that biological determinism and environmental influences interact in a unique way throughout our lives. Individuals take an active part in their own development by building a "mental representation" of the surrounding world, which means that they represent the objects and events of the external world in their memory. He thought that human development results from both biological maturation and the individual's self-development processes. According to this constructivist view,[5] our existing knowledge contributes to the perception, discovery, and memory of new experiences, so we use existing information in our minds in a constructive way to process new information.

Piaget saw the child as a "little scientist," eager to learn about the world, ready to receive environmental stimuli, and actively involved in processing and interpreting them.

According to Piaget's famous theory, there are four stages in the development of the human intellect: sensorimotor development; pre-operational development; concrete operations; and formal operations.

His theory has been and still is the subject of many criticisms. However, it is still generally accepted that integrating and coordinating different perceptions plays a major role in sensorimotor development. During this period, the primitive reflex schemas that the infant possesses at birth and thereafter are first strengthened and then transformed into new schemas through adaptation. (In practice, the integration of primitive reflexes is based on this principle. For example: asymmetrical tonic neck reflex > segmental rolling reflex > crawling reflex > creeping reflex.)

This process requires continuous experience, which is due to the constant perception of sensory stimuli as well as the experience of one's own body movements and actions. The newly acquired experiences assimilate into

5 "Knowledge is built within the child, the exploring person themselves, and then the foundation of new knowledge can be the acquisition of further knowledge."

the existing schema, making it more effective, and if the original schema needs to be modified to incorporate the new experience, Piaget refers to this as the accommodation phenomenon. Piaget placed the sensorimotor stage of development in the first two years of life.

Jerome Bruner (1915–2016), a psychologist and educationist, summarized Piaget's ideas and contributions to the study of cognitive development, stating that Piaget is undoubtedly the most influential personality in this field. According to Bruner, while Piaget is often misunderstood as a psychologist, his true dedication was to epistemology. His primary interest was knowledge itself and how it manifests in different stages of child development. His theory posits that development occurs through cycles of equilibrium and disequilibrium, i.e., accommodation to the environment and assimilation of the environment into an internal schema. Although Piaget's formal descriptions may contain errors, the usefulness and comprehensive power of his descriptive work are of tremendous significance.

In the 1950s, Margaret Rood (1909–1984), who obtained degrees in physical therapy and movement therapy from Stanford University, formulated the three fundamental principles of sensorimotor development. According to the first principle, motor response is always dependent on sensory input. The second principle is that motor activity appears in a predetermined sequence during an individual's development. For example, walking should not precede crawling. The third principle states that stimulation of one sensory area improves the functioning of other sensory areas.

Jane Ayres based her sensory integration therapy on Rood's work. Ayres (1920–1988) was also a movement therapist and earned a PhD in educational psychology from the University of Southern California. In her book *Sensory Integration and the Child*, Ayres distinguished four levels of integration. Although her approach follows a segmented division, she did not provide distinct age boundaries for each stage. The first level is characterized by constant exposure to various sensory stimuli during the early stages of infant development. These stimuli serve as the foundation for later learning processes. Ayres included tactile stimuli (such as maternal touch, stroking, stimulation of the area around the mouth, and breastfeeding), which are crucial for the formation of attachment. Infants enjoy sucking and being picked up, rocked, and stroked. Through these stimuli, they learn that eating and being held provide security.

Ayres noted that vestibular and proprioceptive stimuli provide information to the child about their own movements. These stimuli are critical for regulating eye movements. Without them, focusing or tracking moving objects with the eyes would be impossible. Weak or delayed vestibular and proprioceptive integration can lead to developmental movement disorders. Additionally, children may have difficulty with balance and developing normal muscle tone.

In addition to tactile sensation, another stimulus that is essential for the child's sense of security is gravity. Perception of gravity gives the child a sense of safety. If sensory inputs from the inner ear, muscles, and joints do not integrate properly, then the child will not perceive their spatial position or movement in space well. Uncertainty about gravity not only directly affects movement, but also affects the child's overall personality development.

Ayres considers the development of bodily awareness to be the second level of sensory integration. At this point, the child is able to perceive the position of each body part in relation to the others and can use both sides of their body simultaneously in a coordinated manner, a phenomenon known as bilateral coordination. If the child is unable to use both hands or feet simultaneously, the immaturity of the vestibular (balance) system is often the root of the problem. It is common for the child to need extra effort to use a certain part of their body, and their attention may be weaker than that of their peers who have well-integrated tactile, balance, and proprioceptive functions.

The development of sustained attention is necessary to reach the third level. Without sustained attention, the child is unable to acquire language smoothly. To understand words, the child must pay attention to the speaker and clearly understand the incoming sounds and words. The maturity of the vestibular system is also essential for the child's speech perception and development. It regulates the appropriate tone of the tongue muscles and the movement of the tongue against gravity. It is often observed that when a child has sensory integration problems, their vestibular system is immature, and as a result, they do not feel the spatial position of their tongue or lips, leading to speech difficulties.

Vision, like hearing, is the result of earlier integration and perception processes. Through visual perception, we understand what we see. We first recognize the overall view, then the connection between objects, then distinguish the shape from the background and the parts from the whole. Visual spatial perception helps us understand the position of objects in space. However, the ability to see is not enough for complex perception alone. A lot of experience is needed, during which the child touches, feels, lifts, and puts down objects, gaining a complete picture of their shape, surface texture, weight, and other properties. When a child lifts something, their muscles and joints work against gravity. The vestibular system also plays an essential role in coordinating this process. If a child has vestibular, tactile, or proprioceptive sensory perception or perceptual disorders, they often have difficulty with hand–eye coordination.

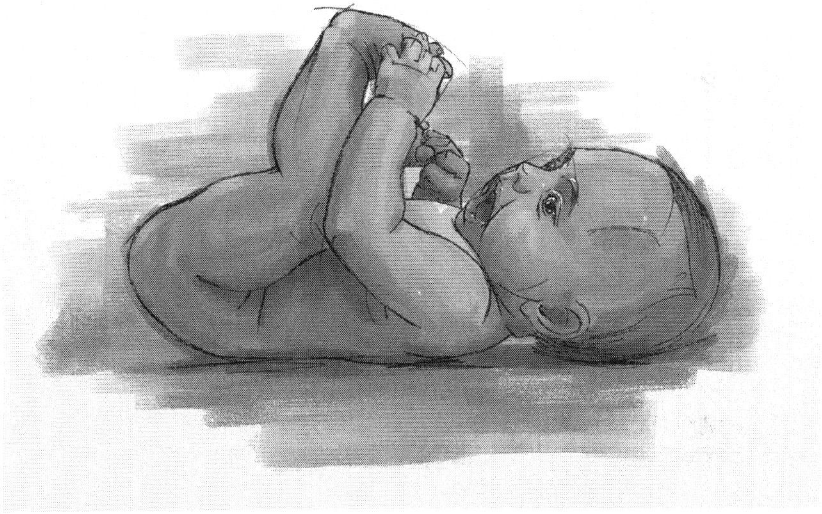

According to Ayres, the fourth level of sensory integration is the complete integration of various sensory sensations and perceptions, specialization of the hemispheres of the brain, and harmonious neural activity through a sufficient number and quality of connections between the two hemispheres. This determines the level of learning abilities such as abstract thinking, inference, fine and gross motor movements, attention regulation, behavior organization, visualization, self-control, and self-confidence.

Rhonda Douglas Brown holds a degree in cognitive psychology and education and is a professor of early childhood education, human development, and cognitive developmental psychology. She currently heads the Developmental and Learning Sciences Research Laboratory at the University of Cincinnati. According to Brown, sensorimotor integration refers to the relationship between the sensory organs (receptors) and the motor system (muscles), which includes communication and coordination between the two. This process lasts from birth to the age of seven.

During sensorimotor integration, the child is constantly involved in the process of cognitive and social interactions. The process starts with the child's involuntary movements, which open the way for experience and learning, leading to more precise and perfect movements. Therefore, for the child movement is how they learn, while their nervous system continues to develop.

The movements become purposeful, and the ability to consciously explore the environment develops. The perception and experience system collaborates with the motor system as a team. If the process of stimulus reception, processing, or motor response is impaired, the response may not occur or may be distorted. According to Brown's cognitive developmental psychology research, learning abilities, behavior, and emotional development are based on the level of sensory-motor integration.

Balance perception, body awareness, and clear and accurate perception not only influence a child's learning abilities but also affect task performance, concentration, and rule-following. Confidence in controlling one's own body enables free movement and thorough exploration of the world. The expanded range of motion opens the mind to further learning, which not only affects cognitive development but also has a positive impact on the child's personality.

If the process of sensory-motor integration occurs slower than necessary or there are "blockages" at different levels of integration, the problem manifests in varying ways in the child's life. The problem may be seen in poor handwriting, reading difficulties, hyperactivity, or attention-deficit. It is possible that even with greater effort, the child may not perform as well as their peers. Often, more time is needed to complete written work, which may cause unwarranted criticism from teachers and parents.

Brown observed that "excessive criticism" or encouragement towards faster and harder task completion leads to emotional problems in children, such as low self-esteem. If constantly reminded that they do not meet expectations, the child may feel worse, as they are doing everything they can but are still not performing adequately. The emotional problem generated is added to the deficit resulting from sensory-motor immaturity, which has a negative impact on the development of the child's social skills.

We have seen that various approaches agree that quick and continuous adaptation to the external and internal environment is necessary for the full realization of motor performance. The nervous system processes, integrates, and filters sensory stimuli for cortical motor responses. Thus, optimal motor planning and behavior can be achieved.

SENSORIMOTOR INTEGRATION

The relationship between sensory processing and primitive reflexes

The process by which a child develops from birth through infancy and into early childhood is nothing short of miraculous. Almost every day, there is a new feat for parents, grandparents, and siblings to marvel at. The baby suckles, gazes at their tiny hands, grasps a rattle—and even shakes it. When spoken to, they turn their head and smile at their parents. When sung to, they become calm and even differentiate between melodies. They become increasingly adept at holding their head up, rolling over, crawling, walking, and eventually uttering their first syllables and words.

The world's doors open to them, and at first hesitantly, then with increasingly determined steps, they enter.

This "miracle" is known as sensorimotor development

It is part of the process of sensorimotor integration, a term that refers to the relationship between the sensory organs and the motor system (muscles) and the process by which these two systems (sensory and motor) communicate with each other. For this to happen seamlessly, sensory processing must first be activated and organized. This means that through their sensory systems, the baby will be able to perceive the stimuli around them and the processes happening within their own body.

After perception, the nervous system processes and interprets the stimuli, combines them, and finally reacts to them. A very important part of the process is filtering out irrelevant stimuli. After a period of time, the nervous system ignores non-relevant information, protecting itself from overload. A good example of this is filtering out background noise. If we were to pay attention to every small sound around us during a conversation on the street, we would be unable to react to what our friend was saying. Our brains would experience significant confusion.

The synthesis of stimuli is a wonderful ability of the nervous system. Imagine how different the processes of vision, hearing, smell, touch, taste, and perception of spatial position in our head are. Our brains can convert different stimuli, such as light, sound, touch, pain, smells, tastes, and spatial perception, into electrical signals. The electrical signal is essentially the "common denominator." Our nervous system classifies, organizes, filters, and reacts to these signals.

As a baby develops, the CNS produces a response that corresponds to the stimuli that affect it, which appears in the form of a series of movements. External environmental stimuli, such as light and heat radiation, air vibrations, gravity, and chemical compounds, are processed by the sense organs and then become images, sounds, tastes, and smells in the appropriate areas of the brain. Stimuli from internal organs, muscles, and tendons also reach the brain through the process of visceroreception and proprioception, where they become sensations.

Piaget established that the process of sensorimotor development is characterized by the appearance of new skills and abilities. According to him, this process occurs during the first two years of life. Indeed, development is very intensive during the period mentioned by Piaget, but sensorimotor development does not end by the age of two—it has now become clear that it extends until the age of six or seven.

What happens in the first year and a half?

After birth, a baby enters a completely foreign world that they must explore using the tools available to them if they want to survive. And they certainly want to. The most peculiar thing is that they don't know the tools necessary for exploration, nor do they really know how to use them. Without instructions, they learn through trial and error which sense, limb, or other body part serves what purpose, and how to use them.

When a baby is born, a "great exploration journey" begins, starting with the perception of gravity. The infant must struggle with this unfamiliar phenomenon because it wasn't necessary when floating in amniotic fluid, in an almost weightless state.

After birth, every muscle movement occurs against gravity, and the functioning of the vestibular (balance) organ located in the inner ear helps to detect the Earth's gravitational pull. This organ senses how the baby's head is positioned in space and what movements it makes, transmitting this information to the CNS. Depending on the received information, the nervous system "sets" the tone of every muscle against gravity.

In the first month, a newborn baby's movement is mostly characterized by innate reflexes. If we approach their eyes, they close them; if they experience sudden noise, light, pain, cold, warmth, or if we put them in their crib, they spread their arms, take a deep breath, and then swing their arms forward. When the corner of their mouth is touched, they turn their head towards the stimulus, or when their lips are touched, they start a sucking movement. If we put our finger in their little hand, they grip it as if they never want to let go. At this point, the baby hardly moves, only performing movements necessary for feeding and excretion with the help of innate reflexes.

During the period from the first to the fourth month, the baby begins to coordinate the experiences gained through perception and also the use of certain motor skills. In the first two weeks, they primarily pay attention to internal stimuli, which helps to monitor internal processes necessary for individual development.

During this period, the baby perceives the sweet taste of breast milk, the scent of their mother, and the touch of her skin while sucking. They hear their parents' voices, which are familiar and comforting. At first, the baby's vision is limited to 25–30 cm and their eyes may occasionally cross or wander off. As time goes by, they begin to move more. They may accidentally start sucking their fingers, and then intentionally repeat this action because they find it pleasant. They also kick with their legs and wave their arms aimlessly. Later, these movements differentiate and integrate into a higher-level pattern. During this period, random movements lead to the execution of a new series of movements.

From the fourth month, the baby increasingly focuses on the world around them. They intentionally repeat activities that result in changes in their environment. From 4–6 months, their visual range increases, and movement becomes increasingly important. Changes in their environment promote new series of movements. If they reach for a rattle or toy hanging above them with their legs or hands, they will do it again and again. Object manipulations also belong to this category. When they grab toys or put them in their mouth and it is pleasurable, they repeat this simple action multiple times. During this phase, one of the baby's most significant achievements is coordinating their hand and eye movements. Object permanence gradually develops.[6] Motor skills become more differentiated, sophisticated, and integrated.

As movement increases, a healthy baby's perception of their internal organs is largely inhibited and is partially replaced by perception of movement, as well as by vision and hearing. If this process is partially or completely obstructed, if perception of internal organs becomes more intense in a later stage of development, or if there is a disorder in movement perception, visceral perception can become dominant again, often leading to various problems.

The period between eight and 12 months is when the child begins coordinating reactions to environmental stimuli. The child now performs clearly deliberate actions. It recognizes the characteristics of individual objects and develops the ability to manipulate relationships between objects. It begins to explore the surrounding world, observing and imitating the behavior of others. During this time, it becomes aware of itself as distinct from its environment. It realizes that it is inside its own skin, wearing clothes on its skin, and other people exist beyond that. The realization of "self" is closely related to the perception and processing of tactile stimuli.

The period from the twelfth to the eighteenth month is the "trial and error" phase. The infant tries to draw attention to itself by making intentional sounds and performing various actions. The primitive application of logic begins, which is evident in manipulating or playing with different objects. During this period, the child can approach a given problem in several different ways.

---

6 According to a study published by Bremner, Slater, and Johnson in 2014, the ability for object permanence is innate but continuously develops during infancy. Over time learning objects requires less time and stimuli.

By the age of one and a half, the child uses symbols to represent the world. Objects and events no longer need to be present for the child to think about them. We can tell a story about a favorite piglet that jumps in a puddle, and the child can imagine it even if the piglet is not there and the storybook is not open to the illustration.

By 18 months, sensorimotor development reaches a level that enables conscious experience and a more conscious understanding of the world, as well as appropriate responses to events. If the process has been smooth, further cognitive, psychological, and motor development can be built on a foundation that provides every opportunity for the child's development to be uninterrupted.

What does sensorimotor integration look like in practice? How can sensory processing work together with primitive reflexes? What will be the result of this cooperation?

Let's take an example from life

Remember that I wrote earlier that primitive reflexes are automatic motor responses to sensory stimuli. Primitive reflexes, genetically encoded in everyone, are activated by specific stimulation at a specific location on the body. The result is a specific, simple, predictable movement pattern. The movement cannot be prevented or influenced by the baby. A given stimulus elicits a single response. When the impulse ceases, the action stops.

Let's use the grasping reflex to look at how sensation and the movement generated by the primitive reflex are related. The grasping reflex can be triggered as early as 24–25 weeks after conception and is active until the baby is four months old. It is also known as the Robinson reflex after its discoverer. When a baby's palm is exposed to tactile stimuli, a specific movement pattern is triggered, i.e., the fingers bend and the hands clench into fists. The pattern is symmetrical, which means that both hands move together, even if only one palm is stimulated.

The grasping reflex allows the baby to hold an object and bring it closer from a distance, for example, from the edge of the cot to their face. After a while, the fingers open, and the object falls out. Over time, the baby touches and holds a variety of textures. A plastic rattle, a soft stuffed animal, the back of the cot, the edge of their blanket, mom's breast. Each experience provides information and a "memory file" is formed in the sensory cortex. The nervous system then recognizes the touch information from the palms as safe and familiar. The reflexive grip becomes less and less necessary, and the grasping reflex becomes less active and less triggered. This involuntary primitive reflex determines the baby's movements less and less.

The baby begins to use its hands in different ways. Its movements, which it can change, become free and flexible, guided by intention, and are no longer automatic. Integrating the grasping reflex opens the way to developing fine motor skills, allowing more complex movements to emerge.

The primitive reflex patterns do not disappear entirely but are integrated into the child's complex repertoire of movements. Throughout life, the grasping reflex is activated only when an immediate, automatic response is needed to protect the child, for example when they fall and need to grab something to prevent injury.

If there is a problem with sensory processing (in the case of the grasping reflex this would mostly relate to tactile sensation), the reflex remains active. The involuntary response to a stimulus will still be triggered. This delays or inhibits the development of controlled, more complex movements. Children must rely on a simple, predictable, unchangeable primitive reflex pattern. This delays the development of the motor cortex in the brain, limits already immature sensory processing, and interferes with the development of fine motor skills in many areas such as independence and the use of tools.

In addition to inadequate sensory processing, there may be problems with reflex deterioration if the reflex is not "strong enough." In this case, the baby cannot grasp objects, so tactile perception will be problematic without sufficient stimulation. If the sensory cortex is not working perfectly, it does not receive enough stimulation and does not store the information that allows it to recognize textures, shapes, etc.

Other reflexes can also affect reflex integration. The grasping reflex is most affected by the sucking reflex and the Moro reflex. If these reflexes do not integrate, then it is likely that the grasping reflex will also not integrate properly. When not integrated in time these primitive reflexes negatively affect the baby's sensory and motor development and can cause problems with fine motor coordination and in processing a wide range of tactile stimuli.

What are these problems?

Persistence of the grasping reflex limits use of the hands. For a baby to develop the ability to use tools, play with different toys, and learn from these activities, it needs to be able to touch and tolerate different textures in many areas of the palm and fingers. Suppose that learning about texture, size, shape, and other properties is not accomplished or is delayed. In that case, there will be a barrier to developing fine motor skills such as buttoning up clothes, tying shoelaces, and drawing. These skills form the basis for developing fine motor and independence skills, which have a strong impact on writing ability.

I mentioned earlier that the pattern of the grip reflex is symmetrical, i.e., both hands are activated when stimulated, even if the stimulus affects only one hand. If the reflex remains active, both hands move together when stimulated, and the brain cannot distinguish between them. This affects the development of the dominant hand and the perception of the body's midline, and causes confusion between the left and right hands. These problems affect laterality, bilateral coordination, reading, and writing.

Above, we have discussed a single primitive reflex and the link with sensorimotor integration. About 100 primitive reflexes have been described. My experience and the literature suggest that 10–15 occur most frequently during the child's life, even when they should have become "dormant." These reflexes block sensorimotor integration and thus hurt the child's physical, emotional, and mental development.

Several problems arise wholly or partly from the persistence of primitive reflexes. Before discussing these in detail, let us look at how sensory perception gives us a complex picture of the world and the processes that occur in us.

It is essential to understand this because the reflexes that help us to gather our experiences of the world from birth for two or three years influence our sensations and perceptions. Imagine that the reflexes are not present with the right intensity and quality in infancy. In that case, they will not be able to fulfill their role in sensorimotor integration, and they will be unlikely to degrade and integrate. In the following few chapters, we will discuss perception, and its role in reflex integration.

THE SYMPHONY OF SENSORY PERCEPTION AND SENSATION

I recently met a very bright seven-year-old boy and his mother. They came to see me about the child's bedwetting. While I was talking to his mother, the boy asked me for a piece of paper because he wanted to draw. Soon, a giant, happy, red apple appeared in the middle of the paper.

The following conversation took place between us:

> *– What a beautiful apple this is. It's almost smiling. Do you like to eat apples?*
> *– Yes. I love apples.*
> *– What do you like about apples?*
> *– I like the crunching sound. When Dad eats apples, I can hear it. He is very good at eating apples.*
> *– Why? How does your dad eat apples?*
> *– First, he rubs it against his clothes. He says it gets the dirt off, but I know he does it to make it shiny. Like apples in fairytales.*
> *– So, you like this fruit because you can hear it crunch. What else do you like about apples?*
> *– The smell. When Dad picks all the apples off the tree and we take them into the kitchen, there's an apple smell everywhere. At Grandma's there is a smell of quince, but I dislike it because it smells "old."*
> *– Yes, apples do smell good. I like them too. What about the taste? I suppose you like the taste of apples too?*
> *– Yeah, I almost forgot. That's the best thing about apples. Do you know that red, yellow, and green apples taste different?*
> *– Yes, I do. Which do you like best?*
> *– The red apple.*
> *– Why red?*
> *– Because it grows on a tree that I can climb. And you know what else I like about apples?*
> *– I don't know, but I'm very curious.*

– I like the fact that they're round. Like this. (He shows with his hand.) Dad and I used to talk about spheres, and I've loved spherical things ever since. Like a ball. But I like apples better.

After our conversation, I thought about how sensory perception and integration is one of the great wonders of nature, beautifully illustrated by this little boy of seven years old.

The spherical shape, the smooth, hard touch, the red color, the taste, the smell, and the crisp sound all come together to form a "whole," which is none other than the apple. As soon as our brain learns that all these elements belong to the apple, just one or two of them are enough for us to recall the others, the whole, that is, the "whole of all the apple's qualities."

The richness and variety of stimuli from the external world and the internal environment are necessary to develop the child's knowledge systems and thus enable them to become as adaptable and practical as possible and to learn. This requires, in addition to the functioning of the nervous system, a flawless sensory system that picks up and transmits information to the place where it is processed.

In the following chapters, we will look at the sensory systems contributing to this process's coherent and integrated nature.

THE SENSE OF BALANCE IN THE LABYRINTH

Ice hockey players don't wobble around on the ice, and they don't just stand still on their skates; they can glide at high speed holding their stick and roll the puck. They know where their teammates are and where the goal is, and they can catch the puck as it moves at lightning speed and shoot at the goal. The goalie can see the incoming puck and usually deflect the shot with his stick. During a game, players are so adept that they rarely or never collide, despite their high speed. Their bodies keep the optimal posture while they zig-zag across the ice from the start to the end of the match.

How is this possible? To sense body position, the coordinated action of several organs is required. The position from which we see our surroundings is essential. Our brain constantly registers which muscles need to contract to maintain the same position or how we can react most quickly to a new situation with our posture and movements.

The organ of body position, and the sense of balance, is the vestibular or balance-sensing organ located inside the inner ear of the petrous bone, which begins to mature in the 8–10th week of fetal life and can sense changes in the position of the head at birth. The vestibular system supports elementary movement patterns such as walking, sitting without support, and crawling.

Continuous adaptation to the Earth's gravitational field is based on a large amount of information from different places, which determines motor adaptation and the motor system's development, as does the direction the stimulus is coming from. From birth, the vestibular system is trained by various stimuli and motor responses. Cradling, rocking, lifting, and putting the baby in the cot all contribute to the development of balance, as do lifting the child's head, turning the child over from their belly to their back and vice versa, and also other types of movement during later stages of development.

This tiny organ, which enables us to overcome the difficulties caused by gravity and to navigate in space, which in turn affects almost every part of our body—how is it built and how does it function?

The vestibular organ comprises the saccule and the utricule, located in the bony vestibule, and the three semicircular arches positioned in three different planes of space.

The utricle and the saccule sense the spatial position of the immobile head. Both organs are hollow, with hair cells inside, covered by a gelatinous sheath. The gelatinous shell contains tiny crystals of calcium carbonate (otoliths). The jelly-like shell bends when the head is tilted—the calcium crystals increase the compressive force, and the hair cell extensions deform and become stimulated.

The semicircular arc ducts are tubular formations found in three perpendicular space planes. In the widening of these are hair cells with a similar gelatinous covering as in the interior of the utricule and saccule.

When the head is displaced, the gelatinous fluid in the arching passage in the plane of displacement moves, and the hair cells bend and are stimulated. The hair cells sense the accelerating or decelerating movement of the head.

From the receptors of the position-sensing organ, the impulse travels along the fibers of the vestibulocochlear, or eighth cranial, nerve, through the brain stem, and then to the thalamus. From the thalamus, the information is transmitted to the primary sensory cortex in the parietal lobe, where the sensation is formed.

The vestibular system has several functions. It is responsible for regulating and maintaining balance and for adjusting muscle tone in response to gravity. Its sensory receptors are located in the sac, sacrococcygeal, and semicircular canals, but it also receives information from the eye, muscles (muscle spindle), tendons (tendon spindle), and skin mechanoreceptors.

The motor centers of the brainstem coordinate and control eye movements regarding changes in the position of the head, and play a role in fixing the gaze.

Each eye is connected to six eye-moving muscles that receive stimuli from the vestibular system. Moving the head repeatedly causes the eyes to adjust. For example, when the head is turned sideways, the eye muscles move the eyeballs parallel to the new position to see clearly. This process helps us to focus.

Related to this is the phenomenon known as nystagmus, which is the involuntary, rhythmic movement of the eyes. Its role is to stabilize the visual field. It can be observed, for example, when looking out of a train window or a car at a passing landscape.

Nystagmus can also be triggered by being spun around or by spinning. Its direction is changed by the position of the stimulated semicircular canals, which is in turn determined by the position of the head and the body. So, if someone is spun in a horizontal direction, for example on a swivel chair, the eyes move horizontally.

Nystagmus plays a significant role in the process of reading and writing. In Western languages, when reading, the eye moves from left to right along the text. At the end of a line, nystagmus helps the sight to automatically jump back to the beginning of the next line, so we only have to look one line down and don't have to search for the start of that line.

Post-rotational nystagmus is often used to test the vestibular system. Róbert Bárány, an Austrian doctor of Hungarian origin, was awarded the

Nobel Prize in 1914 for his research on the vestibular system. The post-rotational test is also called the Bárány test after his name.[7]

Several researchers have addressed the link between post-rotational nystagmus and learning difficulties. Billye Ann Cheatum tested children from 1986 to 1989. Among children with learning difficulties, 61% had inadequate post-rotational nystagmus; for the control group, the figure was just 21%.

The other primary function of the vestibular system is to adjust the tone of the skeletal muscles, and therefore posture, by coordinating visual, balancing, and stretching stimuli. The connection between the balance-sensory system and the cerebellum also plays a role. The cerebellum is also involved in coordinating movements.

The central adjustment of muscle tone applies not only to skeletal muscles but to all muscles, including the muscles of the tongue and face. A child with "weak" or hypotonic tongue and facial muscles often has problems with speech formation or swallowing properly. In addition to articulation problems (forming clear speech), weak tongue and cheek muscles can cause other problems. "Tongue thrust swallowing" may develop, where the child does not press his tongue to the roof of his mouth and push the food back to reach the esophagus, but his tongue "pushes forward," causing his upper incisors to move forward. After a while, this type of swallowing leads to speech formation problems due to persistent misalignment of the teeth. In these cases, braces are not a solution if tongue thrust swallowing persists.

Another problem in children, partly due to inadequate muscle tone adjustment, is bedwetting at night or a weak bladder during the day. If there is no underlying organ dysfunction, the cause of the problem is often that the bladder sphincter is not "strong" enough and does not close properly. Particularly at night, when large amounts of urine are stored in the bladder, the high pressure "opens the gate," and urine flows out.

---

7 Here I note that in the children I have studied, I have found that in those who write letters (b-d, p-q) and numbers (3-Ɛ), and sometimes read words (bed-deb, pub-bup etc.), backward, the eye movement after rotation cannot be triggered by turning to the left (anticlockwise), in the direction that would make the child's eye jump from right to left when reading. Conversely, when the child is spun to the right, there is normal eye movement after the spin, but their eyes automatically jump back to the right from the left. It is assumed they would not have reading difficulties if they could read the text backward.

The malfunction of the balance-sensing system has attracted the attention of several researchers working with children. Dr. Julio B. de Quirós was one of the doctors who discovered a link between vestibular system dysfunction and learning difficulties. de Quirós examined more than 2,000 children in the 1950s and 1960s and followed their development for three years. He found that children with vestibular problems had less motor development, balance, language development, and reading and writing skills than those with a mature and well-functioning vestibular system.

Auxter, Pyfer, and Huetting also stressed that children with poorly functioning vestibular systems have problems with balance perception, gross and fine motor movements, and motor coordination. In particular, weaknesses in eye-hand coordination have been highlighted, which cause problems in learning to write and, later, especially in the first years of school, writing.

Jean Pyfer observed that children who have a delay in developing a good sense of balance also have problems learning new movements (cycling, ball games, skiing, skating), learning to read and write, and learning to understand speech and texts.

The vestibular system's function in regulating muscle tone also explains the relationship between the vestibular system and speech comprehension. Two small muscles are located in the middle ear. One is the eardrum extensor muscle, which is connected to the hammer and keeps the eardrum taut. The stretched eardrum can transmit sound waves with precision. Imagine a drum whose surface is not tight. It is difficult to imagine how a drummer could produce any sound from a drum in this condition. Only a properly tight eardrum can achieve clear hearing.

The other tiny muscle is the stirrup muscle, which connects the stirrup (a tiny bone in the middle ear) and the oval window (a membrane covering the entrance to the cochlea in the inner ear). When exposed to loud noise, the stirrup muscle contracts, making the auditory mechanism stiffer and less conductive. The tone of this muscle can therefore regulate the amount of sound entering the inner ear. If the muscle tone is incorrect, the amount of noise entering the ear is not reduced, which means overload and, together with the previous problem, makes auditory perception more difficult.

Since children learn their mother tongue by hearing only, we can imagine that if they do not hear the voices of the people around them clearly and at the right volume, they will not be able to pronounce words in a clear, straightforward way. This has a significant impact on their speech development and comprehension.

In 1986, de Quirós, who among other things was involved in research into dyslexia (which has a strong connection with disorders of the vestibular system), published a study drawing attention to the link between vestibular system dysfunction and learning difficulties. He suggested ways of alleviating and eliminating the problem. He recommended that special exercises to promote the maturation and development of the vestibular system should be incorporated into the education and development of children with vestibular system problems.

Finally, it is worth mentioning a phenomenon linked to the vestibular system. This is the so-called pre-arousal function. Depending on the nature of the vestibular stimulus (rocking, spinning, sudden turning or shaking of the head), it can be calming or arousing. An excellent example is when young children are tired and they shake their heads, jump around, or run in circles. Or when someone is tired while driving, they shake their head to stay awake and be able to focus. These lively movements stimulate the vestibular system, keeping the brain sharp.

The opposite effect is produced by rocking, swaying, and traveling in a car. These vestibular stimuli have a calming effect on the child's nervous system. They make a baby quiet and often put them to sleep.

In the following, I will list the symptoms that indicate inadequate functioning of the vestibular system, based on Cheatum and Hammond and my own experience:

Vestibular hypersensitivity

- Dislikes watching things that spin in circles such as a carousel or a Ferris wheel
- Dislikes spinning while dancing or on a swivel chair or in the playground, and is reluctant to participate in activities that involve repeated turning
- Feels dizzy when traveling, on a slide, or when jumping
- Does not like to play with playground equipment—swings, slides, roundabouts, trampolines, etc.

- Often loses balance when moving
- Experiences travel sickness
- Prefers to sit in the front seat of a car
- Feels dizzy in lifts or on escalators
- As a small child, did not like being thrown up in the air
- Displays uncoordinated movement
- Usually doesn't like sports
- Usually prefers to read or be in a "quiet corner"

Vestibular hyposensitivity

- Weak muscle tone and body awareness
- Poor sense of balance, frequently trips and falls
- Clumsiness, uncoordinated movements, inability to succeed in sports
- Weak muscle control, inability to sit still on a bench or stand for prolonged periods (e.g., at a ceremony)
- Very fond of spinning, turning, rolling
- Never gets dizzy when spinning
- Has problems with laterality, e.g., coordinating arm and leg movements when skipping or running
- Has speech problems
- Has difficulty reading and/or writing
- Has weak control of the eye muscles, which causes difficulties in learning and sports
- Usually does not like sports

The larger the number of these symptoms present in a child or even an adult, the more you should suspect that something is wrong with the sensory system—in this case, the sense of balance. A symptom does not necessarily mean that the sense is malfunctioning. However, if that problem is very disturbing and is causing the person long-term discomfort, it is worth seeking professional help. This applies to all the senses in general.

THE WORLD OF OUR EYES

Each of our senses has a special role to play in our lives. If any of them get damaged, its function diminishes, or—heaven forbid—it fails entirely, our overall view of the world shatters and falls apart. It takes a long time for the remaining senses to be able to fill in the gaps left by the senses that are no longer functioning.

I once had a young patient who lost all her sight in one eye and 80% in the other. Just as they were getting dressed to go home, the next small child arrived with his mother. This boy, who was almost five years old, noticed that the little girl who was leaving could barely see, but he said nothing. When they came in for his examination, however, the little boy started asking questions.

> *– Mum! Why was the little girl touching the wall?*
> *– Because she couldn't see. Or if she could see, it was very faint.*
> *– But she was wearing glasses. Couldn't she see with them on?*
> *– Unfortunately, glasses don't help everyone.*
> *– But the little girl looked at me. Couldn't she see me?*
> *– No, she couldn't see you. Or at least not the way you saw her.*
> *– Then why was she looking at me? Don't we all see when we look?*
> *– She looks, and she wants to see too. But she can't, because she has a problem with her eyes.*
> *– If I have a problem with my eyes, won't I see?*
> *– I hope your eyes will never be bad.*
> *– But if they are?*
> *– If they are, Mum, you'll be doing my looking for me. You will look hard into my eyes, and then I will see. You will look, I will see. Okay?*
> *– ...*
> *– Look hard, so I can see everything. Because if you miss anything, I'll be angry.*

Obviously, everyone with good eyesight appreciates this extraordinary ability and occasionally thinks about how great it is to see loved ones, a green hilly landscape, the mountains, the ocean, a ladybug, or to watch a movie, see a play, or read a book.

Vision helps us learn, get around, play sports, and avoid dangerous places and situations. How good it is for us to be able to do this! Obviously, people who lack sight have their own "Plan B" to navigate the world, but there is no complete substitute for vision. It occupies a privileged place among our senses for experiencing the world around us.

When? Where? What?

This complex perceptual system provides information in both space and time, as visual stimuli are perceived in time and seen in succession, and simultaneously, we perceive the spatial position, extent, color, and other properties of the living things and objects around us.

Seeing should not be confused with looking, which is "only" a prerequisite for seeing. Looking is not a learned process but an innate ability. Vision, on the other hand, develops as an individual grows. An infant learns to see gradually through experience, as the nervous system analyzes and identifies what it sees. It is in this process that sight becomes a sense.

To understand looking and seeing, think of searching for a pen on a slightly messy desk. We have been looking at the desk for some time and the pen is nowhere to be seen. Then, suddenly, the outline of the pen becomes distinct from the other objects on the desk. Our brain interprets the image of the pen, and we see the object we want to find. We *look* when our eyes are on someone or something, we *see* when we process what we perceive with our eyes, forming an image of it in our mind.

What does a newborn baby see?

From research by Hungarian researcher Emese Nagy and colleagues we know that at a very early stage of sensory development, newborns, and later, infants, can recognize faces and facial expressions. They not only detect them but also imitate them. Some facial expressions can be imitated by the newborn, others only at later stages of infancy. Researchers have also observed that the child not only imitates the facial expression, but after two or three times, begins to repeat it on their own without any stimulus. In newborns, the parent should lean close to the baby due to their short visual range, and later on it is enough to just lean above them.

This suggests that elementary communication skills are already genetically encoded in the child.

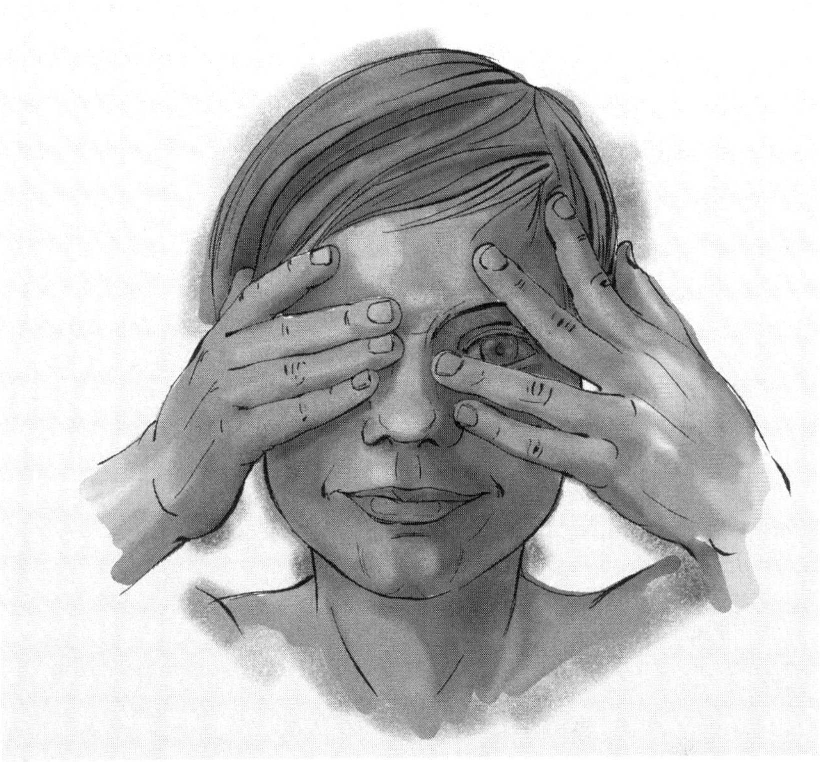

The importance of processing visual stimuli

According to the research team of Cheatum and Hammond, visual stimuli account for 80–90% of the influences on the nervous system. Children with visual perception problems have distorted information coming into the brain. This is combined with vestibular, tactile, proprioceptive, and auditory stimuli perceived simultaneously, leading to disorganization to a greater or lesser extent. As a result, the normal expectations of a child regarding visuality, such as reading and writing, become difficult or impossible to meet.

During the school years, the most apparent problems with vision manifest in reading and writing. Sometimes the axes of the eyes do not converge, or the child's eyes cannot focus, in which case they cannot process visual stimuli correctly or see clearly, even though his or her visual organs are healthy. In other cases, there may be difficulty in distinguishing between shape and background or one part from another. Many young children have poor eye–hand coordination, which, along with the examples mentioned above, is essential for learning to write smoothly.

Several basic skills and abilities related to the process of vision are prerequisites for proper visual functioning. Imagine a simple walk in the woods. You have to look into the distance because your eyes are looking for signs on the trees so you don't get lost, but the next moment you have to look in front of your feet because you don't want to trip. In terms of vision, the same phenomenon happens when a child copies from the blackboard or solves a problem written on the blackboard in his notebook. Their eyes have to focus and refocus quickly between the distant and the nearby.

Let's look at another situation. When we step out of a darkened house into a sunny yard in summer, our pupils must contract quickly to avoid getting too much light on our retinas. If our pupils contract in time and to the proper extent, we can see clearly in bright sunlight.

Both eyes must work correctly to perceive three-dimensional space, movement in space, or the relative position of perceived movements. When we are standing on the side of the road, our vision helps us to know if a car is approaching or driving away, whether it is in the lane near us or further away, slowing down or accelerating, and whether it is red, black, or white.

It is thanks to shape constancy that we are able to recognize our dogs and cats not only from the front but from all directions, even when they are dirty. This ability allows us to identify signs, objects or shapes even if their position, size, or color changes.

Visual memory is the ability to remember images that you have seen before. It enables us to recognize, associate, store and recall images. We can memorize the image of a letter, and we can associate letters with sounds and with other letters in words. We can use visual memory and sequential imagery to recall a scene we have seen, but these skills are also essential for learning and practicing reading and writing.

The eye is just a tool for seeing. To process incoming information with sufficient accuracy, the nervous system must use and process various other sensory and motor information. In the first year after birth, several neural pathways are established between the CNS, the sensory organs, and the body. During visual-sensory integration, the nervous system links and integrates vision with vestibular, auditory, tactile, motor, proprioceptive, and other stimuli.

The link between vision and balance

The vestibulo-ocular system (VOR), or the reflex of the same name, is paramount for vision. When we walk, we hold our heads up and perceive what is happening around us thanks to the VOR reflex. This reflex keeps us balanced even though our head constantly moves, our eyes scanning the environment. This is because when the head moves, the muscles that move the eyes are immediately activated and produce a movement of the same magnitude but in the opposite direction to the head movement. Due to this the nerve membrane stabilizes the visual world.

If the VOR is not functioning properly, vision may become blurred or the image may not be fixed on the retina when the head moves. The person perceives what they see as if the image were "vibrating." Even very slight head movements can distort the recognition of words and letters. Atypical eye movements can blur vision. Because these children and adults read slowly and with difficulty, they are often diagnosed with dyslexia or even dyscalculia (difficulty making calculations).

In these cases, the child's eyes really can't follow words and lines when reading, and their nervous system very quickly gets tired. Depending on their personality type, the child may become anxious or have a variety of behavioral or conduct problems. They drop their pencils, talk to their classmates, and pretend not to care. They usually fall behind in their studies and may even lose interest in attending school because of their failure.

Problems, troubles, difficulties

According to Cheatum and Hammond (2000) and my own experience the following problems may be associated with vision.

1. An "accommodation" disorder, meaning the thickness of the lens of the eye is not able to adjust sufficiently on the target, with the following results:

- focuses the eye too far away or too close instead of the target
- unable to relax when looking close up, for example, when working at a desk
- has difficulty changing focus from the desk to the blackboard and vice versa
- vision can be blurred
- the child uses only one eye
- headaches when looking close up
- double vision
- dry eyes
- drowsiness
- weakness, lack of concentration

2. Problems with fixation, i.e., fixing the gaze in one direction

- children cannot maintain focus
- eyes watering
- fatigue
- stress
- problems during movement and sports
- eyes constantly jumping between target objects
- difficulty in grasping what is happening in the classroom
- short attention span
- often does not know where they are in the text when reading
- reversing letters, reversing words
- retention problems

3. Inability to maintain binocular vision (seeing with both eyes)

- alternating the use of the eyes
- adopts an awkward posture at the desk
- squints
- skips words when reading
- writes numbers and letters in the wrong order in a row or column
- fatigue when focusing
- looks with one eye half open
- difficulty in performing reading and writing tasks
- duplicates letters

- strained posture
- blinks eyes
- props the head up when reading and writing

4. Visual tracking problems

- misses words or letters when reading or writing
- when reading the child moves their head left and right rather than moving their eyes
- when drawing doesn't fill the available space
- low reaction time
- poor aim in sports
- writes numbers, letters, and words in reverse
- skips lines when reading
- difficulty in reading comprehension
- difficulty crossing the midline of the body (especially when looking)
- reserved in the classroom

5. Strabismus

- headaches
- blurred vision in one eye
- double vision
- blindness of one eye when looking
- covering one eye (even by hand)
- no dominant eye
- one or both eyes turned in (cross-eyed)

6. Problems with visual memory

There is a significant correlation between visual memory and reading ability. A simple task such as learning the alphabet can be problematic if visual memory is poor. If a child cannot remember the individual letters, there is little chance that they will be able to recognize and read the letters in a word.

7. Problems with shape versus background discrimination

- difficulty in selecting a figure, word, number, or letter in a picture or text
- difficulty perceiving the relationship between parts of a picture

- difficulty recognizing, connecting, or breaking down letters into their elements
- reserved in the classroom

8. Visual motor problems

- difficulty handling a ball due to double vision
- inability to concentrate on the teacher for a sufficient period of time
- difficulty with focused attention
- difficulty in distinguishing the direction of travel of a moving object (is the ball coming or going?)
- clumsiness, coordination problems
- eye–hand coordination difficulties

When a child is suspected of having a learning disability, an examination is essential to check that the visual system is in order. If the ophthalmologist doesn't find any problems, further investigation should be made into the possibility of sensorimotor integration, maturation, or immaturity issues.

I HEAR, I UNDERSTAND, I ANSWER

"I'm talking to you, don't you understand? Are your ears blocked? Why do I have to say something a hundred times? Do you hear only what you want to hear?"

These phrases may sound familiar. Sometimes, even if we speak to someone in their mother tongue, they don't understand or listen to us, or seem to ignore us.

There are several reasons for this phenomenon. The listener may not be interested in the subject. Other times, the speaker may have poor articulation, a slur, or a speech impediment. Sometimes the background noise is too loud, or the person you are talking to is tired and finds it difficult to stay awake, let alone understand what you are saying. But what if none of these situations apply? How can someone with a perfectly functional hearing organ not seem to understand speech in their native language?

Often, we don't consider that the reason for inattention, behavioral problems, or learning difficulties could be a hearing disorder. But having a clear, precise perception of sounds is essential. Consider that all children learn their mother tongue by hearing alone. They imitate the sounds, syllables, words, and sentences they hear. If an input sound or the speech is distorted, we cannot expect the child to pronounce it clearly and produce intelligible speech. Later, when this young child is learning to read and write, how can they associate a sound with a picture of a letter, when they sometimes hear it one way and sometimes another?

What is hearing?

During the final three months in the womb, the fetus can already hear different noises, speech, and music. A loud sound can produce the so-called orienting response in fetuses in a resting state as early as the 28–29th week of pregnancy, wherein the baby moves and kicks. This phenomenon can be observed frequently during the last few months of pregnancy. The fetus can hear its mother's speech and heartbeat while in the womb, so it comes as no surprise that by the time it sees the light of day, these sounds are familiar to the child. When it comes to perception, the newborn's hearing at birth is almost as complete as an adult's.

Babies react to all sounds when awake. They visibly pay attention when we speak or sing. However, they are startled by unexpected, unfamiliar sounds. It may come as a surprise that they often sleep soundly while surrounded by loud, constant noise. Babies like rhythmic, monotone sounds, and soft melodies that have a calming effect on them. Once the initial restlessness has subsided, the regularly repeating auditory stimulus results in habituation. Such sounds are produced by most household appliances, such as the humming of a dishwasher, hairdryer, or vacuum cleaner. Naturally, it is best if these monotone sounds are soft, soothing music, evenly paced speech, or singing. It is no coincidence that lullabies and bedtime stories calm and lull the child to sleep.

When we speak slowly, in a higher tone of voice, and rhythmically, our experience is that children listen attentively. After all, their initial vocabulary is formed while listening to speech directed toward them. They are able to understand words well before being able to imitate them themselves.

How do sounds reach the auditory nerve? In what way does our brain process auditory stimuli? What protects our nervous system from being overloaded by sounds? How are we able to discern between relevant information and background noise? A rather complex process is involved in this phenomenon, one which has formed through adaptations over the course of several million years and has become increasingly precise.

Hearing is the perception of vibrations in the air at voice frequency, and the subsequent processing of these vibrations. It contributes to the adaptation of living beings, to acquiring information, and to survival. It warns us of danger and promotes communication within and between species. In humans, hearing relates primarily to speech and music.

The strength and pitch of sounds influences the hearing process. The human ear, on average, can hear frequencies in the range of 20 to 20,000 Hertz. The most pleasant range is between 300 and 3,000 Hertz. The pressure of the sound waves on the eardrum depends on the strength of the sound. The greater the pressure, the louder the sound. The threshold for hearing is 0 dB, this being the lowest threshold for sounds heard by the human ear. Anything lower than this is imperceptible to people.

A regular conversation takes place at around 50 dB. The pain threshold is around 120dB—the ear may become damaged at this level, and deafness can occur.

The outer ear starts at the pinna/auricle and goes until the eardrum. The auditory tube, otherwise known as the Eustachian tube, belongs to the middle ear, and it connects the tympanic cavity to the nasopharynx. The most important role of the auditory tube is equalizing pressure between the middle ear and the outer world.

The three ossicles can be found in the tympanic cavity, connected by joints. In order: the eardrum is connected to the hammer, the hammer to the anvil, and finally the anvil to the stirrup. The base of the stapes covers the opening to the inner ear, the "oval window," in which it sits. The sound waves entering the outer ear vibrate the eardrum, and these vibrations travel through the ossicles, amplifying as they go. The vibrations of the ossicles activate the fluid inside the inner ear through the oval window.

The inner ear is located within the bony labyrinth of the temporal bone. This is where the bulk of the work in the hearing process is done since the brain has to unravel, analyze and assign meaning to the complex neural impulses at lightning-quick speed.

Part of the bony labyrinth is the vestibule, to which the cochlea is connected. The organ for balancing is also found here, which was discussed earlier. The bony labyrinth is filled with fluid, and in it lies the membranous cochlea. The lower wall of the membranous cochlea is the so-called basilar membrane, which widens towards the tip of the cochlea, and contains gradually longer coils within. The perception of a sound's pitch depends on the length of the coil. Higher sounds induce stimulation at the base of the cochlea, while deeper sounds do so at the tip.

The "organ of Corti" can be found on the basilar membrane, and is capable of translating sound vibrations into electrical signals. The vibrations cause the tectorial membrane to press against the hair cells sitting on the basilar membrane. Consequently, the hairs bend and an impulse is formed, which travels to the brain through the fibers of the auditory nerve and finally reaches the temporal lobe of the cortex through the auditory pathway. This is where the sensation of sound is formed.

The cochlea is capable of analyzing sound. It reacts differently depending on the pitch and strength of the sound. The stronger the sound, the bigger the deflection in the organ of Corti and the larger the number of electrical impulses, and depending on the frequency of the sound, different sensory cells of the cochlea are stimulated.

Once the information reaches the auditory center, it analyzes the incoming complex sound waves in terms of pitch (frequency) and strength (amplitude). The analyzed waves are then compared with previously heard and stored samples—the echoic or auditory memories. The brain is thus able to recognize the origin of the sound and assign meaning to it. It differentiates between familiar sounds and sounds that signal danger. Auditory memories are so well stored that there may be no other kind of sensory information that can be remembered so accurately at a later time.

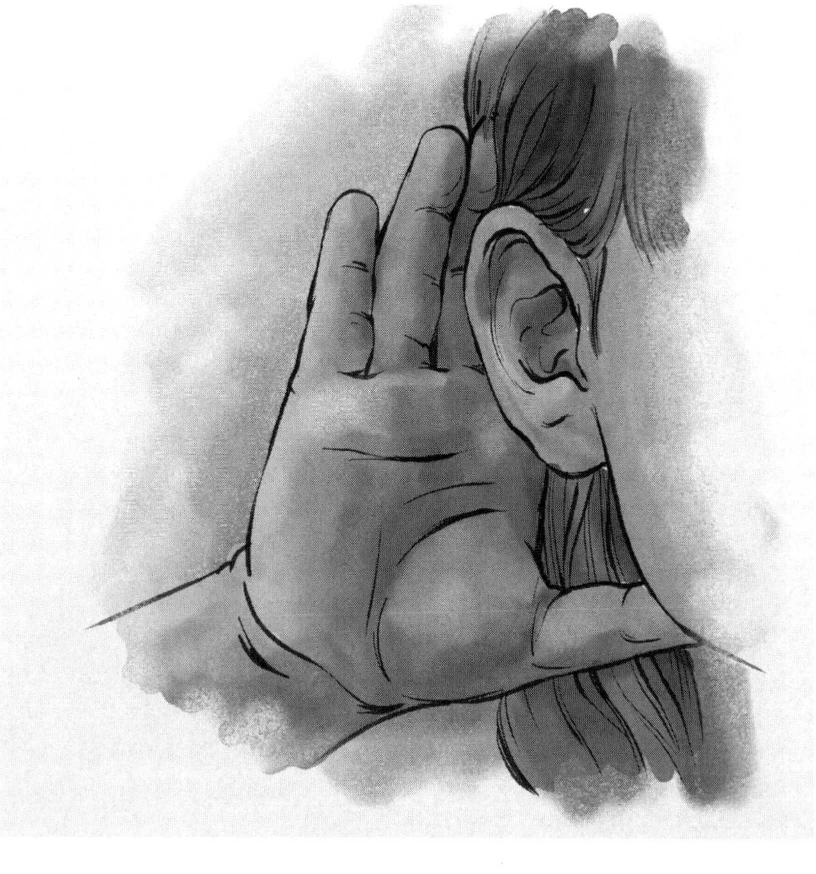

"All ears"

As surprising as it may be, not only does the auditory organ send messages to the brain, but the reverse is also true. When we concentrate hard and we're "all ears," our brain can notify the ears that it needs some sort of "additional" information.

For example, when we sense a faint melody in the distance, and we would like to hear it more sharply, be able to perceive it better and find out what song it is, this is done by the incoming and outgoing nerves and pathways. About 6% of connections between the auditory organ and the brain are outgoing, meaning they travel from the brain to the ear. While incoming nerves and their pathways transmit information toward the brain, the brain can direct the behavior of the basilar membrane in the cochlea thanks to muscle contractions produced by the outgoing nerve pathways. By being able to increase the membrane's sensitivity to certain frequencies, it can influence the quality of hearing, and can help us be "all ears."

Where is this special auditory center, to which we owe countless miracles, located?

The auditory cortex, which can be found in both lobes and is barely bigger than a thumbnail, is located in a gyrus of the temporal lobe. Experiments have proven that there is a sort of division of labor between the two sides of the head. The left center, for example, plays a larger role in recognizing and interpreting acoustic signals, and speech comprehension. The right center is tied to processing melodies. There is constant and intensive communication between the two centers.

Understanding speech

Speech received by the auditory system is nothing more than a convoluted mixture of sound waves. It is an enormous feat by the brain that it can unwind this "ball of sound" so that we can understand what we hear.

Several factors can make understanding speech harder. For example, the pitch of the sound depends on the mood and tone of the speaker, where they place emphasis, differing dialects, and the varying speed of speech. All of the above strongly influence the sound of spoken language, so that each speaker produces completely different sound patterns, even if the sentence is one and the same. Our brain manages these difficulties at an amazing speed when comprehending speech. To date, no computer can keep up with this speed and precision and process heard speech as quickly and reliably as humans.

Distracting signals

To clearly understand what is being said to us, we need to filter out distracting signals. Our hearing faces a great challenge when we are surrounded by a flurry of varied, noisy sounds. When a lot of people talk simultaneously, music is playing in the background, noise is coming in from the street, or children are causing a racket, it becomes difficult for the nervous system to filter out human speech, thus making it harder to understand.

In addition to the auditory centers, the network of the brainstem plays a role in filtering out and ignoring distracting signals. It maintains a level of alertness, which prepares the brain to accept and understand incoming signals. This is the reason why well-rested children are better at hearing and understanding incoming auditory and other sensory information than those who do not get enough sleep. It also explains why a hearing test may provide false information if the child is sleepy. Children cannot be expected to listen attentively and to understand what they're being told if they're tired. (This raises the question: How effective are school lessons during the sixth, seventh or eighth class of the day?)

The above-mentioned problem is referred to as tolerance-fading memory (TFM). The issue is the inability to filter out background noise, which leads to the child becoming fatigued more quickly. Along with the fatigue, weaknesses of auditory sequential memory also appear, for example, the child being unable to recall verbal instructions. At such times, children frequently become aggressive, and "hysterical," or try to cover their ears. In both cases, these are manifestations of fatigue.

In other cases, the child has decoding difficulties. They cannot comprehend the sounds they hear—they're unable to match them to existing experiences and knowledge with the incoming auditory stimuli. They find it difficult to differentiate between similar sounds. Examples of this include the inability to differentiate the sounds b, p, d, and t, or h, k, and g, as well as s, z, and c. This occurs not only in the case of individual sounds but also words that sound similar. Children suffering from this problem have great difficulty assigning a new word to a certain object or action.

Interplay/teamwork

It is not only the two auditory centers that are in constant contact within our brain. The CNS integrates auditory information with other sensory stimuli, such as auditory and motor stimuli, or auditory and visual stimuli, amongst others. This helps us determine, for example, if the sound and its associated object are approaching or moving away, as well as whether we are "coming or going" relative to the source of the sound.

The high level of integration of incoming information can explain our ability to read lips. When we see lips moving in a way that signals speech production, our auditory center switches on, even if no sound can be heard. Surely everyone has felt that they understand better what someone is saying when they can see their mouth at the same time. It's interesting, however, that other means of metacommunication, such as facial expressions, do not influence the activity of the auditory cortex.

Sometimes auditory stimuli are not integrated with other sensory stimuli. At times like this, despite having a healthy auditory organ, the child cannot locate the source of the sound. If the child doesn't know which way to go during hide-and-seek to hide from the seeker, the underlying reason may be that they do not hear the seeker approaching from behind. They can hear that someone is approaching, but they do not know from which direction.

The integration of auditory and sensory stimuli also influences the operation of areas such as bilateral coordination, divided attention, and speech. Communication problems affect the development of the child's social relationships, self-esteem, school performance, and behavior.

Problems, challenges, difficulties

Although we are born with the ability to hear, we must learn to understand what we hear. Problems that present themselves in the learning process affect three main areas: 1) decoding; 2) the ability to filter background noise and the associated weak auditory memory; and 3) problems with auditory integration.

According to the experiences of Cheatum, Hammond, and Kranowitz, together with my own observations, difficulties with hearing often lie behind the following problems:

- Poor attention span
- Problems with auditory attention—difficulty with maintaining focus throughout a story or performance
- Ignores auditory instructions
- Frequently asks for things to be repeated
- Oversensitivity to sudden or jarring sounds
- Gets overly absorbed in an activity
- Does not follow the requested sequence of instructions
- Delayed reaction to sounds or instructions
- Poor sense of balance
- Can't tell the direction of the sound, unable to identify the source and location (close/far) of the sound
- Constantly speaks loudly
- Weak speaking ability
- Delayed speech development
- Poor linguistic ability (both written and spoken)
- Inability to keep track of a sound (e.g., whether a car is nearing or moving further away)
- Weak auditory memory—poor recall of heard texts or instructions, both in the short and long term
- Poor auditory seriality—problems with putting heard information in a logical order; repeating the letters of the alphabet; mixing up conjugations when learning foreign languages
- Weak auditory recognition—poor recognition of various incoming auditory signals, and the subsequent matching of these with known signals, as well as inability to organize them

- Difficulties with auditory discrimination—distinguishing important from irrelevant auditory information
- Associative problems—making associations with already known auditory signals as well as other (e.g., visual, tactile) signals
- Problems with auditory cohesion—difficulties in translating different auditory information into ideas and combining them into a coherent whole. This is also how inferences are made, and how problems, answers, jokes, and puns are understood.

OUTSIDE AND WITHIN

Outside...

Emma sits with her grandfather at the lakeside. They throw pebbles into the water. Water rings form around the pebbles after they land. Emma makes up a game where her grandpa must hit the center of the previous ring of water. Grandpa is very clever and almost always hits the center of the water ring. When they swap, the little girl fails to hit the center. But as time goes by, she gets more accurate.

Grandma is teaching her granddaughter to knit. Luckily the knitting needle is not too sharp because at first, the little girl pokes her finger more than the ball of yarn. But soon the child becomes more precise and skillful with the yarn and the needle. It no longer seems impossible to make a scarf.

Danny wants to be a rower. He has a perfect body for the sport—long arms and legs. Perhaps in a few years, he could compete at a high level. But currently, the situation is disastrous. His arms and legs get tangled, and the boat wobbles. He can't manage to coordinate his four limbs.

Three completely different situations, but with something in common. Each is related to the perception of the body and the position of its parts. Strange as it may sound, the perception of body position and movement also has sensory organs—collectively known as the proprioceptor, which controls the proprioception process. The concept of proprioception was introduced by Sir Charles Scott Sherrington, an English physician, in the early 20th century.

The research results of Ferenc Köteles and his colleagues at Eötvös Loránd University in my homeland Hungary also contributed greatly to international knowledge on proprioception and visceroception. They showed that these have a significant influence on well-being, for example, they found significant connections between visceroception and hypochondria.

Higher, farther, faster, more accurate

This form of sensation (proprioception) coming from the movable parts of our body (muscles, tendons, joints) sends information to the CNS, which constantly monitors and corrects the muscles' position, tone, and movement. By knowing where the parts of your body are in space, you can get an overall picture of your body position. This expresses our perception of ourselves and our understanding of our body as our own.

The perception of the movement of our body is a rather complex function of kinesthesia. Since it would be difficult to detect the stimuli of many different muscles, tendons, and joints simultaneously, most of the stimuli remain below the threshold of perception. Think of how chaotic it would feel if we were aware of our every single tiny movement. If we were running down a hill on a bumpy road, we wouldn't be able to concentrate on the ground because we would be getting information everywhere from our little fingers to our big toes about what every individual part of us was doing.

Unconscious movement

We become conscious of proprioceptive stimuli when we pay attention to them. This happens mainly when learning new movements. Once movements become automatic, perception ceases. Driving a car is a commonly cited example, but also various sports movements, learning music, or writing. A novice driver has to consciously think about when to change gears. A canoer watches how they hold the paddle and coordinate their movements. A pianist watches the fingers on both hands. Once the movement becomes automatic, the driver is not aware of when they changed gears while driving and the canoer isn't conscious of how they hold the paddle while racing, just as the pianist does not concentrate on the movement of their fingers while playing the piano.

What makes it possible to sense our body parts and our body position? The striated skeletal muscle has evolved into signaling systems from restructured muscle cells and special sensory nerve endings found in the joints' inner ligaments and outer capsules.

Various receptors in the joints sense the angle of rotation and, to a lesser extent, the torsion of the joint. From each sensory cell, thick fibers carry the stimulus to the spinal cord, where they make multiple connections. Some of the nerves from the proprioceptors are connected directly or indirectly to the motor nerve cells, forming a reflex loop, which forms the basis of movement control. Another part of the fibers transmits information to different areas of the brain. This allows the position of different body parts to be sensed and their position in space to be corrected almost simultaneously. For example, if we eat ice cream from a bowl on a ship rocking in the waves, our nervous system senses the movement of our hands and body, and adapting to this situation, we can still successfully put the spoon in our mouths.

Emergency alert

Other stimuli, such as pain or abnormal positioning of parts of the body, can also trigger proprioceptive stimuli. In such cases, the stimuli become noticeable, which protects the body, and remain in the conscious mind as long as the emergency persists. In this situation, "proprioceptive awareness" is not only increased in the affected area but also throughout the body.

Awareness of the sense of movement can be achieved by deliberate, cognitive means. This forms the basis of many movement therapies, sports techniques, and playing of instrumental music.

Based on Cheatum, Hammond, Mahler, and my own experience, disorders of proprioceptive perception can result in the following:

- Movement coordination problems
- Body image issues
- Problems with gross motor movements and fine motor movements
- Frequent falls, trips over one's own feet
- Bumps into things and into others
- Pushes the pencil hard into the paper when drawing or coloring; or the opposite, the pencil slips out of the hand
- Plays aggressive games, fights
- Paws around and grabs onto things while walking
- Is never bothered by tight clothing
- Often drops or breaks things
- Bites, scratches

- Needs to be hugged tightly (and hugs others tightly)
- Gnashes teeth
- Dresses with difficulty
- Frequently slams doors, puts things down with a bang
- Unintentionally hurts animals by stroking them with too much force
- Poor self-esteem
- Problems fitting in
- Visual perception and cognition problems
- Frequent injuries
- Causes pain to companions (Sigmundsson, 2005)

... and within

"I'm hungry!"
"I'm thirsty!"
"I have to pee!"
"I have to poop!"

These are perhaps the most common phrases that express the needs of a young child. (Clearly, these are everyone's needs, but at an older age the latter two of these "problems" are not so clearly communicated to the world.)

Hunger, thirst, and the stimulus to urinate or defecate are called visceral sensations, also known as visceroception, which is the name given to the processing of stimuli from the internal organs.

Many others can be included, such as sensing our heartbeat, feeling our stomach or bowels move, or breathing heavily when we run and our side hurts.

Although the innervation of the viscera (the quantity of nerves in the inner organs) is dense and their total surface area is considerable, visceral sensation, the detection of stimuli from the internal organs, is rare. In usual cases we have only a vague feeling of fullness in the stomach or intestines or of urine in the bladder. Although changes in heart rate, lower or higher blood pressure, blood sugar level changes and so on generate some sensation, they can be difficult to identify. However, when we need to go to the bathroom, we now feel the tension of the rectum or bladder and also the tension of the sphincter muscles.

Well-being

We are mostly unaware of our perception of the functioning of our internal organs. We do not feel our kidneys or liver working, so we have no direct knowledge of, for example, blood pressure or changes in blood chemistry. Most of the time, we only get a signal about the state of our gut when something is wrong or when the condition of an organ is different from normal. For example, when our stomachs are empty, or when they are full after a large meal.

However, visceral stimuli can influence our behavior. This can happen in two ways. On the one hand, we can detect general, diffuse, but still characteristic patterns. This is state perception (perception of state). On the other hand, the emotional effect accompanying the stimuli can reach our consciousness, which is subjective perception. An example of state perception is the feeling of hunger or thirst. The infant acquires these at a very early age through learning. Hunger, thirst, or the stimulus to urinate or defecate can also influence behavior in adulthood. Some hungry people, for example, become more irritable, and people who have to go to the toilet frequently cannot pay attention to their work.

We use the term "well-being" to describe the emotional effects generated by our internal organs. In practice, our mood is shaped by perception of our internal organs. This experience leads to a general emotional state. However, we only perceive the pleasant or unpleasant feeling generated within us, not what actually causes it. When all our organs are functioning correctly, we feel good. If there is a problem with one of our internal organs, our well-being changes and becomes bad. We become fussy, moody, irritable, or even apathetic.

The "free-falling stomach"

Research carried out by Jarchow and colleagues in 2003 showed that some of our internal organs, such as the stomach and the vascular system, are involved in the sense of balance, i.e., the spatial position of our head. When we ride a roller coaster, this is the reason for the sensation we experience in our stomach.

To be able to perceive the state of our internal organs correctly, or to ignore it, the receptors and the nervous system must be working correctly. Without it, we would not feel hungry, thirsty, or the need to excrete waste. Or on the contrary, we would jump up with every heartbeat or be unable to sleep because of the movement of our bowels.

TOUCH

On several occasions, a distressed mother or father has complained during an examination that their child refuses to wear certain textures. The fabric must be almost "invisible" and untactile, otherwise, the child will not wear the garment even if they chose it in the shop. Getting dressed in the morning is torture. During our conversation, it almost always turns out that these children do not like playing with plasticine or sand. They also can't stand it if their hands or faces are smeared or sticky.

Other parents complain about the opposite. The child is constantly pawing, touching everything, squeezing everything. You can't take them shopping, or to an exhibition or museum. Sometimes traveling isn't easy because the child grabs everything on the bus, tram, or train. They run their hands over fences, walls, and railings when walking.

In both cases, tactile perception, i.e., perception by touch, is the cause. In the first case, it is about avoiding tactile stimuli; in the second, it is about seeking tactile stimuli.

What is tactile perception?

This form of perception is called the "sense of touch." The organ of touch is the skin because tactile sensation involves the skin meeting the stimulus.

There are seven types of receptors in different layers of the skin that are specialized to receive tactile stimuli. Touch, pressure, temperature, and pain can stimulate these sensory cells. Previously, each sensory cell was thought to respond to a specific stimulus. Nowadays, the more accepted view is that the interaction of all the receptors produces a response to a stimulus.

There is active and passive tactile perception. Active is holding an object, walking barefoot on grass, or touching a hot plate. Passive is when a bug lands on your hand, or someone steps on your foot. In both cases, we sense that something or someone has contacted our skin.

"Seeing" by touching

The tactile sensory system is one of the fastest-evolving sensory systems. Specific tactile sensory processes can be detected as early as seven-and-a-half weeks after conception. The most sensitive areas are the lips, mouth, tongue, fingers, and palms. The mouth can collect most sensory information during fetal life and for a few months after birth. This is one reason why babies put everything in their mouths. Also, at the beginning of life, they "grab" any object they can get their hands on, which is another way of experiencing information from the environment.

The receptors in the skin gather a wealth of information about the world, both as an essential part of the cognitive process and as a warning of danger. Body sensation begins to develop in the womb and is perfected during birth. This stimulates the newborn's mouth to trigger the sucking and rooting reflex, which turns the child's head toward the touch. When the mouth finds and touches the nipple, the sucking reflex is triggered, and sucking begins. During their development, tactile sensation enables the child to distinguish the shape, size, weight, texture, moisture content, and temperature of objects. Touch enables them to learn how to identify strength, location, and quantity. Tactile sensation is the bond between the baby and its caregivers.

Through hugging, rocking, and nursing, the child learns to distinguish between their own body and the outside world. Tactile sensation sends impulses to the nervous system through touch, allowing the child to learn their body schema.[8]

In and beyond the skin

According to Didier Anzieu (1923–1999), the renowned French psychoanalyst, there is a kind of skin-self that plays a role in defining the boundary between the self and the outside world, forming identity and appropriate self-protection. It also has a communicative function.

8 Body schema is a general term for the awareness of one's own body, including the location and orientation of its various parts and their relative motion in space and time.

The child learns to distinguish itself from its mother, but this is not enough to enable it to place itself in its environment. They must learn to separate their body from the environment and its events. They must be able to decide whether events are happening inside their body, on their body, or outside their body, in their environment. If the body's boundaries are not delineated, the self becomes blurred with the environment, and the individual has no sense of how far their boundaries extend. This anomaly applies equally to the physical and personal environment, because private space is not well-defined.

Anzieu's research has shown that if the boundaries of the body are not clear, the boundaries of the self and personal space are also not well defined. The individual is in constant conflict with the environment, as they feel that elements of the environment are invading their own body. In addition, they cannot separate themselves from the noises and visual stimuli in the environment, and their nervous system becomes overloaded and fatigued quickly.

Stinging, hot, sharp, pressure!

The intact tactile sensory system alerts the body to danger, protecting the child from various injuries. The receptors are sensitive to temperature (more specifically heat), cuts, bruises, stings, and pain. Deeper pain receptor cells in the walls of blood vessels, muscles, and periosteum also transmit impulses to the spinal cord and brain. The motor response to pain is very fast: the stimulus immediately triggers a spinal reflex, resulting in a rapid motor response that causes the body part to move away from the source of the stimulation.

It has been observed that how we evaluate pain can be learned to a certain extent and that learning can modify response reactions. The basic pattern is likely acquired in childhood. Individual experiences and major life events can change the basic pattern. Family and parental attitudes to pain play a key role and imprint on the developing nervous system. The basic pattern remains the same or similar, even in different cultural contexts. So, if the mother or father is always jumping to immediately pick up the child who falls on their stomach, the child is conditioned to learn that the fall hurts a lot. This does not mean, of course, that we should not comfort the child when they are in pain, but it is also not worth us crying more than the child when a minor accident occurs (even if it often "hurts us more" than it does our child.)

Tactile perception disorders, in the experience of Cheatum and Hammond, and from my own observations, can result in the following:

- Unable to identify and name parts of the body
- Weak spatial awareness and orientation
- Lack of body schema awareness
- Poor body image
- Weak or incorrect posture
- Clumsiness
- Poor at copying movements
- Seeks physical contact

- Poor sense of balance
- Lack of laterality (differentiation between right and left)
- Mixes directions (up, down, left, right)
- Poor fine and gross motor skills
- Difficulty using scissors
- Difficulty with writing
- Difficulty discovering the texture, shape, and weight of objects
- Dislikes "head over heels" tumbling movements
- Dislikes throwing or catching the ball, dislikes ball games in general
- Does not like to try things that seem dangerous and warns their peers against doing so
- Does not like sitting on things with rough surfaces
- Prefers to be alone
- Uncomfortable with certain types of clothing, especially socks or underwear
- Prefers loose clothes
- Does not like swimming, and dislikes water and hair washing
- Can't stand to get their hands or face dirty
- Doesn't like to stand in a row close to others
- Does not like playing catch
- Does not like to roll over
- Aggressive, hurts others
- Often reacts to touch by hitting out
- Does not like dry towels or freshly ironed bed linen

TASTES, FLAVORS, SMELLS

When we talk about perception, smell and taste are seldom mentioned first. But we love tasty food, pleasant smells, and juicy fruits, and we obviously try to avoid bad tastes and unpleasant, foul smells.

Many writers and poets have written about smells and tastes in novels, poems, and short stories. A great master of this was the Hungarian writer Gyula Krúdy, who even wrote about the cabbage leaves needed for stuffed cabbage in such a delicious way that makes people (who love cabbage) salivate.

> These roots of the cabbage's heart rival the flavors of first love in their youth. You can smell on them the perfume of spring's rivers, and you can feel on them that these clumps, these veins, are selecting from the fresh rains hanging over the gardens, like knowing little farmers' wives, the juices that are suitable for the growing of cabbages.

Of course, as the saying goes, tastes differ, our favorite foods and drinks change throughout our lives, and sometimes we even judge smells differently.

Sometimes it also happens that someone doesn't sense or only partially senses tastes and smells. Their brain misinterprets and misreads them. They don't think of food or scents in the same way as most people. Things that others usually consider pleasant to smell or taste are for them unpleasant. If this phenomenon is significant, it can affect their quality of life or be a symptom, sign, or side effect of an underlying disease or problem.

Anomalies of taste and smell may be caused by problems such as obesity, diabetes, high blood pressure, or an unbalanced or poor diet. Nerve system problems can include Parkinson's disease, Alzheimer's disease, or multiple sclerosis. We have all heard about the loss of smell or taste that can be the result of a COVID-19 infection, or simply a cold or flu.

In the above situations, it rarely happens that the problem starts at birth. It is also common that an immature nervous system or asynchronous functioning of the two hemispheres of the brain may be one of the symptoms of a disturbance in the sense of smell or taste. Often, this is why a child is picky about food, refusing to even taste what their parents find delicious.

We perceive stimuli differently depending on whether they come from the external or internal environment. They can be related to three modalities: olfaction (smell); taste perception; and visceroception, as mentioned earlier. In the first two cases, the stimuli come from the outside world, in the case of visceroception, from inside our body. In all three cases, the trigger is a chemical stimulus. Only soluble compounds are suitable for triggering the stimulus, and the solvent can be of many kinds (e.g., water, alcohol, etc). Chemical stimuli are very rarely pure—they are usually a mixture of substances.

The sense of smell

Because the olfactory receptors are deep in the sinuses, during resting breathing only 10% of the air reaches the olfactory epithelium. Smells are detected only by deeper breathing or by sniffing. Odors can also come from the mouth. Odorants from food contribute to the "flavor" that adds to the enjoyment of food or drink—in fact, flavor is the combination of their taste and smell.

The olfactory system is one of the oldest sensory systems. It has a role in detecting smells and odors and can also alert us to danger. There are evolutionary preferences for odors (such as the smell of a partner or edible fruit) and avoidance (such as the smell of rot). When unpleasant or toxic odors are detected, a smell-related reflex triggers the head to turn and exhale, helping to protect the body from eating toxic foods. Pleasant smells contribute to the enjoyment of eating, providing hedonic pleasure.

Some smells are more complex, others are easier to recognize. This is partly an inherited and learned individual characteristic. Smell recognition plays a vital role in the care of offspring. The mother and the child mutually recognize each other's smell, imprinted in the nervous system. In the animal kingdom, if either of their smells change, the nursing process stops and the offspring dies. This is why, for example, if you pick up a baby bird sitting in a bird's nest and stroke it, the mother bird will often throw it out.

Although the sense of smell plays a much smaller role in humans than in the animal kingdom, many olfactory mechanisms are at work in humans. Smell plays a unique role in the choice of mate, in personal relationships and sexual activity, and in our relationship with food.

We can habituate smells to a certain extent. When in a new olfactory environment (for example, a strange place), the smell strikes us for a few minutes. We feel it for a short time. Then we don't. At first, it may come back with an intense sniff, but later it may not—this is adaptation or adjustment. But when we spend a lot of time in one place, for example, in our home, in our workplace, or in school, that's when habituation, or adaptation, occurs. While adaptation is a peripheral phenomenon occurring at the receptor level so that the same odor does not trigger stimulation in the sensory cells, habituation is a central brain process, involving the olfactory centers.

It is probably due to an evolutionary defense mechanism that unpleasant odors have a stronger impression on us. Still, some pleasant smells can also be imprinted in the memory forever, together with the associated experience or event. Often, a scent will bring back memories associated with it: a smell associated with a doctor's surgery or hospital; a painful or unpleasant event; or, to take more pleasant examples, the smell of apple pie, or a memory of an early autumn afternoon with Grandma.

It has been observed that those diagnosed with autism spectrum disorder have difficulty in recognizing and discriminating (distinguishing) smells. Since smell is essential in selecting preferred foods, the eating problems displayed by autistic people are likely partly due to this.

Taste perception

Taste perception is a contact chemical sensory process that permits the perception of compounds dissolved in water, given that the substance must dissolve in saliva and thus come into contact with the sensory surface. The sensory surface is primarily the tongue, but the soft palate and pharynx (throat) are also involved in the tasting process. The taste receptors are located in the taste buds and vary in number from one taste bud to another. In addition to taste receptors, taste buds also contain mechanical, heat, and pain receptors. The sense of taste is completed by smell, and the result is the overall taste sensation.

Traditionally, four basic tastes are distinguished: sweet, salty, bitter, and sour. (More recently, a fifth basic taste, umami, an intense savory/earthy flavor, has been identified.) Sweet tastes are mainly associated with sugars. Its role is preferred because it is mainly sugar that the body uses for processes that require energy. The bitter taste has a unique role in defense since most toxic substances are bitter. The salty taste is characteristic of chemicals such as sodium and potassium that are needed by the body for conduction. All salty foods are potential sources of sodium and potassium. The sour taste is caused by inorganic and organic acids. Many fruits have a sour taste, which probably plays a role in the search for nutrients. The umami taste is reminiscent of the taste of meat or protein and is involved in regulating meat consumption.

The primary mechanism of taste perception is pattern perception, which occurs when receptors are activated simultaneously. Flavors are not equally stimulating, and one flavor can overwhelm another. An innate taste preference makes infants prefer sweet foods.

Taste perception is influenced by temperature, hunger, time of day, and sex (women's taste perception is more sophisticated). Taste perception can be modified by internal state changes. When hungry, we prefer sweet tastes. When neither hungry nor full, we are neutral to sweet flavors, and when overfed we explicitly lack desire for sweet tastes.

Taste aversion can also occur when the food we ate causes an unpleasant sensation, such as nausea or vomiting. Taste aversion helps us avoid foods that cause illness or are poisonous. A specific form of taste aversion is the avoidance of new tastes or neophobia. People don't like to try new flavors. If they taste something, they taste only a tiny amount of it. If it does not cause any harm, they taste it again several times. This phenomenon is most intense between the ages of two and six and is attributed to the body's defense mechanism, because at this age the child can feed itself. Neophobia prevents them from eating new, possibly poisonous food, or if they do try it, they eat only a little. After the age of six, this condition begins to disappear.

Disorders of smell and taste perception can result in the following:

- Increased seeking of stimuli—smells everything, puts everything in the mouth
- Tastes "inedible" things (eraser, soap, various berries)
- Drinks hot or icy foods and drinks without thinking
- Expressly averse to certain smells
- Refuses to try new tastes (neophobia)
- Difficulty in identifying tastes and smells
- Difficulty distinguishing between tastes and smells

Sensation, perception, processing, response

Sensation and perception are the processes that form the basis of cognition and enable us to make sense of the world. We need our sensory organs and CNS to receive and interpret stimuli from our internal and external environment. The coordinated functioning of these enables us to understand and respond to information from the world.

From birth onwards, the baby's perception becomes more accurate and faster so that sensory information can be processed more accurately and quickly, and the baby can compare, organize, and combine the information in its mind.

Repeated processing of incoming stimuli will result in a change in perception. For example, we can hardly tell them apart when we first meet identical twins. But if we see them several times, we notice more and more differences between them, and we learn to notice differences that seem minor. This process of learning is called perceptual learning, and it is a process that goes on throughout life.

The quality and speed of learning processes, behavior, adaptation, and attitudes to the world are largely determined by how accurately we perceive incoming stimuli and how the nervous system can decode and interpret them and respond appropriately. This makes learning more manageable and makes us feel better about the world.

MOVE IT! ... AND MORE

The term *sensorimotor development* implies that a person receives the correct dose of stimuli through the sensory or motor organs (limbs, head, whole body, toes, etc.) The two are hardly separable, given sensory perception almost always requires muscle work.

Consider the simple case of reading the title of a newspaper article. We have to open our eyes and focus on the letters, follow the line with our eyes, and the axes of the two eyes must be parallel to see clearly. We also use tiny muscles to adjust the curvature of the lens for optimal focus. In addition, we have to hold ourselves against gravity—otherwise, we would collapse and be unable to assume a position where reading is possible.

The sequence

In my experience, sensorimotor development is most effective when we follow the sequence of events during ontogenesis, i.e., the development of the individual. Since the primitive reflexes described earlier help the development of perceptual processes in infancy, it is useful to start from the "home" of these reflexes.

Almost 100 types of infant reflexes have been described by doctors and scientists. Of these, the literature considers the ones I have already mentioned to be the most important for development.

Infant reflexes play an essential role in survival and development in the first year after birth. Think about it. The rooting reflex helps the infant find the mother's breast. The sucking reflex helps the infant eat. The Moro reflex mobilizes the part of the autonomic nervous system that triggers an emergency response in the event of danger. If, for example, the concentration of carbon dioxide in the child's blood rises due to respiratory failure, this reflex is triggered, which releases adrenaline into the bloodstream due to the action of the neuroendocrine system. The adrenaline increases the heart and respiratory rates, among other things, thus improving the child's oxygen supply.

Each infant reflex has a well-defined role in the infant's life, but they are no longer needed as the infant grows older. They have to give way to a higher level of neural activity.

As early as the second half of the 1800s, Jackson described how higher-level neural structures inhibit lower-level areas during individual development. If lower regions are not inhibited, problems in sensory integration can occur.

Sensory integration problems can be accompanied by the persistence or reappearance of primitive reflexes, automatic, involuntary movements, disorganization, and disturbances of higher neural functions, which can cause psychiatric and cognitive dysfunction.

In this case, there is a high probability that the child or adult will have learning difficulties, behavioral problems, problems fitting in, or other unintended consequences. Based on the literature and my own experience, vestibular development and tactile perception exercises should be started simultaneously with reflex integration exercises.

Other sensory stimuli can be included during the development. This includes improving speech perception, developing olfactory discrimination, and increasing the visual field.

Depending on the goal, the sensorimotor development treatment may occasionally need to be supplemented with specific massage exercises. Massage can most often be used effectively for speech initiation or for specific symptoms of autism spectrum disorder.

Also, after successful inhibition of primitive reflexes, it is worthwhile to perform various more complex sensorimotor exercises. These can be done with or without training aids. The best and cheapest tool is a ball, but you can also choose a skipping rope, a hula hoop, or other equipment.

As the primitive reflexes disappear and the vestibular organ matures, the child's motor coordination improves, and they become more successful in mastering basic sports techniques. All young children must have regular participation in sporting activities. Sport should not be understood as a competitive sport but as any physical activity regularly integrated into the child's life.

Why is regular sport important?

Forming new synapses in the nervous system and reorganizing existing neural connections provide the physiological basis for learning. Decades of research have shown that the brain changes its structure during each activity, constantly refining its network of neurons to perform tasks more efficiently. This ability of the brain is called neuroplasticity.[9]

Plasticity persists throughout human life but is of particular importance in childhood. During this sensitive period, new connections between neurons are formed, and existing ones are strengthened or weakened, depending on whether they receive reinforcement. Learning new things in a stimulus-rich environment (both sensory and motor) stimulates the brain's production of brain-derived neurotrophic factor (BDNF).

BDNF supports synaptogenesis, forming connections between nerve cells in brain areas such as the hippocampus, which is considered a key player in the brain for memory, learning, and thinking. The hippocampus is an ancient

9 The term "neuroplasticity" was coined by Polish neuroscientist Jerzy Konorski. Konorski first used it in 1948 to describe changes observed in the structure of neurons. The term did not become widely used until the 1960s (Balleine, 2019).

cortical structure that is indirectly connected to all sensory and associative areas of the cerebral cortex. All sensory information is brought to this brain area and integrated here. Eventually, it travels back to the neocortex, the most advanced part of the cortex, for long-term storage. Although memory traces are stored over the long term by other specific areas of the cortex, the hippocampus imprints the memory traces and associates them with different sensory information.

BDNF, in addition to stimulating new connections between neurons, activates the basal ganglia, the part of our brain involved in processes such as decision-making, goal-directed movement, behavioral switching, procedural learning, working memory, and executive functions. (In procedural learning, we learn to ride a bike, drive a car, tie our shoes, or perform other actions. It takes practice to memorize the sequence of steps.)

It is now known that increasing the number of neurons in the hippocampus and extending the lifespan of existing cells is practically possible. Exercise and learning increase the production and release of BDNF, which triggers neuroplasticity changes such as neurogenesis (the formation and strengthening of synapses). In addition, exercise increases oxygen uptake, improving the oxygen supply to the brain. It has a stimulating effect on the sensory and motor cortex of the brain, thus maintaining sensorimotor functions, which include essential elements such as perception or muscle tone control (affecting all body muscles).

In the following chapter, I would like to list, without claiming to be exhaustive, some research findings that describe and support the relationship between retained primitive reflexes and problems with physical activity, cognitive development, and behavior.

RESEARCH, STUDIES, RESULTS

The study and measurement of children's nervous system and sensorimotor maturity, and the association with different abilities such as behavior, cognitive skills, social skills, and so on, has been a subject of interest for researchers, doctors, and professionals for several years. Some have approached the issue from the view of undeveloped reflexes, others have looked at the maturity of the vestibular system, and still others have considered more complex sensorimotor indicators. They all obtained similar results. They found that the maturity of the nervous system, the profile of primitive reflexes, and vestibular maturation are related to the state of cognitive abilities, behavior, and socialization skills. The more mature the nervous system, the more perfect the reflex profile, the more harmonious the sensorimotor integration, and the better the child functions.

On one hand, research has sought to identify the causes at the root of the problems. Only with these results can effective treatments be found. On the other hand, research has led to the recognition that in most cases, the underlying cause of various symptoms (ADHD, dyslexia, dysgraphia, etc.) is not an organ dysfunction or disease but an immature nervous system.

In my historical review of reflex research, I already pointed out that current knowledge regarding sensorimotor development did not appear overnight but is the result of a long and dedicated effort by many scientists, doctors, and other professionals. This chapter describes some of the results of the research and the conclusions that have been drawn from the deeper exploration of various observations. It is not my aim, of course, to present all the results, but a few examples will provide insight into the scientific background of the topic.

Let's start with Julio B. de Quirós. In a previous chapter, I mentioned that in a large study of 1,902 children during the 1950s and 1960s, he showed that children with vestibular problems displayed lower levels of motor development, balance, language development, reading, and writing skills.

In 1970, Ellenberger made the connection that if infant reflexes are not built up in time during an individual's development, or if they are released from inhibition for some reason, they can be the cause of psychological and cognitive dysfunction. On one hand, sensorimotor integration may not be fully achieved, and on the other hand, automatic, involuntary movements, disorganization, and disturbances of higher neural functions may occur. Ellenberger's hypothesis was confirmed by Meares in 1999.

József Hámori, a renowned researcher into the functional structure of the nervous system and the connections between its elements, described in 1975 the so-called critical periods in the development of the nervous system. During these periods, the correct quantity and quality of stimuli are essential for developing the nervous system's function. Hámori put this period between the ages of two and sixteen.

In 1984, a group of scientists and researchers concluded that many factors could influence the nervous system's maturation. These include injuries, toxic effects, or even psychological stress. Scientists have formulated their observations differently, but the main point is the same—one of the problems underlying deficits in higher motor and cognitive function, and perhaps the most notable, is the persistence of primitive reflexes, i.e., the functioning of retained infant reflexes. Touwen et al. produced this observation.

In 1993, Bushnell and Boudreau concluded that motor development is central to developing cognitive abilities and, thus, a prerequisite for school learning.

Cantell, Smyth, and Ahonen (1994) observed children diagnosed with delayed motor development and motor deficits during neurological examinations at the age of five. They followed their motor status 10 years later, at 15 years of age. They looked at their social relationships, vision for the future, and how they spent their free time. They identified 81 children with delayed motor development and motor problems at age five. Of these children, 54% showed a significant improvement in their motor status by age 15, while the remaining 46% showed deterioration or stagnation. The latter participated much less in social and leisure activities and events than those who showed positive changes in their physical activity. Participation in events was not influenced by whether they were required to take part in physical activities. They were much more likely to be alone and play video games, and socialization was less successful for them.

In 1997, research also showed that physical fitness and motor skills can play a crucial role in healthy brain development, functioning, and academic performance in young people. The study was performed by Etnier et al.

At the turn of the millennium, Diamond, studying children's physical and motor development, found that the maturation of the brain and neural structures has a positive effect on performance and balance perception by increasing the speed and efficiency of information processing.

At the same time, Cheatum and Hammond are credited with several research findings on this topic, emphasizing the importance of the vestibular system in regulating muscle tone and postural regulation (body position.) According to their research, correct functioning of the mature balance organ is essential, as body positioning is involved in sitting, standing, and automatically assuming the position that requires the least energy input during school or home learning to focus the child on the task at hand. They also added that perfect functioning of the vestibular system is essential for competitive sports or recreation.

This line of thought was continued in 2001 by Huettig, Pyfer, and Auxter, who also stressed that children with poor vestibular function have problems with balance perception, gross and fine motor movements, and motor co-ordination. Weaknesses in hand–eye coordination have been highlighted, which cause problems in learning to write, and later, especially in the first years of school, when writing.

McPhillips, Hepper, and Mulhern in 2000, and McPhillips and Jordan-Black in 2007, published a study on the relationship between persistent primitive reflexes and dyslexia. Related to this is the 2003 research by Dordel and Breithecker, who showed that difficulties in concentration and language development skills were associated with being overweight and weakness in coordination tasks. The development of coordination disorders is often (40–90%) accompanied by cognitive impairment.

Subsequently, other researchers have compared academic performance, motor skills and cognitive function. Fields, Diego and Sanders (2001), Kayani et al. (2002), Kim, Iwaki, Imashioya, Uno, and Fujita (2005), Castelli et al. (2007), and Roberts, Freed, and McCarthy (2010) found a strong positive correlation between children's academic achievement and physical abilities and development, looking at different groups of children.

Taylor, Houghton, and Chapman in 2004, and Konicarova and Bob in 2013, described the associations between ADHD symptomology and the presence of primitive reflexes.

Research by Adkins et al. in 2006 showed that cardiorespiratory performance, a significant component of physical fitness, is associated with developing blood vessels and capillaries. Muscle strength and coordination, also essential components of physical fitness, are associated with the growth and maturation of synaptic connections.

As early as 2008, Hillman, Erickson, and Kramer described how imaging techniques in humans show changes in brain structure and function due to regular exercise. Moreover, blood flow to the hippocampus, which plays a major role in verbal learning and memory, increased.

This has been supported by research that found a positive correlation between intelligence quotient (IQ) and the speed of performing a given set of movements (Martin, Tigera, Denckla, and Mahone, 2010), and between crystallized intelligence, motor performance, and working memory (Wassenberg et al., 2005; Davis et al., 2009).

In 2009, Buderath and colleagues, and Ghanizadeh in 2011, found that ADHD is associated with impaired balance perception, which impairs higher motor coordination and executive functions.

Iverson observed in 2010 that as a child's mobility increases, so does the opportunity for social interaction. When a child learns to walk, they become independent of others. They decide who to approach in the playground or to communicate with at daycare. Motor development thus has a significant impact on both the child's cognitive and language development.

2010 proved to be a very fruitful year for research, as Iverson, and Preston, Frost, Mencl, and colleagues showed a link between infants' motor development and language development, which predicts the development of reading skills in school-age children.

In the following years, Westendorp et al. (2011) studied a new group of children. They found learning disabilities were more common and severe among pupils with poor motor skills. Pontifex and colleagues (2011) followed up on these findings by reporting that physical fitness affects working memory, inhibition, delay, control functions, and cognitive processes. In 2012, Chaddock et al. confirmed this by adding to the finding that physical fitness affects school performance.

In 2011, studying the functioning of primitive reflexes, Franz and Gillet showed that these reflexes represent processes at lower evolutionary levels that, when interfering with higher neural activities, cause sensorimotor integration problems.[10]

In 2013, Konicarova and Bob addressed the study of Moro and Galant reflexes in children with ADHD. Their research found that the persistence of these reflexes was significantly higher among children with ADHD than in the unaffected control group. In the same year, they summarized the associations between the ADHD symptom cluster and unintegrated primitive

10 Sensorimotor integration refers to the relationship between the sensory and motor systems (muscles) and the process by which these two systems communicate. Sensorimotor integration is most intense from birth to age seven. There are three sequential parts to the process: (1) a sensory stimulus; (2) nerves carry the information to the brain where the information is interpreted; and (3) the brain then determines what response to make and transmits its instructions to the appropriate group of muscle fibers that will carry out the response. The sensory and motor systems work together in dynamic harmony.

reflexes. They pointed out possible causes of the disturbances in the maturational processes of the CNS, emphasizing the importance of the different stages of ontogenetic development and their temporal sequence in both progress and development.

Also in 2012, Niklasson published a paper presenting the results of his research which concluded that when children are involved in development that includes primitive reflex inhibition, integration, vestibular stimulation, maturation, sensorimotor development (auditory and tactile development), fine motor development, large motor development, and playful exercises, they achieved significantly better results in reading, writing, and mathematics than the control group.

Three years later, Chaddock-Heyman and colleagues found that regular physical activity was beneficial for the brain's white matter. They also noted that exercise made the connections between different cortical grey matter brain regions more active.[11]

In their 2016 study of certain developmental disorders, Dordic, Tubic, and Jaksic observed that deficits in various motor, cognitive, and social skills often co-occur. Motor coordination disorders are usually followed by developmental problems such as attention, speech, and behavioral disorders.

In *Sport and Exercise Psychology Research*, published in 2016, Voelcker-Rehag and colleagues presented a full chapter of research findings that support the hypothesis that physical activity improves both motor skills and cognitive function. They pointed out that regular physical activity influences brain processes and modulates appropriate brain structures. The analysis compared the effects of short-term and long-term physical activity on performance in cognitive tasks and in tasks requiring motor skills.

The research results described above are summarized in Sigafoos et al. (2021). Once primitive reflexes have fulfilled their function and are no longer needed, they are inhibited by cortical processes and become integrated.[12] In

11 Gray matter is named for its pinkish-gray color; it consists of the cell bodies. This brain tissue is abundant in the cerebellum, cerebrum, and brain stem. It also forms a butterfly-shaped portion of the central spinal cord. White matter is composed of bundles of axons, which conduct, process, and send nerve signals up and down the spinal cord and the brain.

12 Recent research shows that over 90% of children aged 4–6 years have at least one persistent infant reflex (Gieysztor, Choińska, and Paprocka-Borowicz, 2018; Pecuch et al., 2020;

normal development, they are replaced by more mature postural reactions that accompany us throughout our lives. Appropriate postural reactions provide the basis for muscle tone adjustment, proper balance, good posture, and motor coordination. The functional maturational dynamics of the CNS allow for the acquisition of higher cognitive skills and thus play a role in learning processes and social interactions. In the same year, this conclusion was also reached by Hickey and Feldhacker, and Goddard and colleagues.

During a 6–8-month period in 2017, I made a study including 776 children aged 5–8. This research investigated whether sensorimotor exercises can be used to develop children's nervous systems in a way that has a measurable effect on sensorimotor development. The second aim of the research was to discover how sensorimotor development relates to auditory and visual skills for learning.

The results demonstrated that the level of sensorimotor maturity could be significantly increased through targeted exercises in an institutional setting like a kindergarten or school (assuming a commitment to perform the training exercises regularly over a suitable duration). It also confirmed the hypothesis that the more mature a child's sensorimotor profile, the higher the level of functioning of their auditory and visual subskills—essential for school learning.

I realize this chapter may have been a little long. The quantity of research far outweighs the number of results presented here. However, I hope the reader received some confirmation that movement development and sensory integration are inseparable from cognitive development, behavior, and how we feel in the world.

Hickey and Feldhacker, 2021; Goddard et al., 2021).

WHEN, WHAT, HOW, AND FOR WHOM?

Immature, primitive reflexes, disturbances in sensorimotor integration, and neurological immaturity can manifest themselves in many different ways in people's lives. Children or adults who present their symptoms to various professionals are often given a "label" or "tag," either symbolically or as a formal "medical code," covering a wide variety of diagnoses. Speech and language problems, dyslexia, dysgraphia, bedwetting, fecal retention, attention-deficit disorder or hyperactivity (or both together), autism spectrum disorder, pervasive developmental disorder, and so on.

A physical problem may well be the cause of some of these disorders. In such situations, sensorimotor development may improve the symptoms, but it will not eliminate the condition that is causing the underlying problem. However, in many cases, the problem is not due to disease, dysfunction, or an issue with an organ or organ system, but is the result of delayed maturation of the nervous system and the resulting sensory and motor blockages. In these cases, there is a good chance that targeted, systematic, and preferably individualized, development therapy will bring about significant positive change within a relatively short period (a few months, perhaps a year, or a year and a half).

For a long time, it was thought that reflex integration or sensorimotor development only made sense until the end of childhood, up to the beginning of puberty. This theory has now been overturned. Research shows, for example, that the severe phase of dementia, during which many infantile reflexes become active again, can be delayed by a few years by using reflex integration or sensorimotor exercises. These "extra" years are "gifts" for both the person and their family.

My experience over many years confirms that exercises can be done at any age and that good results can be achieved. The effect on an individual depends, of course, on many factors. The nature of the symptoms, the person's age, the regularity of the exercises, the accuracy of the exercises, the lifestyle of the person, whether there are other deficits associated with the problem, the responsiveness of the nervous system and its susceptibility to the changes induced by the exercises, and so on, all play a role. In any case, I can tell you that no matter who starts doing the exercises, the results will not be tangible overnight. It requires persistent, regular, and accurate practice.

The following chapters list some of the most essential principles that must be considered in order for the exercises to be effective.

THE PROBLEM, AND CLARIFYING THE ORIGIN OF THE PROBLEM

Inadequate functioning of a particular organ or organ system can produce symptoms similar to those of neurological immaturity, retained primitive reflexes, or "imperfections" in sensorimotor integration. There are two ways to discover what is behind a particular problem. First, medical diagnostic procedures may reveal the cause of the dysfunction. However, if the doctor or specialist cannot find an organic cause or other medically relevant explanation, primitive reflex testing and an assessment of the person's sensorimotor status can help to clarify the origin of the problem.

It should be clear that the first—and perhaps most important—thing is to find out whether the problem is caused by organ dysfunction or disease. If this is not the case, then regular reflex integration or sensorimotor exercises are very likely to help remedy the problem. It is also advisable to start sensorimotor training even if the origin of the problem is "unexplained."

Let's look at some examples.

Everyone has heard of dyslexia, which has several definitions. In my home country Hungary, one of the most widely accepted is Gósy's definition, which states that *"dyslexia is a disorder in which a child has difficulty in learning to read."*

International literature distinguishes two types of dyslexia. The first is called true or developmental dyslexia; the second is acquired dyslexia. It is often complicated to distinguish between the two.

In 1975, the World Federation of Neurologists defined developmental dyslexia:

Developmental dyslexia is a disorder that manifests itself in difficulty in learning to read, despite the fact that reading is taught by appropriate, standard and professionally accepted methods in the language of instruction and the learner's intelligence is within the normal range.

Acquired dyslexia is a condition in which a previously working system is damaged by injury or disease, resulting in reading difficulties or inability to read. This can be partial or complete.

If the ability to read is completely lost, it is no longer called dyslexia but alexia. This usually affects an area of the brain whose role cannot be replaced.

In acquired dyslexia, there is organic damage, in this case to the brain. Although it can happen that a positive change will occur with therapy or massage to stimulate muscles responsible for speech, unfortunately, the chances are lower.

Depending on the nature of developmental dyslexia, there may be problems in many areas of the brain. If someone cannot bring letters together into words, if they have problems reading foreign words, if they read something else instead of what is written, or if they mix up letters and words when reading, the cause of the problem should be looked for elsewhere. In this case, movement or sensorimotor therapy or reflex integration exercises may be effective.

In all cases, the neurological origin of dyslexia should be clarified by a neurologist. An ophthalmological examination can also rule out the possibility that vision problems cause the dyslexic symptoms. If a neurological or ophthalmological problem can be ruled out, it is always worth considering and starting sensorimotor development and reflex integration. Even if the neurological cause is not clearly excluded, it is still worth starting sensorimotor development exercises, as there is a good chance of alleviating or even eliminating reading problems.

The question arises: Is it always possible to rule out that the problem is caused by an organic or functional disorder? There are causes that are well-defined (and thus clearly excludable) and issues that are more difficult to "diagnose."

For example, when a child experiences bedwetting or incontinence, it is clearly worth seeking the advice of a urologist or an endocrinologist. The former is to rule out problems due to the inadequate functioning of the excretory system, and the latter to rule out abnormalities caused by hormonal issues. For example, if a child experiencing bedwetting has a bladder volume that is too small, therapy should be started accordingly and, if still needed, can be supplemented with reflex integration therapy. In cases where the regulation of water balance is not functioning correctly for hormonal reasons, appropriate therapy should also be undertaken. But if everything is well in both these areas, it is very likely that the solution to bedwetting is to be found in reflex integration and sensorimotor development.

Identifying or ruling out the underlying causes of such problems is much more difficult for a child diagnosed with ADHD or autism spectrum disorder.

What can be done for an autistic child, or one with ADHD? It is certainly fortunate if a neurologist or child psychiatrist can see them, but the organic cause of the problem is unlikely to be known at this stage.

Based on a large body of research, researchers have found that many primitive reflexes can be triggered in children and adults who have ADHD and autism spectrum disorder. Although the causal link has not yet been clarified, there is a consensus that it is worth starting sensorimotor development as soon as possible.

The complexity of the underlying problem affects the success of the training, but the principle of "the sooner, the better" also applies here.

What symptoms or groups of symptoms might underly an underdeveloped primitive reflex, sensorimotor integration problem, or divergent neurodevelopment?

If a doctor or specialist did not find any physical reason for the following problems and groups of symptoms, and there are no contraindications to reflex integration or sensorimotor therapy (discussed in a later chapter), it is worth starting sensorimotor development.

- Reading difficulties, dyslexia
- Untidy, disordered handwriting, dysgraphia
- Poor spelling
- Attention-deficit
- Hyperactivity
- ADHD
- Hypersensitivity (to noise, texture, smell, vestibular stimuli, etc.)
- Delayed speech development
- Delayed motor development
- Confused speech and language problems (e.g., "tongue thrust swallowing")
- Uncoordinated, "clumsy" movements
- Bedwetting
- Fecal retention
- Tics
- Autism spectrum disorder
- Very loose or over-tight muscle tone

Each of these problems can be further broken down into "sub-problems." These have already been described in previous chapters, and I will not go into them here.

AGE GROUP

Age must be considered in several respects. On one hand, when choosing the type of exercise to be done and, on the other hand, when determining the amount and frequency of the exercises. Of course, a given age does not necessarily imply a specific level of maturity, fitness, preparation, or motivation. Severity of symptoms must also be taken into account. However, as a starting point, it is still worth following the recommendations below.

Age group	Number of exercises daily	Type of exercise (active = A, passive = P)
Up to 3 years	2–4	P:100%
3–5 years	2–6	A:20% P:80%
5–10 years	4–8	A:60% P:40%
10–16 years	4–12	A:80% P:20%
16+	12–14	A:90% P:10%
Senior citizens	8–12	A:80–90% P:20–10%

It is very important to do the exercises regularly—that is, every day. Together with each exercise in this book, I give guidelines for the number of repetitions, so that the reader can see how many times it is advisable to do a particular activity, depending on the problem and age.

The table above shows how the ratio of active to passive exercises varies with age. Active exercises are where the subject can perform the exercise alone, and passive ones are those where assistance is required. Obviously, an infant cannot be expected to actively perform developmental exercises, so for them, it is mostly a passive activity.

Although it means that the parent or caregiver does the exercises with the baby or toddler, it does not mean the child is "only" a passive participant. Passive participation does not mean that the training is a walk in the park for the baby. It is often very strenuous for the baby to hold its head, or to turn or crawl with the help of an adult.

As we get older, the proportion of active exercise increases. Although children aged 10–16 years are sufficiently mature to perform all the tasks on their own, passive exercises may also occur at this age, mainly related to vestibular stimulation. The same is valid for adults.

Senior citizens, if they do not have dementia or Alzheimer's disease, are usually as capable as adults of performing tasks independently. Obviously, the type of exercises and the level of difficulty will be slightly different for them. In this case, I may deviate from the ratio of active to passive exercises shown above.

PERFORMING THE EXERCISES: WARM-UP, INTENSITY, NUMBER OF REPETITIONS, REST TIME, CORRECTION OF ERRORS, COOL-DOWN

Regular practice is needed to integrate the remaining primitive reflexes through exercises and sensorimotor development. Performing the exercises from this book stimulates the nervous system in order to solve the problem or reduce the symptoms. The various reflex integration movements also have an effect on the areas of the nervous system where the primitive reflex centers are located. This can be achieved in two ways.

In one type of exercise, the movement-induced stimulation runs through the same "pathways" as in infancy, so the reflex inhibition mechanism is similar. These exercises are easier to perform and simpler to execute. Their effect is slightly slower than those of the second group of exercises listed below. However, they are more popular, especially with children, because they are easy to do.

The other type of exercise consists of movements that, when performed, stimulate a higher-level center in the brain. As I mentioned earlier in this book, if the cortex gets enough stimuli it will produce inhibitor neurotransmitters like GABA, which will inhibit the primitive reflex. This is a sign that the cortex has already matured. This type of exercise is very effective, but unfortunately, not all of them are suitable for smaller children.

As mentioned earlier, in the 19th century, the English neurologist John Hughlings Jackson drew attention to the phenomenon that in the complex processes that facilitate the development of the nervous system, ontogenetically younger levels can inhibit the function of more ancient regions. In other words, if development is smooth, the higher levels of neural structures such as the cortex inhibit primitive functions in the brain stem and spinal cord. This means that those primitive reflexes of enormous importance at the beginning of life become inhibited and can no longer be triggered.

Whatever the type of reflex integration exercise, the standard rule of all training applies—begin with a warm-up. A short series of warm-up exercises is necessary before reflex integration training for young children, but especially for adults and the elderly. These exercises prepare the body for movement and the muscles and joints for work. For those who don't have experience with how to loosen the body before exercising, a short warm-up series is included a few chapters later. Of course, you can modify this depending on your preferences, experience, and strength.

These exercises can be done slowly, carefully and regularly, or they can be rushed, sloppy and inconsistent. If you are not consistent and careful, the results may be a long time coming, or may never come at all. The most effective way to achieve the goal is to do the exercises in the most dynamic, focused, and structured way, according to the individual's abilities. The number of repetitions required to have the right effect on the nervous system is adjusted to age, so they should be achievable by everyone in that age group without difficulty. So, put in as much effort as you can, and focus on doing the exercises correctly and without rushing.

Regarding rest time between exercises, variations are possible. The basic principle to follow is that the number of repetitions of an exercise should be performed as recommended. So, if the exercise is 3x8 overhead lifts with 10–15 seconds rest, then this part of the training should be treated as one unit and performed "as one." Don't take a half-hour break between the 3x8 exercises, and do not do all 24 at once in an attempt to finish all the exercises faster.

When the full set of exercises has been completed it is advisable to take some rest. One of the best ways to do this is to do breathing exercises or go for a short walk. Doing the exercises regularly is essential! Exercises should be done daily, in the recommended amount, come rain or shine. In case of illness, especially if it is accompanied by a fever, suspend the exercises until the person is better.

It is best to follow the order of the exercises as shown in each chapter, but if one chooses to deviate from that, it is no major problem.

For how long should the exercises be performed?

The answer to this question could be **until the underlying problem is resolved**. This is obvious, but the situation is not always that simple.

If the problem has disappeared, or if there is a great improvement, it is very likely that the retained primitive reflexes, or at least a large part of them, have been integrated. The chances of reactivation and return are slim in children under 10–12 years of age. Significant physical or psychological stress may have the effect of "reviving" already degraded reflexes, but this is relatively rare. After the program has been finished, one rule to follow is that if the child has a fever or more severe illness, after recovery they should do the exercises again for a week or two. The same applies if a major change occurs in the child's life that may be stressful. I am thinking of the transition from nursery to school, a change of school, the divorce of parents, and so on. It is worth paying attention to this for up to 1–1.5 years after the successful integration of primitive reflexes, i.e., after the problem has disappeared.

For older children, adults, and senior citizens, the same rules apply. Additionally, between the ages of 40 and 50, it is advised to repeat the exercises once every two weeks, and repeat once per week between 50 and 60, because at these ages (according to current research) the nervous system needs to be constantly "reminded." This means doing the same series of exercises repeatedly at regular intervals so the progress made can be maintained.

For people over 60, the literature recommends daily exercise even if a problem has already disappeared, and particularly if the training is for preventive purposes.

Let's return to how long exercises should be carried out. There are two ways of checking whether a particular reflex has been successfully integrated. The first is a physical test; the second is a checklist of symptoms. Tests and symptom checklists are presented in a chapter towards the end of this book. (In the United States therapists often use just a checklist in the case of adults.) If the physical test is negative, i.e., the reflexes cannot be triggered, the training can be stopped, with the caveats described above. When using the checklist, if the symptoms still exist then continue the exercise program.

Of course, it is completely unnecessary to test the child or oneself daily. For children under 12, it is worthwhile to do a test after 4–6 months of performing the exercise program. Between the ages of 12 and 18, it is recommended to do a physical test or review the symptom checklist after 6–8 months, and for adults after 8–12 months. Depending on the results, the exercise program should be continued or can be stopped.

Accurate performance of the exercises, and correcting errors

During the program, attention should be paid to quantitative indicators and quality, i.e., the accurate execution of exercises. For children, this should be monitored by the parent or caregiver. A young child (and sometimes older ones too) cannot be expected to perform the exercises consistently and precisely. Some exercises are more manageable, and some are more difficult. Easier exercises tend to be straightforward, while more complex exercises are not always done accurately even if the child's willingness is strong. Up to the age of 12, it is recommended that a parent always be present during the exercises, even when they are going smoothly. In some cases, physical assistance is necessary; in other situations, gentle but firm guidance about how to do it correctly may be enough.

For older children and adults, body awareness is essential. Without it, it is complicated to perform the exercises accurately. Supervision at the beginning of an exercise session is important. Once you or the child get the hang of the exercises, someone should be asked to check your movements from time to time, especially for slightly more difficult exercises.

As the training progresses, it becomes easier to perform the exercises accurately. However, this does not mean that the primitive reflexes have been integrated.

REGRESSION

Sensorimotor therapies often result in temporary deterioration in movement, behavior, or cognitive functioning. In such cases, existing problems may not only be exacerbated, but new ones may also emerge. These are known as regression symptoms.

Many professionals find that these frighten the parent or carer helping the child perform the exercises, and this can discourage them from continuing.

One of the most significant studies is by a Swedish research group, Vestibular. The group is led by Dr. Mats Niklasson from Karlstad University. In 2010 he and his colleagues observed the onset of regression symptoms in 224 children during reflex-integrating, vestibular, sensorimotor-stimulating exercises.

The brain reorganizes its structure by rewiring its previous "circuits" to reach a more advanced state. Once this is achieved, the higher functioning inhibits the lower-level primitive functioning. This is when a primitive reflex is inhibited, opening the way for sensorimotor integration. While performing sensorimotor development exercises, regression symptoms may occur for a temporary period.

There is no clear pattern for the onset of regression symptoms. They can occur at any time during the performance of the exercises, and symptoms can vary widely from one individual to another. They can manifest themselves in the form of deterioration in movement, behavior, or sensory function, or as the appearance of unpleasant physical symptoms.

Niklasson and his team studied children, their regressive symptoms, and their development over an eight-week period in which there were a total of 16 exercise sessions. On each occasion, new exercises were introduced. In the figure below, the 16 dots represent these 16 sessions. The circles marked with "R*n*" represent the regressions, which were followed in each case by a positive change, which the researchers have represented with "T*n*." Not only was progress interrupted by regression, but there were three or four regressions, most of which were not as "deep" and intense as the previous one.

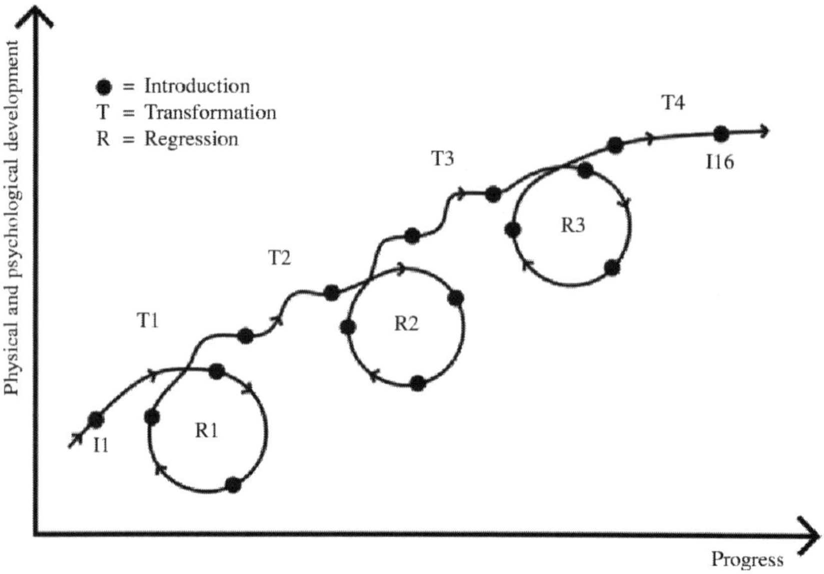

Representation of regression cycles (Vestibular research group, 2010)

It became apparent during the research that the onset of regression symptoms is not age-dependent and can be manifested as much through behavioral, parental, and social processes as through various biological processes.

The most frequently occurring regressive symptoms are listed in the table on the next page.

During the periods in the above diagram marked with "T*n*," the children showed clear sensorimotor and cognitive development. During the process, change was gradual, with positive phenomena becoming more pronounced and persistent over time. The regressive manifestations were described by the researchers as "gateways" to development, through which one must pass to achieve the goal.

Of course, regression periods are stressful not only for the child or adult receiving the training but also for those around them. I primarily mean parents and siblings, but teachers, friends, and the wider social network may also be affected. Parents need understanding, patience, love, and

PHYSICAL SYMPTOMS	PSYCHOLOGICAL SYMPTOMS
Bedwetting	Defiance
Finger sucking	Increased attachment to parents (especially the mother)
Chewing on objects, putting objects in the mouth (T-shirt, pencil, nail, etc.)	Playing with old, worn-out toys
Seeking tactile stimuli (touching everything, touching the parent)	Mood swings
Avoiding tactile stimuli (problems with dressing, avoiding being stroked)	Tantrums, hypersensitivity
Problems with stool retention	Questioning the usefulness of the exercises, increased resistance
Tics	Distraction
Slurring of speech and articulation, "babbling"	Increased alertness, hyperactivity
Sleepiness, desire to sleep with parents	Crying, sadness
Nasal congestion	Unusual cheerfulness, laughing
Complains of difficulty breathing	Changes in social relationships
Motor coordination problems	Restlessness, anxiety
Deterioration of writing and drawing skills	"Pompousness," "couldn't-care-less" attitude

resourcefulness to overcome difficult times. They need to sit down with the child's siblings and explain that this is a temporary situation and they should help the child undergoing development to get through this time, which is not pleasant for anyone. Teachers, sports coaches, and music teachers should be informed that the child is undergoing reflex integration and sensorimotor development, and that this may lead to changes in behavior, attention, motor coordination, etc. Parents should ask the person working with the child to monitor them closely and contact the parent if they notice any concerning changes.

Regression symptoms do not occur with the same intensity in everyone. Some children show almost no signs of problems "on the outside," and others show a spate of problems.

It is better to be prepared from the beginning, because you do not know how your child—or yourself if you are doing the training—will react to it, and what kind of regressive symptoms you will face.

I note here that adult sensorimotor development is not widely practiced, so the regression symptoms adults experience have been little researched. In my experience, adults can have almost the same regressive symptoms as children, with one or two exceptions. For example, none of the adults who have done the series of exercises I put together have ever experienced bedwetting.

Anyone who is involved in any way in sensorimotor development should keep in mind the chart drawn by the Swedish research team and remember that after a difficult period, there will be a significant improvement.

OTHER QUESTIONS RELATED TO THE EXERCISE PROGRAM

Some questions may arise during the exercise program or before starting. I try to answer the most common ones below.

When is it contraindicated to do the exercises?

The first thing that is very important to clarify is whether there are any contraindications to performing these exercises. As they do not put excessive strain on the respiratory and circulatory systems, there is no particular risk. What should always be taken into account, however (if necessary, consult a specialist), is any problem, disease or damage affecting the nervous system or the musculoskeletal system.

Examples of conditions affecting the nervous system are epilepsy and shunts. Exercises should also not be done during the recovery period from a spinal operation or brain surgery.

Among orthopedic disorders, scoliosis, kyphosis, lordosis, and their variations are the most common problems.

This does not mean that a child with scoliosis or epilepsy cannot do the training. However, certain exercises are contraindicated for specific conditions. These will be listed in the next chapter.

Why do two people not develop in the same way when doing the exercises?

Over the years, I have witnessed many times that children with the same problem, of the same age, sex, build, and from very similar family backgrounds, develop at different rates. In fact, even twins have displayed this phenomenon. The individual response of the nervous system explains this.

No two brains are the same, so how each one reacts will be completely different.

The reaction can be influenced by the attitude towards training, motivation, the background and origin of the problem, and the complexity of the problem. A well-motivated child happy to do the exercises will usually improve faster than a child who regards every occasion as torture. If the child was born prematurely, by Caesarean section, with a low Apgar score, the child will likely develop slower than someone born naturally at full term with a 10/10 Apgar score.

And, of course, it matters whether the child "only" wets the bed at night or additionally has delayed speech development and attention-deficit.

Of course, there are different cases. Sometimes the progress is spectacular precisely because the child starts from a very "low" place, and every small positive change is a huge success.

However fast or slow one develops, comparisons should be avoided as much as possible. Every little success should be celebrated. When we exercise with our child, let us share our happiness and praise them highly, as it is the fruit of their labor.

How to communicate?

Related to the previous topic is the challenge of communication and motivation.

By communication, in this case, I mean how to talk to the child about the retention of primitive reflexes and sensorimotor immaturity. There are four things that we need to pay attention to: the age of the child; their intellectual capacity; not frightening the child; but also not trivializing the situation.

Since the pace of maturation of the nervous system in children is the main issue in most cases, perhaps a good analogy is the planting of flower seeds. We can explain to them that when we sow a packet of flower seeds, they do not all sprout, grow and bloom at once. There will be some that will burst into full color sooner, some that are just about to bud, some that haven't even budded yet, and even some that haven't even popped their heads out of the ground. The slower-growing ones will also flourish. They need a little more care, sunlight, water, loosening of the soil around them, and nutrients. The child's situation is similar to that of these flowers.

For older children and adolescents, you also need to sit down and talk to them about what they can expect *from* the training, and what they can expect *during* the training. It is also very important to say that there may be difficult periods, but that these will be temporary because they will be followed by improvement. Improvement will not happen overnight but will take many months of regular work, and we (parents, grandparents, helpers) will be there to help them—they can count on us.

We need to tell children that they are not to blame for anything, just as parents are not to blame for anything in most cases. Many parents have asked me "*"What went wrong?*" and "*What could we have done differently?*" Very rarely, indeed only in a few cases, can the cause of the problem be found somewhere in the past. There are known risk factors for problems with the normal development of the nervous system, but in many cases, none of these factors are present, and yet the problem is still there. Of course, it is good to know the cause of the problem, but finding a solution is more important.

How do we motivate the child or ourselves?

I don't know whether it is easier for an adult to motivate themself or their child.

For adults, I think it's best to incorporate the exercises into your daily routine. Everybody knows and feels what part of the day is the time when they have 15 minutes or half an hour to devote to this small but useful exercise. When times are harder, or you're more tired, or moodier, just think about why you started training in the first place. Do you want to feel better or not? You can listen to music for motivation or, if you have the opportunity, do the exercises outdoors.

Parents often do more for their children than for themselves. In this respect, the parent's task is easier than if they themselves had to exercise every day, because the motivation is strong. You want your child to be happy, healthy, and successful. However, once the novelty has worn off, children often find it a chore to do the exercises daily, and resist when they have to exercise. This is a difficult time for parents, even if they are highly motivated.

Regularity can also help in this case, so building exercise into the child's daily schedule is a good idea. I also suggest taking a notebook and drawing empty circles with your child—10, 15, 20. After each set of exercises, done accurately and without "hysteria," color in a circle or stick a sticker. When 10, 15 and 20 circles are filled, the child can receive a small gift. There is no need to think of something huge because expensive things have no more motivating power than small things.

As parents and helpers, we must always be careful to praise the child whenever possible and whenever the child deserves it. Praise can work wonders. Never threaten a child because that will not move you forward—it creates a negative emotional charge attached to the performance of the exercises and leads to anxiety and resistance.

Finally, can you play sports and do other physical activities alongside the training exercises in the book?

Parents have asked me this question many times. Yes, it is possible. There are no contraindications in the scientific literature to prohibit anyone from doing any physical activity while doing the reflex integration, sensorimotor, and vestibular development exercises.

Sports, games, dancing, hiking, etc. all benefit the nervous system. No one's nervous system will be damaged by exercising regularly and doing 15–30 minutes of exercise a day. The same applies to any physical activity for children. If your child is a fan of a particular sport and likes to go to dance class or some other kind of developmental activity, feel free to go. As a parent, it is also essential to ensure that your child has time for free play, drawing, or whatever they choose to do, as they are still a child.

WHAT YOU NEED TO KNOW BEFORE DOING THE EXERCISES

The composition of the exercises

A problem can be caused by the presence of several unintegrated reflexes, so it is often not just one reflex that needs to be integrated, but three, four, and sometimes more. In the subsequent chapters covering individual conditions, the associated reflexes are listed in the descriptions.

Persistent primitive reflexes have a negative impact in many areas. The basic problems that affect movement, behavior, cognition, and social relationships are listed below:

- They block the development and regulation of optimal muscle tone (e.g., hypotonic or overly tight muscles)
- They lead to perceptual difficulties (affecting virtually all senses)
- They induce involuntary, inappropriate movements (e.g., when a person in whom the grasping and sucking reflexes can be triggered is drawing or writing they stick out their tongue; or as another example, if the ATNR is not inhibited, when they are riding a bicycle and they turn their head to the side, their arm on the same side extends and pulls on the handlebar)
- The development of more advanced reflexes is prevented, e.g., a person whose Moro reflex is not integrated cannot develop the Strauss reflex.

For a detailed description of the negative effects of individual persistent primitive reflexes, see the earlier chapter on reflexes.

Another important thing to note is that a given primitive reflex can be associated with several symptoms and conditions. Let us look at a few examples of this. The ATNR can be triggered in children with ADHD, and also in the case of dyslexia or dysgraphia. The presence of the grasping and sucking reflexes may play a role in dysgraphia but may also cause delayed speech development. The tonic labyrinthine reflexes are present in both bedwetting and fecal retention.

In the subsequent chapters, I recommend the exercises to be performed for each condition. However, as noted, a specific reflex can be associated with multiple conditions. For example, someone with both dysgraphia and a speech development disorder will find the same reflex integration exercises for the grasping and sucking reflexes in both chapters. If the exercises for both conditions are done at the same time, then, of course, the duplicated exercises for integrating the grasping and sucking reflexes can be done just once.

Warm-up

Before performing the exercises in this book, it is wise to get in the right physical and mental mood. The following recommendation is just one of the possible variations. Everyone can develop their own or their child's warm-up routine.

Warming up before the exercises

20–30 seconds of walking in place
2–3 head circles to the right and left
4–5 wrist rotations with both hands
5–6 arm curls back and forth with arms alternating or at the same time
5–6 times bend the torso forward
With hands on hips, 5–6 torso twists right and left
Lean forward with hands on knees, legs slightly bent, 3–4 knee rotations clockwise and anticlockwise
5–6 ankle rotations with each foot
Shake out both feet

Contraindicated exercises

In case of any uncertainty, consult your doctor before performing the exercises in this book.
In cases of the conditions listed below, the following exercises should not be performed under any circumstances.

Epilepsy: illumination of the eye from the side, tumbling head over heels, rotating/spinning in a standing position
Shunt (brain or spinal cord): tumbling head over heels, rolling, rotating/spinning
Scoliosis, kyphosis: tumbling head over heels

If the child is unable to do all the exercises

It is critical to take time to do the exercises *every day*. If the child is however unable to do *all* the exercises each day, I suggest the following approach to divide them across multiple days.

According to the child's ability, decide the number of exercises to be performed in one session. Per age group:

- 3–5 years: either two, three, or four exercises per day
- 6–10 years: either three, four, or six exercises per day
- 11–16 years: six exercises per day
- 16+: 12 or more exercises per day

Then, if doing—for example—three exercises per day, divide the 12 exercises in the appropriate chapter across four days as follows.

- Day 1: perform exercises 1, 5, and 9
- Day 2: perform exercises 2, 6, and 10
- Day 3: perform exercises 3, 7, and 11
- Day 4: perform exercises 4, 8, and 12
- On the fifth day, start again from the beginning

If doing two exercises per day, divide them like this across six days. If four exercises per day, divide them across three days, and if six exercises per day, divide them across two days.

ADHD

Anyone can find it hard to sit still or to pay attention. They may also be more impulsive than they need to be, can be quickly thrown off balance, or often interrupt conversations. Some children and adults experience these symptoms strongly and consistently, making it difficult to manage their family life, or fit into a school or work community, and it harms their work and daily life in general.

Attention-deficit hyperactivity disorder (ADHD) is a neurodevelopmental disorder that affects over 5% of children worldwide and almost 10% of school-age children in the USA. Symptoms persist into adulthood in nearly 80% of cases, meaning inattention, impulsivity, and hyperactivity.

Although people with ADHD can be very successful in life, without proper treatment, this symptom complex has many negative consequences. These may include failure at school, family conflicts, depression, problems with social relationships, excessive drug or substance abuse, delinquency, vulnerability to injury, or failure at work.

ADHD in children was first described by medical science in 1902. Throughout history, the condition has gone by many names—minimal brain dysfunction, childhood hyperkinetic reaction, and attention-deficit disorder with or without hyperactivity.

ADHD symptoms

Symptoms usually appear in early childhood. Many parents report excessive motor activity in early childhood, and later inattention, impatience during play, and lack of perseverance.

There are many symptoms. The most common ones are described below.

Attention-related symptoms:

- Lack of attention to detail
- Makes mistakes due to carelessness when performing a task, not because they cannot do the task well
- It is hard to maintain the child's or person's attention
- Does not seem to pay attention
- Finds it hard to follow instructions
- Difficulty with organization
- Avoids or dislikes tasks that require sustained mental effort
- Forgetful, absent-minded
- Easily distracted

Symptoms of hyperactivity and impulsivity:

- Fatigued by daily activities
- Constantly fidgets with their hands
- Wobbles in the chair
- Finds it hard to stay seated
- Excessive activity in children, extreme restlessness in adults
- Finds quiet activities challenging
- Excessive talking
- Answers before listening or reading the question
- Unable to wait
- Interrupts conversations or cuts in on what others are saying

Symptoms may combine in different ways and change over time. Although hyperactivity tends to decrease, attention-deficit persists.

Severity of symptoms

As symptoms affect different children and adults to different degrees, the severity of ADHD is graded differently. A distinction is made between "mild," "moderate," or "severe" ADHD.

Mild: Relatively few symptoms are present, and symptoms cause only minor deviations from the norm. Symptoms are noticed but usually tolerated by the family, school, or work environment.

Moderate: Symptoms or functional impairments ranging from "mild" to "severe" are present. People are aware that something is wrong. It is common for an individual with ADHD symptoms to be perceived as "absent-minded, head in the clouds, restless, eccentric."

Severe: There are many symptoms, some of which are very severe. The person may have significant problems in the home, school, or work environment, where people find it difficult or impossible to tolerate their behavior.

ADHD in children, adolescents, and adults

Children with ADHD often appear more immature and less independent than their peers. In many cases, ADHD is associated with delayed speech development, poor fine and/or gross motor skills, and maladjustment. They also have a low tolerance for frustration, have difficulty managing their emotions, and are prone to sudden and frequent mood swings.

Children with ADHD are at increased risk in adolescence because of the extra demands placed on them, which they find difficult or impossible to meet without sustained attention. They also battle the difficulties caused by hormonal changes. They often fail in their studies and later at work. They may have problems with social relationships and life skills.

People with ADHD find it difficult to become independent in adulthood and often have problems coping with challenges posed by social situations. Whether as adolescents or adults, they may be irresponsible in sexual relationships and more likely to abuse alcohol or drugs.

Adolescent girls and young adults with ADHD are more prone to eating disorders, bulimia, anorexia, and even morbid obesity due to binge eating compared with their peers without ADHD.

People with ADHD may have problems with working memory, executive functions, and maintaining attention. Executive function is the brain's ability to cope with new, complex, and goal-oriented tasks and to adapt flexibly to environmental changes. It does so by prioritizing and managing thoughts and actions, keeping goals in mind, and eliminating distractions. One of the benefits of this function is that we can consider the long-term consequences of our actions and manage our behavior and decisions more effectively.

Those with problems with executive function may have difficulty carrying out their tasks and may forget or miss important things when making decisions and performing actions.

Co-occurring disorders

More than two-thirds of children with ADHD have at least one other disorder that does not fall under the ADHD umbrella. Delayed speech and motor development have already been mentioned. In addition, ADHD is often associated with a variety of behavioral and conduct disorders, anxiety, depression, tic disorders, Tourette's syndrome, sleep disorders, and learning disabilities.

Some research suggests that ADHD runs in families. Certain environmental factors such as lead and pesticides are believed to increase the likelihood of ADHD. Premature birth, low birth weight, and certain brain injuries also heighten the risk of ADHD.

In the past, scientists thought that maternal stress and smoking during pregnancy might increase the probability of ADHD; however, the results of several studies have questioned this assumption.

The following factors do not cause ADHD but may exacerbate symptoms in susceptible children:

Excessive screen time (TV, monitor, phone, etc.)
Consuming too much sugar
Family stress (poverty, family conflicts)
Traumatic experiences

What can we do?

In recent years, there has been a lot of research into the relationship between immature infant reflexes, impaired sensorimotor integration, and ADHD. There is now clear evidence that many infant reflexes persist in children and adults with ADHD and that, as a consequence, various sensorimotor integration problems exist.

The most common persistent reflexes in ADHD are:

- Symmetrical tonic neck reflex (STNR)
- Asymmetrical tonic neck reflex (ATNR)
- Forward tonic labyrinthine reflex (TLRf)
- Backward tonic labyrinthine reflex (TLRb)
- Spinal Galant reflex

The following exercises should be performed regularly to eliminate these reflexes.

Exercise Videos

A set of videos are available that demonstrate exercises to inhibit the primitive reflexes associated with ADHD. Use the following QR code to go directly to the video package, or visit https://drsarlos.com/videos for more information.

Scan for video!

Exercises for ADHD

1.

STNR

Starting position: Kneel on all fours, with arms extended and palms on the floor, shoulder-width apart. Keep the thighs in a vertical position.
1. Bend the arms, lowering the chin to the floor between the two hands.
2. Extend the arms to return to the starting position.
3. Move the hips back so the bottom is sitting on the heels and the head is between the two shoulders. Keep the arms extended and the palms on the ground.
4. Rise back to the starting position.

Number of repetitions:

3–5 years: 4–5x
5–10 years: 5–6x
10–16 years: 6–8x
16+: 10x

2

ATNR

SP

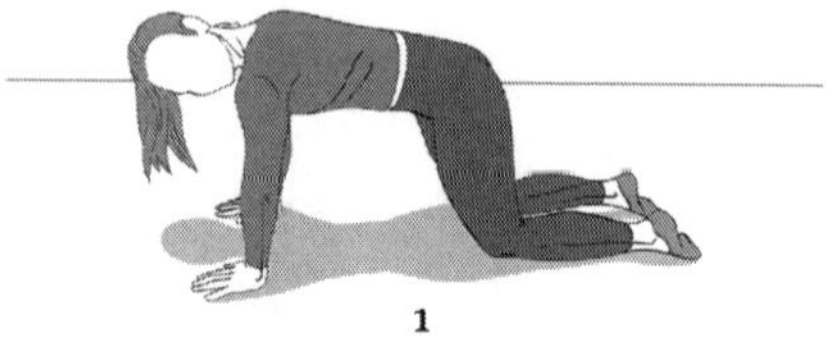

1

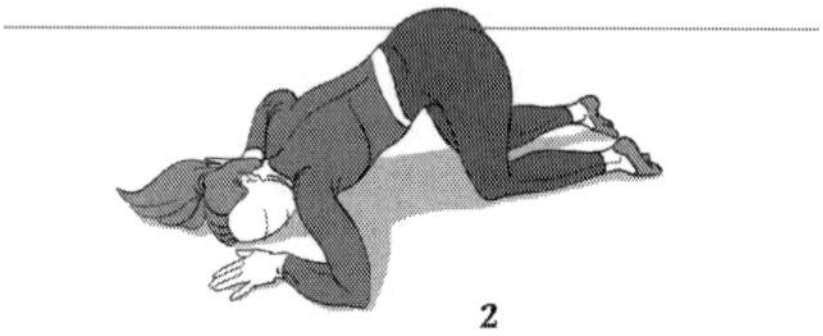

2

3

Starting position: Kneel on all fours, with arms extended and palms on the floor, shoulder-width apart. Keep the thighs in a vertical position.
1. Turn the head to the left so the left ear is aligned with the spine.
Important: Keep the arms extended and the palms on the ground.
2. Bend both elbows simultaneously, lower both shoulders, and place the right ear on the ground.
3. Extend both arms to return to the starting position.
The exercises must also be performed for the stated number of repetitions on the opposite side.

Number of repetitions:
3–5 years: 4–6x
5–10 years: 6–10x
10–16 years: 8–12x
16+: 12–16x

Repeat on each side.

As young children often cannot achieve the starting position due to the triggering of the ATNR reflex, parental assistance may be required for this exercise. In this case, the helper should stand over the child in a straddle position, turning the child's head in the desired direction.

It is almost certain that the arm on the opposite side will bend when the child's head is turned, e.g., if the child looks to the left then the right arm will bend. In this case, gently move the elbow joint to straighten the arm. Additionally, ensure that the hand on the side to which the head moves is fully extended on the ground, not resting on its fingers.

The arm flexion should be initiated from this position, with both elbows bending simultaneously. Assist this by slightly pulling both the child's elbows outward at the same time. This pull will need to be stronger in the direction the child's head is facing, as that arm tends to straighten due to the reflex. (In step 2 of the image above, the left elbow should be pulled more strongly as the head turns left.)

Patience is essential from the parent or helper, as it is difficult for the child to assume and maintain this position. However, when done correctly, this is one of the most effective exercises to help eliminate the ATNR.

3

ATNR

SP

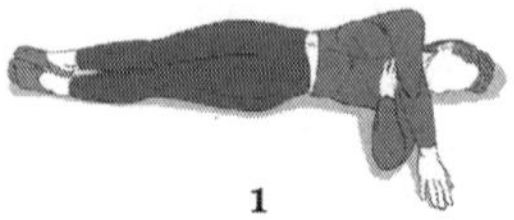

1

2

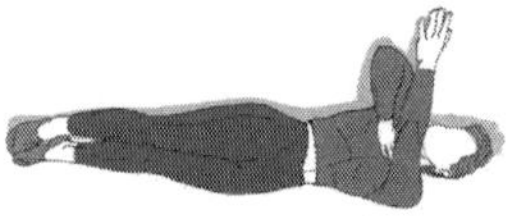

3

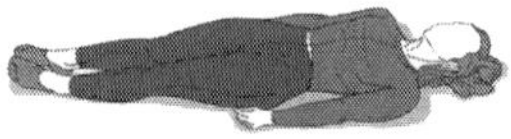

4

Starting position: Lie on the back, gazing upwards.
1. After deep inhalation and exhalation, turn the head and torso to the left. At the same time, bend the left arm by placing the left palm on the chest. Swing the right arm towards the left elbow so that both arms move simultaneously and turn the head and torso. From the navel down, do not move the lower part of the body.
2. Return to the starting position. Rest the arms on the ground beside the body and gaze upwards.
3. Repeat the first movement to the other side.
4. Return to the starting position. Again, rest the arms on the ground beside the body and gaze upwards.

Perform the exercise alternately: to the left, back to the middle, to the right, and again back to the middle.

Number of repetitions:
3–5 years: 6x per side
5–10 years: 10x per side
10–16 years: 12x per side
16+: 15x per side

If it is challenging to do this exercise at first, provide or obtain assistance.

4

ATNR

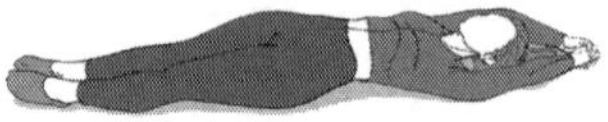

SP

1

2

Starting position: Lie on the back (supine position), with arms on the floor, extended above the head as far as possible, elbows outstretched, and interlocked hands.

1. This exercise is effectively rolling on the floor, with the caveat that crossing the legs should initiate the movement, and the torso and arms follow. So, if lying on the back and rolling to the left, first cross the right leg over the left. Do the opposite if rolling to the right.
2. Then roll over so that the stomach is now on the floor (prone position). Take care during the turn that the legs again become open and parallel. Continue rolling in the same direction, next from prone to supine. Again, the movement starts with the legs crossed, followed by the body and arms. So, if now lying on the front and rolling to the left, first cross the left leg over the right.

If there is enough space, roll as far as possible.
If the room is not large enough, roll back and forth several times until reaching the number of turns listed below.

Number of repetitions:
3–5 years: 4–5 turns in one direction, then backward 3x
5–10 years: 4–5 turns in one direction, then backward 4x
10–16 years: 4–5 turns in one direction, then backward 6x
16+: 4–5 turns in one direction, then backward 6x

5

ATNR TLRB

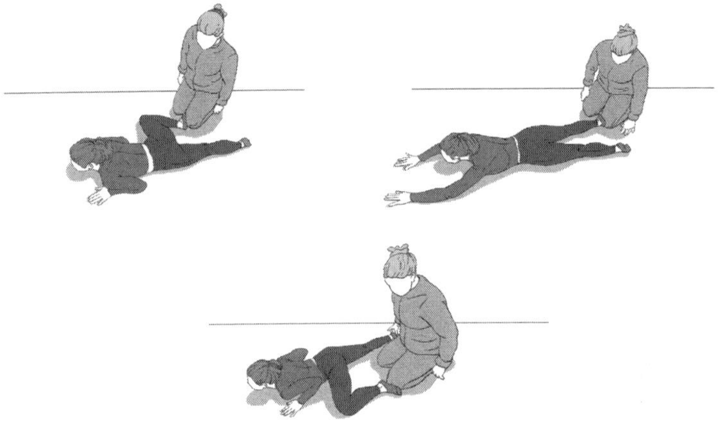

Crawl forward on the floor, keeping the stomach on the ground. After 4–5 crawling movements, stand up, turn around, and open the legs. From this position, tumble "head over heels" and return to the starting position. This can be done on a soft surface, e.g., a carpet or a yoga mat.

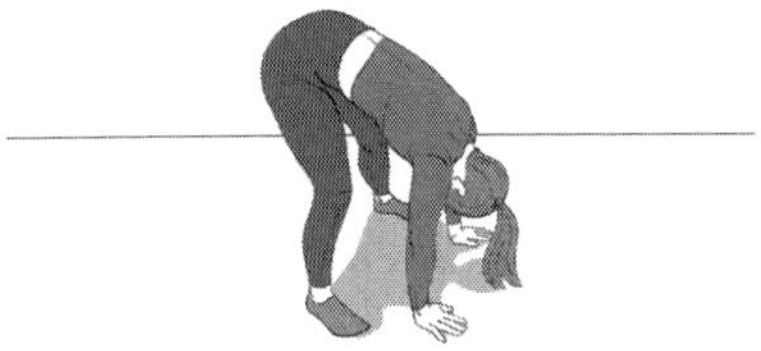

When crawling, pay attention to the following:

- Keep the head off the ground, looking forward. The head should not turn left and right.
- Use both arms and legs when crawling
- Until the bent leg is extended, do not bend the other leg
- Don't lift the hips—keep them on the ground

- Arms should be used to crawl, but don't give advice to use them. It is important to let the crawling movement develop!
- If necessary, help in the way shown in the diagram. With one hand, support the pushing leg, and if the other leg bends, use the other hand to help keep it extended.

When tumbling head over heels, the following points should be observed:

- Start the movement from a straddle position (legs apart)
- Tuck the head in, don't put weight on the top of the head!
- If assistance is given, tilt the head towards the chest with one hand, and with the other hand, support the child's buttocks and thighs, and roll them forward. It's good if the child "rolls like a ball" and doesn't "drop like a log."

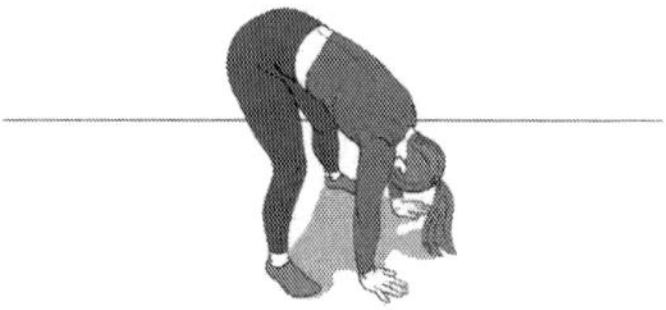

Number of repetitions:
3–5 years: 6x the full sequence of crawling and head over heels
5–10 years: 8–10x the full sequence
10–16 years: 10x the full sequence
16+: 15x: 10x the full sequence

6

TLRF

SP

1

2

Starting position: Lie on the back, with legs bent and feet on the ground. Extend arms, parallel to thighs.

1. Tilt the head forward so that the arms remain extended. The shoulders should not be pulled up into the neck. Maintain this position for the required number of seconds.
2. Lower the head to the ground. If necessary, the arms may be put down on the ground.

Number of repetitions:

3–5 years: 3 x 3, holding the head up for 2–3 seconds (with help if necessary)
5–10 years: 3 x 4–8, holding the head up for 3–6 seconds (with help if necessary)
10–16 years: 3 x 6–8, holding the head up for 5–6 seconds
16+: 3 x 8, holding the head up for 6 seconds

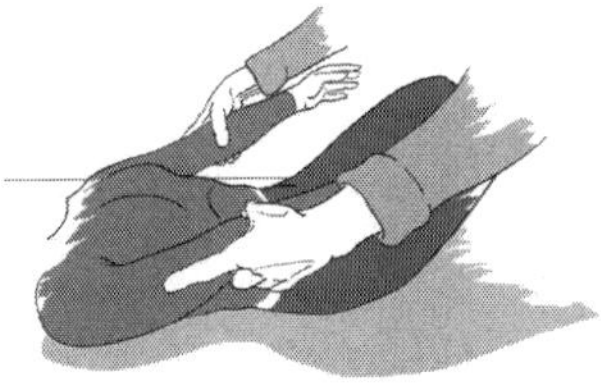

It very often happens that when lifting the head in the above exercise, the arm bends, and the child (and, in many cases, adults too) pulls their shoulder up to the neck.
In these cases, help in the following way.

Sitting at the child's feet, grasp the elbow joint and press down on the elbow with the index finger, preventing the elbow from bending and the shoulder from pulling up to the neck.

7

TLRF

Rock back and forth in the shown position. Arms should be extended, holding the lower legs. The shoulders should not be pulled up into the neck.

Number of repetitions:
3–5 years: 3 x 6 (with help if necessary)
5–10 years: 3 x 8 (with help if necessary)
10–16 years: 3 x 10
16+: 3 x 12

8

TLRF

SP

1

2

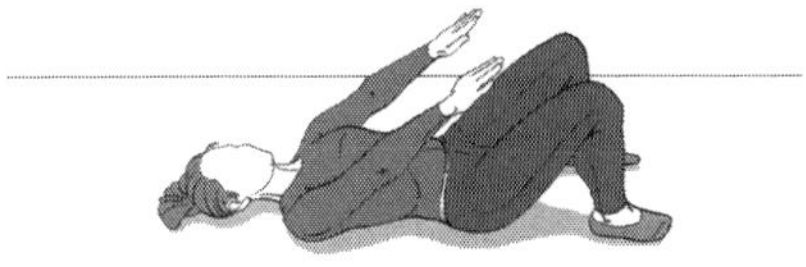

3

Starting position: Lie on the back, with legs bent and feet on the ground. Extend arms, parallel to thighs.

1. Tilt the head forward so that the arms remain extended. The shoulders should not be pulled up into the neck. Maintain this position for the required number of seconds.
2. Raise the shoulders and the back slightly off the ground. Keep the arms extended. The shoulders should not be pulled up into the neck. Maintain this position for the required number of seconds.
3. Lower the head to the ground. If necessary, the arms may be put down on the ground.

Number of repetitions:

3–5 years: 3x, hold in each position for 2 seconds (with help if necessary)

5–10 years: 3–5x, hold in each position for 3 seconds (with help if necessary)

10–16 years: 6–8x, hold in each position for 4–5 seconds

16+: 8x, hold in each position for 6 seconds

9

TLRF

SP

1

2

3

Starting position: Sit cross-legged, palms on the floor, arms outstretched. Rotate the head, don't raise the shoulders, keep arms fully extended and palms on the ground.

Number of repetitions:
3–5 years: two to the left and two to the right; repeat 3x (with help if necessary)
5–10 years: 4 x left and 4 x right; repeat 4x (with help if necessary)
10–16 years: 4 x left and 4 x right; repeat 5x
16+: 4 x left and 4 x right; repeat 6x

10

GALANT

SP

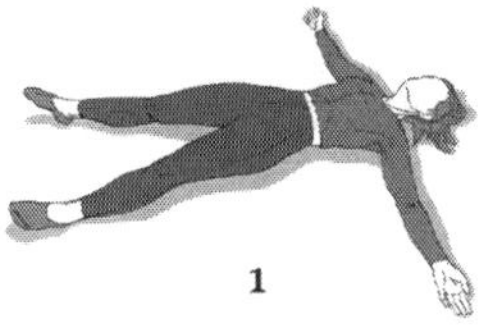

1

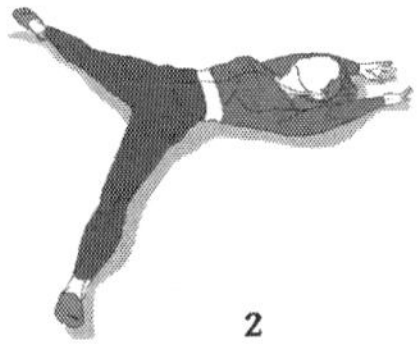

2

3

Starting position: Lie on the back, legs parallel, arms resting on the floor next to the body.
1–2. Spread the legs and slide the arms up to the ears. Do these actions at the same time.
3. Close the legs and simultaneously slide the arms back down to the starting position.

Number of repetitions:
3–5 years: 16–20x
5–10 years: 20–30x
10–16 years: 30–40x
16+: 40x

11

GALANT MORO

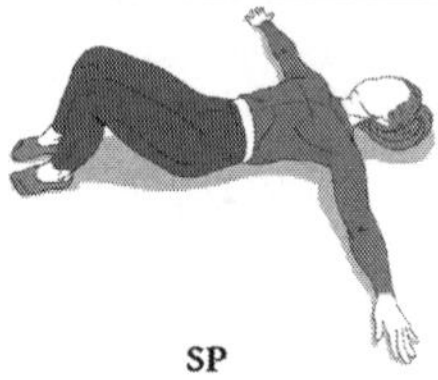

SP

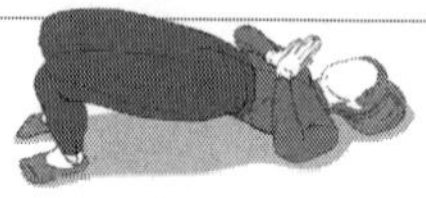

1

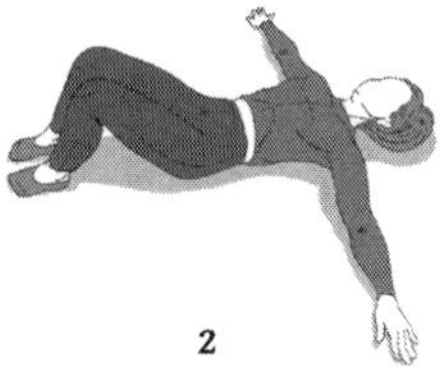

2

Starting position: Lie on the back, knees bent, arms outstretched on the ground.
1. Lift the hips and squeeze the buttocks together, and at the same time bend the elbows and push the palms together. Maintain this position for the required number of seconds.
2. Return to the starting position.
If it is too difficult to coordinate the movement of the arms and legs, it is enough to do only the leg movements for the first 2–3 months.

Number of repetitions:
3–5 years: 4–5x, hold for 3 seconds
5–10 years: 5–6x, hold for 4–6 seconds
10–16 years: 6–8x, hold for 6 seconds
16+: 10x, hold for 6 seconds

12

TLRB

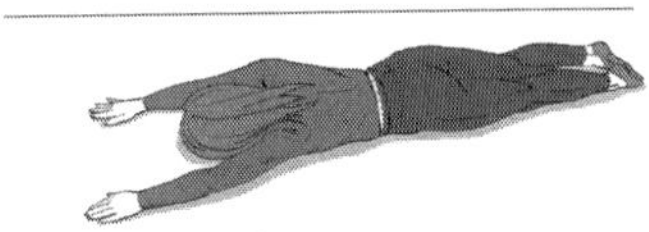

SP

1

2

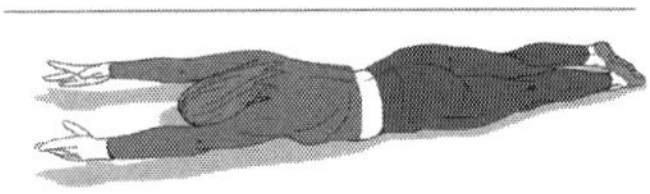

3

4

Starting position: Lie on the stomach, with arms on the ground, extended above the head, forehead resting on the ground.

1. Raise the arms off the ground, extended as far as possible, keeping the forehead on the ground.
2. Raise the head off the ground, keeping the arms fully extended.
3. Lower the head, and return the forehead to the ground.
4. Lower the arms to the starting position.

Number of repetitions:

3–5 years: 6x
5–10 years: 8x
10–16 years: 10x
16+: 12x

Exercises to "wake up" the right hemisphere

In ADHD, it is common for the left hemisphere to function much more intensively than the right. According to the literature and my own experience, this leads to difficulties in controlling emotional-volitional functions (self-control). Impulsiveness, impatience, lack of/poor ability to perform tasks consistently and uniformly, and problems controlling one's behavior are common symptoms.

Performing the following sensory exercises is advisable until the symptoms subside or disappear.

The following sensory stimulation exercises are best done in the evening. If the child or adult is hypersensitive to light or to music (the latter is less common), omit the corresponding exercises.

Exercises should be done daily for 2–3 months. They should reduce symptoms associated with right hemisphere hypofunction. If an improvement in symptoms is observed, it is possible to perform the exercises only every second day and continue in this way for a further 2–3 months.

The results of these sensory stimulation exercises vary from person to person. The most common benefits are: better self-control, fall asleep at night more easily, improved ability to cooperate, reduced sensory sensitivity, and less picky with food choices.

If symptoms recur after these exercises are stopped, the symptoms may be less severe, but it is recommended to recommence the exercises.

1

The child should lie on their back, gazing upwards. From the left side, shine a flashlight into their left eye for about 1 second at a distance of 20 cm (8 in), then turn the flashlight away from the head. Then repeat.

Number of repetitions:
3–5 years: 6–8x
5–10 years: 8x
10–16 years: 10x
16+: 12–16x

2

The child should lie on their back, gazing upwards. They should listen to classical music (Mozart, Vivaldi, Schubert, etc.) with their left ear, i.e., position the speaker or phone on the left side of the head.

Number of minutes for which to listen:
3–5 years: 1 minute
5–10 years: 1–2 minutes
10–16 years: 2–3 minutes
16+: 3–5 minutes

3

The child should lie on their back. Lift the head slightly and turn it to the left, then back to the center. Repeat.

Adults should assist children with this exercise.

Number of repetitions:
3–5 years: 6–8x
5–10 years: 8–10x
10–16 years: 10–16x
16+: 10–16x

4

The child should lie on their back. Using the left hand only, clench the fingers into a fist, or squeeze a small ball for 1–2 seconds. Then release, and repeat.

Number of repetitions:
3–5 years: 6–8x
5–10 years: 8–10x
10–16 years: 10–12x
16+: 16–20x

5

The child should lie on their stomach. Stroke or massage the left side of the body (e.g., the back, the leg). Although this exercise ideally requires another person to perform the task, adults can massage their own feet and hips using an aid such as a small smooth stone, a massage roller, or a massage tool.

Number of repetitions:
3–5 years: 20x
5–10 years: 20–30x
10–16 years: 30x
16+: 30x

FECAL RETENTION

There are many factors associated with the intensity and frequency of a person's bowel movements: genetics, diet, social habits, comfort, cultural beliefs, family relationships, the timing of daily activities, and the state of development of the nervous system.

The frequency of bowel movements varies naturally with age. Babies poop on average four times in the first week of life. By age two, you can expect to defecate about two times a day; by age four, it typically decreases to once daily. Healthy babies fed exclusively on breast milk may not defecate for over a week.

We talk about fecal retention when a child holds back stools for days or more than a week. Because of their efforts to prevent defecation, they often clench their legs, tighten their buttock muscles, and hold their torsos tight and straight, resulting in a noticeable posture.

We speak of functional fecal retention when there is no objective, organic obstruction to the passage of feces. This condition is most often the result of painful defecation experiences. Given that the child wants to avoid further pain, they try not to poop.

Prolonged retention of stool results in an increase in stool size. As it stays longer than necessary in the large intestine, where water is absorbed, it becomes harder and harder. Eventually, it must pass out; large amounts of hard stool will lead to another painful experience.

This reinforces stool retention, and the child will repeatedly do everything possible to avoid pooping.

Even though they may not poop for days on end, it is still common for their underwear to become stained. Although the child can retain feces for a long time, the gaseous metabolites are still passed out. When the child relaxes their bottom to let the gases out, it causes fluid around the retained feces to leak out and soil the underpants. As feces accumulate in the intestinal tract, the child becomes more irritable and does not want to eat. When the stool finally passes, the child becomes liberated and gobbles up food to make up for missed meals. This continues until the whole process starts over again.

Diet rarely affects functional bowel control because the problem is no longer just constipation but the child's fear of painful bowel movements. Nevertheless, it is worth paying attention to diet because if the child "gets the urge" to go to the toilet early, there is some chance of avoiding another painful experience.

Enemas and suppositories are often only temporary solutions. They do not help the child to learn to poop regularly as they are not in control of when they need to go to the bathroom. Moreover, these methods often provoke resistance in children.

To resolve this problem, parents should understand some key things about functional bowel movements. The following information should also be shared with the child, taking into account their age and level of understanding:

1) Fecal retention is not a disease, despite being the most common pediatric gastroenterological problem
2) The situation almost always improves if the child decides of their own free will to go to the toilet when they feel the urge to poop
3) It is not dangerous. It never causes cancer, the colon will not "burst," and toxins will not be released back into the bloodstream.
4) In most cases, 100% improvement can be achieved by doing specific reflex integration exercises.

Which primitive reflexes are associated with regular defecation, and how?

At least three reflexes influence normal defecation: the forward tonic labyrinth reflex (TLRf); the backward tonic labyrinth reflex (TLRb); and the spinal Galant reflex.

The function of the first two is related to the vestibular system in the inner ear. This system senses the spatial position of the head and its movement in space.

The nervous system uses the spatial position of the head as a basis for adjusting the body's muscle tone to deal with gravity. This mechanism is critical. If there is not complete consistency, muscle tone may be too loose (hypotonic) or too tight. This regulation mechanism affects all the muscles in our body, including those that enable our internal organs to function, thereby influencing, among other things, stomach and bowel movements or bladder contractions. These organs need to contract and relax. This dynamic work is crucial for the organs to function in perfect harmony.

There is a relationship between visceroception, the sensation of our internal organs, and the sense of balance. Poor balance perception (which may be caused by the presence of TLRb and TLRf) leads to poor visceroception. This may manifest as poor stimulus perception as well as hypersensitivity, and may be compounded if the spinal Galant reflex is not integrated since this reflex also affects the mechanism of defecation and urination.

Hence, it easily happens that a child fails to feel the need to poop in time, since they have retained tonic labyrinthine reflexes and a poor sense of balance, resulting in suboptimal muscle tone and visceral sensation.

To better understand the mechanism of defecation, let's go through the steps.

1) The rectum is empty. There is no urge to defecate.
2) Stool enters the rectum and dilates the rectal wall, causing a feeling of fullness
3) Pressure on the rectal wall causes a reflexive relaxation of the internal anal sphincter, allowing feces to pass on to the next stage of the intestinal tract. This movement signals the need to "poop."
4) The muscles of the pelvic floor contract to prevent pooping, causing the feces to move "backward"
5) If the stool remains in the rectum after the pelvic floor returns to its resting state, the stool no longer makes contact with the anus. The wall of the rectum relaxes, and pressure is reduced.
6) Fecal evacuation occurs when the pelvic floor relaxes and the pressure in the rectum is greater than that of the external anal sphincter and the pelvic floor. The feces move from the higher-pressure section of the bowel to the lower-pressure area. The increased pressure causes the feces to cross the anus.
7) The pelvic floor contracts again when the stool is no longer in contact with the anus, forcing the remaining stool outwards.

8) A larger mass of feces accumulates if the child repeatedly fails to feel the pressure or resists the urge to poop. Over time, it becomes large, or, because of the absorption of water by the intestine, it becomes hard and too solid for the child to pass without pain.

At least two of the three primitive reflexes noted above were present in all the children who have come to me with fecal retention problems. Once the reflexes were fully integrated, the difficulties with stool retention disappeared. Therefore, if a child has not pooped for days and the problem persists despite several solutions having already been tried, it is always worth examining the status of the primitive reflexes. If the reflexes have not been integrated, it is recommended to begin the exercises with the child as soon as possible.

Finally, I would like to point out that the same primitive reflexes are often present in irritable bowel syndrome (IBS). The perception of the bowels' state and the strength and density of bowel movements can be attributed to several causes, one of which is poor muscle tone or a disturbance in visceral perception. Therefore, I recommend a daily exercise routine for adults who suffer from IBS.

Exercise Videos

A set of videos are available that demonstrate exercises to inhibit the primitive reflexes associated with fecal retention. Use the following QR code to go directly to the video package, or visit https://drsarlos.com/videos for more information.

Scan for video!

Exercises for fecal retention

1

ATNR GALANT

Starting position: Sit on the floor with legs stretched, hands on hips.
1. Move forward using just the buttocks for 1.5–2.5 meters/yards.
2. Turn over onto all fours and put the forearms fully on the floor.
3–5. Keeping the forearms down, crawl back to the starting point.

Number of repetitions:
3–5 years: 4–6x the full sequence
5–10 years: 6–8x the full sequence
10–16 years: 8–10x the full sequence
16+: 10–12x the full sequence

2

GALANT

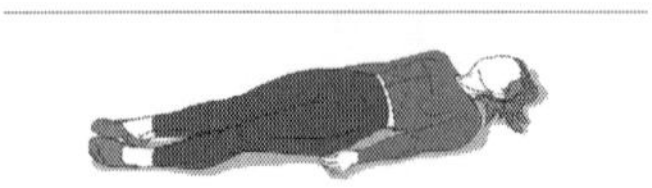

SP

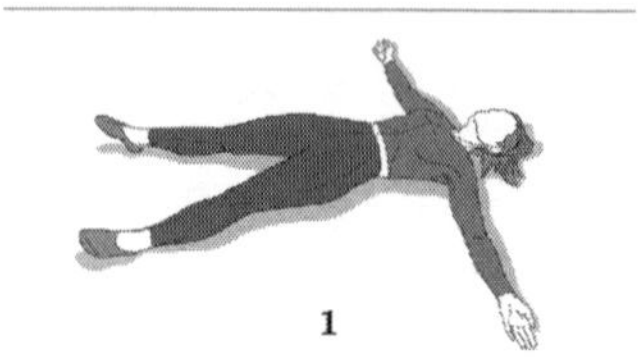

1

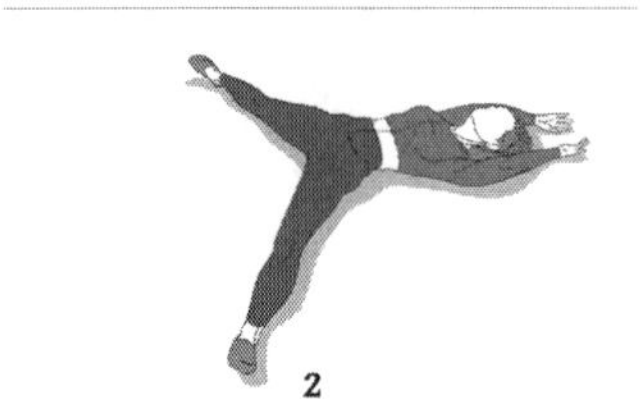

2

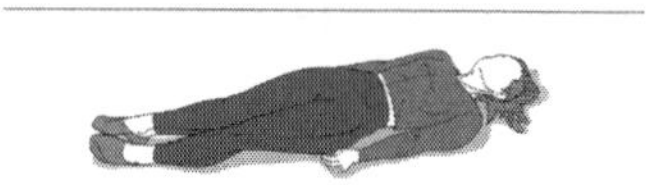

3

Starting position: Lie on the back, legs parallel, arms resting on the floor next to the body.

1–2. Spread the legs and slide the arms up to the ears. Do these actions at the same time.

3. Close the legs and simultaneously slide the arms back down to the starting position.

Number of repetitions:

3–5 years: 16–20x

5–10 years: 20–30x

10–16 years: 30–40x

16+: 40x

3

ATNR GALANT TLRB

1. Tumble forward "head over heels."

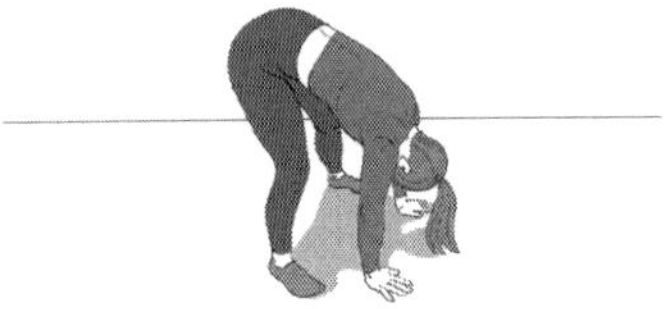

2. "Crab climb" backwards to the starting point.

3. In each alternate sequence, "spider walk" forwards to the starting point (instead of crab climbing).

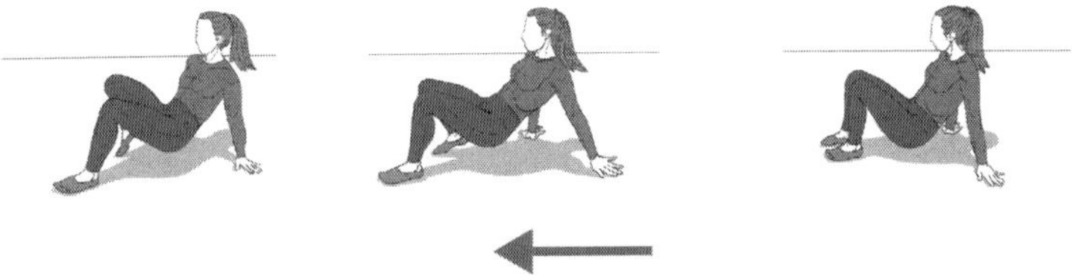

For adults, if tumbling forward is difficult or impossible, just go forward and back with alternating crab-climbing and spider-walking.

When tumbling head over heels, the following points should be observed:

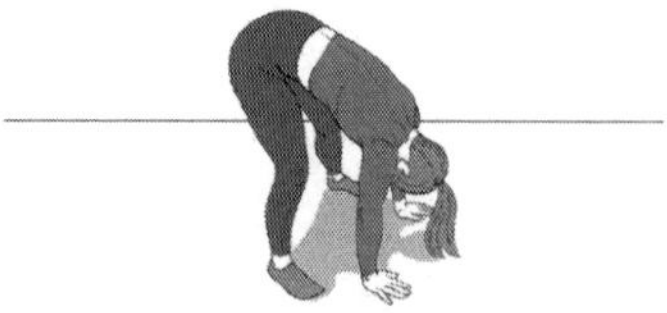

- Start the movement from a straddle position (legs apart)
- Tuck the head in—don't put weight on the top of the head!
- If assistance is given, tilt the head towards the chest with one hand, and with the other hand, support the child's buttocks and thighs, and roll them forward. It's good if the child "rolls like a ball" and doesn't "drop like a log."

Number of repetitions:
3–5 years: 4–6x the full sequence
5–10 years: 6–10x the full sequence
10–16 years: 10x the full sequence
16+: 10 the full sequence

4

GALANT

Starting position: Lie on the back, legs slightly bent.
Make a "cycling" movement, tilting the hips to each side as the legs make the cycling action.
Older children and adults can do this exercise on their own. They should place their hands under their waist for support, and perform the cycling movement with a slight sideways hip sway.
Children under 10 should do the exercise with parental assistance. The parent should push and pull the legs and tilt the child's hips to the side to make the cycling movement.
One full left and right rotation counts as a single repetition.

Number of repetitions:
3–5 years: 3x20
5–10 years: 4x20
10–16 years: 4x20
16+: 4x20

5

GALANT

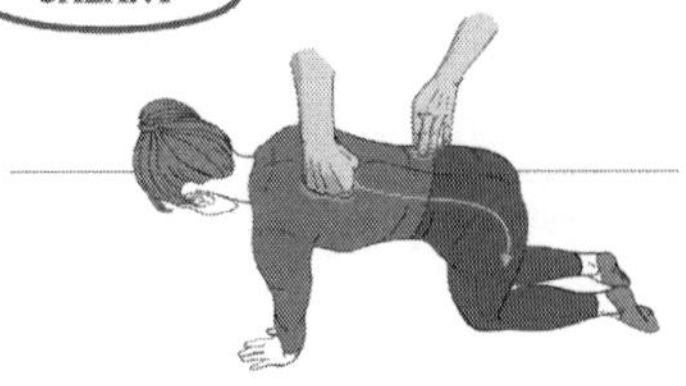

SP

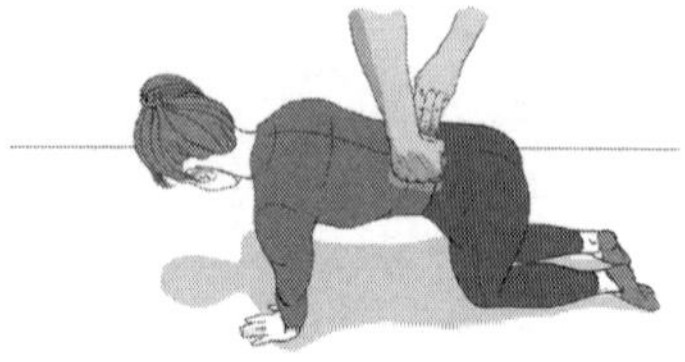

1

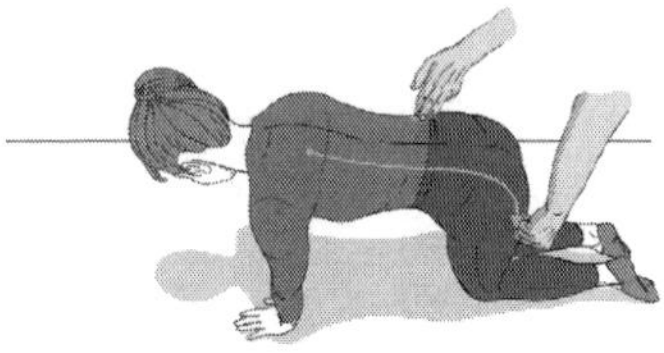

2

Starting position: Kneel on all fours.
A parent or assistant should massage the area next to the spine from the shoulder blade down to the thigh.
The person doing the massage should clench their hand into a fist and massage back and forth with the "middle point" of the fingers, moving parallel to the spinal column, 3–4 cm (1–1½ inches) away from the spine.

Number of repetitions:
3–5 years: 15–20x on each side of the body
5–10 years: 20x on each side of the body
10–16 years: 20–25x on each side of the body
16+: 25–30x on each side of the body

6

GALANT

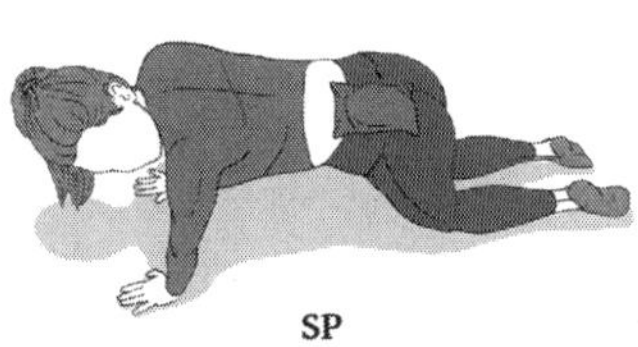

SP

1

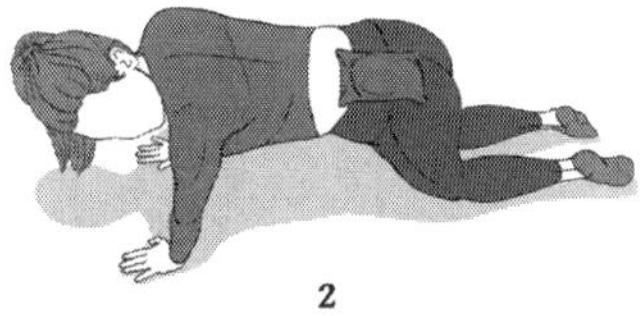

2

Starting position: Kneel on all fours, with palms on the floor. Place a small beanbag on the hip area.

1. On the side with the beanbag, push the hip to the side, and look back over the shoulder towards the beanbag. Keep the palms and knees firmly on the ground.
2. Return the hips and head to the starting position.

Number of repetitions:

3–5 years: 4–6x on each side
5–10 years: 6–10x on each side
10–16 years: 10–15x on each side
16+: 15x on each side

7

TLRF

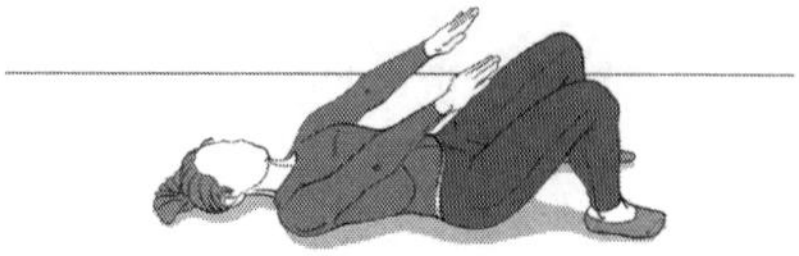

SP

1

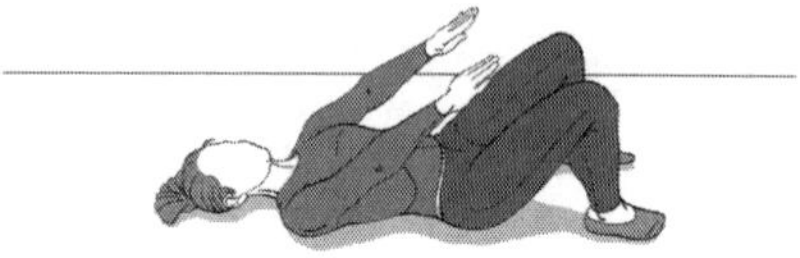

2

Starting position: Lie on the back, with legs bent and feet on the ground. Extend arms, parallel to thighs.
1. Tilt the head forward so that the arms remain extended. The shoulders should not be pulled up into the neck. Maintain this position for the required number of seconds.
2. Lower the head to the ground. If necessary, the arms may be put down on the ground.

Number of repetitions:
3–5 years: 3 x 3, holding the head up for 2–3 seconds (with help if necessary)
5–10 years: 3 x 4–8, holding the head up for 3–6 seconds (with help if necessary)
10–16 years: 3 x 6–8, holding the head up for 5–6 seconds
16+: 3 x 8, holding the head up for 6 seconds

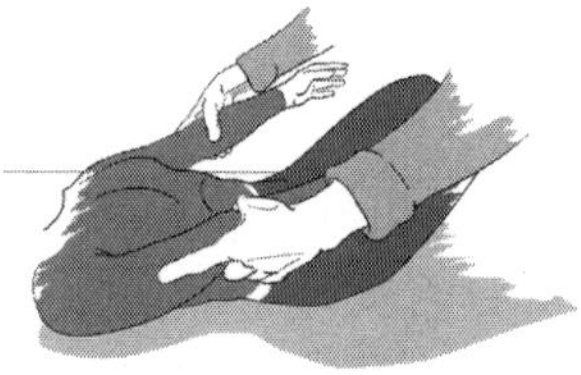

It very often happens that when lifting the head in the above exercise, the arm bends and the child (and, in many cases, adults too) pulls their shoulder up to the neck.
In these cases, help in the following way.

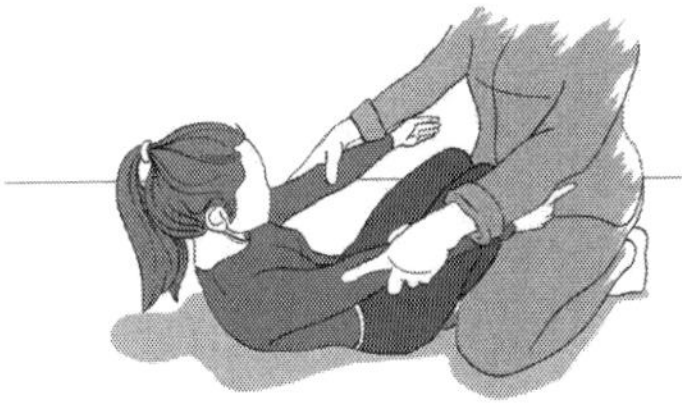

Sitting at the child's feet, grasp the elbow joint and press down on the elbow with the index finger, preventing the elbow from bending and the shoulder from pulling up to the neck.

8

TLRF

Rock back and forth in the shown position. Arms should be extended, holding the lower legs. The shoulders should not be pulled up into the neck.

Number of repetitions:
3–5 years: 3 x 6 (with help if necessary)
5–10 years: 3 x 8 (with help if necessary)
10–16 years: 3 x 10
16+: 3 x 12

9

TLRF

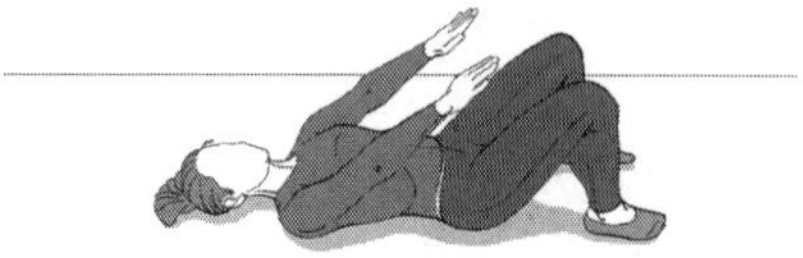

SP

1

2

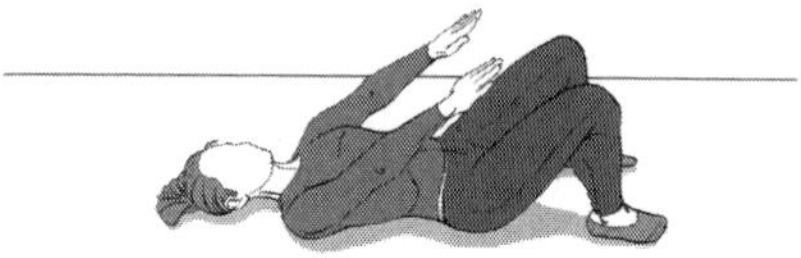

3

Starting position: Lie on the back, with legs bent and feet on the ground. Extend arms, parallel to thighs.

1. Tilt the head forward so that the arms remain extended. The shoulders should not be pulled up into the neck. Maintain this position for the required number of seconds.
2. Raise the shoulders and the back slightly off the ground. Keep the arms extended. The shoulders should not be pulled up into the neck. Maintain this position for the required number of seconds.
3. Lower the head to the ground. If necessary, the arms may be put down on the ground.

Number of repetitions:

3–5 years: 3x, hold in each position for 2 seconds (with help if necessary)
5–10 years: 3–5x, hold in each position for 3 seconds (with help if necessary)
10–16 years: 6–8x, hold in each position for 4–5 seconds
16+: 8x, hold in each position for 6 seconds

10

TLRF

SP

1

2

3

Starting position: Sit cross-legged, palms on the floor, arms outstretched. Rotate the head, don't raise the shoulders, keep arms fully extended and palms on the ground.

Number of repetitions:
3–5 years: two to the left and two to the right; repeat 3x (with help if necessary)
5–10 years: 4 x left and 4 x right; repeat 4x (with help if necessary)
10–16 years: 4 x left and 4 x right; repeat 5x
16+: 4 x left and 4 x right; repeat 6x

11

TLRF TLRB

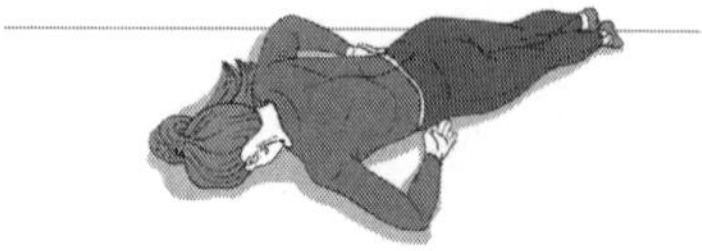

SP

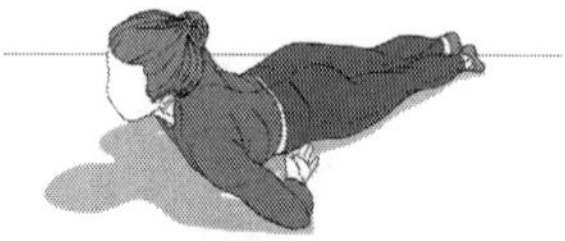

1

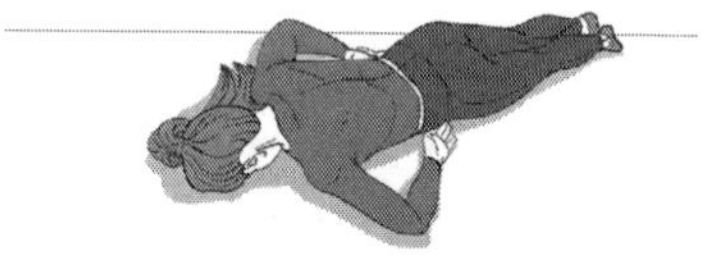

2

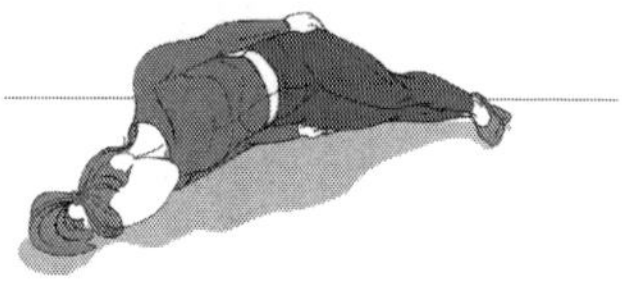

3

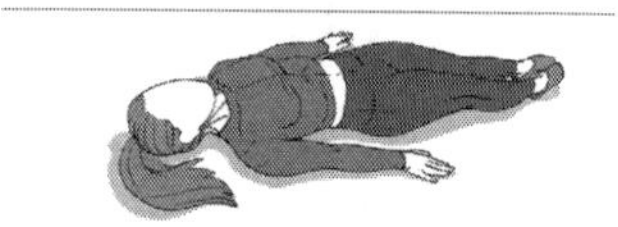

4

5

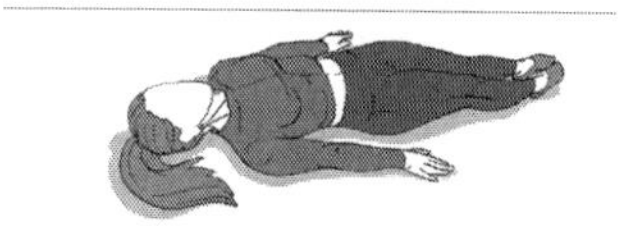

6

7

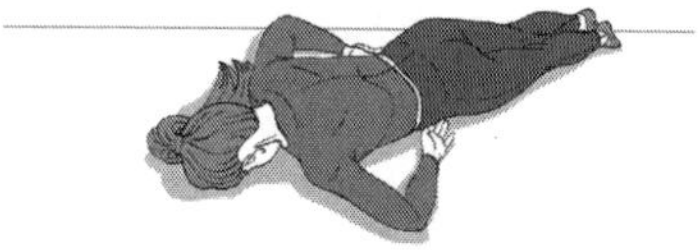

8

Starting position: Lie on the front, forehead on the floor, arms next to the body with elbows bent.

1. Lift the torso, keeping the arms bent.
2. Lower the torso back to the starting position.

3–4. Stretch the arms out straight and roll over onto the back.

5. Raise the head, keeping the arms extended.
6. Lower the head back to the ground.

7–8. Now roll back onto the front, and bend the arms to return to the original starting position.

Number of repetitions:
3–5 years: 4x the full sequence
5–10 years: 6x the full sequence
10–16 years: 8x the full sequence
16+: 10x the full sequence

12

MORO

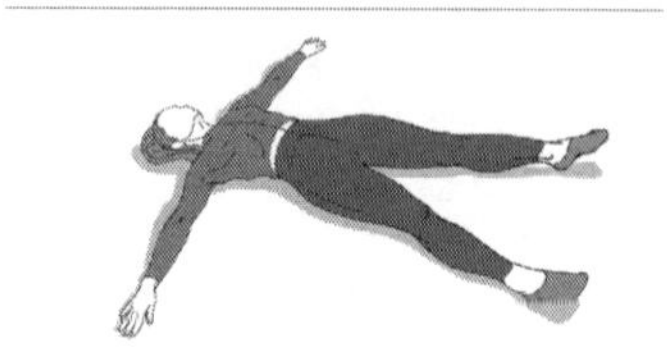

SP

1

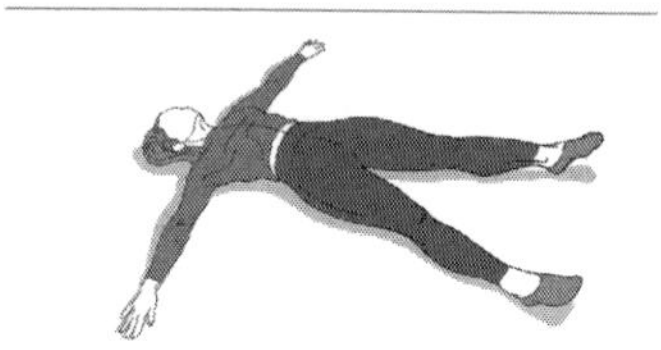

2

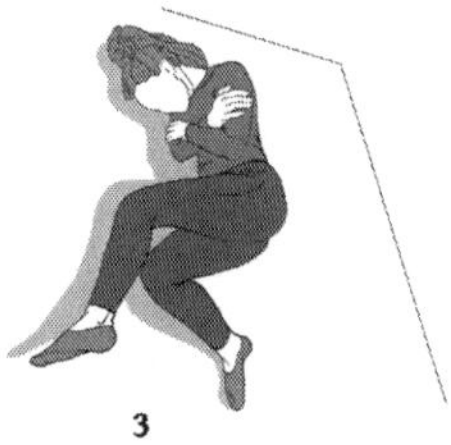

3

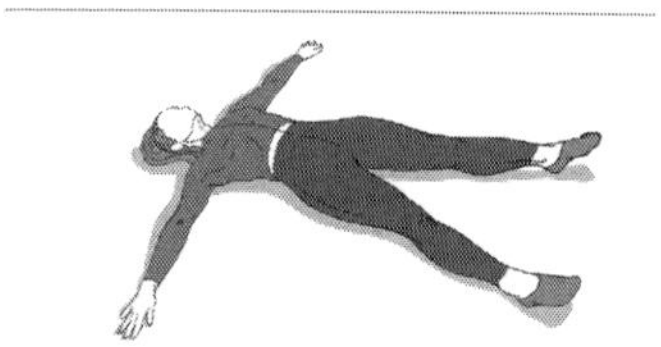

4

Starting position: Lie on the back, arms stretched out to the side, legs open on the floor.

1. Turn onto the left side into the "fetal position" with forearms and legs crossed. When turning left, move the right forearm over the left, and the right lower leg over the left.
2. Return to the starting position.
3. Turn onto the right side into the "fetal position" with forearms and legs crossed. When turning right, move the left forearm over the right, and the left lower leg over the right.
4. Return to the starting position.

Number of repetitions:

3–5 years: 12x (6x to the left, 6x to the right, alternating)
5–10 years: 16x (8x to the left, 8x to the right, alternating)
10–16 years: 20x (10x to the left, 10x to the right, alternating)
16+: 30x (15x to the left, 15x to the right, alternating)

Tips to help with fecal retention

In addition to performing reflex integration exercises, it is worth paying attention to the following:

- Drunk prune (plum) juice. Prune juice can be mixed with other liquids, such as apple juice, if the taste is too strong for your child. It is also essential that both younger and older children drink enough water.
- Eat foods rich in fiber. Oatmeal, barley, whole grains, and foods containing them, help digestion and bowel movements.
- Reduce consumption of foods that cause constipation. Reduce the quantity of food that can cause constipation, such as cheese, bananas, rice, and chocolate.
- If possible, take your child for a 30-minute walk every day, or for older children a 20–30-minute run. Regular physical activity can stimulate bowel movements.
- Reduce the focus on toileting. Take a break if you suspect your child is bothered by having to try to make a bowel movement every day. Being relaxed can be effective in this case.
- It is advisable to perform a 10–15-minute massage every day or two, specifically on the back and torso. Gently massage the abdomen using a circular motion, going up on the right side and down on the left side.

BEDWETTING

Country-level global data is not available on nocturnal enuresis, commonly known as bedwetting. However, a survey in the United States found that 30% of children aged 3–7 years, around 5% of children aged 7–10 years, and 2–3% of people over 18 years of age have what is known as the primary form of the problem, which is defined as the last night-time bedwetting having occurred within the past six months.

Secondary nocturnal bedwetting is when full potty training has been achieved, meaning that there has been no wetting during the night or the day, but the problem suddenly appears or returns.

When do we talk about bedwetting at night? For most children, full potty training is a gradual process, in most cases between 2½ and 4½ years of age. This means that they will not wet their underpants or pajamas during the day or night and will be able to hold their urine. Some more permissive literature states that bedwetting is only a problem if the child is over seven years old and wets the bed twice or more weekly for at least three months. Surveys show that primary night-time bedwetting is more common in boys.

No matter how you look at it, night-time bedwetting can cause stress and fatigue for the child and those around them after a while. Regular night-time wakings, changing pajamas, and changing bed linen can put a strain on the whole family. Children who wet the bed may feel ashamed or embarrassed. Naturally, they do not want to sleep anywhere else than at home, so they are reluctant to go on school trips or to summer camps for fear of wetting the bed.

There is usually no single cause for bedwetting at night but a combination of factors. Fortunately, it is rarely an organ problem.

What are the possible causes of bedwetting?

- **Prevalence within the family:** Children are more likely to have nighttime bedwetting when one or both parents have struggled with nocturnal urinary retention.
- **Sensory disturbance:** The extra pressure of feces within the rectum can interfere with the nerve signals sent to the brain by the bladder. A rectum full of stool can reduce the amount of urine the bladder can hold. It can also prevent the bladder from emptying completely during urination.
- **Hormones:** A hormone called vasopressin, produced in large nerve cells in the hypothalamus and delivered to the pituitary gland's posterior lobe via the pituitary axon, limits the amount of urine the body produces during the night. It does this by sucking water from the excretory ducts back into the bloodstream so that less urine is released into the bladder. Children who do not produce enough vasopressin are more likely to wet the bed.
- **Low functional bladder capacity:** Children with a low functional bladder capacity have a normal-sized bladder but feel that their bladder is full even when it can hold more urine. They tend to go to the toilet very often during the day. They often run to pee suddenly because they feel that if they don't hurry, they will have an accident. They are more likely to urinate at night.
- **Deep sleep:** Sometimes children cannot wake up in time to go to the bathroom. As the bladder fills with urine, it sends a signal to the brain, which sends a signal back to the bladder to relax so it can hold more urine. A full bladder continues to send alerts to the brain to wake the child up. Bedwetting occurs when the child has not yet learned to respond to these internal signals and cannot wake from a deep sleep.
- **Psychological or emotional problems:** Emotional stress caused by traumatic events or disruption of the child's regular routine may cause bedwetting. For example, moving to a new home, enrolling in a new school, the death of a loved one, or the divorce of their parents may lead to bedwetting that becomes less frequent or ceases over time.
- **Sexual abuse:** In some cases, children who have been fully toilet trained and who start bedwetting at night again may be victims of sexual abuse. Fortunately, this is rare and associated with other symptoms. Other signs of abuse include:

- Vaginal or urinary tract infections
- Vaginal pain
- Itching
- Sexually transmitted diseases

- **Health or organ problems:** Disorders associated with bedwetting include
  - Urinary tract infections
  - Diabetic disorders
  - Sickle cell anemia
  - Sleep apnea
  - Neurological problems
  - Kidney or bladder disorders

If a child was never successfully toilet-trained, the reasons listed above could be the cause of bedwetting. If this is not the case, it is likely that the underlying problem is the immaturity of the nervous system.

Four immature reflexes may be responsible in this case:

- Tonic labyrinthine reflex, forward (TLRf)
- Tonic labyrinthine reflex, backward (TLRb)
- The spinal Galant reflex
- Asymmetrical tonic neck reflex (ATNR)

I describe the negative effects of the retained reflexes that can cause nocturnal enuresis in the chapter discussing fecal retention.

As a supplement, I would like to note that the visceral sensation must be working correctly to feel that the bladder is full. When it is "underactive," even if the bladder is full, the person does not feel the tightening sensation. In addition, at night, the stimulus threshold is slightly raised to allow us to sleep peacefully, making it even more difficult to feel a full bladder. In addition, muscle tone is inadequate, in almost all cases hypotonic. This means the bladder sphincter is not "strong enough" to hold the increased urine pressure. A high volume of urine and a weak sphincter are enough to cause nocturnal enuresis.

Exercise Videos

A set of videos are available that demonstrate exercises to inhibit the primitive reflexes associated with bedwetting. Use the following QR code to go directly to the video package, or visit https://drsarlos.com/videos for more information.

Scan for video!

Exercises for bedwetting

1

GALANT MORO

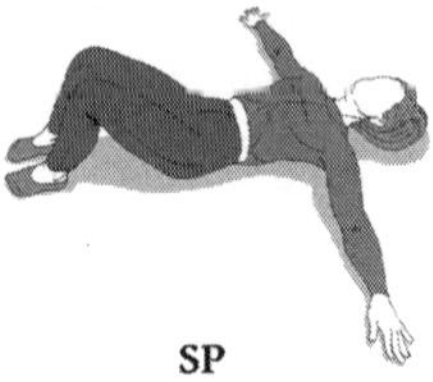

SP

1

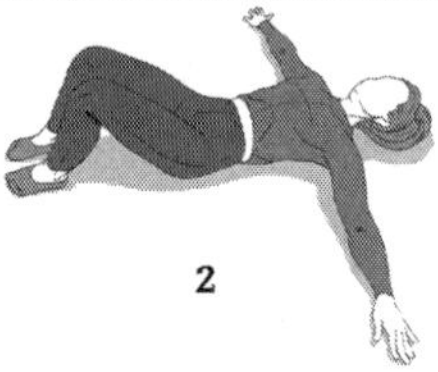

2

Starting position: Lie on the back, knees bent, arms outstretched on the ground.
1. Lift the hips and squeeze the buttocks together, and at the same time bend the elbows and push the palms together. Maintain this position for the required number of seconds.
2. Return to the starting position.

If it is too difficult to coordinate the movement of the arms and legs, it is enough to do only the leg movements for the first 2–3 months.

Number of repetitions:
3–5 years: 4–5x, hold for 3 seconds
5–10 years: 6–8x, hold for 4–6 seconds
10–16 years: 8–10x, hold for 6 seconds
16+: 12x, hold for 6 seconds

2

GALANT

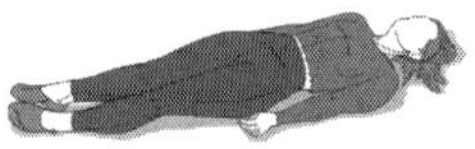

SP

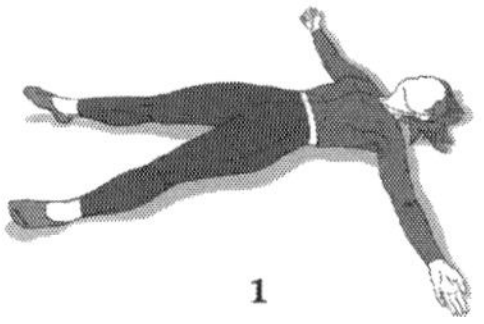

1

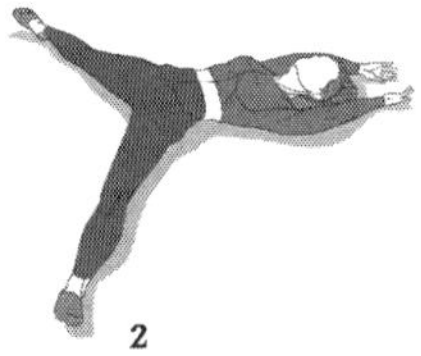

2

3

Starting position: Lie on the back, legs parallel, arms resting on the floor next to the body.
1–2. Spread the legs and slide the arms up to the ears. Do these actions at the same time.
3. Close the legs and simultaneously slide the arms back down to the starting position.

Number of repetitions:
3–5 years: 16–20x
5–10 years: 20–30x
10–16 years: 30–40x
16+: 40x

3

ATNR GALANT TLRB

1. Tumble forward "head over heels."

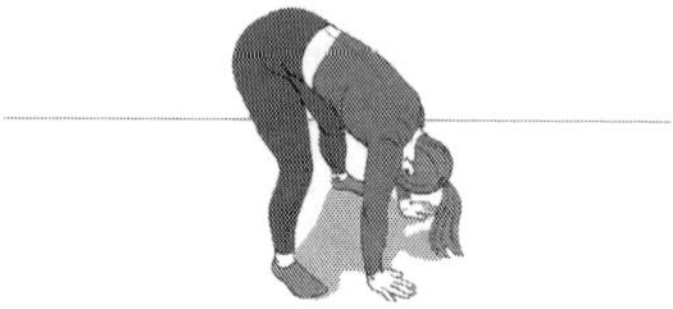

2. "Crab climb" backwards to the starting point.

3. In each alternate sequence, "spider walk" forwards to the starting point (instead of crab climbing).

For adults, if tumbling forward is difficult or impossible, just go forward and back with alternating crab-climbing and spider-walking.

When tumbling head over heels, the following points should be observed:

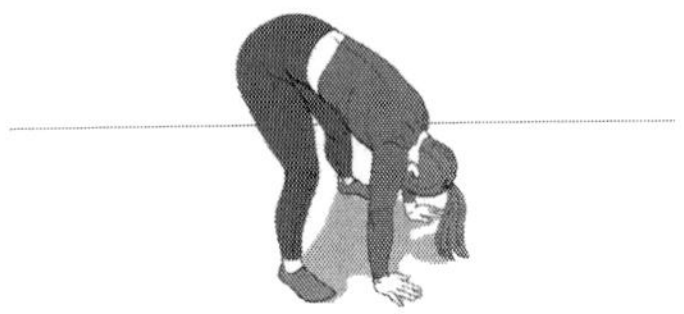

- Start the movement from a straddle position (legs apart)
- Tuck the head in—don't put weight on the top of the head!
- If assistance is given, tilt the head towards the chest with one hand, and with the other hand, support the child's buttocks and thighs, and roll them forward. It's good if the child "rolls like a ball" and doesn't "drop like a log."

Number of repetitions:
3–5 years: 4–6x the full sequence
5–10 years: 6–10x the full sequence
10–16 years: 10x the full sequence
16+: 10 the full sequence

4

GALANT

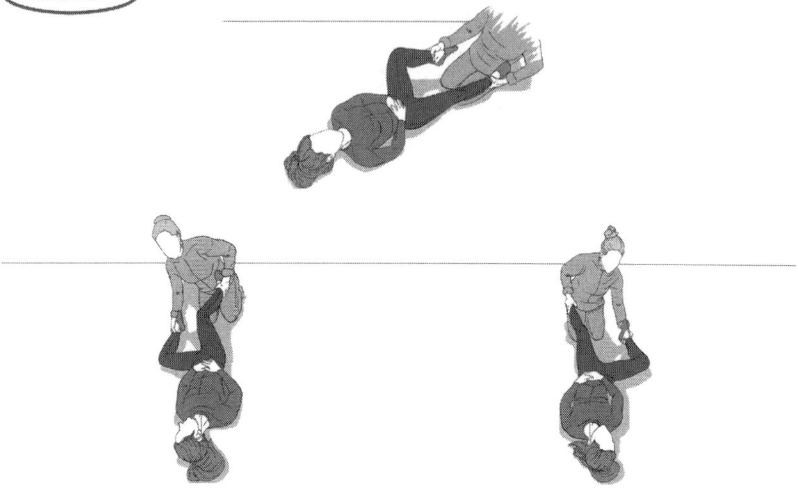

Starting position: Lie on the back, legs slightly bent.
Make a "cycling" movement, tilting the hips to each side as the legs make the cycling action.
Older children and adults can do this exercise on their own. They should place their hands under their waist for support, and perform the cycling movement with a slight sideways hip sway.
Children under 10 should do the exercise with parental assistance. The parent should push and pull the legs and tilt the child's hips to the side to make the cycling movement.
One full left and right rotation counts as a single repetition.

Number of repetitions:
3–5 years: 3x20
5–10 years: 4x20
10–16 years: 4x20
16+: 4x20

5

GALANT

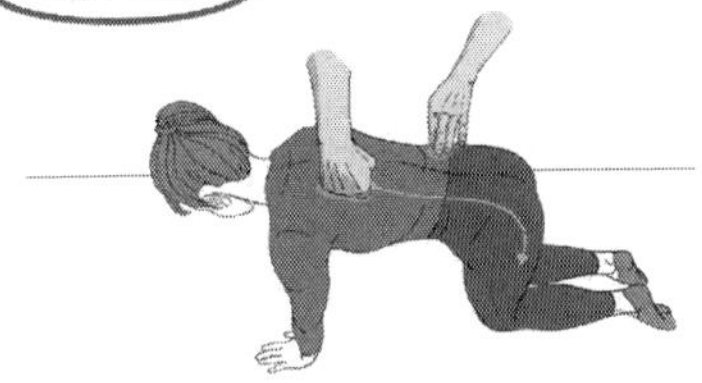

SP

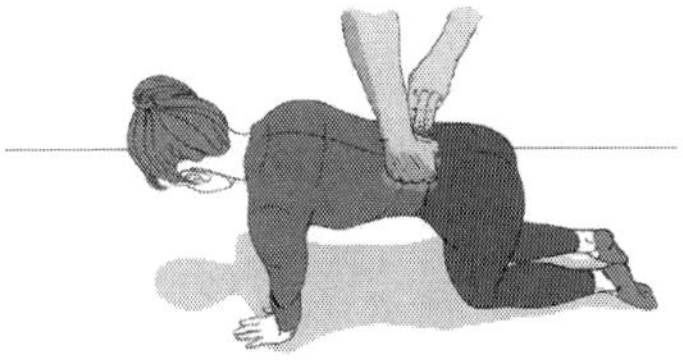

1

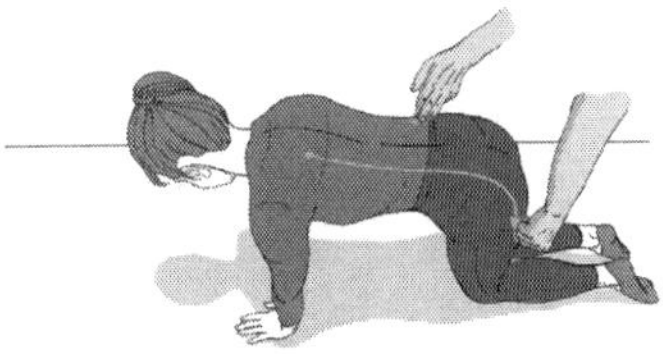

2

Starting position: Kneel on all fours.
A parent or assistant should massage the area next to the spine from the shoulder blade down to the thigh.
The person doing the massage should clench their hand into a fist and massage back and forth with the "middle point" of the fingers, moving parallel to the spinal column, 3–4 cm (1–1½ inches) away from the spine.

Number of repetitions:
3–5 years: 15–20x on each side of the body
5–10 years: 20x on each side of the body
10–16 years: 20–25x on each side of the body
16+: 25–30x on each side of the body

6

GALANT

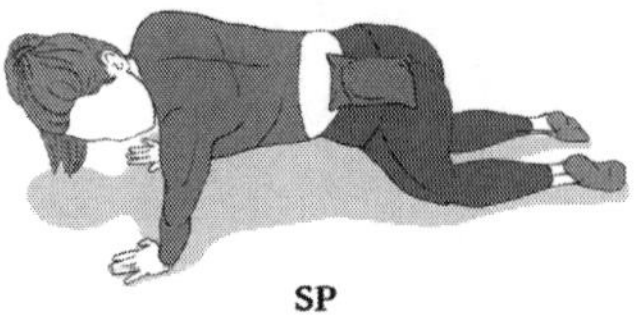

SP

1

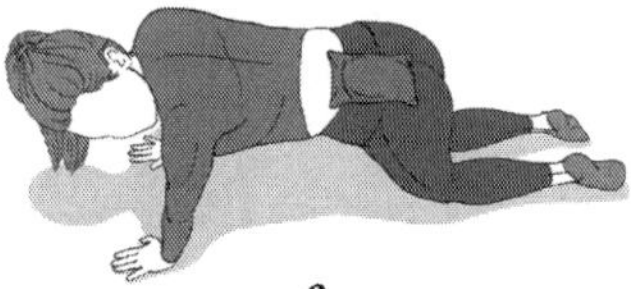

2

Starting position: Kneel on all fours, with palms on the floor. Place a small beanbag on the hip area.
1. On the side with the beanbag, push the hip to the side, and look back over the shoulder towards the beanbag. Keep the palms and knees firmly on the ground.
2. Return the hips and head to the starting position.

Number of repetitions:
3–5 years: 4–6x on each side
5–10 years: 6–10x on each side
10–16 years: 10–15x on each side
16+: 15x on each side

7

TLRF

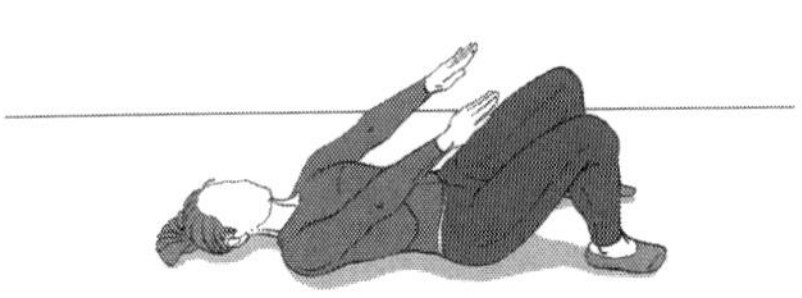

SP

1

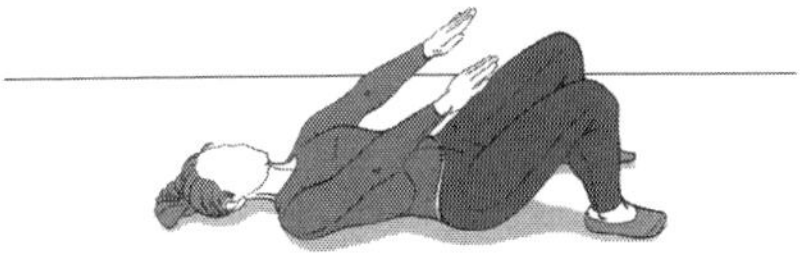

Starting position: Lie on the back, with legs bent and feet on the ground. Extend arms, parallel to thighs.

1. Tilt the head forward so that the arms remain extended. The shoulders should not be pulled up into the neck. Maintain this position for the required number of seconds.
2. Lower the head to the ground. If necessary, the arms may be put down on the ground.

Number of repetitions:

3–5 years: 3 x 3, holding the head up for 2–3 seconds (with help if necessary)

5–10 years: 3 x 4–8, holding the head up for 3–6 seconds (with help if necessary)

10–16 years: 3 x 6–8, holding the head up for 5–6 seconds

16+: 3 x 8, holding the head up for 6 seconds

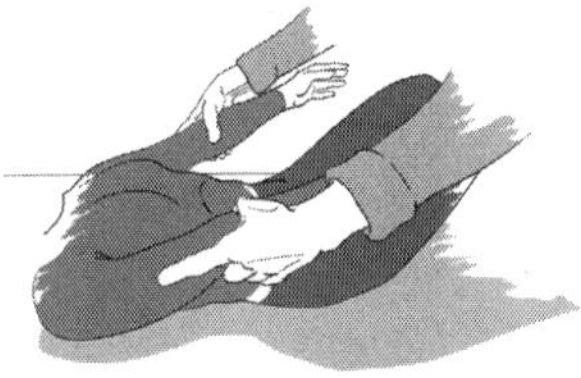

It very often happens that when lifting the head in the above exercise, the arm bends, and the child (and, in many cases, adults too) pulls their shoulder up to the neck.
In these cases, help in the following way.

Sitting at the child's feet, grasp the elbow joint and press down on the elbow with the index finger, preventing the elbow from bending and the shoulder from pulling up to the neck.

8

TLRF

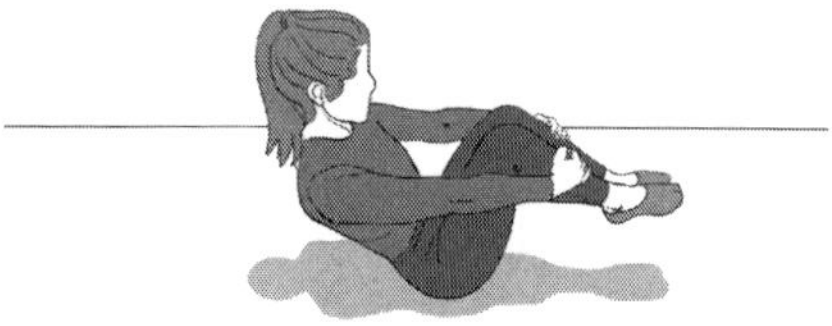

Rock back and forth in the shown position. Arms should be extended, holding the lower legs. The shoulders should not be pulled up into the neck.

Number of repetitions:
3–5 years: 3 x 6 (with help if necessary)
5–10 years: 3 x 8 (with help if necessary)
10–16 years: 3 x 10
16+: 3 x 12

9

TLRF

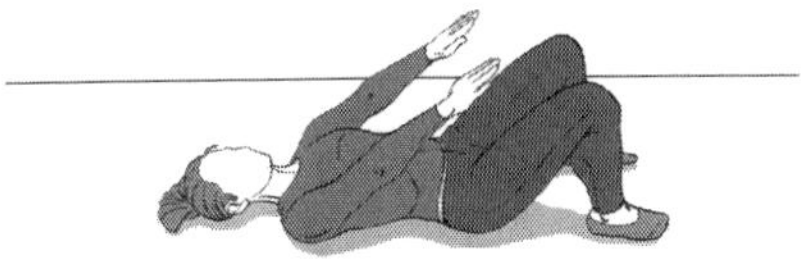

SP

1

2

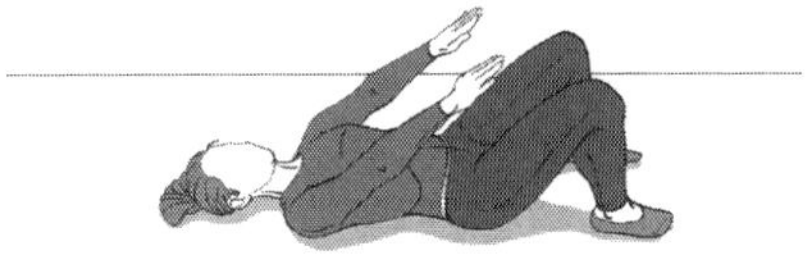

3

Starting position: Lie on the back, with legs bent and feet on the ground. Extend arms, parallel to thighs.

1. Tilt the head forward so that the arms remain extended. The shoulders should not be pulled up into the neck. Maintain this position for the required number of seconds.
2. Raise the shoulders and the back slightly off the ground. Keep the arms extended. The shoulders should not be pulled up into the neck. Maintain this position for the required number of seconds.
3. Lower the head to the ground. If necessary, the arms may be put down on the ground.

Number of repetitions:

3–5 years: 3x, hold in each position for 2 seconds (with help if necessary)
5–10 years: 3–5x, hold in each position for 3 seconds (with help if necessary)
10–16 years: 6–8x, hold in each position for 4–5 seconds
16+: 8x, hold in each position for 6 seconds

10

TLRF

SP

1

2

3

Starting position: Sit cross-legged, palms on the floor, arms outstretched. Rotate the head, don't raise the shoulders, keep arms fully extended and palms on the ground.

Number of repetitions:

3–5 years: two to the left and two to the right; repeat 3x (with help if necessary)

5–10 years: 4 x left and 4 x right; repeat 4x (with help if necessary)

10–16 years: 4 x left and 4 x right; repeat 5x

16+: 4 x left and 4 x right; repeat 6x

11

TLRF TLRB

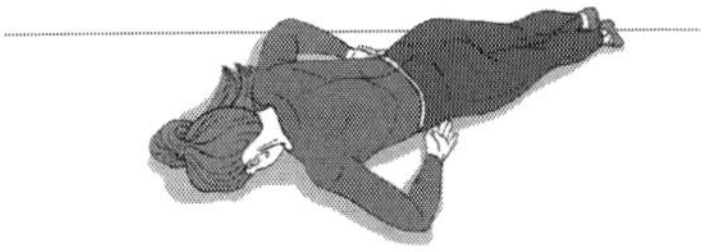

SP

1

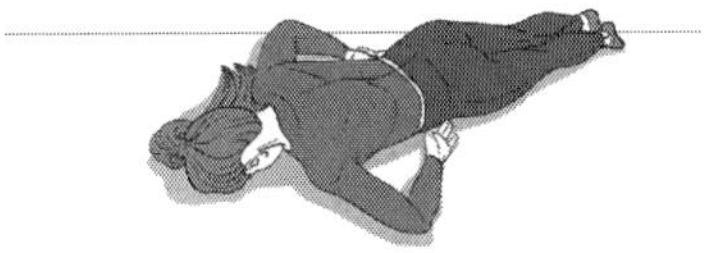

2

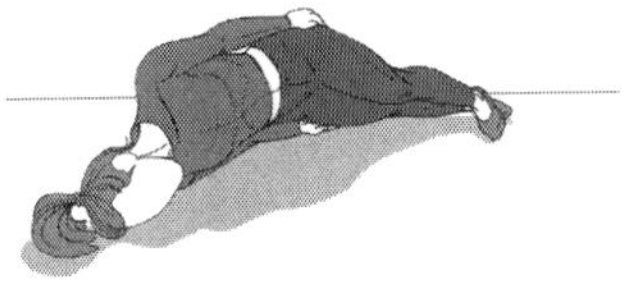

3

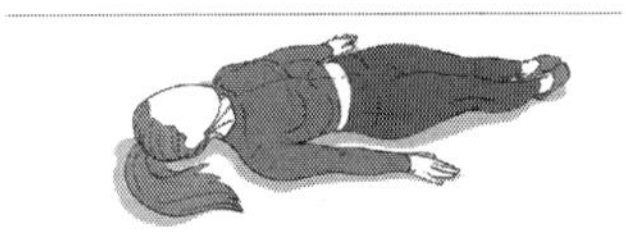

4

5

6

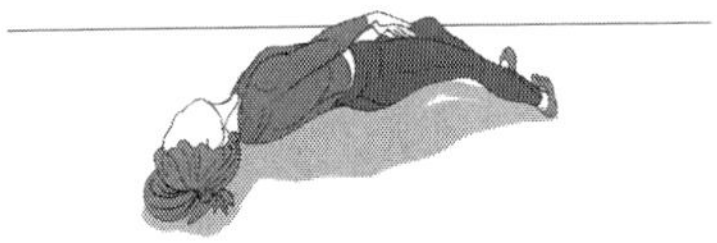

7

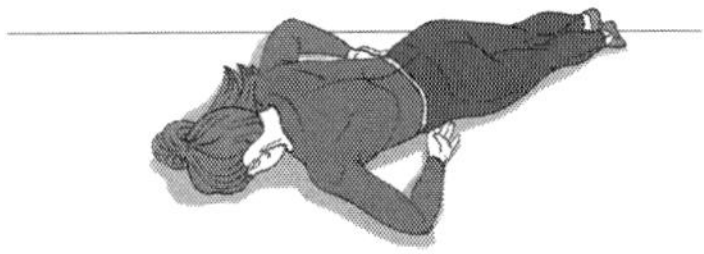

8

Starting position: Lie on the front, forehead on the floor, arms next to the body with elbows bent.

1. Lift the torso, keeping the arms bent.
2. Lower the torso back to the starting position.

3–4. Stretch the arms out straight and roll over onto the back.

5. Raise the head, keeping the arms extended.
6. Lower the head back to the ground.

7–8. Now roll back onto the front, and bend the arms to return to the original starting position.

Number of repetitions:
3–5 years: 4x the full sequence
5–10 years: 6x the full sequence
10–16 years: 8x the full sequence
16+: 10x the full sequence

12

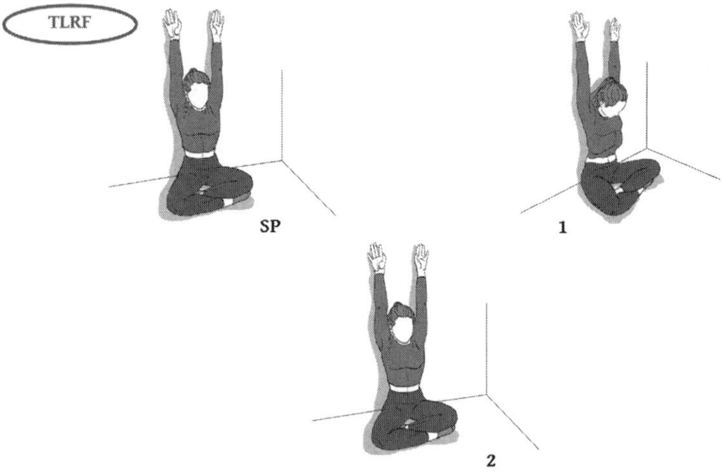

Starting position: Sit with back against the wall, cross-legged, arms outstretched over the head and against the wall.
1. Bend the head down, keeping the arms up against the wall.
2. Lift the head up back to the starting position.

Number of repetitions:
3–5 years: 6–8x
5–10 years: 8–10x
10–16 years: 10–16x
16+: 16x

Tips to help with bedwetting

- Limit fluid intake before bedtime: ensure your child drinks plenty of fluids during the day, but do not give them a drink within the two hours before bedtime
- Urinate before bedtime: make sure your child goes to the toilet and empties their bladder
- Pee twice before bedtime: first pee before getting ready for bed (bathing, dressing, saying goodnight, brushing teeth, combing hair, etc.) and then again, with some effort, immediately before bedtime. This way, the child can squeeze out any "leftover" urine.
- Bladder therapy: this approach aims to gradually increase the functional capacity of the bladder by telling the child how often they must go to the toilet. Usually, the doctor sets the duration after a medical examination. Increasing the time between peeing helps increase the bladder's capacity to hold more urine. Of course, adequate fluid intake must be ensured.
- Intermittent urination: in this case, the child stops peeing, then starts again and continues until the bladder is empty. This "exercises" the bladder's sphincter and improves its contractility, i.e., its ability to contract.
- Appropriate clothing for the night
- Counseling: psychological counseling can be effective in cases where the child has experienced a traumatic event or has low self-confidence due to bedwetting.

DELAYED SPEECH AND LANGUAGE DEVELOPMENT, AND OTHER PROBLEMS RELATED TO SPEECH FORMATION

The first three years of life are the most intensive period for acquiring speech and language skills. Ideally, the child's nervous system and senses are intact and they are growing up in an environment rich in sounds and visual experiences, constantly listening to the people around them and the language they speak.

There are sensitive periods in infants' and young children's speech and language development when the brain is most receptive to language acquisition. When these critical periods pass without the infant hearing human speech, language becomes increasingly difficult to learn. In a bilingual family, it is recommended for each parent to speak to the child in their own language from birth, tell stories, and sing. Even if such parents communicate together in just one language, it is advisable that the mother consistently speaks to the child in the "mother tongue" and the father in the "father tongue." In this way, both languages are integrated and developed at the mother tongue level during the child's speech and language development, and importantly for the child, there isn't much (or no) mixing of vocabulary and grammatical structure between the two languages.

What are the milestones in the development of speech and language?

The first signs of communication appear when an infant realizes that crying brings food, comfort, and companionship. At a very early stage, newborn babies begin to recognize important sounds in their environment, such as their mother's or primary caregiver's voice. As they grow, they learn to pick out the speech sounds that make up the words of the language spoken around them. As a result, by six months, most babies recognize the basic sounds of their mother tongue.

As with all developmental processes, the rate of speech and language development varies from one individual to another. However, for everyone, the acquisition of language skills follows a similar, natural "timetable." The table below shows the milestones in the normal development of speech and language skills from birth to age five. It is natural that individual children show faster and slower rates of development; however, if there is a significant difference, it is always advisable to consult a professional to identify the causes of the delay and help find a solution.

From birth to 5 months	• Making baby noises • Makes different sounds when happy, pleased, or unhappy (laughs, giggles, cries, or whimpers) • When spoken to, makes a noise or sound
6 to 11 months	• Says "no-no" when spoken to • Rather than understanding, repeats simple syllables: "be-be-be," "ma-ma," or "da-da" • Tries to communicate through gestures or actions • Attempts to repeat certain sounds • Recites the first word
12 to 17 months	• Gives non-verbal responses to simple questions • Speaks two or three words to name a person or object (pronunciation may not be clear or perfect) • Tries to imitate simple words • Has an active vocabulary of 8–10 words
18 to 23 months	• Vocabulary of 50 words, pronunciation often unclear • Calls common foods by name • Makes sounds that are unusual, such as "moo," "woof-woof" • Starts to combine words, e.g., "more milk" • Begins to use pronouns, e.g., "mine" • Uses two-word phrases

2 to 3 years	• Knows some concepts of space, for example, "in" or "to" • Knows some pronouns, such as "you," "I" or "he" • Uses adjectives such as "big," "small," and "many" • Uses three-word sentences • Speech is becoming more precise, but words may end with a slur or a trailing-off, and strangers may not understand much of the speech • Answers simple questions • Begins to use more pronouns • Uses questioning stress when asking a question • Starts to use plurals and the past tense
3 to 4 years	• Begins to group things, such as food or clothes • Identifies colors • Uses most speech sounds, but may distort some of the more difficult sounds, such as l, r, c, cs, s, s, v, z—these are difficult to fully master before the age of seven or eight • Uses consonants at the beginning, middle, and end of words. Some of the more difficult consonants may be slurred, but an effort is made to pronounce them • Strangers can understand a lot of what is said • Can describe the use of objects such as "spoon" or "car" • Entertained by language; enjoys poetry and recognizes linguistic absurdities, e.g., "Do you have donkey ears?" • Can express thoughts and feelings, rather than just talking about the surrounding world • Using more and more verbs • Answers simple questions such as "What do you do when you are hungry?" • Asks questions, often asking "Why?" • Repeats sentences • Understands concepts that express spatial relationships, such as "behind" or "next to"
4 to 5 years	• Understands complex questions • Speech is mostly understandable but sometimes makes mistakes when pronouncing long or complicated words. For example: hippopotamus; caterpillar; helicopter. • Describes how to do things, e.g., paint a picture • Lists items in a category, such as animals, fruits, or vehicles • Answers "why" questions

5 years	• Begins to understand sequences in time (for example, what happened first, second, or third) • Can carry out a sequence of three instructions • Understands and enjoys listening to rhyming poems and sayings • Likes to join in a conversation • Uses sentences of up to eight words or more • Uses simple and complex sentences • Describes objects • Lives with imagination, makes up stories

Source: Stanford Children's Health.

What is the difference between a speech disorder and a language disorder?

Children with difficulty understanding what others say or difficulty communicating their thoughts may have a language disorder. Specific language impairment (SLI) is developmental dysphasia, a language disorder that delays the acquisition of language skills. A child with SLI may not start speaking until the third or fourth year of life.

The generally accepted view is that SLI is a developmental disorder without hearing loss and other peripheral problems, without impairment of non-verbal cognitive functions, without mental deficits, and without neurological or social issues. In developmental dysphasia, the only problem is a delay in language development.

Children with difficulty forming correct speech sounds, searching for words, or stuttering may have a speech disorder. Apraxia of speech is a speech disorder that makes it difficult to put sounds and syllables in the correct order to form words.

What might be behind the problem?

There can be external environmental problems and internal causes:

- Environmental harm: the lack of an appropriate, linguistically rich environment for full communication, which may result from neglectful parenting or caring, poor speech examples (for example, if the parents are themselves speech impaired or hearing impaired), excessive listening to audiovisual material, living in state care
- Hearing loss: as speech and language learning in children are auditory, hearing loss of more than 60 dB causes significant problems in speech formation and speech. Therefore, if this problem persists, the baby should be fitted with hearing aids in the first weeks after birth. In many cases, early use of hearing aids can help development, and the hearing aid can be subsequently abandoned. However, such good results cannot be expected when used after 6–8 months of age. If a hearing aid is used, it should be monitored continuously to see if any adjustment in strength is necessary.
- Dyslexia hinders young children from learning metacommunication (tone of voice, stance, facial expression, hand gestures, etc.) and makes it difficult to incorporate metacommunication cues into communication functions. In addition, the inability to follow the movement of the lips hinders the child's ability to provide visuomotor feedback.
- Acoustic agnosia: a disorder of discrimination of acoustic stimuli with intact peripheral hearing linked to a dysfunction of the cortical areas of the auditory pathways
- Intellectual disability: this is often associated with symptoms involving different pathways, courses, and functioning of speech and language development, sometimes associated with a genetic disorder
- Apraxia: a symptom associated with a disorder of output, processing, motor control, and motor inhibition due to CNS damage, in which voluntary speech movements are inhibited or defective. Dyspraxia is a milder form of apraxia and is a common feature of articulation errors and dysarthria.
- Encephalopathic lesions of the motor system (affecting the brain): in many cases, articulation, chewing, and swallowing functions are inhibited
- Organic disorders of the peripheral speech organs: these include lesions of the organs necessary for speech (e.g., lowered tongue, cleft lip and palate, cleft palate, laryngitis)
- Disabilities of speech that are familial, with a family history
- Other factors: mutism, autism, other mental disorders, and speech developmental features associated with psychiatric disorders

- Some residual infant reflexes: sucking, rooting, grasping, forward TLR, and backward TLR.

In many cases, the reflexes listed in the final point above cause delayed speech and language development and issues related to speech formation. If this is the case, regular practice of the following exercises may help to solve the problem.

Exercise Videos

A set of videos are available that demonstrate exercises to inhibit the primitive reflexes associated with issues of speech development. Use the following QR code to go directly to the video package, or visit https://drsarlos.com/videos for more information.

Scan for video!

Exercises for speech development

1

GRASPING SUCKING

SP

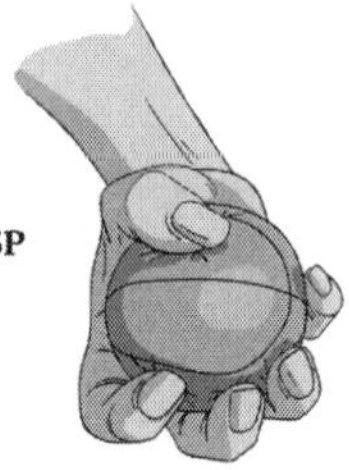

Starting position: Hold a sponge ball with the thumb facing the other four fingers.
Squeeze the ball for a second, then relax. Repeat.
Make sure to grip the ball with the last joints of each finger bent as shown. Some children find this difficult at first, either because the thumb keeps sliding back alongside the other fingers, or they cannot bend the last joint of the fingers. In this case, they need help to make the correct grip. Between the ages of three and five, they can hold their own forearm to help, as shown below.

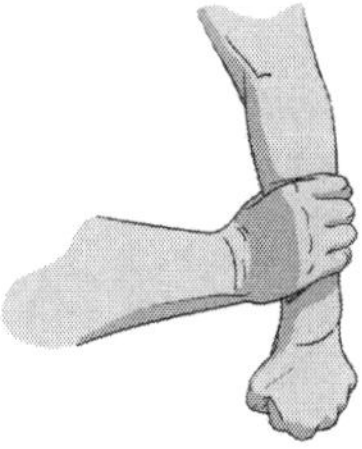

Number of repetitions:
3–5 years: 3 x 8–10 with both hands, alternating
5–10 years: 3–4 x 10 with both hands, alternating
10–16 years: 4 x 10 with both hands, alternating
16+: 4–5 x 10 with both hands, alternating

2

GRASPING SUCKING

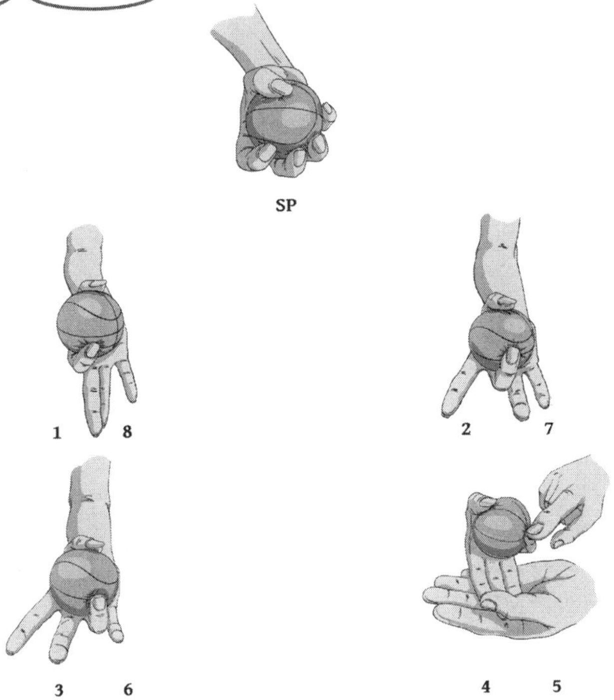

Starting position: Hold a sponge ball in the palm, with the thumb and index finger bent and facing each other, resting on the ball.

1. Grip the ball with the thumb and index finger.
2. Grip the ball with the thumb and middle finger.
3. Grip the ball with the thumb and ring finger.
4. Grip the ball with the thumb and little finger.

5–8. Repeat the previous steps in reverse order, beginning with the little finger and ending with the index finger.

This exercise should be performed with both the right and left hands.
In young children—and sometimes older persons, too—it happens that all the fingers bend in, not just the one that should be active. In this case, another person can help, as in the image above showing the little finger and thumb gripping the ball.

Number of repetitions:
3–5 years: two sequences, back and forth, with both hands
5–10 years: three sequences, back and forth, with both hands
10–16 years: four sequences, back and forth, with both hands
16+: five sequences, back and forth, with both hands

3

GRASPING SUCKING

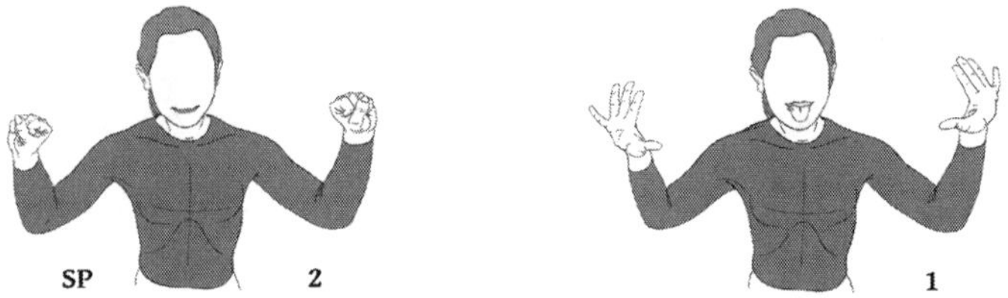

Starting position: Clench the fingers of both hands into fists, with the thumb resting on the outside of the other fingers.
1. While stretching the fingers and extending them backward, stick out the tongue as far as possible.
2. Close the fingers back into a fist, retract the tongue behind the teeth, and close the mouth.

Number of repetitions:
3–5 years: 3 x 6–10 both the above steps
5–10 years: 3 x 10 both the above steps
10–16 years: 4 x 10 both the above steps
16+: 5 x 10 both the above steps

4

GRASPING SUCKING

Starting position: Bring the tips of the index finger and the thumb of both hands together so that they form an "O" shape.

1. While stretching the fingers and extending them backward, stick out the tongue as far as possible.
2. Now, bring the middle fingers and thumbs together, forming an "O" shape.

The exercise is performed back and forth with each finger: index, middle, ring, and little finger, then back in sequence from the little finger to the index. Between each touching of fingertips, stretch the fingers back, and stick the tongue out strongly.

Number of repetitions:

3–5 years: one full sequence, using both hands, back and forth
5–10 years: three full sequences, using both hands, back and forth
10–16 years: 3–4 full sequences, using both hands, back and forth
16+: 3–4 full sequences, using both hands, back and forth

5

TLRF

SP

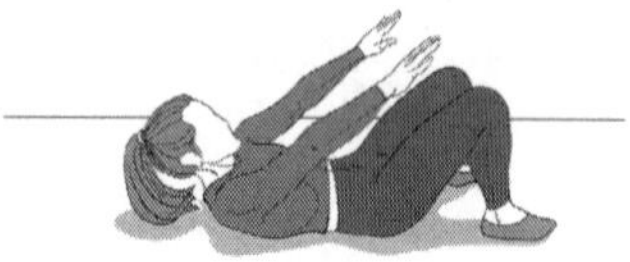

1

2

Starting position: Lie on the back, with legs bent and feet on the ground. Extend arms, parallel to thighs.

1. Tilt the head forward so that the arms remain extended. The shoulders should not be pulled up into the neck. Maintain this position for the required number of seconds.
2. Lower the head to the ground. If necessary, the arms may be put down on the ground.

Number of repetitions:

3–5 years: 3 x 3, holding the head up for 2–3 seconds (with help if necessary)

5–10 years: 3 x 4–8, holding the head up for 3–6 seconds (with help if necessary)

10–16 years: 3 x 6–8, holding the head up for 5–6 seconds

16+: 3 x 8, holding the head up for 6 seconds

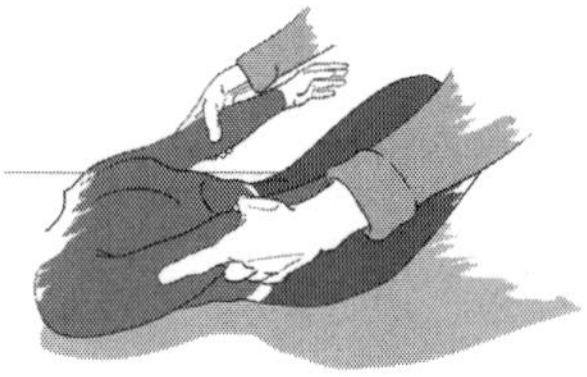

It very often happens that when lifting the head in the above exercise, the arm bends, and the child (and, in many cases, adults too) pulls their shoulder up to the neck.

In these cases, help in the following way.

Sitting at the child's feet, grasp the elbow joint and press down on the elbow with the index finger, preventing the elbow from bending and the shoulder from pulling up to the neck.

6

TLRF

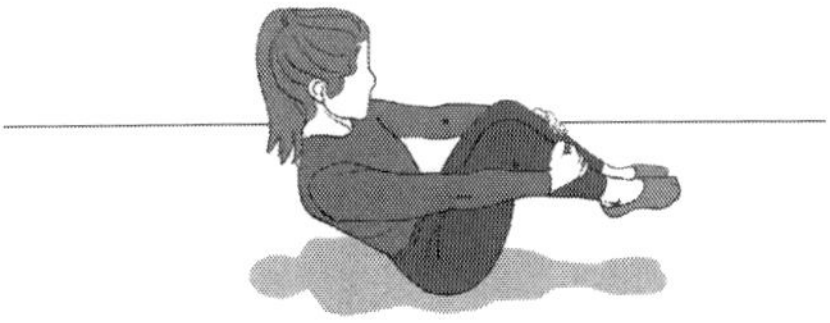

Rock back and forth in the shown position. Arms should be extended, holding the lower legs. The shoulders should not be pulled up into the neck.

Number of repetitions:
3–5 years: 3 x 6 (with help if necessary)
5–10 years: 3 x 8 (with help if necessary)
10–16 years: 3 x 10
16+: 3 x 12

7

TLRF

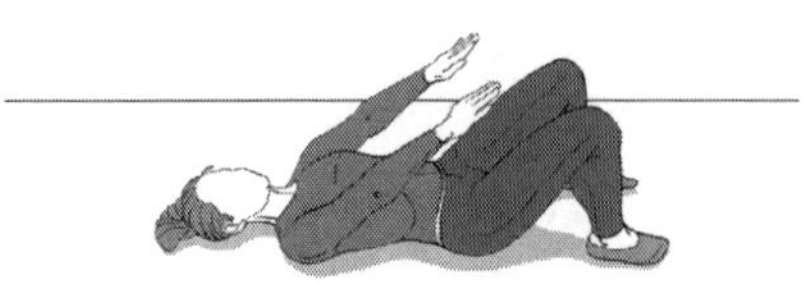

SP

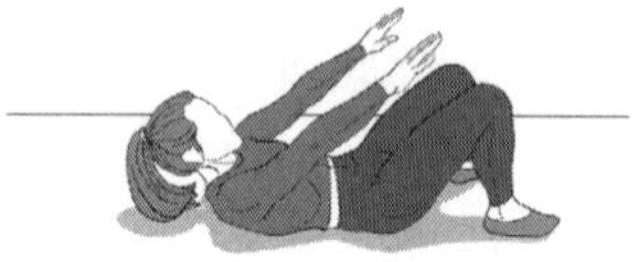

1

2

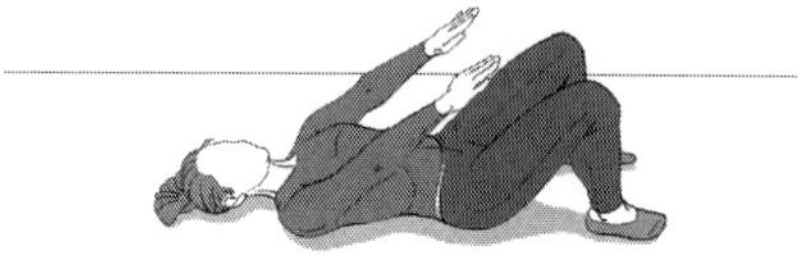

3

Starting position: Lie on the back, with legs bent and feet on the ground. Extend arms, parallel to thighs.
1. Tilt the head forward so that the arms remain extended. The shoulders should not be pulled up into the neck. Maintain this position for the required number of seconds.
2. Raise the shoulders and the back slightly off the ground. Keep the arms extended. The shoulders should not be pulled up into the neck. Maintain this position for the required number of seconds.
3. Lower the head to the ground. If necessary, the arms may be put down on the ground.

Number of repetitions:
3–5 years: 3x, hold in each position for 2 seconds (with help if necessary)
5–10 years: 3–5x, hold in each position for 3 seconds (with help if necessary)
10–16 years: 6–8x, hold in each position for 4–5 seconds
16+: 8x, hold in each position for 6 seconds

8

TLRF

SP

1

2

3

Starting position: Sit cross-legged, palms on the floor, arms outstretched. Rotate the head, don't raise the shoulders, keep arms fully extended and palms on the ground.

Number of repetitions:

3–5 years: two to the left and two to the right; repeat 3x (with help if necessary)
5–10 years: 4 x left and 4 x right; repeat 4x (with help if necessary)
10–16 years: 4 x left and 4 x right; repeat 5x
16+: 4 x left and 4 x right; repeat 6x

9

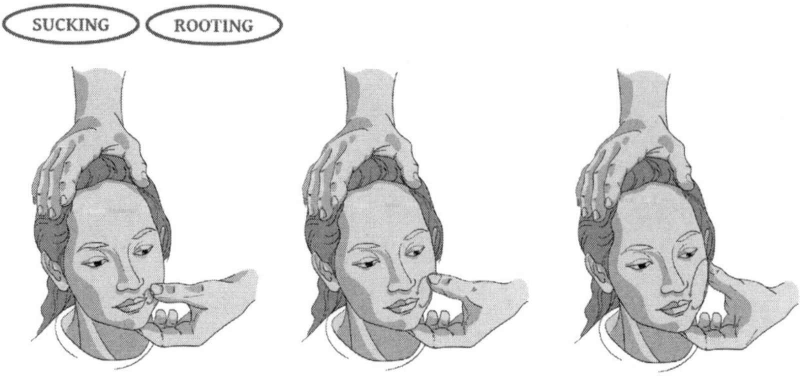

Massage the face around the mouth in three semi-circular arcs of increasing length. In each case, the massage starts between the mouth and the nose and ends in the area under the lower lip. Each line should be massaged 5–6 times, not pressing too hard. Adults and older children can do the massage themselves, but in this case, it is better to massage the face with a smooth pebble rather than use their own fingers.

Number of repetitions:

3–5 years: five times each arc, on both sides of the face, 2x
5–10 years: five times each arc, on both sides of the face, 3x
10–16 years: six times each arc, on both sides of the face, 3–4x
16+: six times each arc, on both sides of the face, 4x

10

GRASPING SUCKING

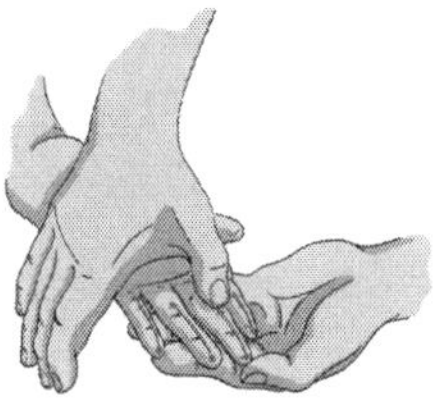

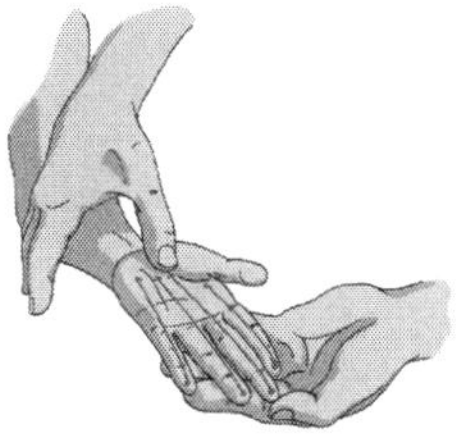

Massage the palm from the fingers towards the wrist. As with massaging the face, older children and adults can do the massage themselves, but they should use a smooth pebble rather than use their own fingers.

Number of repetitions

3–5 years: 4–5 times per finger on both the left and right palm, 2x
5–10 years: 5 times per finger on both the left and right palm, 3x
10–16 years: 6 times per finger on both the left and right palm, 3–4x
16+: 6 times per finger on both the left and right palm, 4x

11

TLRB

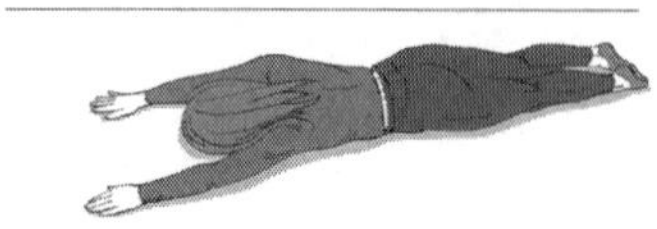

SP

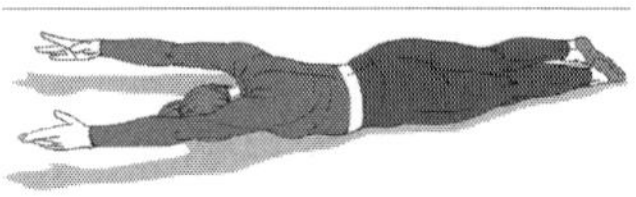

1

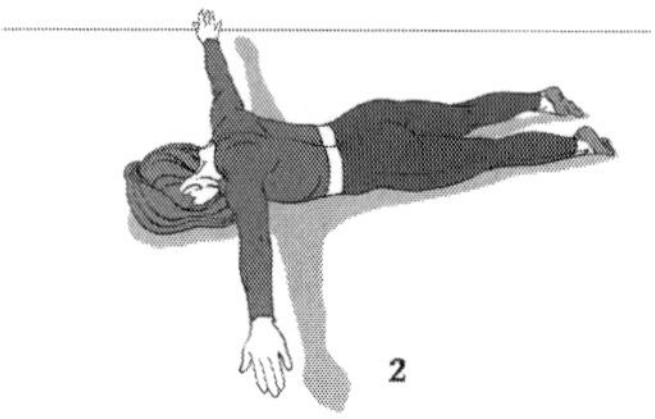

2

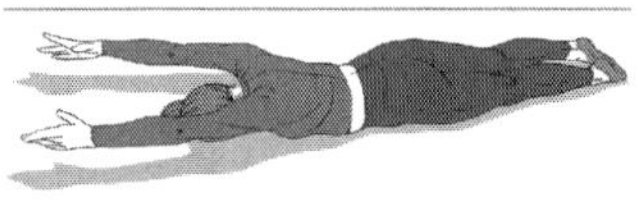

3

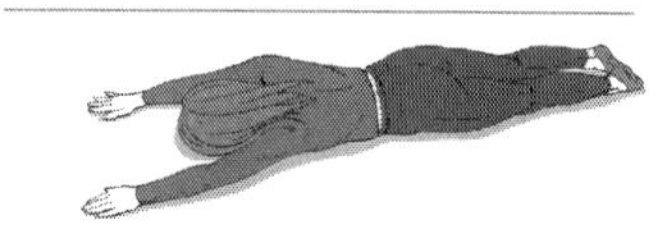

4

Starting position: Lie on the stomach, with arms on the ground, extended above the head, forehead resting on the ground.

1. Raise the arms off the ground, extended as far as possible, keeping the forehead on the ground.
2. Move the arms to the side of the body, keeping the arms fully extended.
3. Return the arms to above the head, still keeping the arms extended.
4. Lower the arms to the starting position.

During the exercise, always keep the forehead on the ground, and the legs stretched out and on the ground.

Number of repetitions

3–5 years: 6x (with help if necessary)

5–10 years: 8x

10–16 years: 10x

16+: 10x

12

ATNR GALANT TLRB

1. Tumble forward “head over heels.” Pay attention to the following:

- Start the movement from a straddle position (legs apart).
- Tuck the head in—don’t put weight on the top of the head!
- If assistance is given, tilt the head towards the chest with one hand, and with the other hand, support the child’s buttocks and thighs, and roll them forward. It’s good if the child “rolls like a ball” and doesn’t “drop like a log.”

2. While leaning on the forearms, crawl backwards to the starting position.

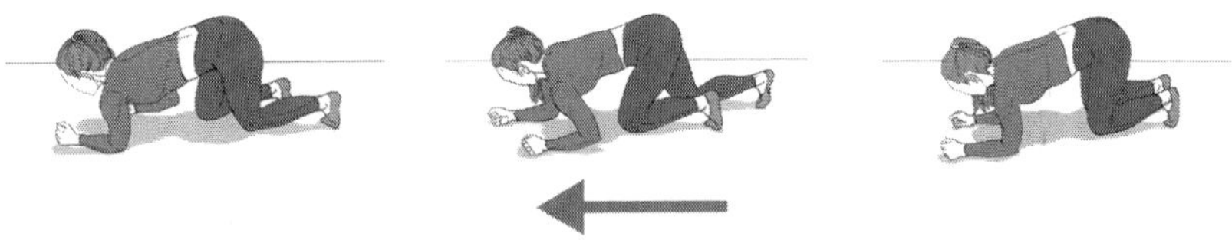

While crawling backwards, keep the head slightly raised with the eyes always looking forward.

Number of repetitions

3–5 years: the full sequence 4–6x (with help if necessary)
5–10 years: the full sequence 6–10x
10–16 years: the full sequence 10x
16+: the full sequence 10x

Massage exercises to support the development of speech

The subject should lie on their back for these massage exercises. Each exercise should be performed for 20–60 seconds, depending on the ability of the person receiving the massage to tolerate the activity. These exercises should be performed daily. Doing them all at once is unnecessary, but you should try to do them in threes or fours. If a child is very reluctant, one or two exercises a day may be sufficient at the beginning of the training. In this case, it is advisable to do the different massages in the order shown and progress from the first exercise to the fifteenth exercise before starting again from the first.

1. Massage the area around the collarbone from the sternum to the shoulders.

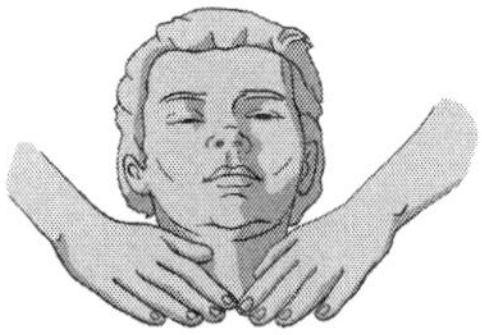

2. Gently turn the head from right to left.

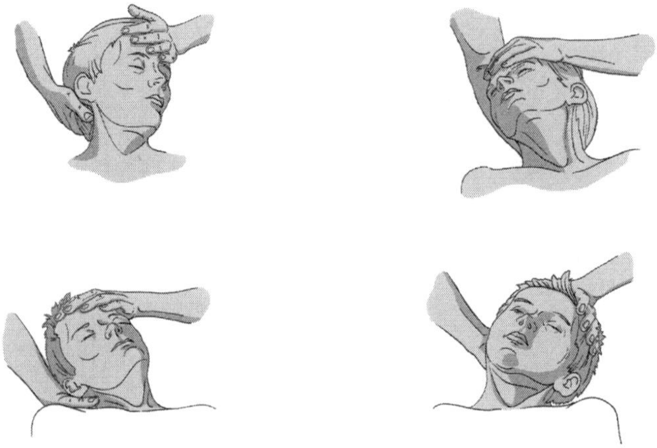

3. Put the fingers together on the chin and massage the face sideways towards the ear, applying light pressure.

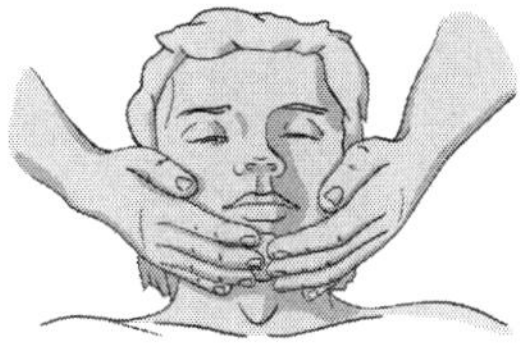

4. Gently massage the entire face and mouth as shown in the diagram, from the mouth towards the ears.

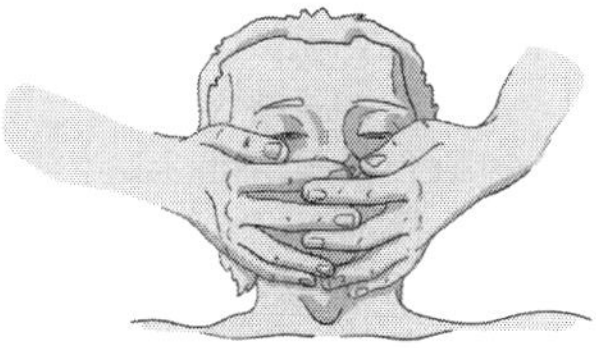

5. Apply light pressure to the face and make a circular massage from the mouth towards the ears.

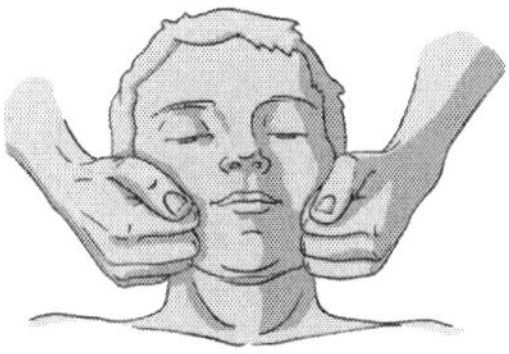

6. Massage the muscles of the face from the chin "upwards" while gently pulling the mouth slightly apart.

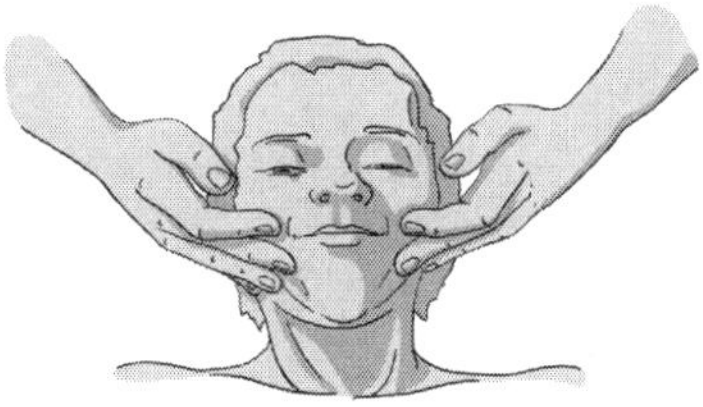

7. As shown in the picture, take a cotton handkerchief in the right hand and gently put your index and middle fingers into the child's mouth. Using your thumbs, massage the face from under the eyes downwards in a spiral motion. Start on the side of the face above the ear and work inwards. Repeat on the other side. Use the non-massaging hand to support the head.

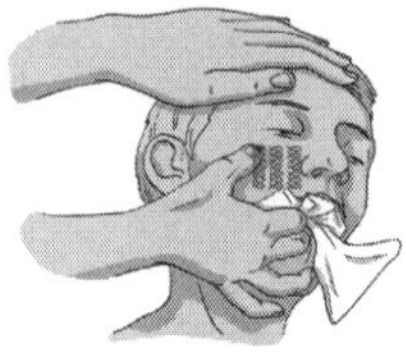

8. Perform a gentle circular massage of the jaw joint. Do the exercise on both sides of the face.

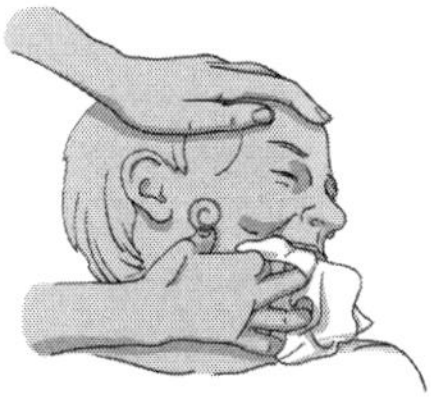

9. Massage the upper and lower lips as shown below.

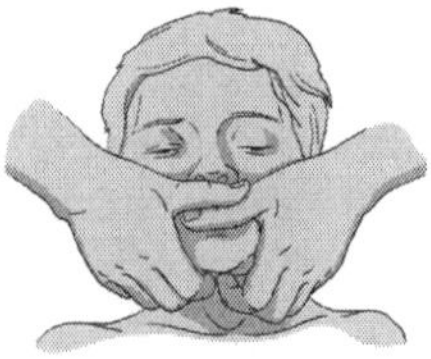

10. Pinch the upper lip with two fingers and press the lips together. Then repeat with the lower lip.

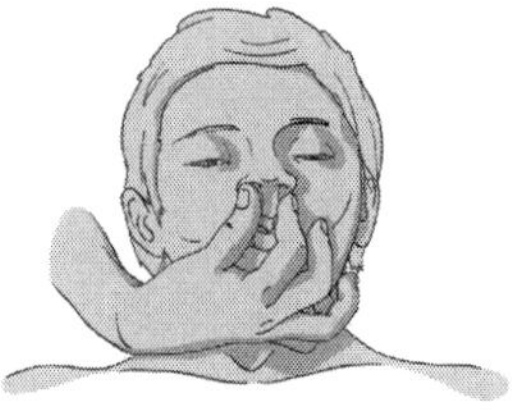

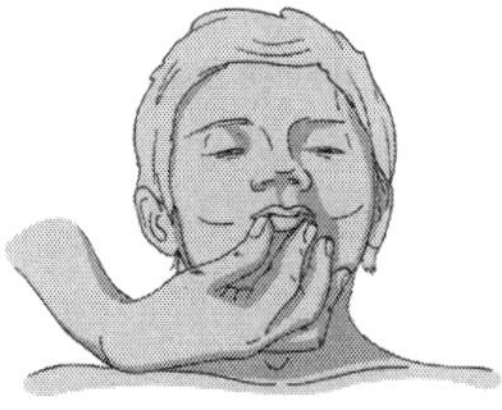

11. Press the two cheeks inwards, and then relax.

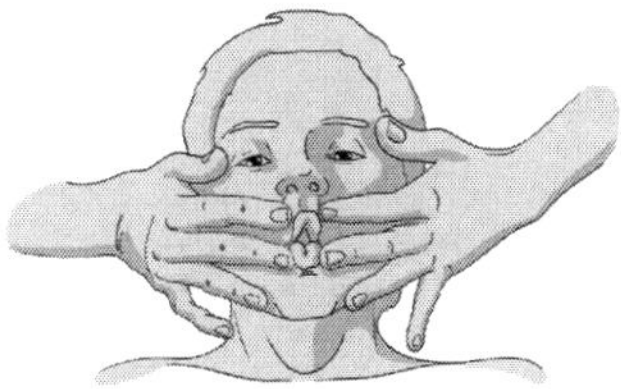

12. Pull the mouth up and then down as shown in the diagram.

13. Lick a small spoon alternately on the right side and on the left side of the face.

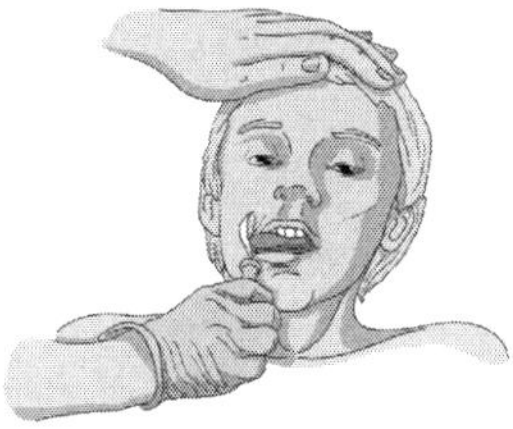

14. Carefully hold the tongue with one hand, and with the other hand massage the tongue right and left. First on one side, then repeat on the other side.

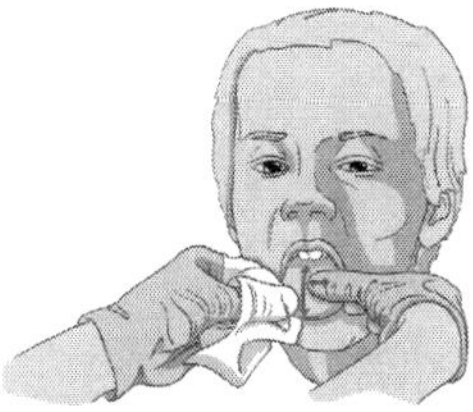

Exercises to "wake up" the left hemisphere

The following sensory stimulation exercises are best done in the evening. If the child or adult is hypersensitive to light or to music (the latter is less common), omit the corresponding exercises.

Exercises should be done daily for 2–3 months. They should reduce symptoms associated with left hemisphere hypofunction. If an improvement in the symptoms is observed, it is possible to perform the exercises only every second day and continue in this way for a further 2–3 months.

The results of these sensory stimulation exercises vary from person to person. The most common benefits include improved speech understanding, speech formation, and development in reading, writing, and some mathematical skills. These exercises lead to more improvement when combined with reflex integration exercises.

If symptoms recur after these exercises are stopped, the symptoms may be less severe, but it is recommended to recommence the exercises.

1.

The child should lie on their back, gazing upwards. From the right side, shine a flashlight towards the right side of their face for 1 second at a distance of 20 cm (8 inches), then turn the flashlight away from the head for a second. Then repeat.

Number of repetitions:
3–5 years: 6–8x
5–10 years: 8x
10–16 years: 10x
16+: 12–16x

2.

The child should lie on their back, gazing upwards. They should listen to a metronome at 60 beats per minute (BPM) with their right ear, i.e., position the speaker or phone on the right side of the head. Metronome apps can be easily downloaded.

Number of minutes for which to listen:
3–5 years: 1 minute
5–10 years: 1–2 minutes
10–16 years: 2 minutes
16+: 2–3 minutes

3.

The child should lie on their back. Lift the head slightly and turn it to the right, then back to the center. Repeat.

Adults should assist children with this exercise.

Number of repetitions:
3–5 years: 6–8x
5–10 years: 8–10x
10–16 years: 10–16x
16+: 10–16x

4.

The child should lie on their back. Using the right hand only, clench the fingers into a fist, or squeeze a small ball for 1–2 seconds. Then release, and repeat.

Number of repetitions:
3–5 years: 6–8x
5–10 years: 8–10x
10–16 years: 10–12x
16+: 16–20x

5.

The child should lie on their stomach. Stroke or massage the right side of the body (e.g., the back, the leg). Although this exercise ideally requires another person to perform the task, adults can massage their own feet and hips using an aid such as a small smooth stone, a massage roller, or a massage tool.

Number of repetitions:
3–5 years: 20x
5–10 years: 20–30x
10–16 years: 30x
16+: 30x

AUTISM SPECTRUM DISORDER

Today, April 2, as I write this chapter, is World Autism Awareness Day. When I was young, I knew almost nothing about autism. I have a memory of the movie *Rain Man*, made legendary by Dustin Hoffmann's unforgettable performance. He played Ray Babbitt, whose character was based on a real person, Laurence Kim Peek.

Peek was not, in fact, a "high-functioning autistic," as Babbitt is known in the film, but suffered from a rare genetic disorder that, among other anomalies, prevents the development of a cortex connecting the two hemispheres of the brain. Peek also showed symptoms of savant syndrome, "thanks to which" he had outstanding gifts. He was brilliant at mental calculation and knew all of Shakespeare's works by heart. Many people think that all autistic people have above-average abilities, are amazing at math, have an incredible memory, or can even compose an eight-part piece of music on the first attempt. But the situation is not so simple.

A series of articles on the film have dealt with the manifestations of autism and other related symptoms. Autism can appear in "pure form" or it can appear mixed with other symptom groups, developmental disorders, and anomalies. According to some measures, one in 10 people diagnosed with autism spectrum disorder (ASD) has a prominent gift—called savant syndrome—associated with autistic symptoms.

It can happen that people with Down syndrome, intellectual disability, ADHD, and other conditions show symptoms similar to those of autism. The true number of autistic people as a proportion of the total population is almost unknown, as they are classified into different groups.

In my home country Hungary, according to the website of the National Association of Autistic People, one in 100 people are autistic. Due to the reasons mentioned before, this proportion varies in countries around the world. In the United States, according to a 2018 report by the Johns Hopkins Institute of Public Health, based on 2016 data, one in 59 children have autism. Although these figures depend on the classification criteria, there are internationally agreed recommendations. The autistic *Triad of Impairment* has the following components:

1. Autistic loneliness, a type of intellectual solitude in which the person avoids company
2. Significantly limited range of activities and narrow interests
3. Specific impairment in communication ability, either in all situations or in social interactions and activities requiring imagination.

There is agreement across countries that boys are four times more likely than girls to have this condition.

What is autism spectrum disorder?

ASD is a developmental disorder affecting the nervous system that significantly impacts social relationships and how the affected child or adult interacts with others, communicates, and behaves. This may be accompanied by other sensory, motor, and sensorimotor symptoms. Although autism can be diagnosed at any age, it is described as a "developmental disorder" because symptoms usually appear in the first two years of life.

According to the American Psychiatric Association (APA) guidelines, people with ASD often match the following statements:

- They have severely limited communication and social interaction with other people
- They have limited interests, often repeating action sequences and behavioral patterns
- They exhibit severe symptoms that negatively affect their performance in preschool, school, work, and daily life.

These are essentially identical to the autistic triad of impairments mentioned above.

The term "spectrum" is used in ASD because there is a wide variation in the type and severity of symptoms experienced, from very mild problems, to complete withdrawal from social relationships.

What are the most typical symptoms of ASD?

Depending on exactly where the child or adult diagnosed with ASD is positioned on the spectrum, the appearance, intensity, and quantity of the following symptoms may vary:

- Low or inconsistent eye contact
- May appear to not pay attention to those who are talking to them
- Rarely shows emotion
- Rarely or never shares their interests with others, does not show others the toys or objects they play with or use
- Does not respond to questions, or, when spoken to does not react to their name
- Difficulty making conversation
- Can talk at length about their favorite subject without realizing that others are not interested. Does not give another person a chance to intervene in their "monologue."
- Improper metacommunication, e.g., facial expressions, lack of body language, or gestures that do not match what is being said
- Unusual tone of voice. Often "sing-songy" or monotone.
- Unable to understand the actions of others. Has difficulty listening to and accepting another person's point of view.
- Difficulty in accepting the rules of social interaction
- Difficulties with making friends, especially when involved in games requiring creativity and imagination
- Repetition of certain behaviors and movements
- Repetition of words or phrases (echolalia)
- A sustained intense interest in specific subjects such as numbers, dinosaurs, trains, etc.
- A narrow range of interests. Obsessed with a single topic and can talk about it in detail for hours.
- Slight changes in daily routine cause upset. Difficulty with changes in routine, for example, replacing winter boots with light shoes in the springtime.
- Hypersensitivity or hyposensitivity (lower sensitivity) to sounds, light, clothing, temperature, or other sensory stimuli.

As you can see, autistic traits, the manifestations of autism, are extremely varied. Symptoms range from merely "slightly eccentric" behavior, to sitting in one place all day, rocking back and forth, and being unable to speak. The traits also depend on other disorders the autistic individual may have. There is no consensus on the percentage of people with autism who have, for example, an intellectual disability. Some statistics suggest that autistic symptoms are associated with intellectual disability in 30% of cases. Others suggest 60%. It is also common to have signs of disability in some cases, and Savant syndrome with above-average performance in others.

Obviously, the more problems accumulate, the more the diagnosis shifts toward the severe end of the spectrum.

How is Asperger's syndrome linked to ASD?

The term "Asperger's syndrome" is not used in more recent literature. This is partly because the symptoms are largely the same as those of high-functioning autism and partly because of Hans Asperger's history.[13]

However, as the term Asperger's syndrome is still used in many countries worldwide, it is necessary to say a few words about it. The literature considers Asperger's syndrome to be a mild form of autism, the main difference being in the severity and number of symptoms and communication skills, particularly in the use of speech. Individuals diagnosed with Asperger's syndrome can communicate. They usually recognize that they are different from others and try to fight it, with varying degrees of success.

Unfortunately, so-called high-functioning autistic people struggle to integrate into society. Despite many of them graduating from university, they cannot find jobs that match their skills, and their "eccentricity" often leads them into uncomfortable situations, turning them into "misunderstood geniuses." Most of them can reach their full potential with a little help, understanding, and support. It should not be for them to understand the "majority". They should not be forced to adapt to their environment—that is what they are struggling with. Rather, the "majority" must learn to understand and accommodate them.

13 Prize-winning historian Edith Sheffer: Asperger's Children (W.W. Norton, 2018)

What is the cause of ASD?

The development of ASD cannot be attributed to a single cause. Most researchers agree that hereditary factors (influenced by multiple genes rather than a single gene) and certain environmental influences combine to cause the condition.

Research suggests that the following are more likely to produce ASD:

- An autistic sibling or parent
- Older parents, over the age of 40. Some research suggests that the likelihood of developing ASD is also higher if there is a significant age difference between a young mother and an older father.
- The presence of other conditions, such as Down syndrome
- Very low birth weight
- Researchers at Columbia University in New York studied second children born within three years of the birth of their older sibling. The results showed that if the second-born child was born within one year, they were three times more likely to develop autism than the average risk, and if born within two years, they were twice as likely to develop autism.
- Industrial pollution, air pollution (e.g., from exhaust fumes), certain herbicides, and pesticide additives are also significant risk factors.

Research in Hungary suggests that there may be a link between the risk of developing autism and taking certain antidepressants and anti-epileptic drugs during pregnancy.

In addition to the above, I would like to mention a few things and share the questions that I have in my own mind. It has been the subject of many studies and theses that people diagnosed with ASD have *sensory integration* problems, that is, a dysfunction in processing *sensory* stimuli. Given this evidence that many of their primitive reflexes were not inhibited in time, questions like the following arise:

1. Are primitive reflexes possibly not inhibited in time because they were not present in sufficient quantity and quality during infancy?

2. If the movement elicited by primitive reflexes was not sufficiently intense, could it have affected sensory ***perception*** *so significantly that it could have led to* ***integration*** *delays?*

Through *tactile perception* the baby learns its own physical boundaries and where the world begins. They learn that they exist within their skin, on their skin are clothes, and, beyond that, everything else. If the baby's tactile perception is disturbed, the sensory fields in the cerebral cortex do not develop an optimal balance between the sensory functions of the different organs.

I want to illustrate this with an example. It is well known that the lips, tongue, fingertips, and thumb are extremely sensitive to *tactile stimuli*. This is no wonder, since in the first months of life, the baby is exposed to a huge quantity of tactile stimuli through the lips and tongue because of feeding, which usually means sucking. Accordingly, the lips and tongue represent a significant area in the sensory field. In infancy, the sucking reflex is closely related to the grasping reflex (the Babkin response), so when a baby sucks, it also grasps with its hands. (This combination is still noticeable in adulthood in people with undeveloped infantile reflexes: when they are drawing, creating something, or manipulating objects with their fingers, their tongues roll around in their mouths or rub the edges of their mouths.)

Often, a weak sucking reflex is accompanied by a weak grasping reflex. Thus, the sensations from the thumb and finger will not result in an appropriate representation in the sensory cortex. So, the question is:

3. Can the proportion of representation of each organ in the sensory cortex be affected by stalled, defective ***tactile perception****?* The next question is related.

4. Is there a correlation between the accurate differentiation between "self" and the external world, and the structure of the sensory cortex? This question is interesting because it is known that our brain learns to distinguish between ourselves and the world through the processing of tactile stimuli.

Since primitive reflexes influence the baby's perception of each of its sensory organs, it is conceivable that the infant's muscle tone is suboptimal, either hypotonic or too tight. In this case, the level of perception is suboptimal and the synthesis, coordination, and interaction of sensory experiences cannot be realized.

5. Can inaccurate perception or lack of sensory integration cause sensory over- or under-sensitivity?

There is evidence from several studies that in ASD and ADHD, there is under-activity of certain right hemisphere functions compared with left hemisphere functions. For example, the person understands speech literally, does not respond to jokes, does not understand irony, and does not see the underlying meaning of texts. They are unable to abstract meanings. The left hemisphere performs speech comprehension (*what* is said), but interpreting speech-related emotions and other non-verbal expressions of emotion is the work of the right hemisphere. Not only the interpretation of speech (*how* something is said) but also our emotions such as joy, sorrow, anger, fear, rage, and excitement is attributed to the right hemisphere.

6. Does the right hemisphere develop less or more slowly as a result of autism, or are the autistic symptoms a result of the underdeveloped right hemisphere?

There are no completely ready answers to the above questions. However, there are research results and practical experiences which suggest that, on the one hand, not all autistic symptoms are autism spectrum disorders, and on the other hand, autistic symptoms can be alleviated by specific exercises.

In my experience, as I have already stated regarding other disorders, the earlier the training starts, the faster the results. Unfortunately, because the physiological background of autism is not clear, it is also difficult to combat and prevent it. However, some procedures and exercises can reduce, in many cases significantly, the severity of symptoms.

Specifically, which symptoms?

1) Persistent primitive reflexes
2) Lack, or weakness, of coordinated processing of sensory stimuli
3) Weak/weaker functioning of the right hemisphere
4) "Disconnection" from the world
5) Difficulty processing vestibular stimuli
6) Absence or severely delayed development of speech.

When carrying out the training exercises, it should be borne in mind that each child or adult with ASD will respond differently. Some people can do all the exercises, while others may dislike some of them. In the latter case, in the first and second months choose those they prefer. After that, it is a gradual process of adding more and more exercises to the daily routine.

Sometimes autistic symptoms are "misleading" and are not actually an ASD but a sensory integration blockage due to immaturity of the nervous system.

This is clearly established when the problem disappears as a result of training. If we are dealing with "true" ASD, although there may be significant improvement in some areas, the nature of the problem as a whole will not be resolved.

Which infant reflexes are not inhibited in ASD?

When I examine children with ASD, the 13 infant reflexes I test for are all present in 90% of cases. They are the symmetrical tonic neck reflex (STNR), asymmetrical tonic neck reflex (ATNR), backward tonic labyrinthine reflex (TLRb), forward tonic labyrinthine reflex (TLRf), the core tendon guard reflex (CTGR), fear paralytic reflex (FPR), and the spinal Galant, grasping, sucking, rooting, Moro, and Babinski reflexes.

If you go back to the chapter on reflexes and re-read the undesirable effects of some of the primitive reflexes, you can get a rough idea of the hour-to-hour struggle of the child or adult who retains these reflexes. And that's without even mentioning other problems such as sensory integration disorders or vestibular immaturity arising due to uninhibited primitive reflexes.

Exercise Videos

A set of videos are available that demonstrate exercises to inhibit the primitive reflexes which are commonly observed in children with ASD symptoms. Use the following QR code to go directly to the video package, or visit https://drsarlos.com/videos for more information.

Scan for video!

Exercises for ASD

1

ATNR

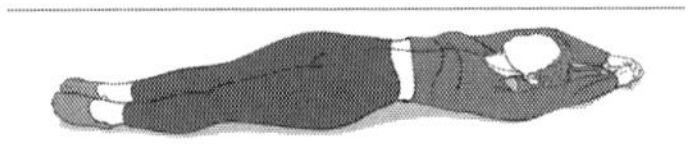

SP

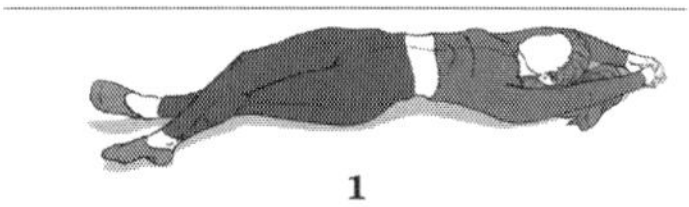

1

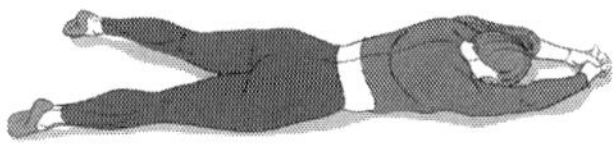

2

Starting position: Lie on the back (supine position), with arms on the floor, extended above the head as far as possible, elbows outstretched, and hands interlocked.

1. This exercise is effectively rolling on the floor, with the caveat that crossing the legs should initiate the movement, and the torso and arms follow. So, if lying on the back and rolling to the left, first cross the right leg over the left. Do the opposite if rolling to the right.
2. Then roll over so that the stomach is now on the floor (prone position). Take care during the turn that the legs again become open and parallel.

Continue rolling in the same direction, next from prone to supine. Again, the movement starts with the legs crossed, followed by the body and arms. So, if now lying on the front and rolling to the left, first cross the left leg over the right.

Roll as far as possible in the space available.
If the room is not large enough, roll back and forth several times until reaching the number of turns listed below.

Number of repetitions:
3–5 years: 4–5 turns in one direction, then backward 3x
5–10 years: 4–5 turns in one direction, then backward 4x
10–16 years: 4–5 turns in one direction, then backward 6x
16+: 4–5 turns in one direction, then backward 6x

2

ATNR

Starting position: Kneel on all fours, with arms extended and palms on the floor, shoulder-width apart. Keep the thighs in a vertical position.
1. Turn the head to the left so that the left ear is aligned with the spine.
Important: Keep the arms extended and the palms on the ground.
2. Bend both elbows simultaneously, lower both shoulders, and place the right ear on the ground.
3. Extend both arms to return to the starting position.
The exercises must also be performed for the stated number of repetitions on the opposite side also.

Number of repetitions:
3–5 years: 4–6x
5–10 years: 6–10x
10–16 years: 8–12x
16+: 12–16x

Repeat on each side.

As young children often cannot assume the starting position due to the triggering of the ATNR reflex, parental assistance may be required for this exercise. In this case, the helper should stand over the child in a straddle position, turning the child's head in the desired direction.

It is almost certain that the arm on the opposite side will bend when the child's head is turned, e.g., if the child looks to the left then the right arm will bend. In this case, gently move the elbow joint to straighten the arm. Additionally, ensure that the hand on the side to which the head moves is fully extended on the ground, not resting on its fingers.

The arm flexion should be initiated from this position, with both elbows bending simultaneously. Assist this by slightly pulling both the child's elbows outward at the same time. This pull will need to be stronger in the direction the child's head is facing, as that arm tends to straighten due to the reflex. (In step 2 of the image above, the left elbow should be pulled more strongly as the head turns left.)

Patience is essential from the parent or helper, as it is difficult for the child to assume and maintain this position. However, when done correctly, this is one of the most effective exercises to help eliminate the ATNR.

3

ATNR

SP

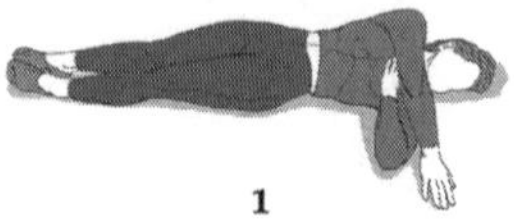

1

2

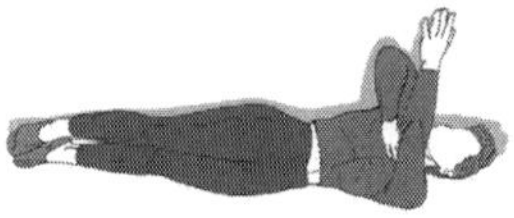

3

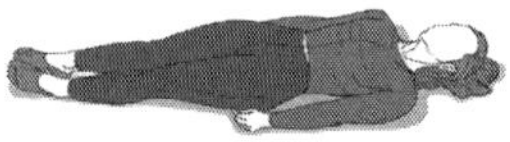

4

Starting position: Lie on the back, gazing upwards.
1. After deep inhalation and exhalation, turn the head and torso to the left. At the same time, bend the left arm by placing the left palm on the chest. Swing the right arm towards the left elbow so that both arms move simultaneously and turn the head and torso. From the navel down, do not move the lower part of the body.
2. Return to the starting position. Rest the arms on the ground beside the body and gaze upwards.
3. Repeat the first movement to the other side.
4. Return to the starting position. Again, rest the arms on the ground beside the body and gaze upwards.

Perform the exercise alternately: to the left, back to the middle, to the right, and again back to the middle.

Number of repetitions:
3–5 years: 6x per side
5–10 years: 10x per side
10–16 years: 12x per side
16+: 15x per side

If it is challenging to do this exercise at first, provide or obtain assistance.

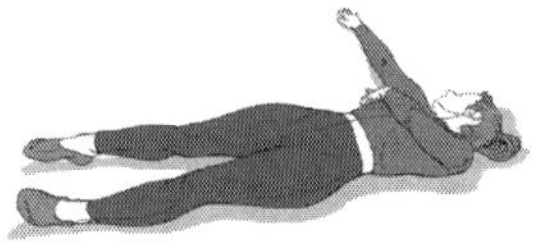

4

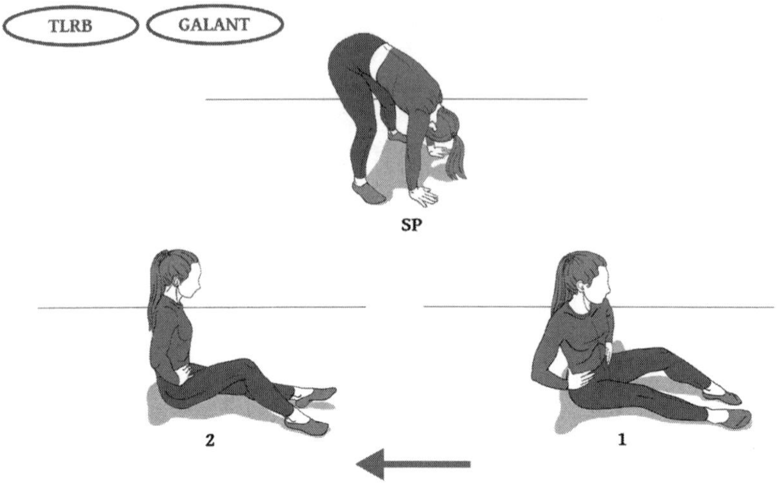

Starting position: Tumble forward "head over heels."
1–2. Move backward using just the buttocks.

When tumbling head over heels, the following points should be observed:

- Start the movement from a straddle position (legs apart)
- Tuck the head in—don't put weight on the top of the head!
- If assistance is given, tilt the head towards the chest with one hand, and with the other hand, support the child's buttocks and thighs, and roll them forward. It's good if the child "rolls like a ball" and doesn't "drop like a log."

Number of repetitions:
3–5 years: 4x
5–10 years: 8x
10–16 years: 10x
16+: 12x

5

GALANT

SP

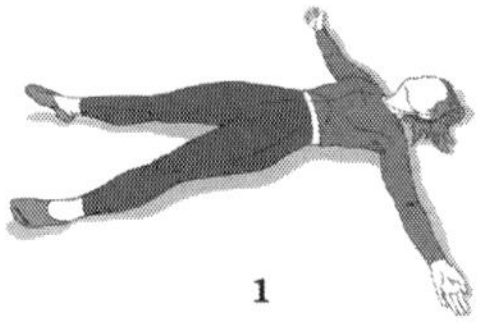

1

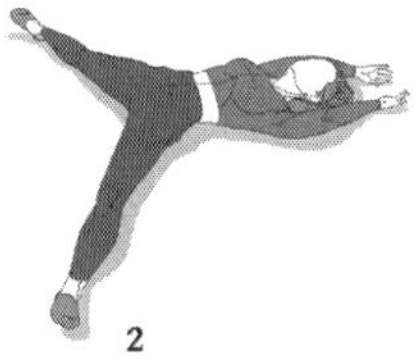

2

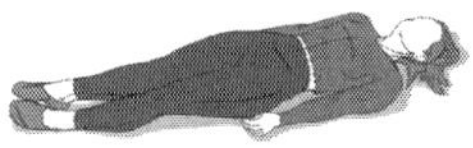

3

Starting position: Lie on the back, legs parallel, arms resting on the floor next to the body.

1–2. Spread the legs and slide the arms up to the ears. Do these actions at the same time.

3. Close the legs and simultaneously slide the arms back down to the starting position.

Number of repetitions:

3–5 years: 16–20x (with assistance if necessary)

5–10 years: 20–30x

10–16 years: 30–40x

16+: 40x

6

TLRF

SP

1

2

Starting position: Lie on the back, with legs bent and feet on the ground. Extend arms, parallel to thighs.

1. Tilt the head forward so that the arms remain extended. The shoulders should not be pulled up into the neck. Maintain this position for the required number of seconds.

2. Lower the head to the ground. If necessary, the arms may be put down on the ground.

Number of repetitions:

3–5 years: 3 x 3, holding the head up for 2–3 seconds (with help if necessary)

5–10 years: 3 x 4–8, holding the head up for 3–6 seconds (with help if necessary)

10–16 years: 3 x 6–8, holding the head up for 5–6 seconds

16+: 3 x 8, holding the head up for 6 seconds

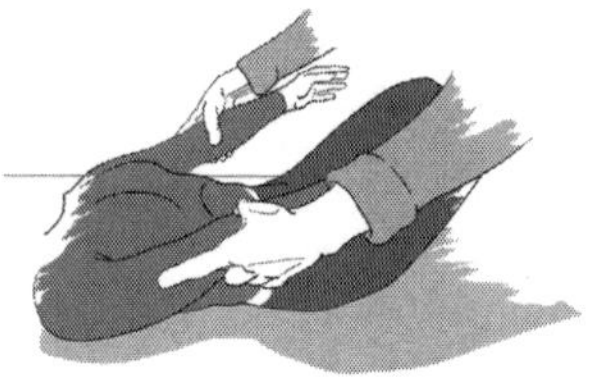

It very often happens that when lifting the head in the above exercise, the arm bends, and the child (and, in many cases, adults too) pulls their shoulder up to the neck.

In these cases, help in the following way.

Sitting at the child's feet, grasp the elbow joint and press down on the elbow with the index finger, preventing the elbow from bending and the shoulder from pulling up to the neck.

7

TLRF

Rock back and forth in the shown position. Arms should be extended, holding the lower legs. The shoulders should not be pulled up into the neck.

Number of repetitions:
3–5 years: 3 x 6 (with help if necessary)
5–10 years: 3 x 8 (with help if necessary)
10–16 years: 3 x 10
16+: 3 x 12

8

GRASPING SUCKING

SP

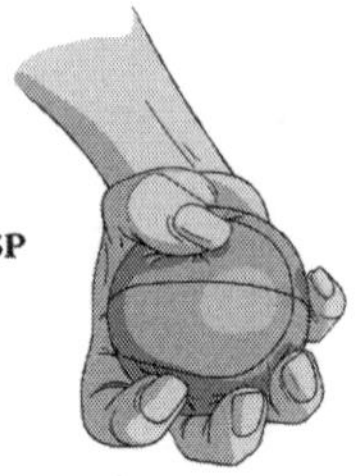

Starting position: Hold a sponge ball with the thumb facing the other four fingers.

Squeeze the ball for a second, then relax. Repeat.

Make sure to grip the ball with the last joints of each finger bent as shown. Some children find this difficult at first, either because the thumb keeps sliding back alongside the other fingers, or they cannot bend the last joint of the fingers. In this case, they need help to make the correct grip. Between the ages of three and five, they can hold their own forearm to help, as shown below.

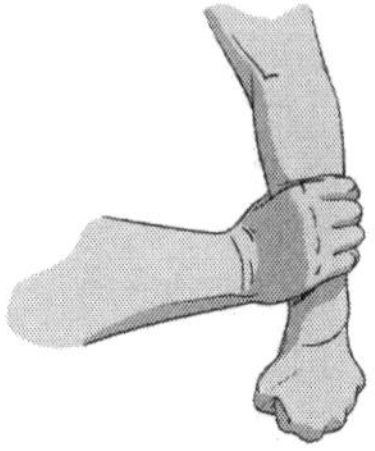

Number of repetitions:
3–5 years: 3 x 8–10 with both hands, alternating
5–10 years: 3–4 x 10 with both hands, alternating
10–16 years: 4 x 10 with both hands, alternating
16+: 4–5 x 10 with both hands, alternating

9

TLRB

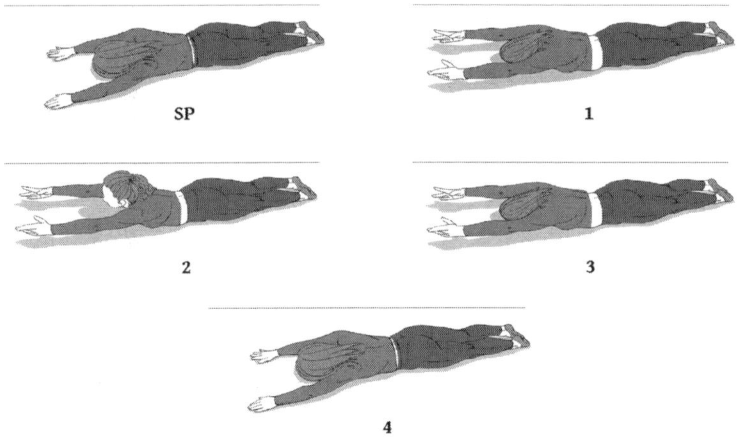

Starting position: Lie on the stomach, with arms on the ground, extended above the head, forehead resting on the ground.

1. Raise the arms off the ground, extended as far as possible, keeping the forehead on the ground.
2. Raise the head off the ground, keeping the arms fully extended.
3. Lower the head, and return the forehead to the ground.
4. Lower the arms to the starting position.

Number of repetitions:

3–5 years: 6x
5–10 years: 8x
10–16 years: 10x
16+: 12x

10

GRASPING SUCKING

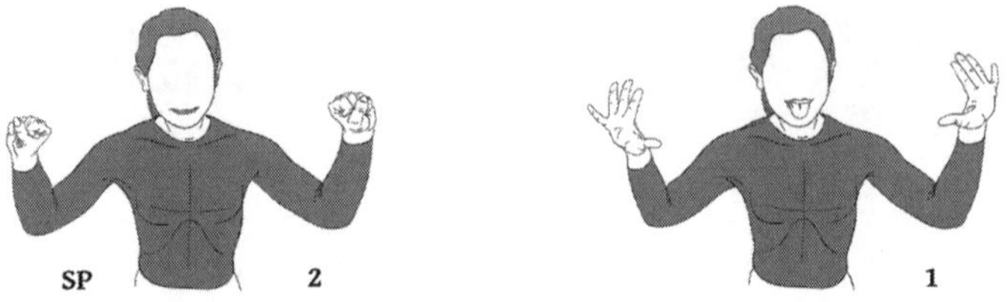

Starting position: Clench the fingers of both hands into fists, with the thumb resting on the outside of the other fingers.
1. While stretching the fingers and extending them backward, stick the tongue out as far as possible.
2. Close the fingers back into a fist, retract the tongue behind the teeth, and close the mouth.

Number of repetitions:
3–5 years: 3 x 6–10 both the above steps
5–10 years: 3 x 10 both the above steps
10–16 years: 4 x 10 both the above steps
16+: 5 x 10 both the above steps

11

MORO

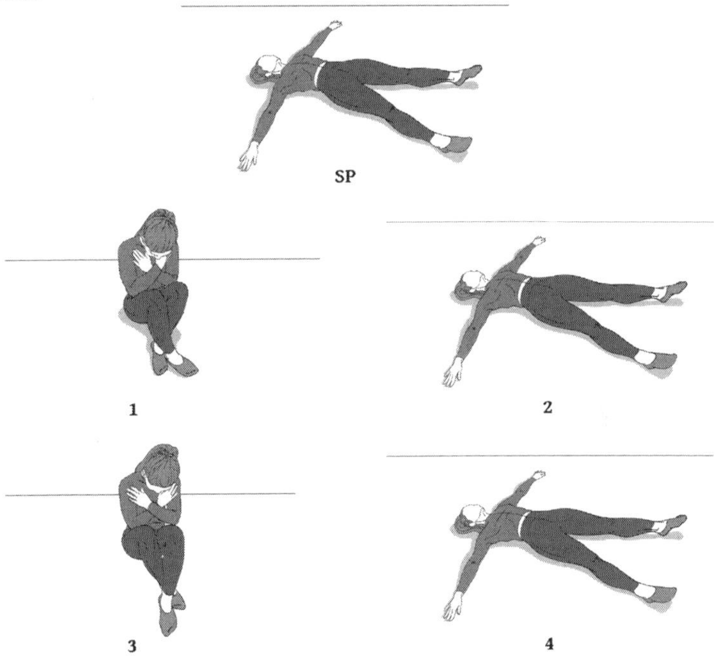

Starting position: Lie on the back, arms outstretched to the side, legs spread apart.

1. Sit up into a bent position, head tucked in, legs crossed, and arms crossed with hands lightly gripping the shoulders. The *right* foot and *right* forearm must be forward, i.e., further from the body.
2. Return to starting position.
3. Again sit up into a bent position, head tucked in, with legs crossed and arms crossed with hands lightly gripping the shoulders. This time the *left* foot and *left* forearm must be forward, i.e., further from the body.
4. Return to starting position.

If it is very difficult to sit up, support the upper body with bean bags or pillows.

Number of repetitions:

3–5 years: 8x
5–10 years: 16–20x
10–16 years: 20–24x
16+: 20–24x

12

MORO

Starting position: Stand with back against the wall, legs apart, arms outstretched to the side.

1. Keeping the right foot in place, cross the left foot in front of the right foot, and at the same time cross the arms. The *left* foot and *left* forearm must be in front, i.e., further from the body.
2. Move the left foot back to the starting position, stretching out the arms.
3. Now, keeping the left foot in place, cross the right foot in front of the left foot, and at the same time cross the arms. This time the *right* foot and *right* forearm must be in front, i.e., further from the body.
4. Move the right foot back to the starting position, stretching out the arms.

Number of repetitions:

3–5 years: 12–16x
5–10 years: 20–30x
10–16 years: 30x
16+: 40x

13

Do this exercise every second day.

On each foot, pull the big toe towards the body 10–12 times. Repeat 3–4 times.

CTGR

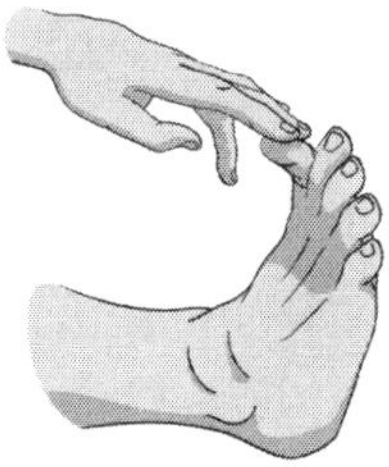

For a child, a parent or helper can also perform this action.

14

Do this exercise every second day.

Massage the Achilles tendon and calf muscle, 10–12 times on one leg and then on the other. Repeat 3–4 times.

CTGR

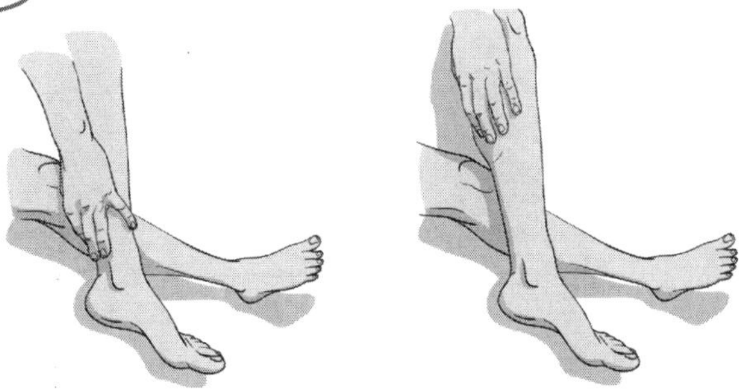

For a child, a parent or helper can also perform this action.

Exercises to "wake up" the right hemisphere

The following sensory stimulation exercises are best done in the evening. If the child or adult is hypersensitive to light or music (the latter is less common), omit the corresponding exercises.

Exercises should be done daily for 2–3 months. They should reduce symptoms associated with right hemisphere hypofunction. If an improvement in symptoms is observed, it is possible to perform the exercises only every second day and continue in this way for a further 2–3 months.

The results of these sensory stimulation exercises vary from person to person. The most common benefits are: easier to fall asleep at night, improved ability to cooperate, reduced sensory sensitivity, and less picky with food choices.

If symptoms recur after these exercises are stopped, the symptoms may be less severe, but it is recommended to recommence the exercises.

1.

The child should lie on their back, gazing upwards. From the left side, shine a flashlight towards the left side of their face for one second at a distance of 20 cm (8 inches), then turn the flashlight away from the head for a second. Then repeat.

Number of repetitions:
3–5 years: 6–8x
5–10 years: 8x
10–16 years: 10x
16+: 12–16x

2.

The child should lie on their back, gazing upwards. They should listen to classical music (Mozart, Vivaldi, Schubert, etc.) with their left ear, i.e., position the speaker or phone on the left side of the head.

Number of minutes for which to listen:
3–5 years: 1 minute
5–10 years: 1–2 minutes
10–16 years: 2–3 minutes
16+: 3–5 minutes

3.

The child should lie on their back. Lift the head slightly and turn it to the left, then back to the center. Repeat.

Adults should assist children with this exercise.

Number of repetitions:
3–5 years: 6–8x
5–10 years: 8–10x
10–16 years: 10–16x
16+: 10–16x

4.

The child should lie on their back. Using the left hand only, clench the fingers into a fist, or squeeze a small ball for 1–2 seconds. Then release, and repeat.

Number of repetitions:
3–5 years: 6–8x
5–10 years: 8–10x
10–16 years: 10–12x
16+: 16–20x

5.

The child should lie on their stomach. Stroke or massage the left side of the body (e.g., the back, the leg). Although this exercise ideally requires another person to perform the task, adults can massage their own feet and hips using an aid such as a small smooth stone, a massage roller, or a massage tool.

Number of repetitions:
3–5 years: 20x
5–10 years: 20–30x
10–16 years: 30x
16+: 30x

Tactile stimulation; me and the world

The following exercises are recommended if you can commit to doing them daily and can maintain the recommended number of repetitions.

Tactile stimulation can be used with children and adults who do not show sensory (tactile) hypersensitivity during the exercises, i.e., those who seem to tolerate and even request massage and stroking.

The exercises can be performed over several months. Depending on where the child is on the ASD spectrum, how sensitive their nervous system is to tactile stimuli, at what age they start the exercises, and how precisely they can follow the prescribed frequency and number of repetitions, a positive change in condition can be expected.

1. Massage or stroke (whichever feels best) three times a day—morning, afternoon, and evening—for 30 seconds per body part.
Parts of the body: thumbs, fingertips, mouth (upper and lower lips separately), and the tip of the tongue (if the subject allows). Perform for six minutes in total on each occasion.

2. Massage or stroke twice daily—morning and evening—for 12–15 seconds per body part.
Parts of the body: limbs, abdomen, chest, face, forehead, chin, scalp, ears, neck, palms, and soles. Perform for four minutes in total on each occasion.

3. Once a day—in the evening—massage or stroke for 5–6 seconds per body part.
Parts of the body: Back, hips, buttocks, back of the hands, and back of the feet. Perform for a total of 25–30 seconds.

During this tactile stimulation, name the body parts that are being massaged or stroked! For example, "*Now I'm going to massage your thumb.*"

Vestibular stimuli

The following stimuli can be varied at will depending on the preference of the person doing the exercises. It is advisable to choose just two per day, with the vestibular organ receiving the stimulus from different directions.

1) Rock forward and back, right and left
2) Roll on the floor, right and left
3) Tumble forward head over heels. For those physically capable of doing so, try tumbling backward.
4) Spin around while standing or sitting in a swivel chair
5) Balance on a disc or balance board
6) Jump on a trampoline
7) Spin the head right and left
8) Bend the head up and down, and from side to side
9) Standing in a straddle position (legs apart), rotate the neck in a circle, alternating directions
10) Standing in a straddle position, move the upper body in a circular movement, alternating directions.

Exercises to stimulate the start of speech

These exercises should be performed daily. If some exercises are not liked by the child or adult, select those which they prefer. The younger the child, the better the results.

1

GRASPING SUCKING

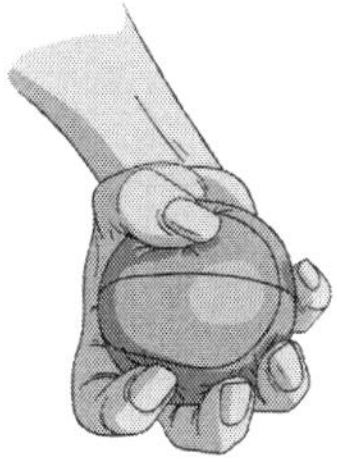

Starting position: Hold a sponge ball with the thumb facing the other four fingers.
Squeeze the ball for a second, then relax. Repeat.
Make sure to grip the ball with the last joints of each finger bent as shown. Some children find this difficult at first, either because the thumb keeps sliding back alongside the other fingers, or they cannot bend the last joint of the fingers. In this case, they need help to make the correct grip. Between the ages of three and five, they can hold their own forearm to help, as shown below.

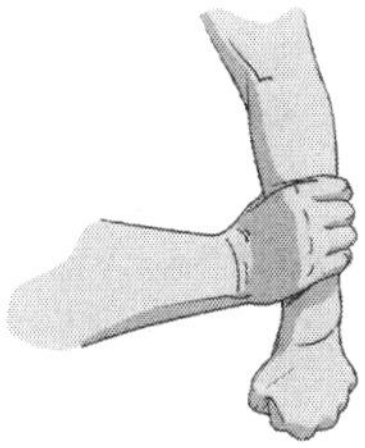

Number of repetitions:
3–5 years: 3 x 8–10 with both hands
5–10 years: 3–4 x 10 with both hands
10–16 years: 4 x 10 with both hands
16+: 4–5 x 10 with both hands

2

GRASPING SUCKING

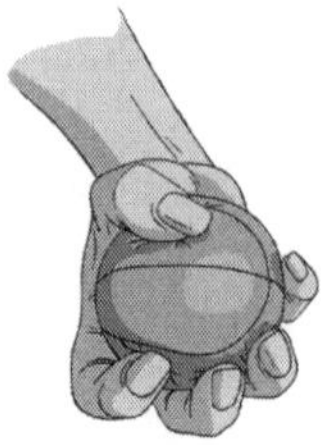

SP

1 8

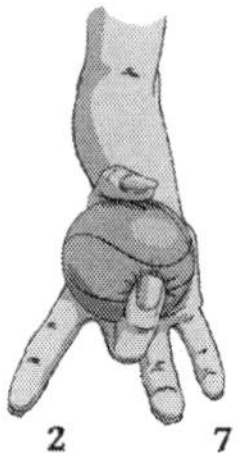

2 7

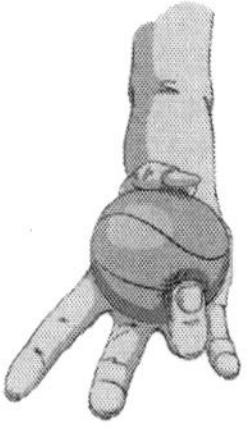

3 6

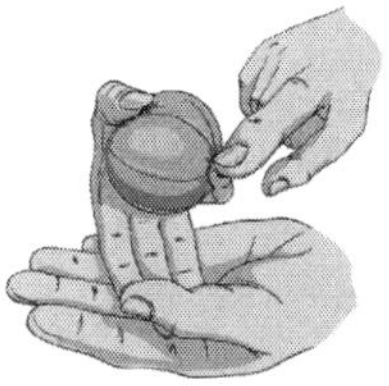

4 5

Starting position: Hold a sponge ball in the palm, with the thumb and index finger bent and facing each other, resting on the ball.
1. Grip the ball with the thumb and index finger.
2. Grip the ball with the thumb and middle finger.
3. Grip the ball with the thumb and ring finger.
4. Grip the ball with the thumb and little finger.
5–8. Repeat the previous steps in reverse order, beginning with the little finger and ending with the index finger.

This exercise should be performed with both the right and left hands.

In young children—and sometimes older persons, too—it happens that all the fingers bend in, not just the one that should be active. In this case, another person can help, as in the image above showing the little finger and thumb gripping the ball.

Number of repetitions:

3–5 years: two sequences, back and forth, with both hands
5–10 years: three sequences, back and forth, with both hands
10–16 years: four sequences, back and forth, with both hands
16+: five sequences, back and forth, with both hands

3

GRASPING SUCKING

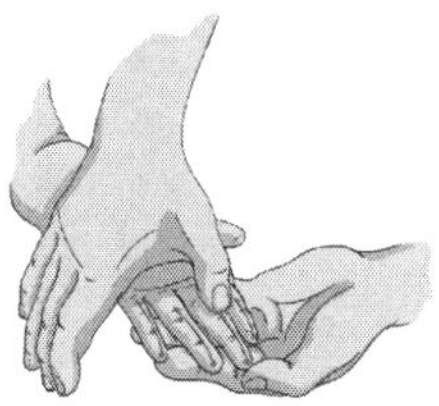

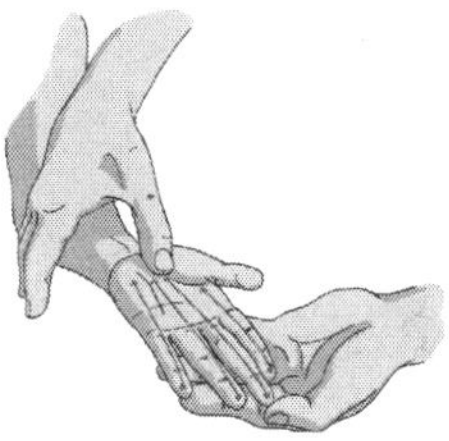

Massage the palm from the fingers towards the wrist. Older children and adults can do the massage themselves, but they should use a smooth pebble rather than their own fingers.

Number of repetitions

3–5 years: 4–5 times per finger on both the left and right palm, 2x
5–10 years: five times per finger on both the left and right palm, 3x
10–16 years: six times per finger on both the left and right palm, 3–4x
16+: six times per finger on both the left and right palm, 4x

4

For this and the subsequent massage exercises in this section, the child lies on their back.

Place your palms on the collarbone and press gently, then release.

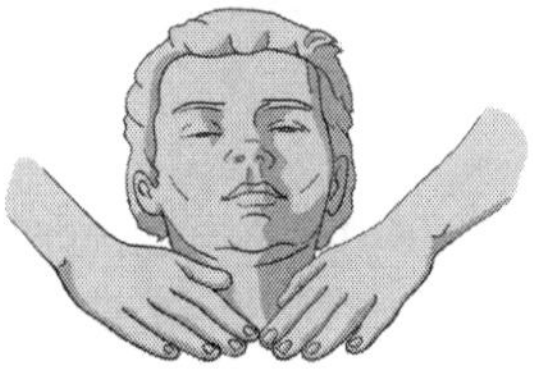

Number of repetitions:
3–5 years: 10–16x
5–10 years: 16–20x
10–16 years: 20–30x
16+: 20–30x

5

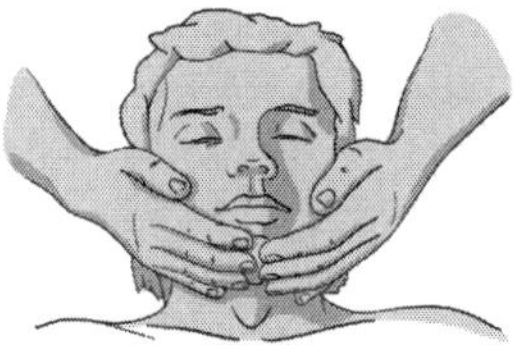

Put the fingers together on the chin and massage the face sideways towards the ear, applying light pressure.

Number of repetitions:
3–5 years: 10–16x
5–10 years: 16–20x
10–16 years: 20–30x
16+: 20–30x

6

Gently massage the entire face and mouth as shown in the diagram, from the mouth towards the ears.

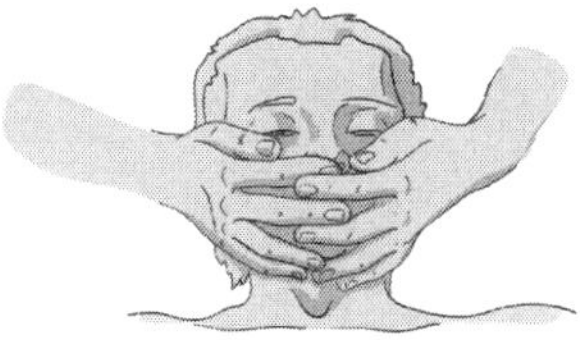

Number of repetitions:
3–5 years: 10–16x
5–10 years: 16–20x
10–16 years: 20–30x
16+: 20–30x

7

Apply light pressure to the face and make a circular massage from the mouth towards the ears.

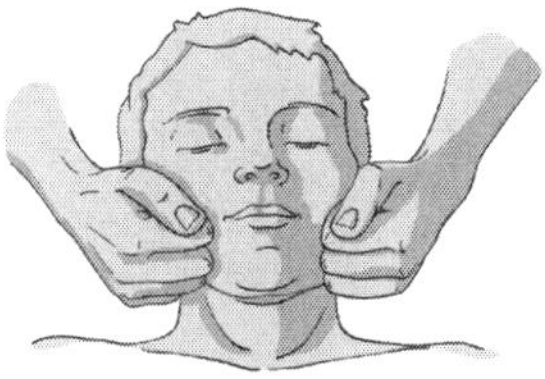

Number of repetitions:
3–5 years: 10x in one direction
5–10 years: 16x in one direction
10–16 years: 20x in one direction
16+: 20x in one direction

8

As shown in the picture, take a cotton handkerchief in the right hand and gently put your index and middle fingers into the child's mouth. Using your thumbs, massage the face from under the eyes downwards in a spiral motion. Start on the side of the face above the ear and work inwards. Repeat on the other side. Use the non-massaging hand to support the head.

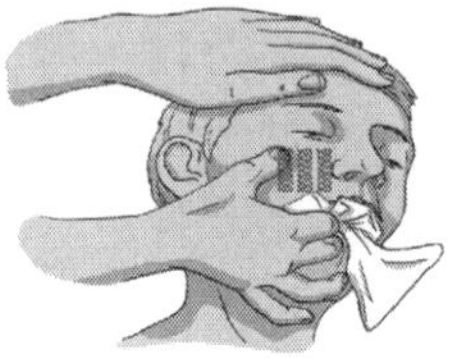

Number of repetitions:
3–5 years: 2–3x on each side
5–10 years: 4–5x on each side
10–16 years: 10–12x on each side
16+: 10–12x on each side

9

Perform a gentle circular massage of the jaw joint. Do the exercise on both sides of the face.

Number of repetitions:
3–5 years: 10x in one direction and 10x in the other direction
5–10 years: 10x in one direction and 10x in the other direction
10–16 years: 15x in one direction and 15x in the other direction
16+: 15x in one direction and 15x in the other direction

10

Massage the upper and lower lips as shown below.

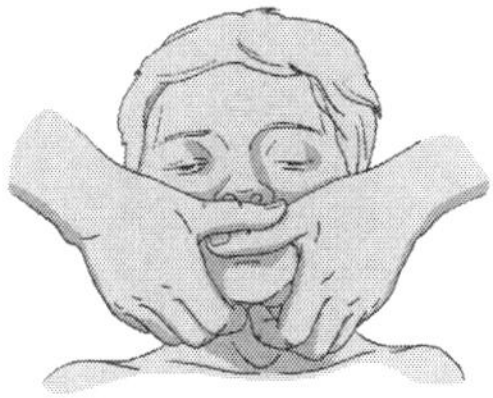

Number of repetitions:

3–5 years: 10x
5–10 years: 12–20x
10–16 years: 20x
16+: 20x

11

Pinch the upper lip with two fingers and press the lips together. Then repeat with the lower lip.

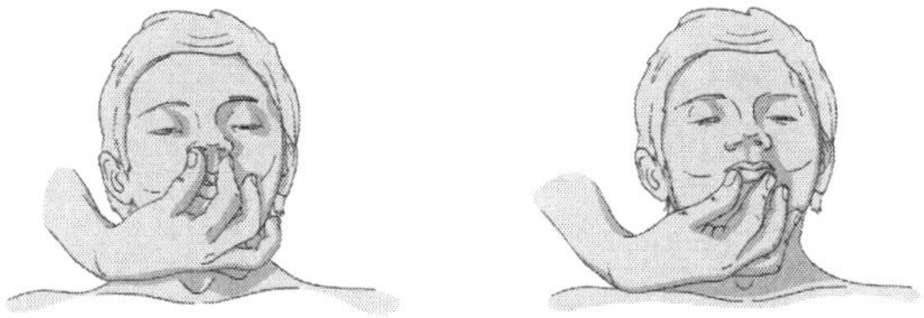

Number of repetitions:

3–5 years: 10x above the mouth, 10x below
5–10 years: 16x above the mouth, 16x below
10–16 years: 20x above the mouth, 20x below
16+: 20x above the mouth, 20x below

12

Lick a small spoon alternately on the right side and on the left side of the face.

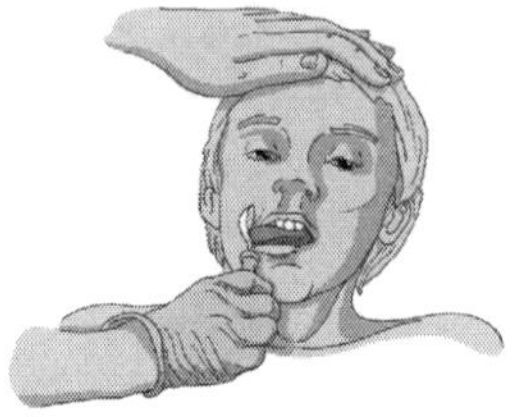

Number of repetitions:
3–5 years: 6x left side, 6x right side
5–10 years: 8x left side, 8x right side
10–16 years: 10–12x left side, 10–12x right side
16+: 12x left side, 12x right side

13

Press the two cheeks inwards, and then relax.

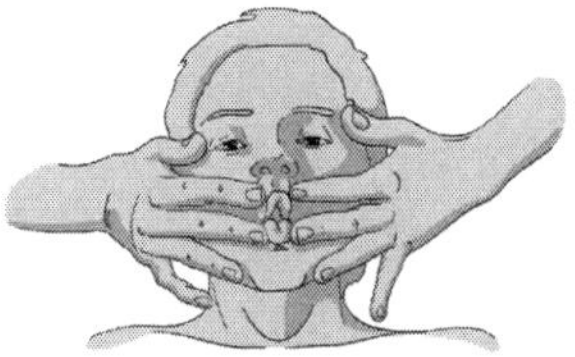

Number of repetitions:
3–5 years: 8x
5–10 years: 10x
10–16 years: 12–16x
16+: 16x

14

Pull the mouth up and then down as shown in the diagram.

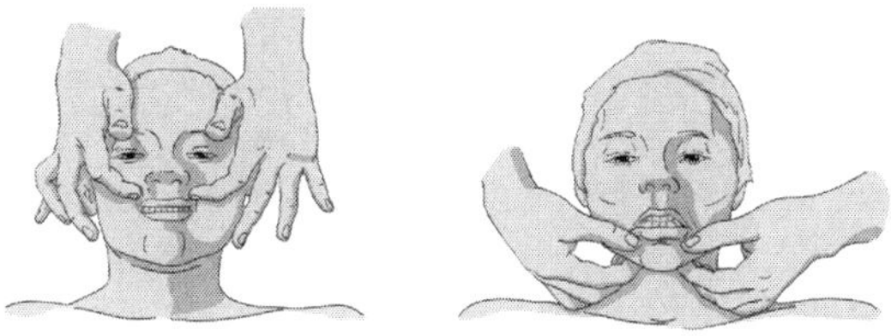

Number of repetitions:
3–5 years: 6x up, 6x down
5–10 years: 8–10x up, 8–10x down
10–16 years: 10–12x up, 10–12x down
16+: 12x up, 12x down

15

Carefully hold the tongue with one hand, and with the other hand massage the tongue right and left. First on one side, then repeat on the other side.

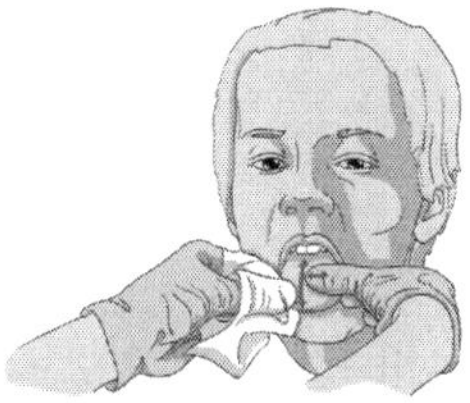

Number of repetitions:
3–5 years: 4–5x on each side
5–10 years: 5–8x on each side
10–16 years: 8x on each side
16+: 10x on each side

DYSLEXIA AND DYSGRAPHIA

I'm sure many people have heard the terms dyslexia, dysgraphia, and dyscalculia. But being precise about what they mean is a challenging task because there are many definitions and explanations. In addition these active areas of research and new results are constantly appearing and changing our understanding of these conditions.

For now, let's just say that dyslexia refers to difficulty in learning to read and comprehend written text. Dysgraphia is difficulty in learning to write. And dyscalculia refers to difficulties with mathematical concepts and calculations. What they have in common is they are independent of intelligence, socio-cultural environment, teaching methods, and practice.

We are not all the same

Children learn to read and write in different ways and at varying speeds because they do not have the same abilities or the same maturity when they enter school. This is true even when they are around the same age. They may develop at different rates, inherit different abilities from their parents, or have very different family backgrounds. This is confirmed by research showing that children of the same biological age differ in terms of cognitive abilities as well as physical parameters (age, weight, etc). The neurological maturity of a seven-year-old child may in some cases be only at the level of a 4–5-year-old child, while in other cases may exceed that of an 8-9-year-old. The maturity of a child's nervous system and their physical maturity naturally influence learning processes, including those for reading and writing.

Sometimes a young child is already reading stories when they start school. Others are unable to read consistently and comprehensively at the end of second grade (around 7–8 years old). Some will still not be able to do so as adults. Several researchers argue that the end of second grade is the "watershed." If the child is not reading fluently by the end of second grade, the parent should take it seriously and look for the cause of the problem. Fortunately, not all second-graders who cannot read will have a lifelong problem. But certain warning signs must be taken seriously.

The first is **family traits**. A group of researchers has been looking into the causes of dyslexia in families across a 20-year period. They found that if a child has dyslexia, there is a 50% greater-than-average chance that his or her sibling will also have reading problems.

The second warning sign is **delayed speech development**. When learning to read, a child needs to hear the differences between sounds. The ability to break down words into their constituent parts, i.e., sounds and syllables, is called phonological awareness.

Phonological awareness is specific to spoken language and not to writing. When a child is unable to break words into sounds and syllables—which is often a consequence of delayed speech development—phonological awareness is low, and they are likely to have reading problems.

In the case of a child with delayed speech development who does not pronounce sounds clearly, if they receive speech therapy, there is a chance that they will speak clearly and articulate well.

However, clear speech alone does not mean that there will be no reading difficulties. Nor is it a guarantee that they will be able to break words down into phonemes, put them in a different order, and form different words.

The meaning of the word "phoneme" may need some explanation. To simplify the definition slightly, it means nothing more than the elements of spoken language, i.e., the speech sounds that are made according to the rules of the language in which they are spoken.

Since the breakdown of a word into phonemes, or the role of operations on phonemes, is a deeper level of processing than that of articulation, it can happen that the child may be able to speak clearly but still be unable to read.

A third warning sign is the **confusion of letters, numbers, and signs**. One example is mixing similar letters (e.g., b and d). Another is forgetting the spelling of a word and repeating this error again and again. Similarly, reading words backward. There are two observable symptoms of this problem, which appear to be closely related and would be worth investigating in a scientific context.

The first is when a child writes letters in "mirror writing" such as shown below. Such children fall into the at-risk category.

DAD = ᗡAᗡ

The second is testing for horizontal post-rotational nystagmus. Normally the nervous system tends to move in a way that adjusts the eyeballs to the correct position using the eye-moving muscles. If you spin a person to their left, i.e., anticlockwise, while spinning, their eyes will jump back in a left-to-right direction. When they stop spinning, the eye movement changes direction so there is now a rapid movement of the eyes from right to left. This is the normal situation. When reading, this right-to-left movement allows the eye to jump from the end of a line back to the beginning of the line and then move to the next line, so that we don't have to search through the text to find where we are. However, in the case of many children with reading difficulties, I observed the phenomenon that when I perform this test, it is not possible to trigger this eye movement (or only to a minimal extent). After they stop spinning, their eyes stay stationary and don't jump from right to left.

Some children show a preference to write or read "backward," from right to left. Imagine what happened when I tried spinning such a child in a *clockwise* direction. After they stopped spinning, the result was the opposite of what should happen after spinning anticlockwise. Their eyes would jump from left to right. So, one imagines that if such children would read texts written right to left, their eyes would be able to naturally jump from the end of one line to the start of the next. (I am familiar only with Western languages. An interesting topic to explore in this context would be reading difficulties in Semitic languages with a right-to-left writing direction.)

The fourth warning sign to watch out for is **a refusal to listen to stories and, later, aversion to reading.** In early childhood, the majority of children love to be read to, they can't get enough of stories. Over time, they become interested in books, numbers, and letters.

Many young children pretend that they can read or write. They open a story book, pull their index finger under the letters and invent a story. Others draw wavy lines and "write" their secrets in a little notebook. They recognize the first letter of their name. Before school age, some of them have been taught to write their names or can read.

Experts say that the opposite is true for children who do not like stories. As they progress toward school age, they are not interested in letters and numbers and are likely to have challenges with reading and writing.

In many cases, the line is between "a little late" and a true problem. It is very important that the parent or professional recognizes early on the signs that predict a reading disability. All the more so because, in a significant number of cases, these are not organic problems but delayed neurodevelopment, and this can be treated.

What is the difference between the organic origin of dyslexia and immature neurological reading problems?

If the problem has an organic cause, i.e., the brain or the structure of the sensory organs, in particular the visual and auditory organ systems, then specific methods and exercises for learning to read can help to make reading easier and smoother.

But in this case, the underlying problem is not solved. In the case of organic damage, the structure of the brain of a dyslexic person is different from a "normal" brain. This includes asymmetry of the temporal lobes and underdevelopment of the area of the brain connecting the two hemispheres (the corpus callosum) or abnormal organization of the temporal-occipital regions. Several researchers have found that if the left hemisphere is damaged it can cause "dysfunction" of the connections between these areas, leading to dyslexia.

Depending on which area of the brain is affected, different functions may be impacted. Among others, these include memory, attention, executive functions, visual processing, auditory processing, and motor functions.

In other cases, the nervous system does not have any organic damage in the regions mentioned above, but rather a deficiency in sensorimotor function, combined with neurological immaturity, or rather a lack of maturity of the nervous system.

Several experiments have shown that individuals with dyslexic symptoms have difficulty in synchronizing auditory and visual stimuli and in performing tasks involving balance and motor coordination.

My mother was a physical education teacher for over 40 years. When I was starting my career I often sat in on her classes. I remember her drawing my attention on several occasions to the close link between children's motor coordination and learning abilities. Those who were unable to coordinate the movement of their arms and legs when running and skipping, were unable to perform a simple four-part exercise sequence, make a regular basket throw in basketball, or who got their hands and feet tangled during a sports game or while simply running, were almost certainly the children who had trouble reading and writing.

The relationship between sensorimotor function and primitive reflexes was discussed in the chapter on sensorimotor integration. Primitive reflexes play an essential role in sensorimotor development, but their persistence over time hinders the optimal development of further sensorimotor processes.

Some primitive reflexes significantly complicate learning to read or reading if they are not inhibited in time. One much-studied reflex is the ATNR. In 2006, a school in Northern Ireland studied 739 children aged 7–9 years. They found that among those studied, those with a retained ATNR were significantly more likely to have reading difficulties. Recall that this reflex has no place in the child's life after the age of 6 months!

According to a study conducted in Egypt in 2021, dyslexia-affected 6–9-year-old children have significantly higher levels of ATNR, STNR, forward or backward TLR, and the grasping reflex. Research conducted in the USA in 2017 came to the same conclusion, adding the sucking and rooting reflexes to the list.

Difficulties with handwriting, dysgraphia

Before moving on to the exercises, let's look at dysgraphia, a handwriting disorder.

Whether it's forming the letters, correctly sequencing them, or the speed of writing, poor or weak handwriting can interfere with learning how to spell words and produce written text.

In 2019, researchers in Pakistan studied 666 children aged 13, 409 of whom were enrolled in public schools and 257 in private schools. In the study, 33% of the participants showed dyslexia, 48% dysgraphia, and 45% dyscalculia;

30% of the children had both dyslexia and dysgraphia, 26% had dyslexia and dyscalculia, and 36% had dysgraphia and dyscalculia.

In the USA, a 2008 survey found that 30–47% of people with reading difficulties also have difficulties with writing and math. The problems are probably explained by the fact that all three disorders (dyslexia, dysgraphia, dyscalculia) are largely based on common cognitive structures.

What causes dysgraphia?

Several studies point to the fact that for learning to read and write, the dominant side of the brain must develop first. In modern understanding, the development of dysgraphia in children is due to the lateralization of brain functions (i.e., certain functions are specialized to either the right or left side of the brain), including speech and language.

The lateralization should be completed by the start of school. If it is delayed and a child uses the right hand but is, in fact, a "hidden left-hander," then cortical control will be impaired (and vice versa).

Research carried out so far has shown that the so-called orthographic coding in working memory is linked to handwriting and is often impaired in the case of those with dysgraphia. Orthographic coding refers to the fact that written words are stored in the working memory while the individiual letters are analyzed. So, when we write the word "SCHOOLCHILD," the whole word is "there" in working memory. At the same time, the pencil forms and writes the letters one by one in the correct order, paying attention to the correct spelling.

It is not necessary to think about how to spell a word—we can retrieve it automatically from our memory.

Children with dysgraphia may have developmental motor disorders, although this is not always the case. However, it is true that almost all children who have difficulties with writing have difficulty coordinating continuous finger movements. They have difficulty grasping and guiding a pencil or pen if they are not looking at their fingers. In most cases, a fundamental problem is that they cannot turn their thumbs to face (oppose) the other fingers.

Regarding persistent reflexes, my experience with children with dysgraphia symptoms is almost the same as for children with dyslexia. In 85–90% of cases, the following reflexes are present: the STNR, the ATNR, the forward or backward TLR, the grasping reflex, and the sucking reflex. I would add to this the so-called Babkin response, which is a combination of the grasping and sucking reflexes.

The grasping reflex is more intense and more difficult to integrate in children with dyslexia, and their palms are particularly ticklish and sensitive. If it is the case with one hand, it will be the same with the other. Among other things, this reaction makes it difficult to develop a stable laterality (dominant side of the body), which is a prerequisite for writing.

Exercise Videos

A set of videos are available that demonstrate exercises to inhibit the primitive reflexes associated with dyslexia and dysgraphia. Use the following QR codes to go directly to the relevant video packages, or visit https://drsarlos.com/videos for more information.

Scan for video!

Scan for video!

Exercises for dyslexia and dysgraphia

1

Starting position: Kneel on all fours, with arms extended and palms on the floor, shoulder-width apart. Keep the thighs in a vertical position.

1. Bend the arms, lowering the chin to the floor between the two hands.
2. Extend arms to return to the starting position.
3. Move the hips back so the bottom is sitting on the heels and the head is between the two shoulders. Keep the arms extended and the palms on the ground.
4. Rise back to the starting position.

Number of repetitions:

3–5 years: 4–6x
5–10 years: 6–8x
10–16 years: 8–10x
16+: 12–16x

2

ATNR

Starting position: Kneel on all fours, with arms extended and palms on the floor, a shoulder-width apart. Keep the thighs in a vertical position.
1. Turn the head to the left so that the left ear is aligned with the spine.
Important: Keep the arms extended and the palms on the ground.
2. Bend both elbows simultaneously, lower both shoulders, and place the right ear on the ground.
3. Extend both arms to return to the starting position.
The exercises must also be performed for the stated number of repetitions on the opposite side.

Number of repetitions:
3–5 years: 4–6x
5–10 years: 6–10x
10–16 years: 8–12x
16+: 12–16x

Repeat on each side.

As young children often cannot achieve the starting position due to the triggering of the ATNR reflex, parental assistance may be required for this exercise. In this case, the helper should stand over the child in a straddle position, turning the child's head in the desired direction.

It is almost certain that the arm on the opposite side will bend when the child's head is turned, e.g., if the child looks to the left then the right arm will bend. In this case, gently move the elbow joint to straighten the arm. Additionally, ensure that the hand on the side to which the head moves is fully extended on the ground, not resting on its fingers.

The arm flexion should be initiated from this position, with both elbows bending simultaneously. Assist this by slightly pulling both the child's elbows outward at the same time. This pull will need to be stronger in the direction the child's head is facing, as that arm tends to straighten due to the reflex. (In step 2 of the image above, the left elbow should be pulled more strongly as the head turns left.)

Patience is essential from the parent or helper, as it is difficult for the child to assume and maintain this position. However, when done correctly, this is one of the most effective exercises to help break down the ATNR.

3

ATNR

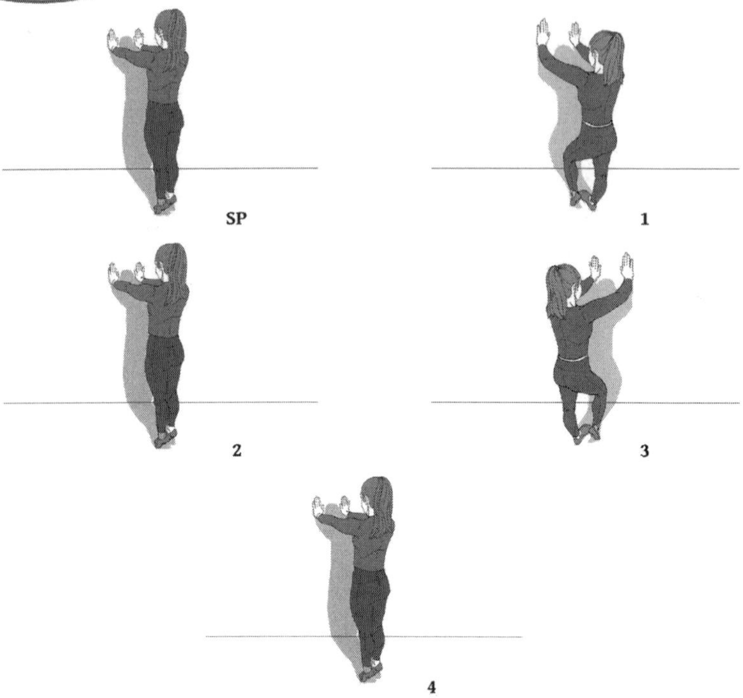

Starting position: Stand on tiptoe facing the wall, arms extended at shoulder height, with palms resting on the wall, fingers pointing up.

1. Lower the right heel to the ground and in the same movement bend both the left knee and left elbow. Keep looking forward, palms against the wall.
2. Return to the starting position, straightening the left knee and elbow, and move the right foot back to tiptoe.
3. Now the other side. Lower the left heel to the ground and in the same movement bend both the right knee and right elbow. Keep looking forward, palms against the wall.
4. Again return to the starting position, straightening the right knee and elbow, and move the left foot back to tiptoe.

Number of repetitions:

3–5 years: 10x, alternating sides
5–10 years: 20x, alternating sides
10–16 years: 20–30x, alternating sides
16+: 30x, alternating sides

4

ATNR TLRB

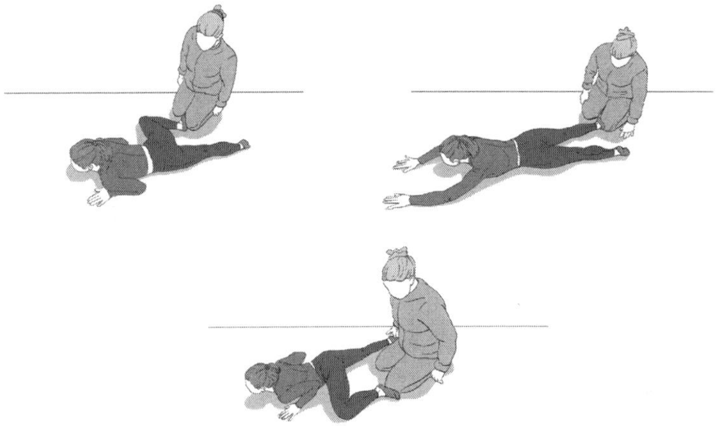

Crawl forward on the floor, keeping the stomach on the ground. After 4–5 crawling movements, stand up, turn around, and open the legs. From this position, tumble "head over heels" and return to the starting position. This can be done on a soft surface, e.g., a carpet or a yoga mat.

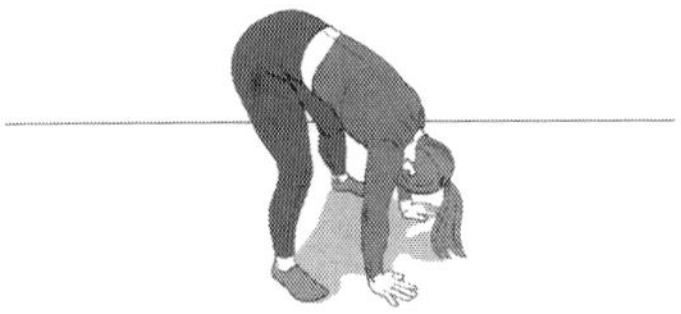

When crawling, pay attention to the following:

- Keep the head off the ground, looking forward. The head should not turn left and right.
- Use both arms and legs when crawling
- Until the bent leg is extended, do not bend the other leg
- Don't lift the hips—keep them on the ground
- Arms should be used to crawl, but don't give advice to use them. It is important to let the crawling movement develop!
- If necessary, help in the way shown in the diagram. With one hand, support the pushing leg, and if the other leg bends, use the other hand to help keep it extended.

When tumbling head over heels, the following points should be observed:

- Start the movement from a straddle position (legs apart)
- Tuck the head in—don't put weight on the top of the head!
- If assistance is given, tilt the head towards the chest with one hand, and with the other hand, support the child's buttocks and thighs, and roll them forward. It's good if the child "rolls like a ball" and doesn't "drop like a log."

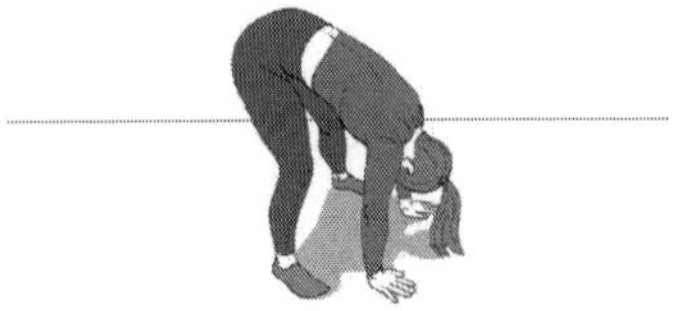

Number of repetitions:

3–5 years: 6x the full sequence of crawling and head over heels
5–10 years: 8–10x the full sequence
10–16 years: 10x the full sequence
16+: 15x: 10x the full sequence

5

TLRF

SP

1

2

Starting position: Lie on the back, with legs bent and feet on the ground. Extend arms, parallel to thighs.

1. Tilt the head forward so that the arms remain extended. The shoulders should not be pulled up into the neck. Maintain this position for the required number of seconds.
2. Lower the head to the ground. If necessary, the arms may be put down on the ground.

Number of repetitions:

3–5 years: 3 x 3, holding the head up for 2–3 seconds (with help if necessary)
5–10 years: 3 x 4–8, holding the head up for 3–6 seconds (with help if necessary)
10–16 years: 3 x 6–8, holding the head up for 5–6 seconds
16+: 3 x 8, holding the head up for 6 seconds

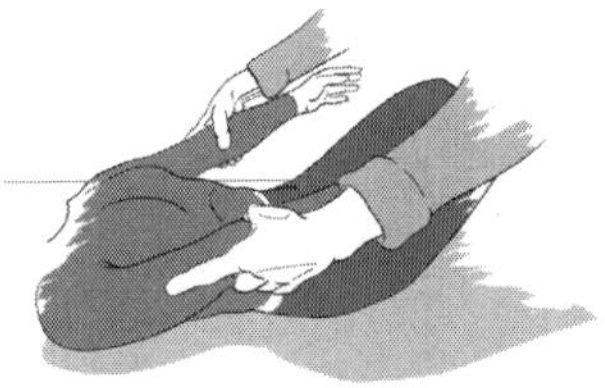

It very often happens that when lifting the head in the above exercise, the arm bends, and the child (and, in many cases, adults too) pulls their shoulder up to the neck.

In these cases, help in the following way.

Sitting at the child's feet, grasp the elbow joint and press down on the elbow with the index finger, preventing the elbow from bending and the shoulder from pulling up to the neck.

6

TLRF TLRB

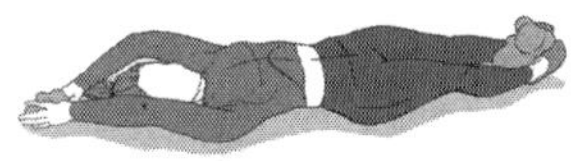

SP

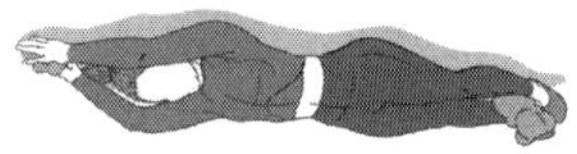

1

2

3

Starting position: Lie on the back, holding stuffed animals between both the ankles and the palms of the hands. Keep the legs straight. Extend the arms on the floor above the head.

Roll on the floor, holding on to the stuffed animals so that they do not fall out from between the ankles or the hands. Repeat the exercise back and forth.

Number of repetitions:

3–5 years: 4–5 turns in one direction, then backward 3x

5–10 years: 4–5 turns in one direction, then backward 4x

10–16 years: 4–5 turns in one direction, then backward 6x

16+: 4–5 turns in one direction, then backward 6x

7

ATNR

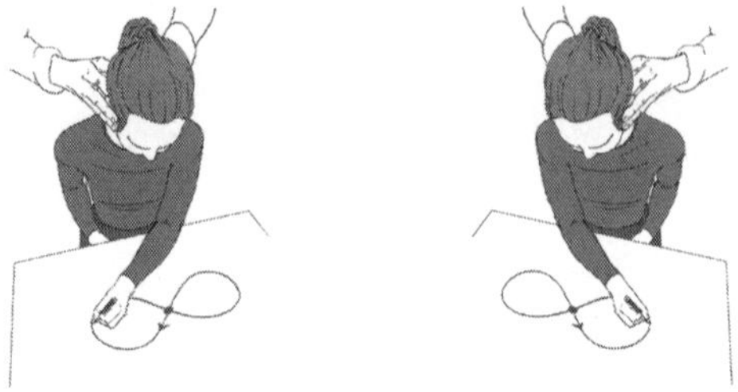

For this exercise, use a sheet of paper, at least ledger size (A3), and for an older child ideally larger. On the sheet, first draw an infinity symbol with a larger dot in the center.

Starting position: Sit at the table with the nose directed towards the dot. Move a pencil smoothly along the line with the eyes following the pencil, making sure that the head does **not** move right or left. Keep the nose directed at the point in the center of the infinity symbol.

Perform the task with **both** left and right hands.

For children aged 3–5, stick the paper to the wall so that the center of the infinity symbol is at the height of the child's nose. The child should use a crayon, not a pencil. If even this is difficult, hold the child's arm outstretched and run their finger along the line.

The parent can help both younger and older children keep their heads still. It is not necessary to hold their head, just gently push it back to the middle if it moves.

Number of repetitions:
3–5 years: 3–8 rotations with both hands
5–10 years: 8–10 rotations with both hands
10–16 years: 10–15 rotations with both hands
16+: 15–20 rotations with both hands

8

a)

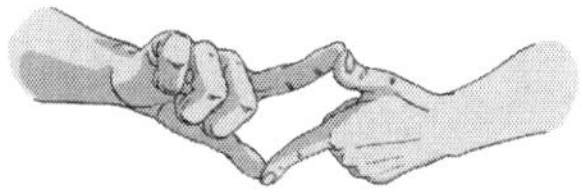

Starting position: Touch the thumb of the right hand to the index finger of the left hand, and the thumb of the left hand to the index finger of the right hand.

From this starting position, release the thumb of the left hand and the index finger of the right hand, and while keeping the other thumb and index finger together, rotate both hands so that they face the opposite direction, and again touch together the thumb of the left hand and the index finger of the right hand. Repeat this "stepping" motion.

When this exercise can be done without difficulty, do it with the other fingers instead of the index finger: thumbs and middle fingers; thumbs and ring fingers; thumbs and little fingers.

When you can do the task with all your fingers, then move to the "next level." Now, each finger touches the thumb only once as you progress from the index fingers to the little fingers and back. While doing this, you can say out loud which finger is touching the thumb.

Number of repetitions:
3–5 years: 4–5x forward and back
5–10 years: 6–8x forward and back
10–16 years: 8–10x forward and back
16+: 10x forward and back

b)

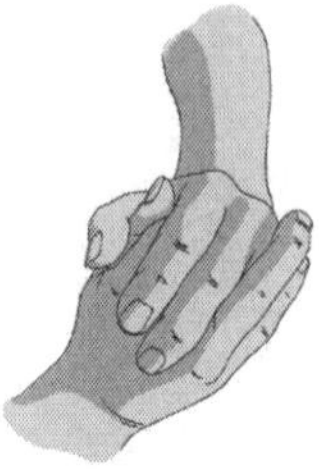

Starting position: The backs of the hands should face upwards (towards the ceiling). Put the thumb, index, and middle fingers of one hand on top, and the ring and little fingers of the other hand on top, as shown in the diagram.

Then continuously and smoothly alternate this position, so that whichever fingers are on top are moved underneath, and vice versa. Always keep the backs of the hands facing upward!

When this exercise can be done well, modify which fingers are on top. For example, start with the thumb of the left hand on top, the middle and index fingers of the right hand on top, and the ring and little fingers of the left hand on top.

The exercise should be done by people over 10 years old. Although younger children can try it too, for them I instead suggest the next exercise.

Number of repetitions:
10–16 years: 8–10x
16+: 10x

c)

This is an alternative to the previous exercise, for children under 10 years.

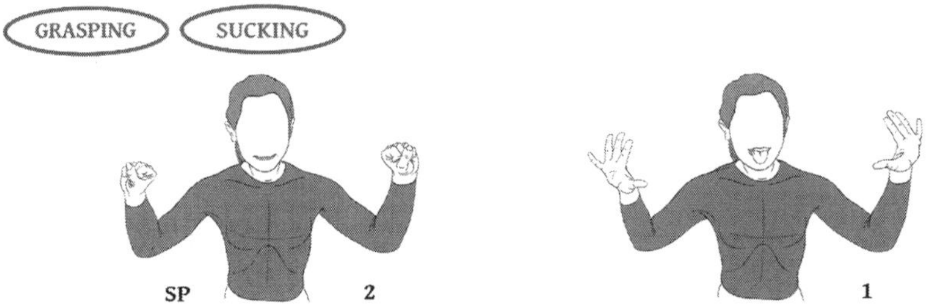

Starting position: Clench the fingers of both hands into fists, with the thumb resting on the outside of the other fingers.
1. While stretching the fingers and extending them backward, stick out the tongue as far as possible.
2. Close the fingers back into a fist, retract the tongue behind the teeth, and close the mouth.

Number of repetitions:
3–5 years: 3 x 6–10 both the above steps
5–10 years: 3 x 10 both the above steps

9

GRASPING SUCKING

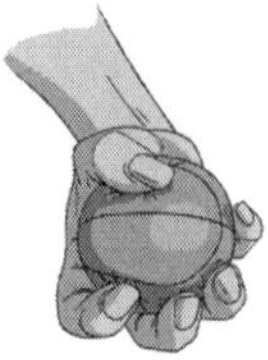

Starting position: Hold a sponge ball with the thumb facing the other four fingers.

Squeeze the ball for a second, then relax. Repeat.

Make sure to grip the ball with the last joints of each finger bent as shown. Some children find this difficult at first, either because the thumb keeps sliding back alongside the other fingers, or they cannot bend the last joint of the fingers. In this case, they need help to make the correct grip. Between the ages of three and five, they can hold their own forearm to help, as shown below.

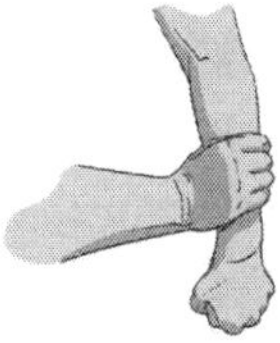

Number of repetitions:
3–5 years: 3 x 8–10 with both hands, alternating
5–10 years: 3–4 x 10 with both hands, alternating
10–16 years: 4 x 10 with both hands, alternating
16+: 4–5 x 10 with both hands, alternating

10

a)

SUCKING ROOTING

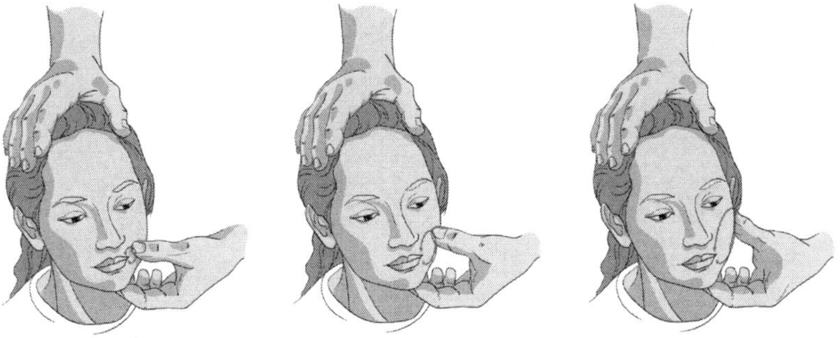

Massage the face around the mouth in three semi-circular arcs of increasing length. In each case, the massage starts between the mouth and the nose and ends in the area under the lower lip. Each line should be massaged 5–6 times, not pressing too hard. Adults and older children can do the massage themselves, but in this case, it is better to massage the face with a smooth pebble rather than use their own fingers.

Number of repetitions

3–5 years: five times each arc, on both sides of the face, 2x
5–10 years: five times each arc, on both sides of the face, 3x
10–16 years: six times each arc, on both sides of the face, 3–4x
16+: six times each arc, on both sides of the face, 4x

b)

GRASPING SUCKING

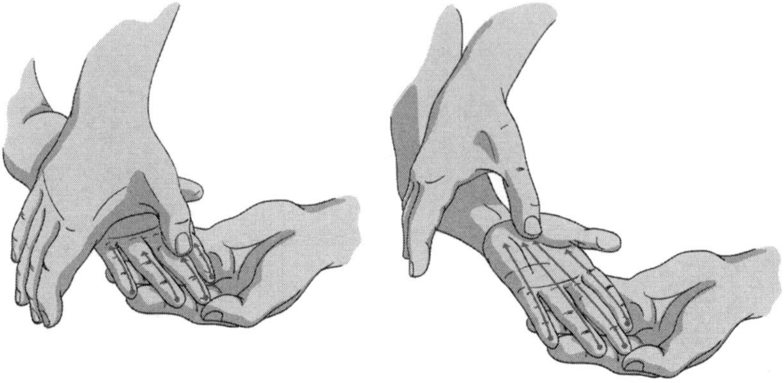

Massage the palm from the fingers towards the wrist. As with massaging the face, older children and adults can do the massage themselves, but they should use a smooth pebble rather than their own fingers.

Number of repetitions

3–5 years: 4–5 times per finger on both the left and right palm, 2x
5–10 years: five times per finger on both the left and right palm, 3x
10–16 years: six times per finger on both the left and right palm, 3–4x
16+: six times per finger on both the left and right palm, 4x

11

GRASPING SUCKING

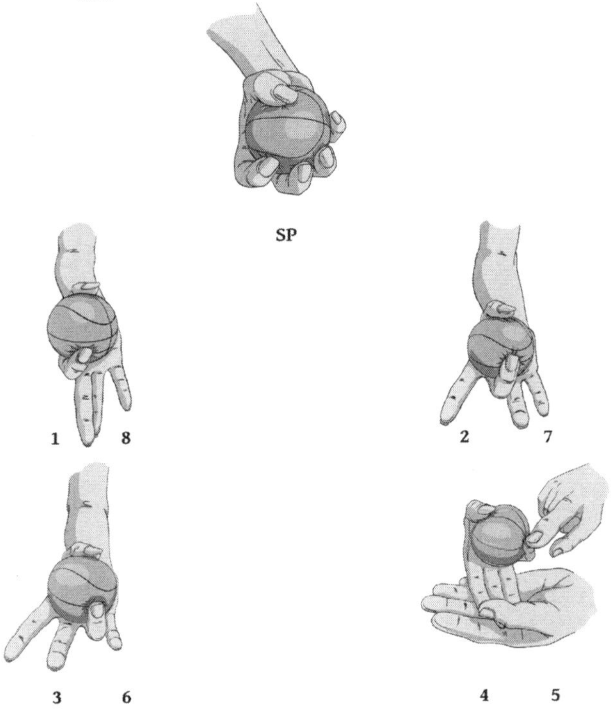

Starting position: Hold a sponge ball in the palm, with the thumb and index finger bent and facing each other, resting on the ball.

1. Grip the ball with the thumb and index finger.
2. Grip the ball with the thumb and middle finger.
3. Grip the ball with the thumb and ring finger.
4. Grip the ball with the thumb and little finger.

5–8. Repeat the previous steps in reverse order, beginning with the little finger and ending with the index finger.

This exercise should be performed with both the right and left hands.

In young children—and sometimes older persons, too—it happens that all the fingers bend in, not just the one that should be active. In this case, another person can help, as in the image above showing the little finger and thumb gripping the ball.

Number of repetitions:
3–5 years: two sequences, back and forth, with both hands
5–10 years: three sequences, back and forth, with both hands
10–16 years: four sequences, back and forth, with both hands
16+: five sequences, back and forth, with both hands

12

MORO

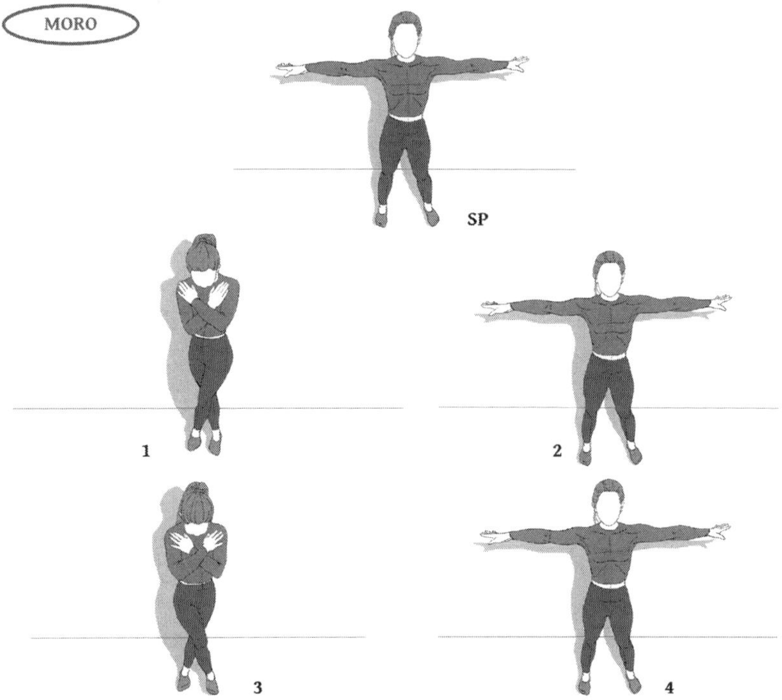

Starting position: Stand with back against the wall, legs apart, arms outstretched to the side.

1. Keeping the right foot in place, cross the left foot in front of the right foot, and at the same time cross the arms. The *left* foot and *left* forearm must be in front, i.e., further from the body.
2. Move the left foot back to the starting position, stretching out the arms.
3. Now, keeping the left foot in place, cross the right foot in front of the left foot, and at the same time cross the arms. This time the *right* foot and *right* forearm must be in front, i.e., further from the body.
4. Move the right foot back to the starting position, stretching out the arms.

Number of repetitions:

3–5 years: 10x
5–10 years: 20x
10–16 years: 30x
16+: 40x

Exercises to "wake up" the left hemisphere

The following sensory stimulation exercises are best done in the evening. If the child or adult is hypersensitive to light or to music (the latter is less common), omit the corresponding exercises.

Exercises should be done daily for 2–3 months. They should reduce symptoms associated with left hemisphere hypofunction. If an improvement in the symptoms is observed, it is possible to perform the exercises only every second day and continue in this way for a further 2–3 months.

The results of these sensory stimulation exercises vary from person to person. The most common benefits include improved speech understanding, speech formation, development in reading, writing, and some mathematical skills. These exercises lead to more improvement when combined with reflex integration exercises.

If symptoms recur after these exercises are stopped, the symptoms may be less severe, but it is recommended to recommence the exercises.

1.

The child should lie on their back, gazing upwards. From the right side, shine a flashlight towards the right side of their face for one second at a distance of 20 cm (8 inches), then turn the flashlight away from the head for a second. Then repeat.

Number of repetitions:
3–5 years: 6–8x
5–10 years: 8x
10–16 years: 10x
16+: 12–16x

2.

The child should lie on their back, gazing upwards. They should listen to a metronome at 60 beats per minute with their right ear, i.e., position the speaker or phone on the right side of the head. Metronome apps can be easily downloaded.

Number of minutes for which to listen:
3–5 years: 1 minute
5–10 years: 1–2 minutes
10–16 years: 2 minutes
16+: 2–3 minutes

3.

The child should lie on their back. Lift the head slightly and turn it to the right, then back to the center. Repeat.

Adults should assist children with this exercise.

Number of repetitions:
3–5 years: 6–8x
5–10 years: 8–10x
10–16 years: 10–16x
16+: 10–16x

4.

The child should lie on their back. Using the right hand only, clench the fingers into a fist, or squeeze a small ball for 1–2 seconds. Then release, and repeat.

Number of repetitions:
3–5 years: 6–8x
5–10 years: 8–10x
10–16 years: 10–12x
16+: 16–20x

5.

The child should lie on their stomach. Stroke or massage the right side of the body (e.g., the back, the leg). Although this exercise ideally requires another person to perform the task, adults can massage their own feet and hips using an aid such as a small smooth stone, a massage roller, or a massage tool.

Number of repetitions:
3–5 years: 20x
5–10 years: 20–30x
10–16 years: 30x
16+: 30x

Vestibular stimulation

Spin counterclockwise, either in a standing position or in a swivel chair. Keep the eyes open and face forwards.

Children and adults with dysgraphia and dyslexia do not usually feel dizzy while spinning and do not feel symptoms such as nausea or "stomach upset." This is the case 80% of the time. In such cases the movement is safe—just take care not to fall or tip the chair over.

For the other 20% of people, who may become unwell from spinning, skip the exercise altogether or do it very slowly and do it less, e.g., about two-thirds the number of repetitions.

In either case, allow a half- or one-minute break between spins.

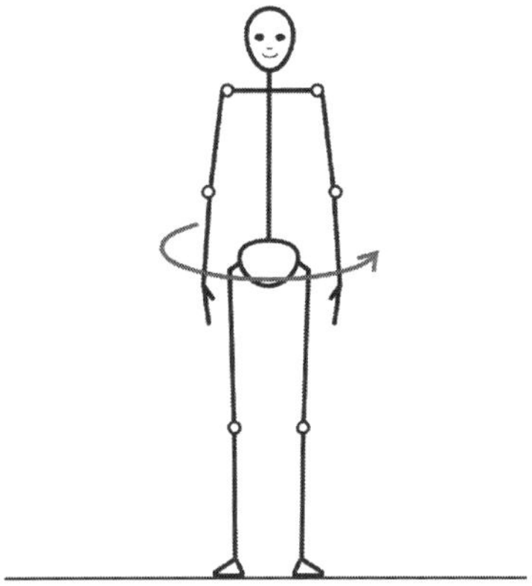

Number of repetitions:
3–5 years: 2–3 x 8
5–10 years: 2–3 x 10
10–16 years: 3 x 10–15
16+: 3x 10–15

In addition to spinning, all games and forms of movement are recommended that involve changes to the spatial position of the head. This includes playground games, dance, certain martial arts, gymnastics, ice skating, and skiing.

CLUMSINESS

When a young child doesn't talk, still wets the bed at the age of six, is unable to sustain attention for long periods, or seems to have little contact with the outside world, parents or teachers who know the child usually turn to a specialist for help.

However, the situation is quite different when the child "only" smears their food all over their face at every meal, trips when walking, has difficulty using scissors, or cannot tie their shoes properly or unbutton their shirt. In cases like these, it is rare for anyone to seek professional help. What would parents say? *"Doctor, my child keeps tripping over himself."* The answer, with few exceptions, would be *"Come on, they'll grow out of it."*

Although in rare cases there may be spontaneous improvement, it is much more common that the "clumsy" movements accumulate and the number of issues increases. The child will have difficulty learning basic sports techniques, will fail to learn a musical instrument, will be first to be "out" when playing dodgeball at school, or the one who is laughed at in dance class.

Parents and professionals should take more seriously these "minor" motor difficulties suffered by children. A survey in the USA found that around 6% of school-age children have coordination problems that hinder their academic performance and integration into communities.

Most of these problems can be detected as early as the end of preschool or early school years when performing simple motor tasks such as running, buttoning a cardigan, or using scissors. There is growing evidence that these problems will not be solved in time without proper training. Rather than improving during childhood, they persist into adulthood. In fact, due to body growth and hormonal changes during adolescence, the original motor coordination problems become even more severe. The clumsier a child is, the more vulnerable they are to ridicule and the less likely they are to experience success compared with peers who do not have to deal with such problems. In their teenage years, these children will have higher rates of learning difficulties, adjustment issues, and behavioral and emotional problems. In addition, poor motor coordination is often associated with disorders such as attention-deficit and hyperactivity, various learning disabilities, and poor handwriting, drawing skills, and emotional immaturity.

In some countries, a standardized test is used by pediatricians to screen for "clumsiness," and the results are used to refer the child to appropriate therapy. Unfortunately, this does not yet exist in all countries. With appropriate intervention many more children could experience success in sports, music, learning, and life.

There is a term for this condition—clumsy child syndrome—coined by Professor Sasson Gubbay in 1972. Into this category, he classified those normal or highly intelligent children who had no identifiable medical or neurological disorder but who had poor coordination skills affecting their academic performance and/or their ability to socialize.

More recently, the term clumsy child syndrome has been replaced by developmental coordination disorder (DCD); in the research literature, the two terms are used interchangeably.

Frequency of occurrence of the problem

Data show that 6–7% of the population is affected by "clumsiness." The problem is more common in boys than in girls. It is unrelated to the educational attainment or socio-economic status of the child's family. Affected children are usually diagnosed between the ages of six and 12, and occasionally before the age of five.

What might be behind clumsiness?

The problem is complex, and although the exact causes are unknown, many theories have been put forward to explain its roots. Researchers who have studied motor control difficulties in clumsy children have hypothesized that motor execution is one of the main problems. Other researchers have suggested that such children have deficits in proprioception, sensory integration, and visual processing, which causes them to become clumsy.

The greater the number of other problems co-occurring with clumsiness—learning disability, behavioral problems, psychosomatic pains, illnesses—the less likely it is that "spontaneous recovery" can be expected; therefore, intervention is needed to ensure the child's continued development and well-being.

It is very important that the parent takes it seriously if they feel something is wrong with their child. Parents are very rarely wrong when it comes to the development and maturation of their children. A young child's clumsiness or motor delay should not be ignored to the point that it prevents them from learning to ride a bike, go swimming, or throw and catch a ball. If this happens, then sooner or later others don't want to play with the child because they see them as clumsy, and they slowly become isolated from their peers. Weakness in fine motor skills affects the child's ability to dress, manipulate objects with their hands and fingers, and do schoolwork.

Unfortunately, more and more school-age children struggle to master motor skills that their peers already have. This is why parents need to listen to their children, and if their instincts tell them that "something is not right," don't listen to those who say, "they will grow out of it." Start to address the problem as early as possible; the results will soon begin to show.

The table below shows various development milestones by age. If your child differs significantly from these, e.g., if they are 6–12 months behind, or even more, it is advisable to consult a professional and/or do the exercises in this book.

4 years	• Can button and unbutton their cardigan or coat
4½ years	• Can dress and undress independently (except for tying shoelaces) • Can ride a bicycle with training wheels • Can cut a sheet of paper in two with scissors • Can stay inside the lines when coloring
5 years	• Can draw a square • Can stand on one foot (both right and left) for 15 seconds
5½ years	• Can tie their shoelaces • Can write at least their first name in block capitals • Can repeatedly jump forward on both feet at the same time • Can smoothly and continuously touch their thumbs to their other fingers one after another to form a circular shape • Can correctly hold a pencil or spoon

6 years	• Can cycle without training wheels • Can eat with a knife and fork
7 years	• Can draw the diagonal of a square or rectangle
8 years	• Can tell which finger has been touched with their eyes closed • Can hop in place on alternate legs
9 years	• Can tap the table with their fingers one after another, from thumb to little finger and back, at a relatively fast pace • Can draw a cross with lines of equal length
10 years	• Can stand with eyes closed on an imaginary line for 10 seconds with one foot in front of the other, the toes of the rear foot touching the heel of the front foot

Source: Virginia Commonwealth University School of Medicine

The most common reflexes related to clumsiness are the STNR, the ATNR, the forward TLR, the Galant reflex, and the Moro reflex.

Exercise Videos

A set of videos are available that demonstrate exercises to inhibit the primitive reflexes associated with clumsiness. Use the following QR code to go directly to the video package, or visit https://drsarlos.com/videos for more information.

Scan for video!

Exercises for clumsiness

1

TLRB STNR ATNR GALANT

In each "round," first tumble forward head over heels, and then return to the starting position in one of four ways. In the first round bunny hop back to the start, in the second round spider walk, in the third crab crawl, and in the fourth bear crawl. These movements are described in more detail below.

1) Out: Tumble forward head over heels

When tumbling head over heels, the following points should be observed:

Start the movement from a straddle position (legs apart)

Tuck the head in—don't put weight on the top of the head!

If assistance is given, tilt the head towards the chest with one hand, and with the other hand, support the child's buttocks and thighs, and roll them forward. It's good if the child "rolls like a ball" and doesn't "drop like a log."

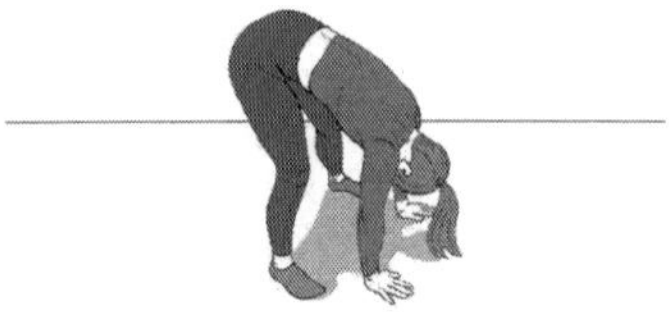

2) Back:

Round I: Bunny hop

Round II: Spider walk

Round III: Crab crawl

Round IV: Bear crawl

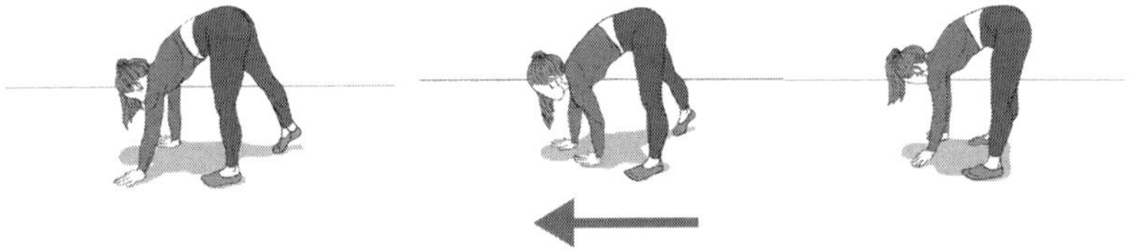

Number of repetitions:

3–5 years: 1x the full sequence of out and back in each of the four ways
5–10 years: 1–2x the full sequence
10–16 years: 2x the full sequence
16+: 15x: 3x the full sequence

2

STNR

Starting position: Kneel on all fours, with arms extended and palms on the floor, shoulder-width apart. Keep the thighs in a vertical position.

1. Bend the arms, lowering the chin to the floor between the two hands.
2. Extend the arms to return to the starting position.
3. Move the hip back so the bottom is sitting on the heels and the head is between the two shoulders. Keep the arms extended and the palms on the ground.
4. Rise back to the starting position.

Number of repetitions:

3–5 years: 4–5x
5–10 years: 5–6x
10–16 years: 6–8x
16+: 10x

3

ATNR

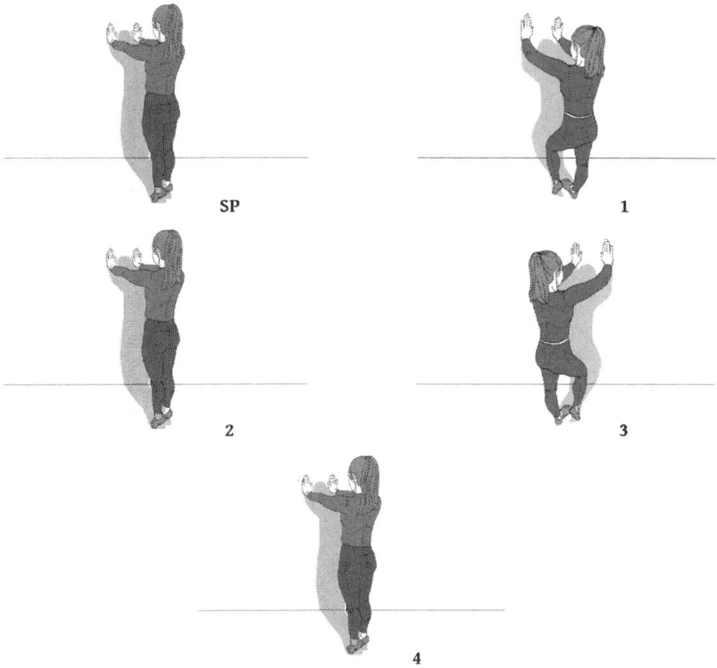

Starting position: Stand on tiptoe facing the wall, arms extended at shoulder height, with palms resting on the wall, fingers pointing up.
1. Lower the right heel to the ground and in the same movement bend both the left knee and left elbow. Keep looking forward, palms against the wall.
2. Return to the starting position, straightening the left knee and elbow, and move the right foot back to tiptoe.
3. Now the other side. Lower the left heel to the ground and in the same movement bend both the right knee and right elbow. Keep looking forward, palms against the wall.
4. Again return to the starting position, straightening the right knee and elbow, and move the left foot back to tiptoe.

Number of repetitions:
3–5 years: 10x, alternating sides
5–10 years: 20x, alternating sides
10–16 years: 20–30x, alternating sides
16+: 30x, alternating sides

4

ATNR

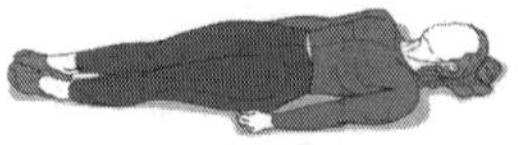

SP

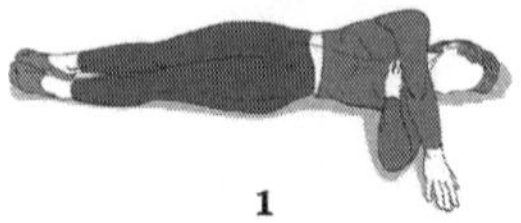

1

2

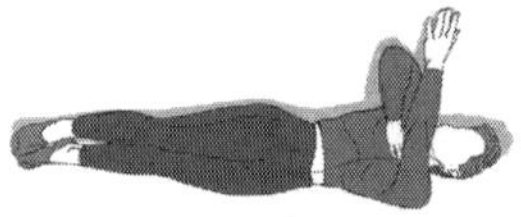

3

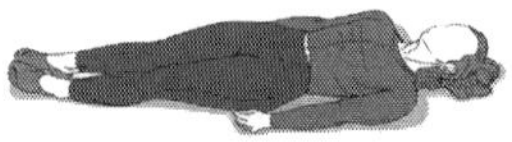

4

Starting position: Lie on the back, gazing upwards.

1. After deep inhalation and exhalation, turn the head and torso to the left. At the same time, bend the left arm by placing the left palm on the chest. Swing the right arm towards the left elbow so that both arms move simultaneously and turn the head and torso. From the navel down, do not move the lower part of the body.

2. Return to the starting position. Rest the arms on the ground beside the body and gaze upwards.

3. Repeat the first movement to the other side.

4. Return to the starting position. Again, rest the arms on the ground beside the body and gaze upwards.

Perform the exercise alternately: to the left, back to the middle, to the right, and again back to the middle.

Number of repetitions:
3–5 years: 6x per side
5–10 years: 10x per side
10–16 years: 12x per side
16+: 15x per side

If it is challenging to do this exercise at first, provide or obtain assistance.

Alternatively, younger children can do the exercises as shown below. Simply modify the exercise to turn the head in the direction of the arms.

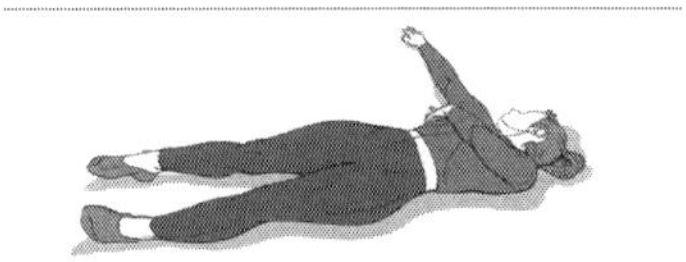

5

ATNR

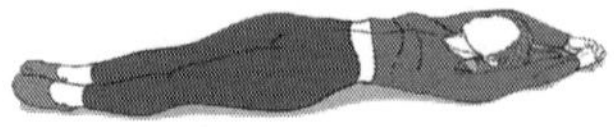

SP

1

2

Starting position: Lie on the back (supine position), with arms on the floor, extended above the head as far as possible, elbows outstretched, and interlocked hands.

1. This exercise is effectively rolling on the floor, with the caveat that crossing the legs should initiate the movement, and the torso and arms follow. So, if lying on the back and rolling to the left, first cross the right leg over the left. Do the opposite if rolling to the right.

2. Then roll over so that the stomach is now on the floor (prone position). Take care during the turn that the legs again become open and parallel.

Continue rolling in the same direction, next from prone to supine. Again, the movement starts with the legs crossed, followed by the body and arms. So, if now lying on the front and rolling to the left, first cross the left leg over the right.

Roll as far as possible in the space available.

If the room is not large enough, roll back and forth several times until reaching the number of turns listed in the table below.

Number of repetitions:
3–5 years: 4–5 turns in one direction, then backward 3x
5–10 years: 4–5 turns in one direction, then backward 4x
10–16 years: 4–5 turns in one direction, then backward 6x
16+: 4–5 turns in one direction, then backward 6x

6

TLRF

Rock back and forth in the shown position. Arms should be extended, holding the lower legs. The shoulders should not be pulled up into the neck.

Number of repetitions:
3–5 years: 3 x 6 (with help if necessary)
5–10 years: 3 x 8 (with help if necessary)
10–16 years: 3 x 10
16+: 3 x 12

If necessary, help in the following way.

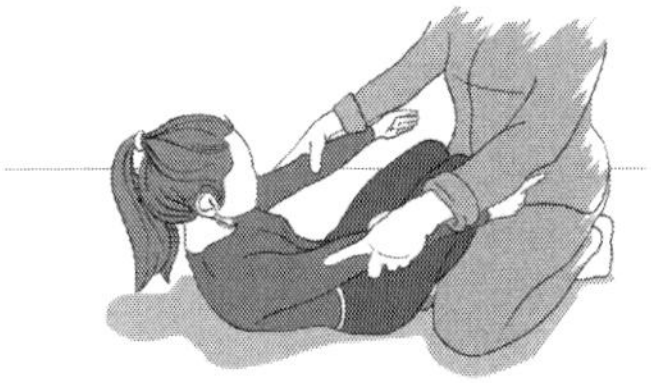

Sitting at the child's feet, grasp the elbow joint and press down on the elbow with the index finger, preventing the elbow from bending and the shoulder from pulling up to the neck.

7

TLRF

SP

1

2

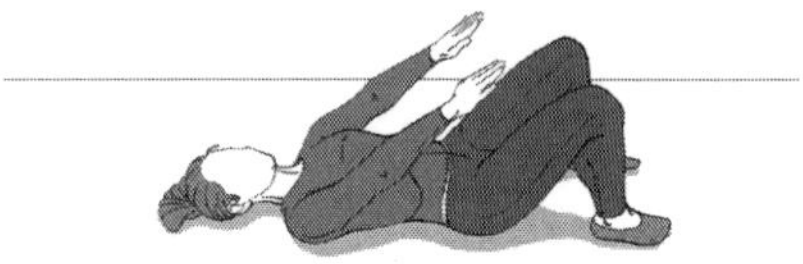

3

Starting position: Lie on the back, with legs bent and feet on the ground. Extend arms, parallel to thighs.

1. Tilt the head forward so that the arms remain extended. The shoulders should not be pulled up into the neck. Maintain this position for the required number of seconds.
2. Raise the shoulders and back slightly off the ground. Keep the arms extended. The shoulders should not be pulled up into the neck. Maintain this position for the required number of seconds.
3. Lower the head to the ground. If necessary, the arms may be put down on the ground.

Number of repetitions:

3–5 years: 3x, hold in each position for 2 seconds (with help if necessary)
5–10 years: 3–5x, hold in each position for 3 seconds (with help if necessary)
10–16 years: 6–8x, hold in each position for 4–5 seconds
16+: 8x, hold in each position for 6 seconds

The assistance is the same as in exercise 6.

8

MORO

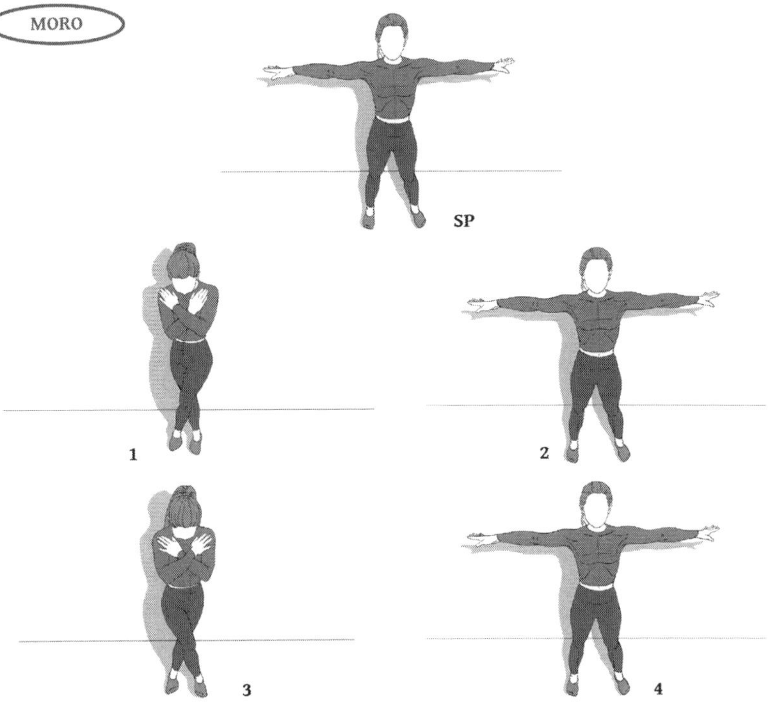

Starting position: Stand with back against the wall, legs apart, arms outstretched to the side.

1. Keeping the right foot in place, cross the left foot in front of the right foot, and at the same time cross the arms. The *left* foot and *left* forearm must be in front, i.e., further from the body.
2. Move the left foot back to the starting position, stretching out the arms.
3. Now, keeping the left foot in place, cross the right foot in front of the left foot, and at the same time cross the arms. This time the *right* foot and *right* forearm must be in front, i.e., further from the body.
4. Move the right foot back to the starting position, stretching out the arms.

Number of repetitions:

3–5 years: 10x
5–10 years: 20x
10–16 years: 30x
16+: 40x

9

MORO

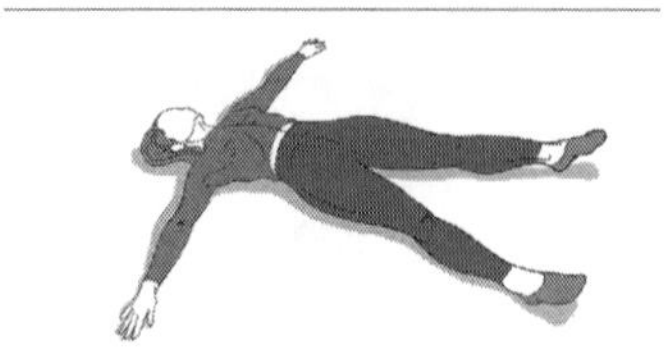

SP

1

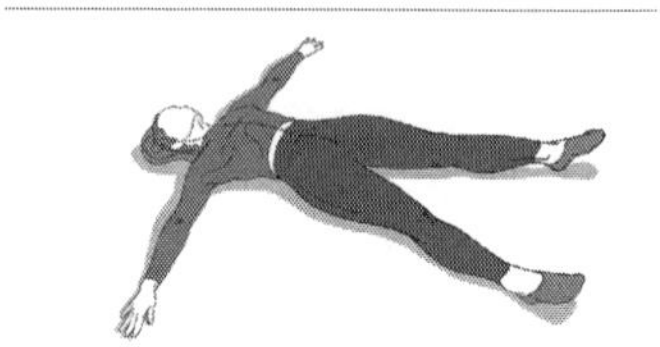

2

3

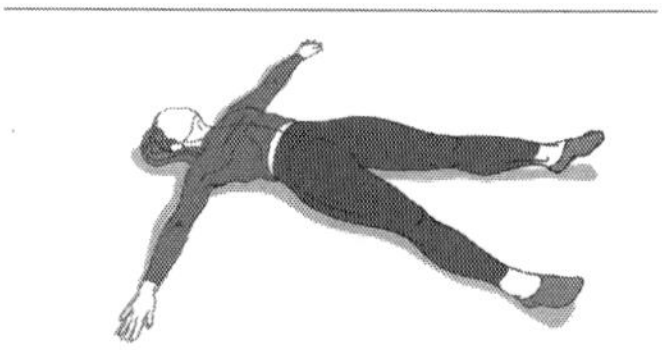

4

Starting position: Lie on the back, arms stretched out to the side, legs open on the floor.

1. Turn onto the left side into the "fetal position" with forearms and legs crossed. When turning left, move the right forearm over the left, and the right lower leg over the left.
2. Return to the starting position.
3. Turn onto the right side into the "fetal position" with forearms and legs crossed. When turning right, move the left forearm over the right, and the left lower leg over the right.
4. Return to the starting position.

Number of repetitions:

3–5 years: 12x (6x to the left, 6x to the right, alternating)
5–10 years: 16x (8x to the left, 8x to the right, alternating)
10–16 years: 20x (10x to the left, 10x to the right, alternating)
16+: 30x (15x to the left, 15x to the right, alternating)

10

MORO

Starting position: Lie on the back, arms outstretched to the side, legs spread apart.

1. Sit up into a bent position, head tucked in, legs crossed, and arms crossed with hands lightly gripping the shoulders. The *right* foot and *right* forearm must be forward, i.e., further from the body.
2. Return to starting position.
3. Again sit up into a bent position, head tucked in, with legs crossed and arms crossed with hands lightly gripping the shoulders. This time the *left* foot and *left* forearm must be forward, i.e., further from the body.
4. Return to starting position.

If it is very difficult to sit up, support the upper body with bean bags or pillows.

Number of repetitions:

3–5 years: 8x

5–10 years: 16–20x

10–16 years: 20–24x

16+: 20–24x

11

TLRF

SP

1

2

3

Starting position: Sit cross-legged, palms on the floor, arms outstretched. Rotate the head, don't raise the shoulders, keep arms fully extended and palms on the ground.

Number of repetitions:
3–5 years: two to the left and two to the right; repeat 3x (with help if necessary)
5–10 years: 4 x left and 4 x right; repeat 4x (with help if necessary)
10–16 years: 4 x left and 4 x right; repeat 5x
16+: 4 x left and 4 x right; repeat 6x

12

TLRF TLRB

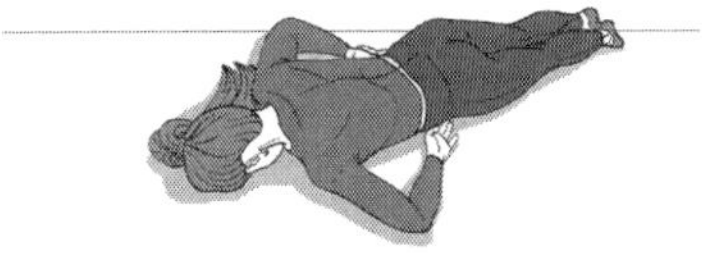

SP

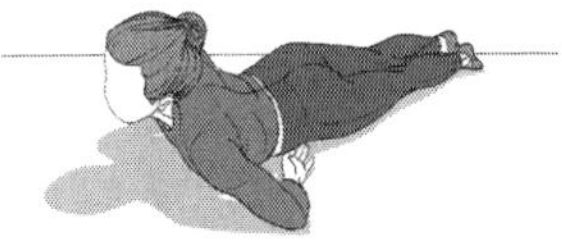

1

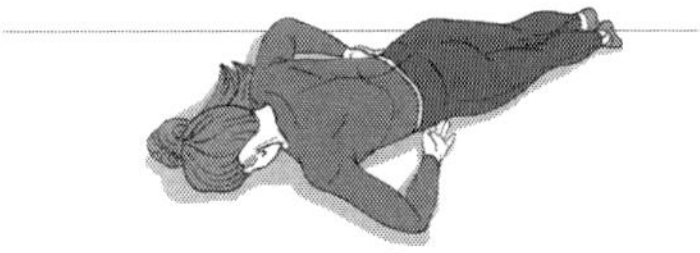

2

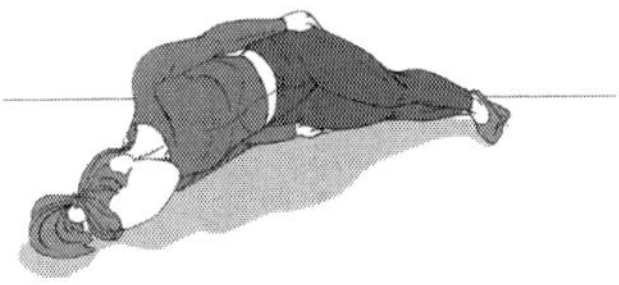

3

4

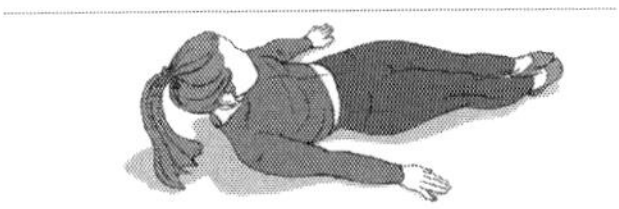

5

6

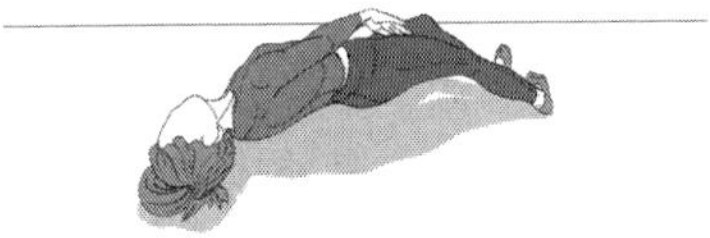

7

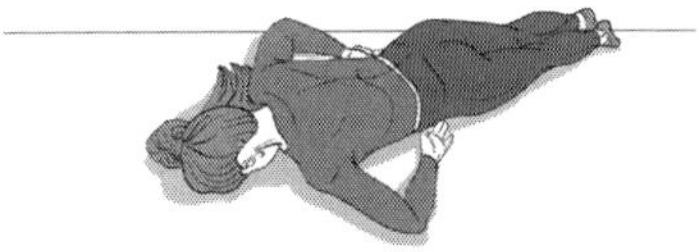

8

Starting position: Lie on the front, forehead on the floor, arms next to the body with elbows bent.

1. Lift the torso, keeping the arms bent.
2. Lower the torso back to the starting position.

3–4. Stretch the arms out straight and roll over onto the back.

5. Raise the head, keeping the arms extended.
6. Lower the head back to the ground.

7–8. Now roll back onto the front, and bend the arms to return to the original starting position.

Number of repetitions:
3–5 years: 4x the full sequence
5–10 years: 6x the full sequence
10–16 years: 8x the full sequence
16+: 10x the full sequence

ANXIETY, EXCITEMENT, SLEEPLESS NIGHTS

Childhood anxiety is, unfortunately, not an uncommon phenomenon. Signs of a child's seemingly unwarranted anxiety can even be detected shortly after birth. Reacting to a new stimulus is a natural phenomenon, but a calm equilibrium should be restored once the stimulus has passed.

When an infant suddenly freezes, holds its breath, and does not move in response to noise or light, it means that a reflex has been activated that should have been "merged" before birth into the Moro reflex. During a baby's development, the reflex that precedes the Moro reflex is the fear paralysis reflex (FPR), which can also be called the freezing reflex.

In the animal kingdom, fright and threatening situations can trigger three different states. One is freezing, i.e., the animal pretends to be dead. This is an attempt to "fool" the threat, usually the predator attacking it. The other two options are to flee from the danger or to confront it. In the latter two cases, the body's energy reserves are mobilized, and the animal either runs away or fights back.

The three reactions serve the same purpose but trigger completely different mechanisms in the body. All three reflexes are linked to the autonomic nervous system. The freezing reflex produces parasympathetic effects, i.e., a significant decrease in respiration rate and blood flow from the skeletal muscles to the internal organs. Heart function and blood pressure reduce, causing a lower blood supply to the brain. Also, the mouth often salivates. While in the womb, this is a normal phenomenon. When the mother is under stress or exposed to a strong external stimulus, such as a loud noise, the fetus reacts by freezing because it wants to remain "invisible." But this reflex has no place in the baby's life after birth! Some research has attributed "cot death," which is caused by the baby's respiratory and circulatory systems stopping, to the freezing reflex. Fortunately, this horrific event is rare, and many baby monitoring devices are now available to parents to help prevent the tragedy.

The freezing reflex can also cause many problems later in life. The most common of these are:

- Low tolerance to stress
- Anxiety that appears to be unrelated to reality
- Hypersensitivity to touch, sound, specific frequencies of sound, and visual stimuli
- Dislikes change and surprise
- Hard to adapt to new situations and people
- Fatigue
- Selective mutism—unwillingness to talk in certain situations
- Holds their breath or often feels "short of breath"
- Fear of social interactions, especially in situations perceived as uncomfortable
- Does not feel safe
- Lack of confidence
- Social isolation
- Overly attached to certain people or, conversely, unable to accept or show affection easily
- Avoids nursery, school, and communities
- Compulsive behavior
- Pessimistic, negative attitude
- Difficulty trying new activities, or never tries
- Avoids situations where it is necessary to compete against others
- Frequent depression
- Tantrums
- Likes to control others
- Resistant behavior, especially in the home environment
- "Paralyzed" by stress—cannot think and move simultaneously
- Hypotonic muscles in many cases
- Nutritional disorders
- Constant need for attention
- Aggressive behavior due to frustration and confusion
- Poor sense of balance.

Another reflex also has a connection with freezing, the inability to act. In English literature, it is referred to as the core tonic guard reflex (CTGR).

The CTGR is an involuntary reaction in response to a sudden threat, surprise event, or significant stress. Although it appears in infancy, it is not classified as a primitive or postural reflex. It is nothing more than a generalized muscular response to stress. During the activation of the CTGR, the muscle response starts at the toes and extends throughout the body. The muscle contractions extend from the big toes through the sole of the foot to the Achilles tendon, then up the back of the legs to the hamstrings, through the lower back to the neck, and into the back of the head. The tension in the tendons and muscles causes a change in posture.

CTGR is a normal response to nerve-muscle function. When activated, it causes the person to stop. We hold our breath and become still, paying increased attention to what we see and hear. We scan our surroundings, motionless, looking for the source of danger. If there is a real danger, we act accordingly. But if there is no real danger or if the danger has passed, our muscles and tendons relax, and stress hormone levels return to normal. In an infant, it is during the change between the two states (calm and agitated) that the nervous system and the muscular system develop their cooperation. CTGR not only supports motor development but also contributes to cognitive development.

What if the frozen state is not followed by relaxation and calm? What if the reflex is locked in a continuously activated "mode"? In this case, the neuro-hormonal system linkage causes hormones to be released into the bloodstream that reinforce the "emergency." The activity of the CTGR causes the calf muscles to contract and the person to rise on tiptoe. The person leans forward slightly, and the rest of the body adjusts to the new position, trying to maintain equilibrium. The lower back and neck muscles contract, creating a homogenous posture. If the process described above does not resolve after the "emergency" has passed, the muscles of the leg, back, and neck remain in tension, leading to incapacity.

It has been observed that children with speech development delays and/or autistic symptoms frequently have the tendency to walk on tiptoe. If the CTGR is persistent and does not disappear after the perceived or real danger has passed, not only can the child be observed to tiptoe, but their torso, shoulder, and neck muscles also become tense. In this state, sensory perception is reduced, and the child can only pay attention to small details, and not perceive exactly what is happening around them.

Difficulties associated with a chronically active CTGR may include:

- Poor posture and balance
- Foot and leg cramps
- Back pain
- Poor motor coordination
- Difficulty walking and running
- Walking on tiptoe
- Delayed speech development and/or speech impairment
- Fear or anxiety, stress
- Gets excessively absorbed in a task
- May appear to "switch off" at times, not listen when spoken to
- Excessive shyness
- Hyperactivity
- Hypervigilance—frequent freezing-up when faced with a challenge or in competitive sports.

The third reflex, triggered by unexpected stimuli in the first six months of life, is the Moro reflex. This reflex was described in detail earlier in this book. It is important to note that the Moro reflex has the opposite effect of the FPR and CTGR. This is because the Moro reflex is associated with the sympathetic part of the autonomic nervous system causing alarm symptoms as a response. The heart starts beating faster, pumping more blood to the skeletal muscles to prepare the body for escape. The skeletal muscles need more oxygen, so the respiratory rate increases. The liver releases sugar, which is also important for increased muscle function. At the same time, the blood supply to the skin and internal organs decreases. The pupils dilate to allow more accurate and easier perception of visual stimuli. Saliva production is reduced, but the sweat glands work more intensively. This explains why our palms sweat when we get excited.

This reflex must be present in the first six months of life. After the baby is six months old, it gradually integrates and is replaced by the startle (Strauss) reflex. If the Moro reflex is not integrated at the right time and to the right extent, the slightest unexpected event (sometimes it is enough to imagine a "scary" situation) triggers the sympathetic reactions described above, generating permanent tension and anxiety. In addition, the following symptoms may occur due to an underdeveloped Moro reflex:

- Easily distracted attention
- Hypersensitivity to light, sound, or touch. (Hypersensitivity to touch includes the refusal to wear clothes of different materials and an aversion to combing one's hair.)
- Nausea or sickness in a car or moving vehicle
- Overreacting to certain situations
- Impulsive and aggressive
- Emotional immaturity, low empathy
- Excessively withdrawn or shy
- Disturbed sensory perception
- Difficulty forming relationships
- Depression
- Dyslexia
- Some allergic reactions, food intolerances, and certain types of asthma
- Unreasonable anger or emotional outbursts
- Poor sense of balance, weak coordination of movements, or poor ball handling skills.

The above symptoms are the most characteristic symptoms of a retained Moro reflex. Other problems may also occur. The symptoms may appear individually, but they may often appear together.

During the development of the individual, the FPR, CTGR, and Moro reflex are closely related and may be present together or separately. The symptoms can exist in a myriad of combinations.

If I had to identify the three most frequent symptoms of these immature reflexes, I would say that, based on the children I worked with, anxiety is the most common, hypersensitivity is the second, and insecurity is the third.

The exercises to integrate these reflexes are listed below.

Exercise Videos

A set of videos are available that demonstrate exercises to inhibit the primitive reflexes associated with anxiety. Use the following QR code to go directly to the video package, or visit https://drsarlos.com/videos for more information.

Scan for video!

Exercises for anxiety

1

Push the ring fingers together for six seconds.

MORO

Number of repetitions:
3–5 years: 4–5x
5–10 years: 6–8x
10–16 years: 8–10x
16+: 12x

2

MORO

Starting position: Stand with back against the wall, legs apart, arms outstretched to the side.

1. Keeping the right foot in place, cross the left foot in front of the right foot, and at the same time cross the arms. The *left* foot and *left* forearm must be in front, i.e., further from the body.
2. Move the left foot back to the starting position, stretching out the arms.
3. Now, keeping the left foot in place, cross the right foot in front of the left foot, and at the same time cross the arms. This time the *right* foot and *right* forearm must be in front, i.e., further from the body.
4. Move the right foot back to the starting position, stretching out the arms.

Number of repetitions:

3–5 years: 10x
5–10 years: 20x
10–16 years: 30x
16+: 40x

3

MORO

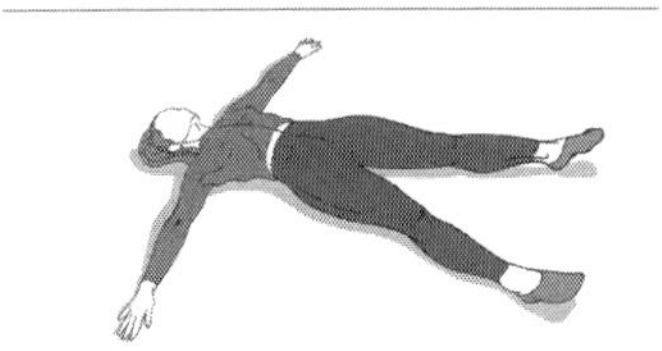

SP

1

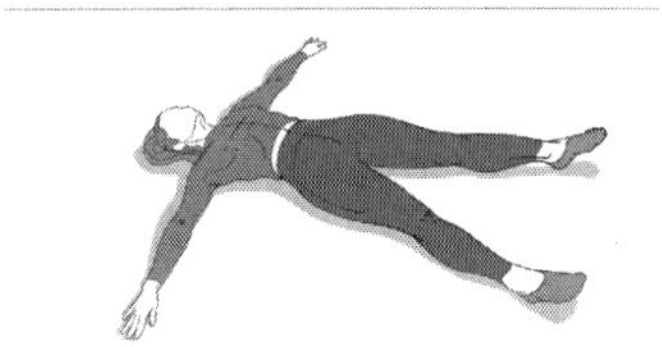

2

3

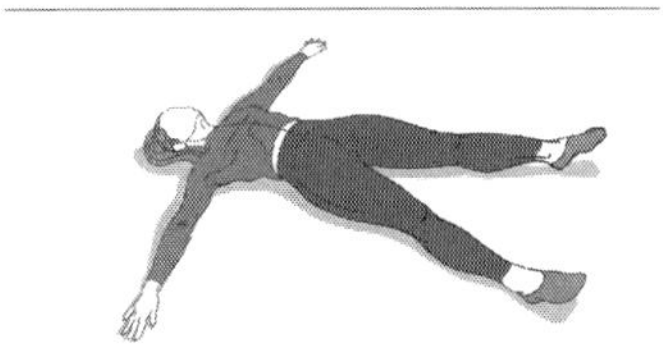

4

Starting position: Lie on the back, arms stretched out to the side, legs open on the floor.

1. Turn onto the left side into the "fetal position" with forearms and legs crossed. When turning left, move the right forearm over the left, and the right lower leg over the left.
2. Return to the starting position.
3. Turn onto the right side into the "fetal position" with forearms and legs crossed. When turning right, move the left forearm over the right, and the left lower leg over the right.
4. Return to the starting position.

Number of repetitions:

3–5 years: 12x (6x to the left, 6x to the right, alternating)
5–10 years: 16x (8x to the left, 8x to the right, alternating)
10–16 years: 20x (10x to the left, 10x to the right, alternating)
16+: 30x (15x to the left, 15x to the right, alternating)

4

GALANT MORO

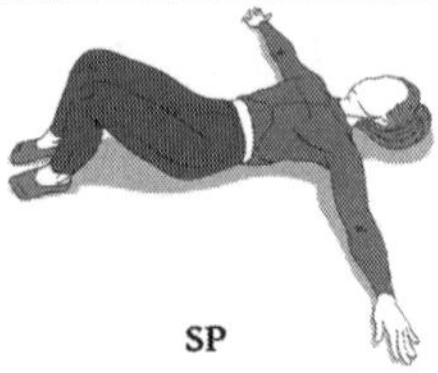

SP

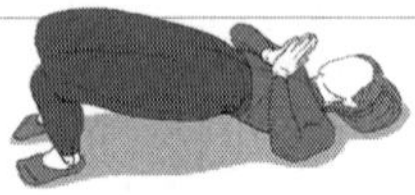

1

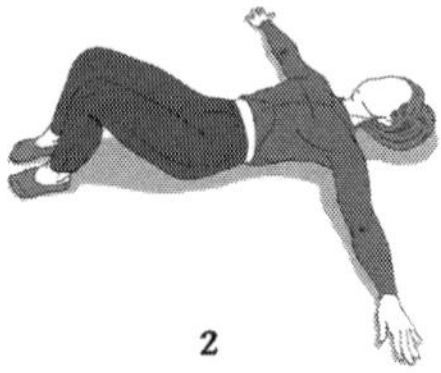

2

Starting position: Lie on the back, knees bent, arms outstretched on the ground.

1. Lift the hips and squeeze the buttocks together, and at the same time bend the elbows and push the palms together. Maintain this position for the required number of seconds.
2. Return to the starting position.

If it is too difficult to coordinate the movement of the arms and legs, it is enough to do only the leg movements for the first 2–3 months.

Number of repetitions:

3–5 years: 4–5x, hold for 3 seconds
5–10 years: 6–8x, hold for 4–6 seconds
10–16 years: 8–10x, hold for 6 seconds
16+: 12x, hold for 6 seconds

5

MORO

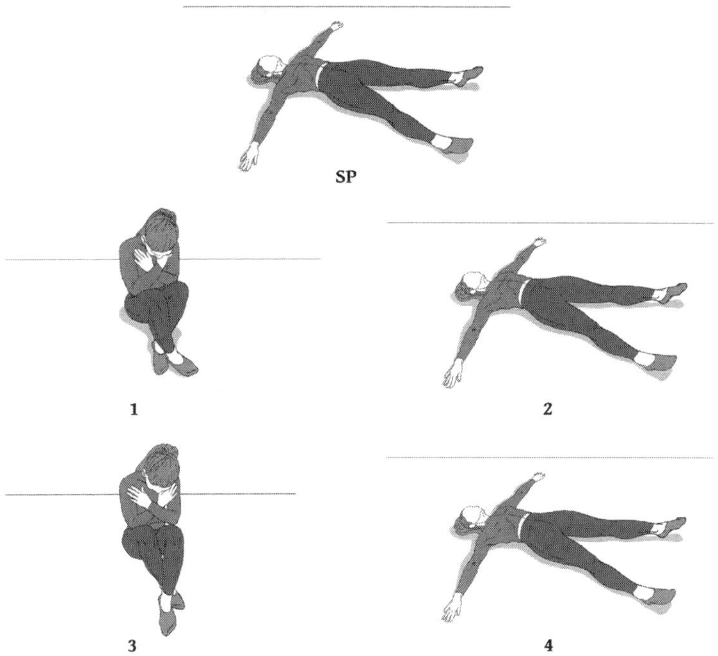

Starting position: Lie on the back, arms outstretched to the side, legs spread apart.

1. Sit up into a bent position, head tucked in, legs crossed, and arms crossed with hands lightly gripping the shoulders. The *right* foot and *right* forearm must be forward, i.e., further from the body.

2. Return to starting position.

3. Again sit up into a bent position, head tucked in, with legs crossed and arms crossed with hands lightly gripping the shoulders. This time the *left* foot and *left* forearm must be forward, i.e., further from the body.

4. Return to starting position.

If it is very difficult to sit up, support the upper body with bean bags or pillows.

Number of repetitions:
3–5 years: 8x
5–10 years: 16–20x
10–16 years: 20–24x
16+: 20–24x

6

CTGR

Starting position: Stand on some stairs, with one foot entirely on the stair and the other foot only having the front half on the stair and the heel hanging off the edge.
The task is to push the heel down 10–12 times.
Then switch and repeat with the other foot.

Number of repetitions:
3–5 years: 3–4x with each foot
5–10 years: 4–5x with each foot
10–16 years: 5–6x with each foot
16+: 6x with each foot

7

Do this exercise every second day.

On each foot, pull the big toe towards the body 10–12 times. Repeat 3–4 times.

CTGR

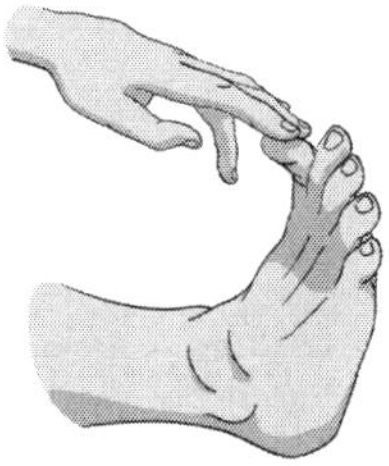

For a child, a parent or helper can also perform this action.

8

Do this exercise every second day.

Massage the Achilles tendon and calf muscle, 10–12 times on one leg and then on the other. Repeat 3–4 times.

CTGR

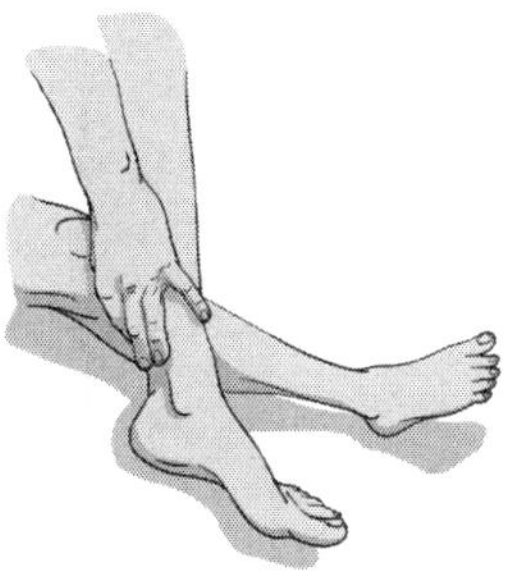

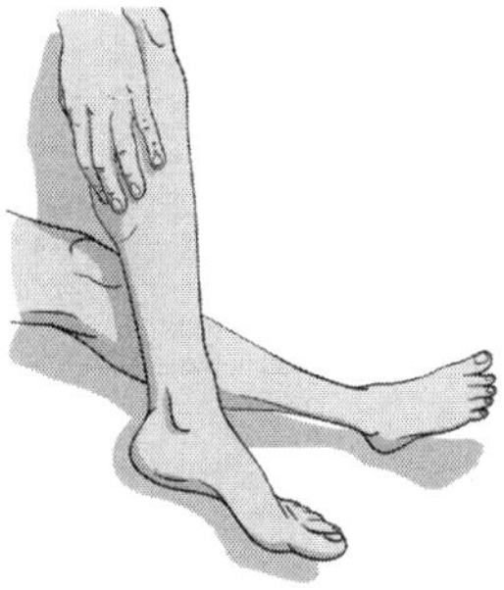

For a child, a parent or helper can also perform this action.

9

FPR

Starting position: Stand in a comfortable position.

A helper stands behind the "subject" and claps (lightly taps) the "subject" on different parts of their body, to the rhythms listed below.

1) on the shoulders
2) on the arms
3) on the hip from the side
4) on the legs
TA-TA TI-TI-TA TI-TI-TI-TI TA-TA
(TA is longer, TI shorter)

Number of repetitions:
3–5 years: 2x
5–10 years: 2x
10–16 years: 4x
16+: 4x

10

Starting position: Stand comfortably. Put both hands on the navel.
1. Inhale deeply.
2. Hold your breath for a short time.
3. Exhale the air in small bursts, making "P" sounds. Each exhalation should consist of at least 5–6 bursts.

Number of repetitions:
3–5 years: 4x
5–10 years: 6x
10–16 years: 8x
16+: 8x

11

GRASPING SUCKING FPR

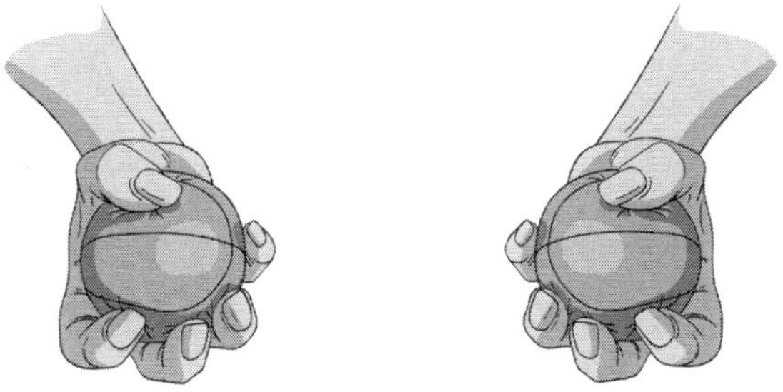

Starting position: Sit comfortably, holding a small sponge ball in each hand.

A "helper" stands behind the person doing the exercise.

When the helper claps, the person doing the exercise squeezes the balls, preferably with the last joints of the fingers bent.

Number of repetitions:
3–5 years: 6x claps
5–10 years: 10x claps
10–16 years: 12x claps
16+: 12x claps

12

GRASPING SUCKING

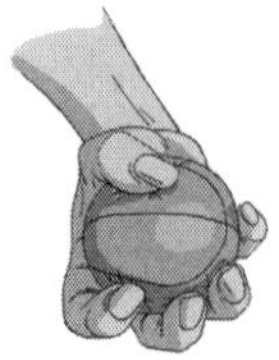

Starting position: Hold a sponge ball with the thumb facing the other four fingers.

Squeeze the ball for a second, then relax. Repeat.

Make sure to grip the ball with the last joints of each finger bent as shown. Some children find this difficult at first, either because the thumb keeps sliding back alongside the other fingers, or they cannot bend the last joint of the fingers. In this case, they need help to make the correct grip. Between the ages of three and five, they can hold their own forearm to help, as shown below.

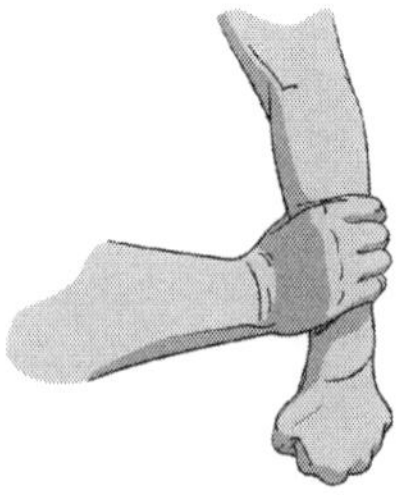

Number of repetitions:
3–5 years: 3 x 8–10 with both hands, alternating
5–10 years: 3–4 x 10 with both hands, alternating
10–16 years: 4 x 10 with both hands, alternating
16+: 4–5 x 10 with both hands, alternating

"YOUR TINY LITTLE HAND FITS PERFECTLY IN MINE"

According to Raymond Trevo, a practicing pediatrician and professor of child development neuroscience in Canada, parents must be listened to carefully. Their every word, their fears, and their intuition will bring the doctor or specialist closer to finding the cause of the problem. The parents' concerns are probably not unfounded. Their accounts often paint a more nuanced picture than clinical observations. Parents should be taken seriously because early detection of problems is very important, as brain development is best shaped early in life.

What Trevo writes is very important. There is a wealth of information about child development available these days. There is a plethora of internet sites and textbooks that describe the age-related stages of development.

After the birth of the first child, parents have little else to rely on other than the sources mentioned above. However, the experiences of grandmothers, grandfathers, aunts, and uncles sometimes provide new mothers and fathers with information on the child's developmental pace. By the second or third child, there is already a basis for comparison.

I hear stories like this one every week:

Luke, at the age of one, could say ba-ba-ba or ma-ma-ma, took a few steps and, although he was still breastfeeding, he accepted the solid food I gave him on a spoon and ate it with relish. But Mimi is 16 months old now and she doesn't say any syllables at all, just babbles nonsensically—and even then, only sometimes. She crawls on all fours (although she never crawled on her stomach) but can't stand up, let alone walk. She won't breastfeed, only takes a bottle, and now she will only drink her formula if it is thin enough for her to easily suck out of the bottle. She won't go near a spoon, even just for play. The nurse told me not to worry—she will catch up.

But the mother didn't relax. She went to the professionals and was told, *"Don't worry mum! Children do not develop in the same way. Mimi will start talking and moving. Don't worry about the eating, your little girl is too plump anyway."*

A whole book of case studies could be written about children whose parents took them to professionals with complaints and worries and got "reassuring" answers. Some parents believe these unconditionally because "he" or "she" is the trained professional. Others, like Mimi's mum, won't let it go. They take their children everywhere until finally they find a person who helps, or at least tries to help. Unfortunately, it is not uncommon that months and sometimes years pass between the first attempt and the solution. Remember the quote from Dr. Trevo: *"Brain development is best shaped early in life."* This should never be forgotten by anyone, not by parents, not by professionals.

Professor Ferenc Katona, a developmental neurologist in Hungary who is 98 years old at the time of writing, and the savior of many premature babies, started a hospital ward in 1975 at the St. Margaret Hospital in Budapest, where he still works. It has been operating ever since according to the diagnostic and therapeutic principles he developed, and the current head of the department is Dr. Marianne Berényi. Why am I mentioning their names?

In addition to their extraordinary professionalism and humanity in helping to create the conditions for a fuller, better, and happier life for premature babies, the website of the department they founded and run reads as follows:

"An early diagnosis and the resulting neurotherapy can permit the elimination of symptoms that have already developed and the achievement of a complete cure or a high degree of improvement. Early treatment is also a preventive measure."

Dear parents, below are the warning signs. Don't let yourselves be pushed back! Get to the bottom of the problem. Please note, although I have grouped the symptoms by age, some children may show these signs two weeks to a month later. For example, in the 2–3 months age range, it could actually be up to 3½ or even nearly four months.

2–3 months of age

- At 2–2½ months the baby already "rolls around" (possibly due to overtight muscle tone)
- Does not seem to respond to loud noises
- Weak sucking ability
- Does not follow moving objects with their eyes
- Does not smile in response to mom's or dad's voice
- Does not grasp or hold small objects
- At four months, does not smile back when someone smiles at them
- At 3–4 months, cannot hold their head up when lying on their tummy
- After four months, they do not touch or hold toys when they are handed to them
- Uses only one hand
- At four months, does not put objects in their mouth (e.g., teething toys, rattle, etc.)
- Up to 3–4 months, the child should make a walking motion when held up on a flat surface. However, it's a problem if this continues after four months. (After four months of age, this so-called elementary movement pattern should no longer be triggered. Later the child will naturally learn to walk.)
- Has difficulty moving one or both eyes in every direction
- Crosses their eyes during most of their waking hours. (Occasional crossing is normal in the first months.)

4–7 months of age

- Muscles appear very stiff and tight. Often slouches when lying on their back.
- Looks very loose and flabby, like a "rag doll"
- After five months of age, when lifted from lying on their back to a sitting position, their head still hangs. (Up to five months of age, the head may follow the body with a slight delay.)
- Does not show emotion towards those who care for them
- Cries or tetchy around people. Seem to dislike and reject company.
- One or both eyes constantly turn inwards or outwards
- Eyes are watery and sensitive to light
- Unresponsive to nearby sounds

- One side is more active than the other
- They have difficulty putting, or never able to put, objects in their mouth
- After four months, does not turn their head towards sound
- By six months, does not turn from tummy to back
- Can't sit unaided (not alone!)
- By six months, does not laugh or giggle
- By six months, does not actively touch objects
- Unable to follow moving objects with both eyes at the same time
- At five months, they still have the so-called elementary walking movement pattern described above.

7–12 months

- Doesn't crawl
- Crawls asymmetrically or pulls on one side of the body while crawling (over a period of more than one month)
- Uses only arms when crawling
- Gets hysterical if helped in any way
- Does not look for hidden objects, even their favorite toy
- Does not say any words (e.g., "mom" or "nana")
- Does not learn to use gestures such as waving or shaking their head
- At 10 months, does not sit stably
- At eight months, shows no interest in playing peek-a-boo or clapping
- At eight months, does not repeat syllables (e.g., "dadada", "bababa", "mamama")
- After seven months, sit on their legs in the "W" position
- One side is more active than the other.

12–24 months

- At 18 months, cannot walk
- Does not develop a mature heel-to-toe gait or walks exclusively on their toes after more than one month of walking
- At 18 months, doesn't talk, not using around 15 words
- At two years old, not using 50 words
- At two years of age, no two-word sentences (e.g., "give me," "come here," "baby eats," "baby claps")

- By 15 months, does not seem to know the names of everyday objects (e.g., brush, phone, table, fork, spoon, potty) or their function
- At 24 months, does not imitate actions or words
- At 24 months, does not follow simple one-step instructions (Come here! Pick it up! Put it down! Drink it!)

24–36 months

- Frequently falls
- Difficulty walking up stairs. Even when walking uphill they "lag behind."
- Drools a lot (not only when teething)
- Completely unintelligible speech
- Can't build a tower of Duplo more than four stories high
- Has difficulties manipulating small objects like Lego, beads, and pebbles
- At three years, can't draw or copy a circle
- Unable to communicate in short phrases
- Does not engage in role-playing games or role-play with dolls or stuffed animals
- Does not understand simple instructions
- Does not show interest in other children
- Hard to separate from their mother, father, or primary caregiver.

Other warning signs

- Reversal from a stage of development already reached. For example, the child has already spoken syllables or words but suddenly speech development stops.
- Becomes antisocial and aggressive
- Muscles are too tight (hypertonic) or toneless (hypotonic)
- After 24 months, primitive reflexes can be triggered.

Sources:

Early Childhood Direction Center, C/O Women & Children's Hospital of Buffalo, 219 Bryant St., Buffalo, New York.
Raymond Tervo, MD, Neurodevelopmental Pediatrician and Medical Director of Pediatrics at Gillette Children's Specialty Healthcare.

If as a parent you have any doubts about a child's development, consult your child's doctor or a pediatric neurologist. If the child is not responding to sounds, a hearing test should be requested, and likewise an eye examination for any vision problems. If there is any disagreement, it is advisable to seek the opinion of two or more specialists.

If the neurological findings are negative, and if no abnormalities are found in the sensory tests, the problem may be caused by a slower neurological maturation for the age of the child. In this case, it is recommended that gymnastic exercises and age-appropriate sensory exercises are regularly introduced into daily life.

In addition to nervous system immaturity, the child could also have sensory or neurological organic problems. In this case, YOU MUST ALWAYS SEEK THE OPINION OF A PEDIATRICIAN OR SIMILAR PROFESSIONAL IN CONNECTION WITH PERFORMING THESE EXERCISES!

Exercise Videos

A set of videos are available that demonstrate primitive reflex integration exercises for children aged 3 to 5. Use the following QR code to go directly to the video package, or visit https://drsarlos.com/videos for more information.

Scan for video!

Exercises for small children

If the young child cooperates well, try to do all of the exercises each day. If doing all the exercises daily is too difficult, you can divide the exercises into parts, e.g., half one day, half the next. The most important thing is to do at least two or three exercises EVERY DAY—this is the way to make progress.

1

Starting position: Sit on a bed or in a comfortable chair with the child on your lap.

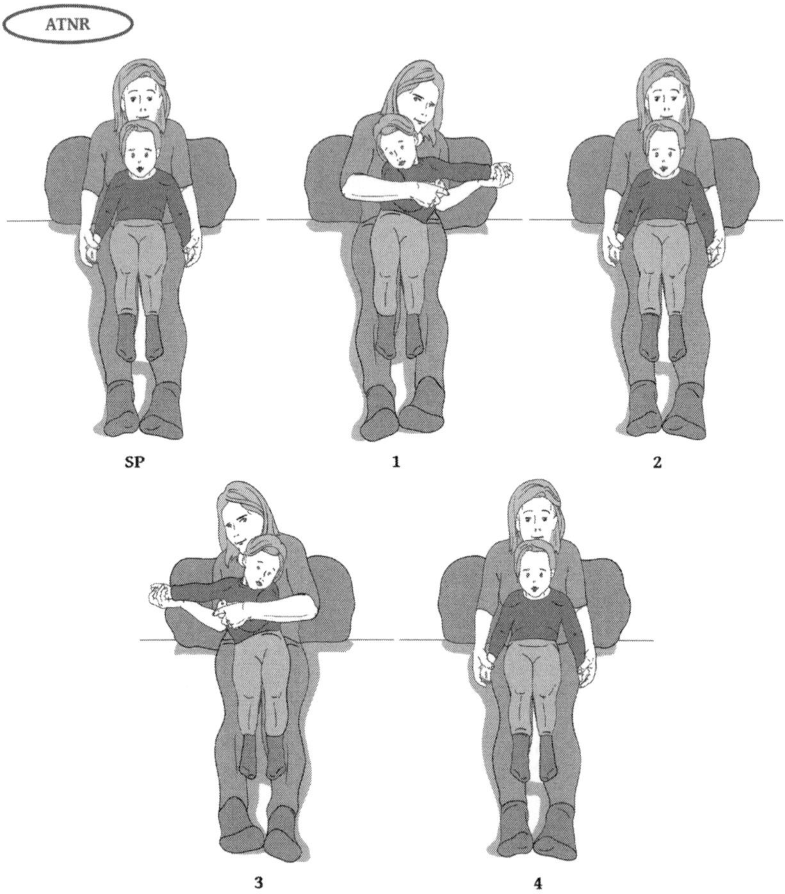

Hold their hands and do the following exercise while saying a rhyme. Keep time with the rhythm while performing the movements.

1. Swing **both** of the child's arms to the left.
2. Return both arms to the starting position.
3. Swing **both** of the child's arms to the right.
4. Return both arms to the starting position.

Repeat the exercise 2–4 times, depending on the length of the rhyme.

2

ATNR GALANT

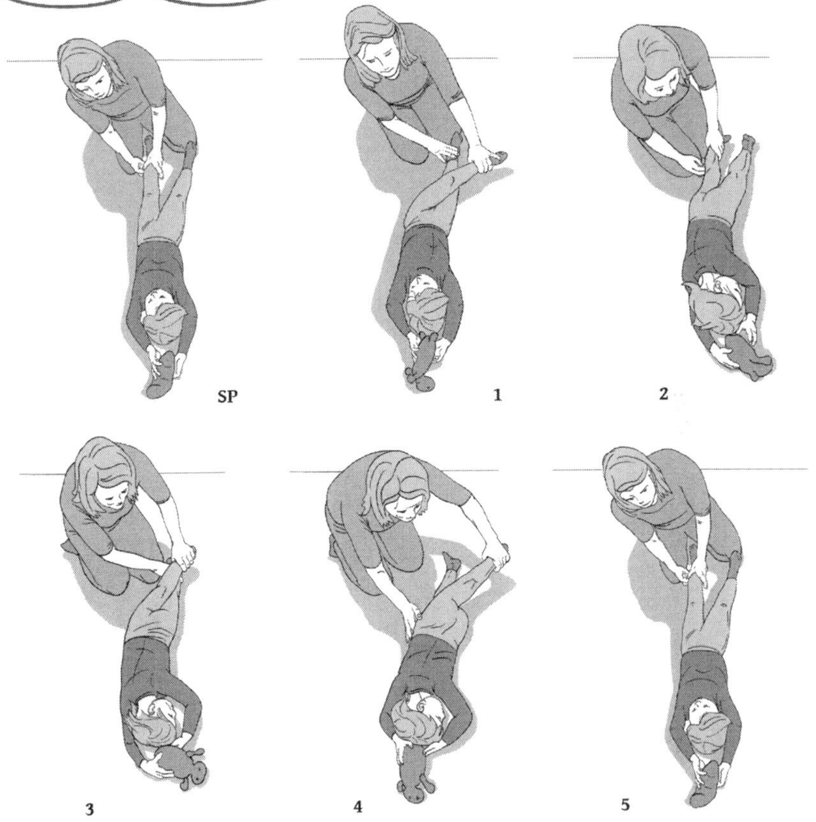

Starting position: The child should lie on their back on the floor or on a bed.

Hold their feet as shown in the diagram and roll their body over, so that the roll of the upper body is preceded by crossing the legs. In this way, the child rolls over from tummy to back, from back to tummy. Continue until you run out of space, then repeat the exercise in the opposite direction. If you can do four to five rolls (180°) in one direction, four repetitions are enough.

While doing this exercise, you can say a rhyme.

3

Starting position: The child should lie on their back with knees bent and feet on the ground. Kneel facing them and hold their arms so that they cannot bend their elbows.

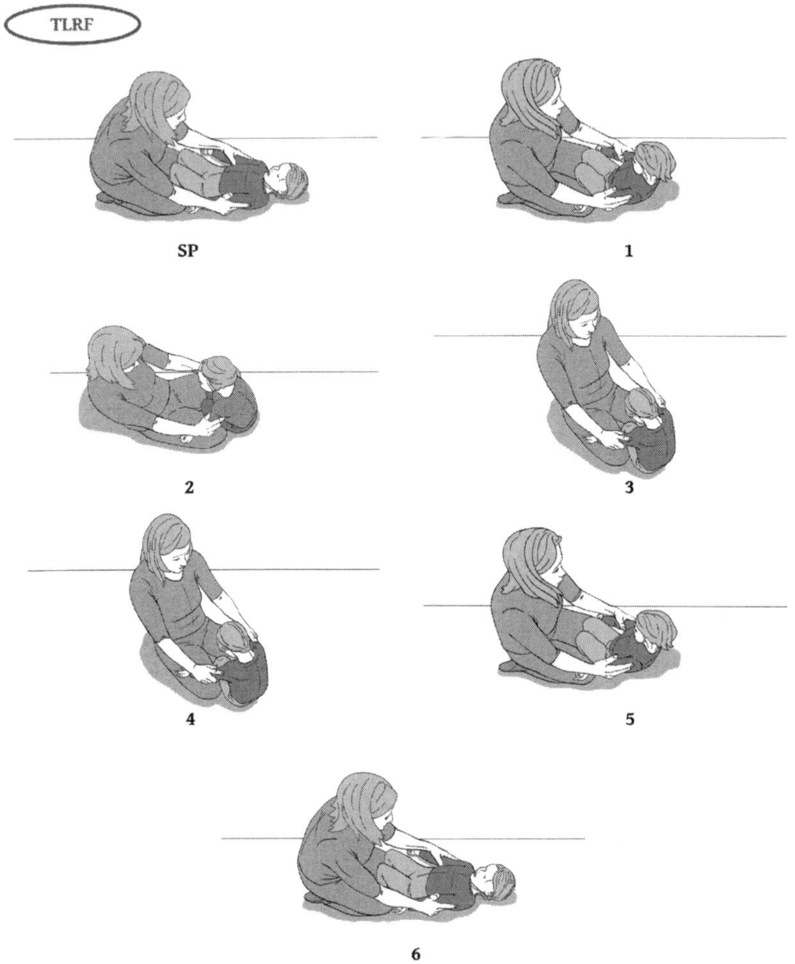

Use your index finger to gently press down on the child's upper arm so that they do not pull their shoulders up into their neck. Pull the child up into a sitting position and then slowly lower them back to the ground.

While doing this exercise, you can tell a rhyme.

The child may bend their head backward. Don't worry about this, but when you put them down, make sure that their head returns comfortably back to the starting position.

Repeat the exercise 1–3 times, depending on the length of the rhyme.

4

This exercise should be performed only by children aged 3 or older.

Starting position: The child should stand with legs open, their torso leaning forward, and palms on the ground.

With one of your hands, tilt the child's head forward so that their chin touches (or almost touches) their chest. Wrap your other arm around their thighs, under the buttocks. Then turn the child over so that they tumble forward "head over heels" in a smooth rolling (not dropping) movement.

TLRB

Repeat 4–5 times.

5

Starting position: The child should lie on their back on the floor. Kneel opposite them and hold their ankles or feet.

Open their legs wide, and then bring them back together.

While doing this, tell a rhyme, matching the rhythm to the movement of the legs.

GALANT

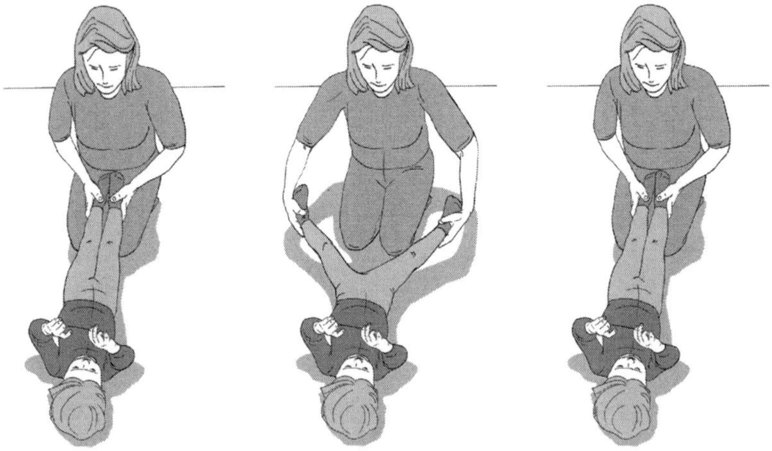

Repeat 2–3 times depending on the length of the rhyme.

6

Starting position: The child should lie on their back on the floor. Kneel opposite them and hold their ankles or feet.

Move their legs in a cycling motion, while rotating their hips from right to left.

Again, you should accompany this with a rhyme.

GALANT

Repeat 2–3 times depending on the length of the rhyme.

7

Starting position: Sit on a bed or in a comfortable chair with the child on your lap. Hold their hands.

MORO

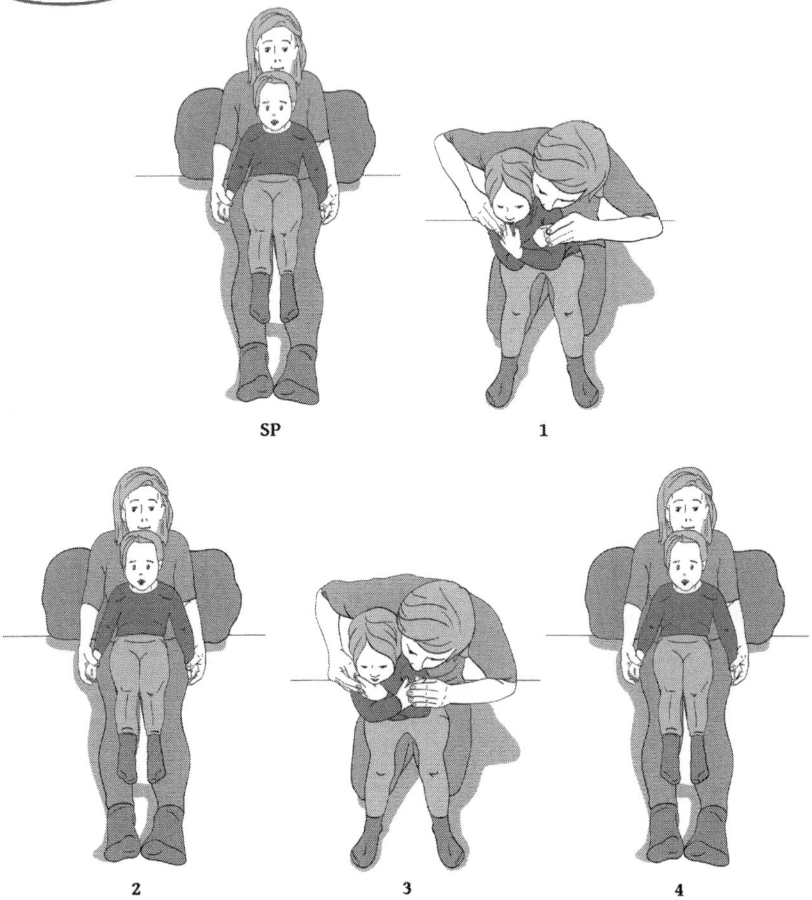

Do the following exercise while telling a rhyme:

1. Bend slightly forward and cross the child's forearms over their chest, with the left forearm over the right, as shown in the diagram.
2. Return to the starting position.

3. Again, bend slightly forward and cross the child's forearms, this time with the right forearm over the left.
4. Return to the starting position.

Repeat 2–3 times depending on the length of the rhyme.

During this exercise, it doesn't matter what the child does with their feet because the emphasis is on the arm movement.

8

Massage the face around the mouth in three semicircular arcs of increasing length, as shown in the diagram.

In each case, start the massage in the area between the mouth and nose, and finish in the area under the lower lip. Each arc should be gently massaged 5–6 times.

Do this 1–2 times on each side of the face.

SUCKING ROOTING

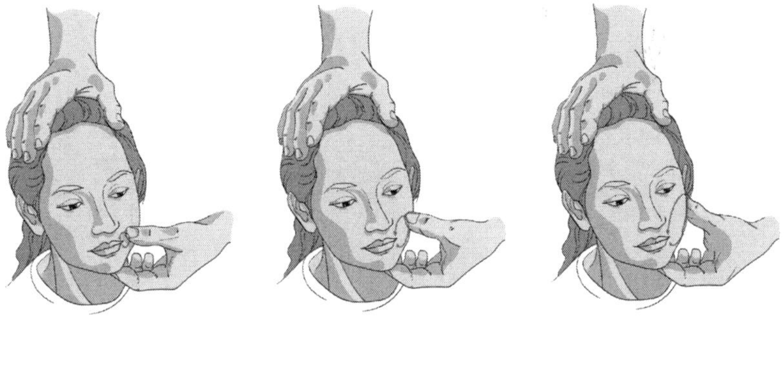

9

GRASPING SUCKING

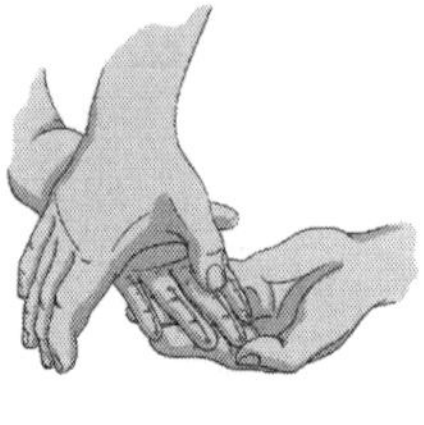

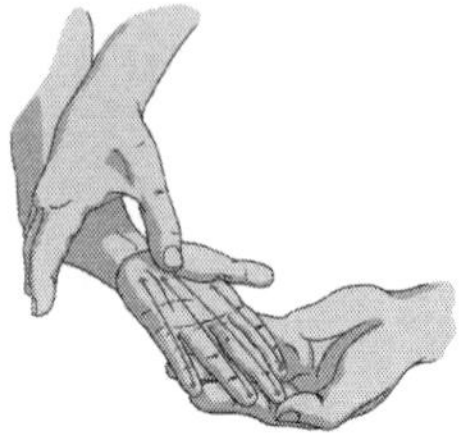

Massage the palm from the fingers towards the wrist. This exercise is the same as massaging the face.

Repeat 1–2 times on both hands.

A suitable rhyme to accompany this exercise is "This little piggy went to market. . ."

10

Starting position: The child should sit comfortably. Hold one of their feet and pull the big toe towards their body for a second at a time. Do this 8–10 times, then continue on the other foot.

CTGR

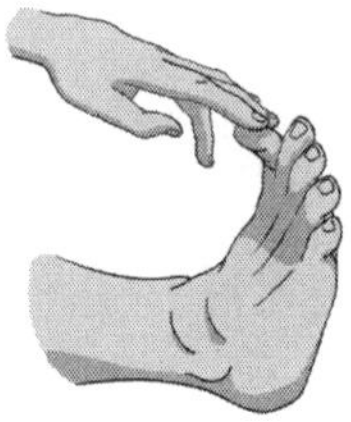

Repeat 2–3 times on both feet.

11

Starting position: Sit on a bed or in a comfortable chair with the child on your lap.

Hold their hands and do the following exercise while saying a rhyme. Keep time with the rhythm while performing the movements.

ATNR

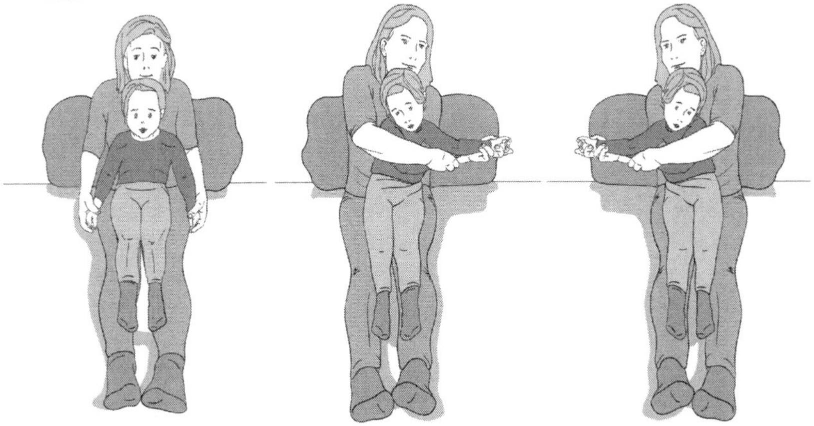

1. Swing **both** of the child's arms to the left.
2. Swing **both** of the child's arms to the right.

Swing the arms continuously—don't return the arms to the starting position in between sides.

Do the exercise while repeating the rhyme 2–4 times, depending on its length.

12

With assistance, the child should crawl forward on the floor. This can be done on a soft surface, e.g., carpet or a yoga mat.

ATNR GALANT

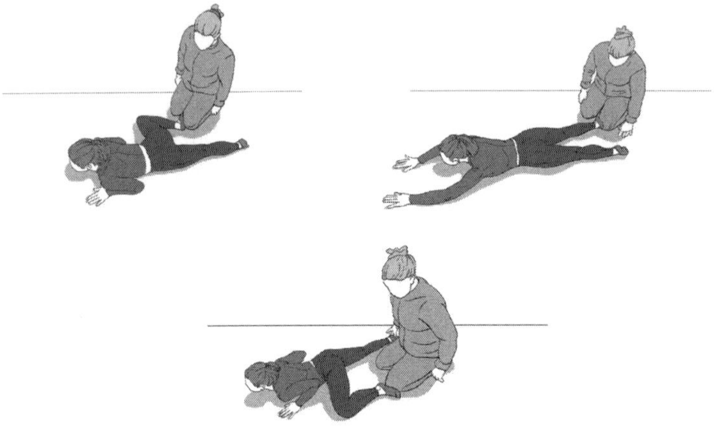

Pay attention to the following:

- Until the bent leg is extended, the other leg should not be bent.
- Don't let the hips lift—keep them on the ground.
- Help in the way shown in the diagram. With your knee, or with one of your hands, support the child's pushing leg, and if the child's other leg bends, use your other hand to help keep it extended.
- Encourage the child to use their arms!
- The movement should be as symmetrical as possible.

After 4–5 crawling movements, turn around, or return to the starting point, and repeat the exercise 2–3 times.

AN OLD MAN IS NOT AN OBSOLETE MAN

I recently read a lovely article about how primitive reflexes "lead" us into the world and then out of the world at the end of our lives. These special reflexes are present at birth and for a few months afterward, and then gradually disappear from our lives, giving way to higher neural activities. However, they slowly creep back in at the twilight of life, and many of them are present when we leave this world.

With people living longer lives, it has become possible for scientists to study aging changes more and more extensively. As of 2020, Europe's average life expectancy is 77.5 for men and 83.2 for women.[14] In the USA, the figures from 2021 are 73.2 for men and 79.1 for women.[15] It should be noted that in both regions, these statistics show a decrease in average life expectancy compared with previous years, although the COVID-19 pandemic will have played a role in this.

If we assume that the final 20% of our lives is the age at which signs of decline, such as reduced motor coordination, deterioration in gross and fine motor movements, reduced muscle tone, balance disorders, return of infantile reflexes, attention or memory problems, become more pronounced, this means that the first symptoms in the above regions may appear in men after the age of 60 and in women after the age of 64.

Of course, these are average numbers, and in reality, there are significant variations. People who lead mentally and physically active lives, who do not have chronic illnesses, who can afford to eat healthily and consciously, who do not have harmful addictions such as smoking, excessive alcohol consumption, or the use of various legal and illegal drugs, can expect to see the signs of decline later—in some cases, much later. On the other hand, an inactive or self-destructive lifestyle can have the opposite effect.

14 https://ec.europa.eu/eurostat/web/products-eurostat-news/-/ddn-20220427-1

15 https://www.cdc.gov/nchs/pressroom/nchs_press_releases/2022/20220831.htm

Aging is a natural part of life, but the quality of life for the "aging person," and for their family, will not be the same. It is also a question of luck, but it is largely up to us whether we spend the last fifth of our lives active, healthy, and happy.

I wrote about the need for exercise and its effects on the body in the third chapter of this book, which discussed the importance of movement. Now I want to talk about the primitive reflexes that return with aging. It is perhaps no accident that old age is often referred to as the second childhood. If one lives to a ripe old age, one may experience a return of primitive reflexes.

The reader may remember that the reflex centers of primitive reflexes are located in the brain stem, and having fulfilled their mission, they "merge" and integrate into a higher level of neural activity. They can no longer be triggered because they are inhibited by a higher-level system, which is the cerebral cortex. With aging, the cortical inhibition presumably weakens, and the primitive reflexes first start to "revert" and then return permanently. They can be triggered in the same way as in a young child under two years of age.

The aging person will notice that from time to time they make a mess on their clothes, accidentally bump into a table or chair, lose their balance, things fall out of their hands, they lick their lips more and more when manipulating objects with their fingers, and they may have problems with the retention of feces. Of course, while there may be reasons other than primitive reflexes, research shows that primitive reflexes do have a significant impact on quality of life in this age group. Studies over the past 10–15 years have shown that the more primitive reflexes appear as we age, the greater the chance of developing dementia.

Dementia is—rightly—a fear for many people. But how many people are doing something about it? And what is dementia? It is not a single well-defined disease but a group of symptoms, or in other words a syndrome. One of the leading symptoms is memory loss, but it can also affect other cognitive functions. There are often stumbling blocks in language use or the sufferer may experience impairments in spatial perception, numeracy, judgment, abstract thinking, attention, and other functions. Symptoms such as disruptive behavior, personality changes, delusions, or hallucinations are common. These often erupt to such an extent that they affect interpersonal relationships and the ability to work and lead a normal life.

There are several known manifestations of dementia, depending on the underlying problem. Often, the first classification is whether it is due to degenerative changes in brain cells or problems with the vascular system supplying the brain. Within the two groups, there are several "subsystems." The good news is that almost any form of dementia can be slowed down or prevented.

It has been repeatedly shown that regular, low-to-moderate intensity, aerobic (i.e., using oxygen) exercise for 30–60 minutes a day has a markedly positive effect on cognitive performance, delays decline, and may even prevent it in some forms of dementia.

Ten years ago, a team of researchers in Connecticut—Sara M. Gregory, Beth Parker, and Paul D. Thompson—set out to analyze and summarize the research findings on the links between exercise and cognitive function and between exercise and dementia.

As the figure below from their research shows, exercise is just one component that helps our brains to function quickly and efficiently. However, it is an essential component that influences many other elements.

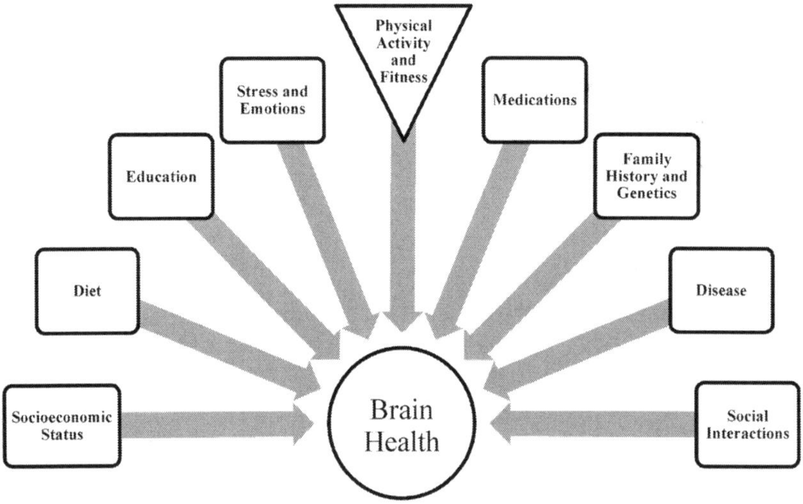

Source: Gregory et al., 2012.

Exercise advice for those who want to keep both their mind and their body active

It's best if you've been exercising all your life rather than spending your days snacking in front of the TV. In this case, continue the lifestyle you've been leading and add a few simple reflex integration exercises. If you haven't led a very active lifestyle, start with the following:

1) Visit your general practitioner/primary care physician and ask for advice on regular exercise. In particular, ask if any conditions need special attention or make a particular form of exercise inadvisable.
2) If there is no medical barrier, do 30–60 minutes of active exercise a day, taking care to avoid experiencing breathing difficulties. Walking, swimming, hiking, Nordic walking, yoga, walking the dog, or gardening, if you have a garden, are all good forms of exercise.
3) Eat healthily as much as you can
4) Keep your mind fresh. Read short stories, and novels, solve puzzles, play chess, cards, and board games, learn a language, learn poems or songs, or learn to play an instrument.
5) Socialize. For example, cultural activities for the older generation, outings, community center activities, exhibitions, theater or concert visits, or arts and crafts activities are all great.
6) Choose from the sensory exercises for children in this book. If your grandchild or a young child in your neighborhood does the exercises, you can do them together, even "competing" in some activities.
7) Find a hobby and cut back on TV watching as much as possible
8) Perform reflex integration exercises that delay the return of primitive reflexes. The exercises suggested specifically for older age groups are mostly designed to be done sitting at a desk. If you want to do more than these, you can do any of the exercises in the book, according to the condition of your musculoskeletal and nervous systems.

The following are some of the main symptoms and problems that can be avoided or prevented from developing or worsening by doing the exercises:

- Weakening of hand strength, difficulty in performing fine motor movements
- Disorders of hand–eye coordination
- Dribbling and swallowing difficulties

- Difficulty following the lines while reading
- Problems associated with changes in muscle tone, for example, fatigue, reflux symptoms, urination difficulties, and stool retention
- "Clumsiness," falls, and motor coordination problems
- Unexplained nervousness and anxiety.

Exercise Videos

A set of videos are available that demonstrate reflex integration exercises designed to delay the return of primitive reflexes. Use the following QR code to go directly to the video package, or visit https://drsarlos.com/videos for more information.

Scan for video!

Exercises

All the exercises in this chapter should be done carefully, at a tempo that does not cause problems. Once you become more comfortable with the exercises, you can do more than the stated number of repetitions.

If you can do all the exercises in one session, that's great. But don't despair if you can't do them all at once. You can split it into two, three, or even more parts. In fact, the 12 exercises in this section can be spread over three days. Doing any of them is better than doing nothing at all.

1

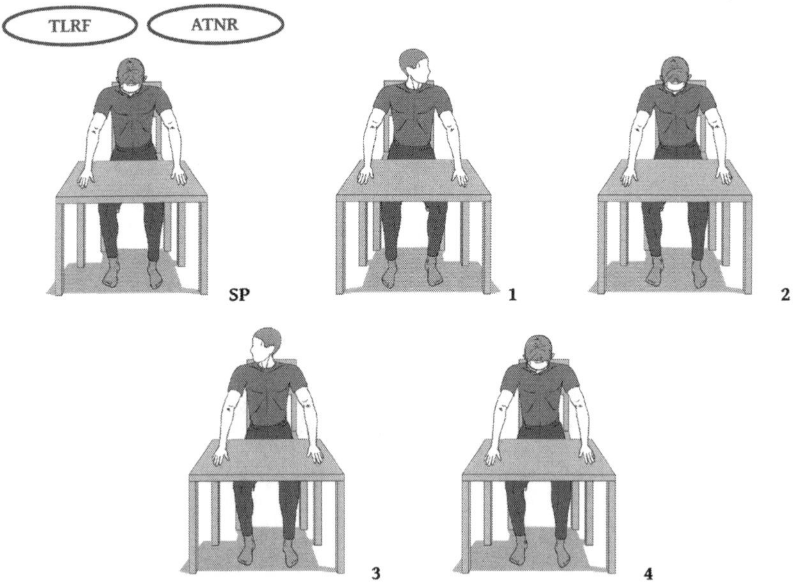

Starting position: Sit at a table. Place your palms on the table, with your arms extended comfortably. Bend your head down.
1. Lift your head up, then slowly turn it to the left.
2. Bring your head back to the center and bend it down again.
3. Lift your head up, then slowly turn it to the right.
4. Once again, return your head to the center and bend it down.
During the task, keep your arms extended.
Repeat the exercise 10 times (5x left and 5x right).

2

ATNR

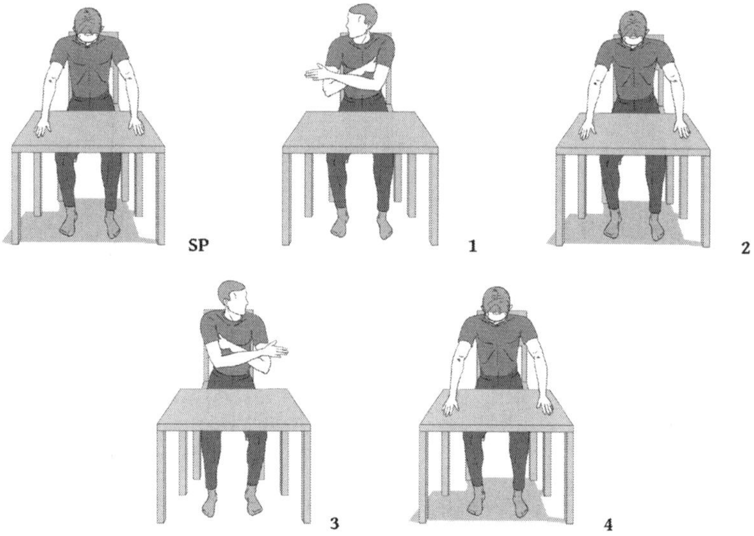

Starting position: Sit at a table. Place your palms on the table, with your arms extended comfortably. Bend your head down.

1. Lift your head up and turn it to the right. At the same time, swing your left arm to the right side of your body, bend your right arm, and place your right palm on your chest.
2. Return to the starting position, with your arms back on the table, your head in the center and bent down.
3. Now the opposite side. Lift your head up and turn it to the left. At the same time, swing your right arm to the left side of your body, bend your left arm, and place your left palm on your chest.
4. Again return to the starting position.

Repeat the exercise 10 times (5x left and 5x right).

3

MORO

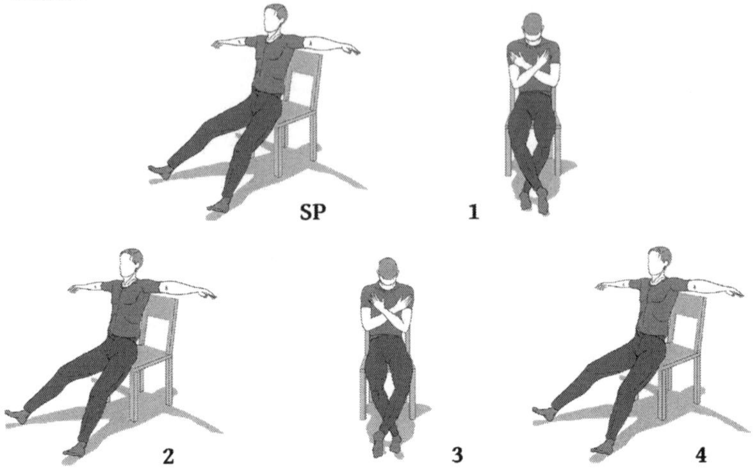

Starting position: Sit on a chair with your arms out to the sides and your legs open, preferably extended.

1. Tilt your head forward and simultaneously cross your arms in front of your chest and cross your legs by bending your knees, so that your right forearm and right leg are over the left. See the diagram.
2. Spread your legs and raise your arms to your sides, returning to the starting position.
3. Again tilt your head forward and simultaneously cross your arms in front of your chest and cross your legs by bending your knees, but now your left forearm and left leg are over the right.
4. Once again, spread your legs and raise your arms to your sides, returning to the starting position.

Repeat the exercise 10–12 times.

4

GALANT

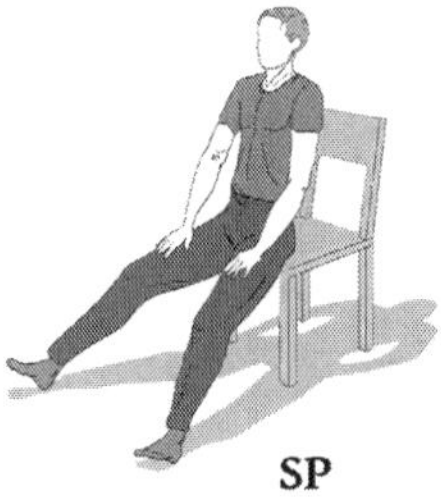

SP

1

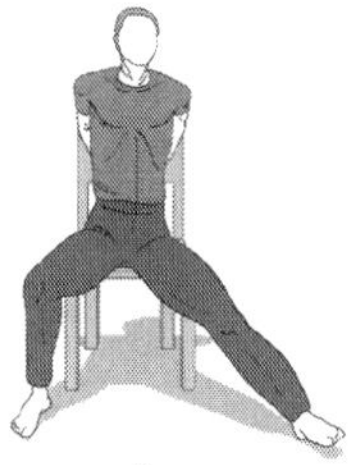

2

Starting position: Sit on a chair or bedside with legs slightly extended. Support your back with your arms for balance.

1. Bend your left leg while keeping your right leg extended.
2. Stretch out your left leg and simultaneously bend your right leg.

Repeat the exercise 12–16 times.

5

Hold a small soft ball or similar object, such as a rolled-up sock, in one hand. Squeeze it for a second or two, so that the final joints of your fingers are bent.

Repeat the exercise 10 times with one hand, then 10 times with the other. Repeat the full sequence three times.

GRASPING SUCKING

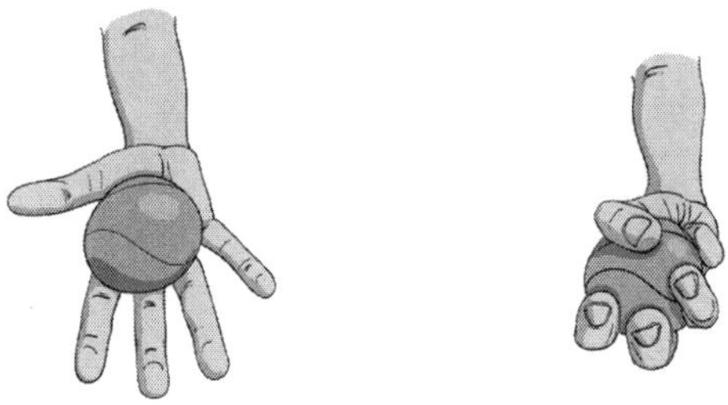

6

Place a small ball or similar object in both hands.

GRASPING SUCKING

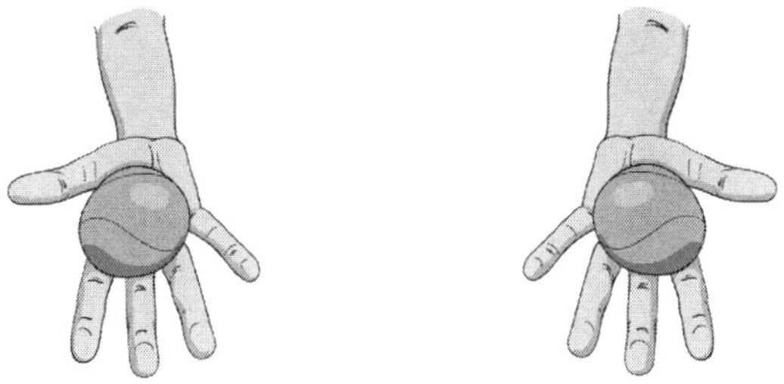

Squeeze the ball with your right hand while opening the fingers of your left hand. This is shown below.

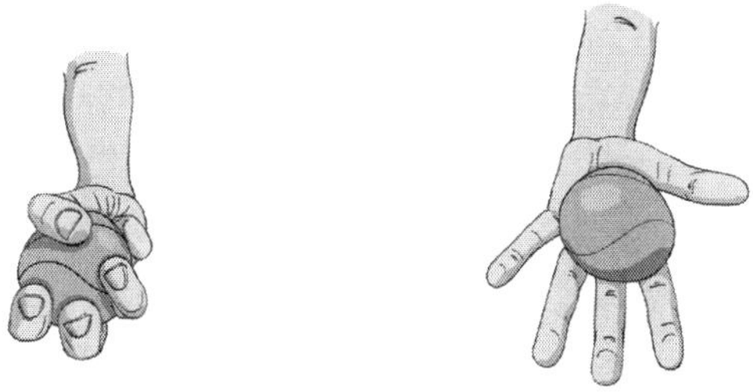

Then do the opposite. Squeeze the ball with your left hand while opening the fingers of your left hand.

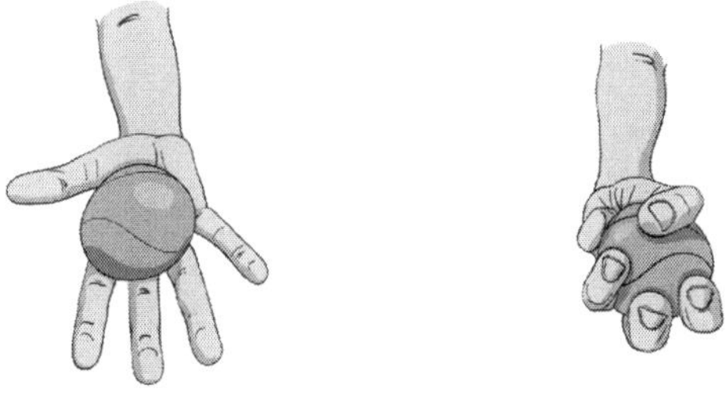

Repeat the sequence 20 times.

7

GRASPING SUCKING

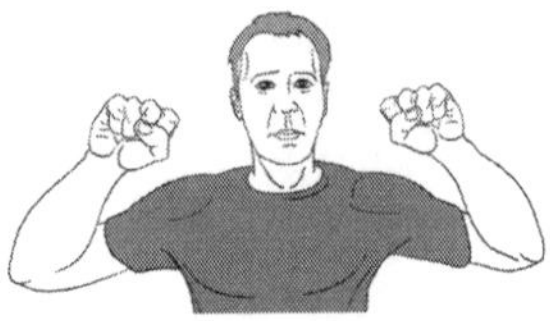

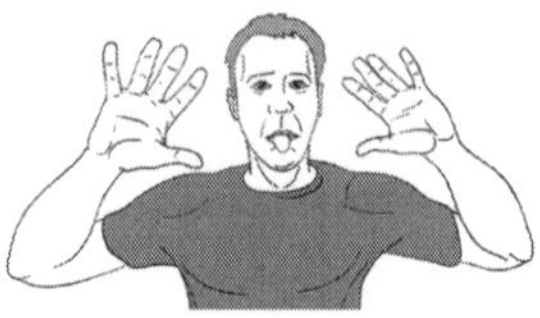

Starting position: Clench the fingers of both hands into fists, with the thumb resting on the outside of the other fingers. Close your mouth with your tongue behind your teeth.

1. While stretching your fingers and extending them backward, stick out your tongue as far as possible.
2. Close your fingers back into a fist, retract your tongue behind your teeth, and close your mouth.

Repeat the exercise 15–20 times.

8

STNR

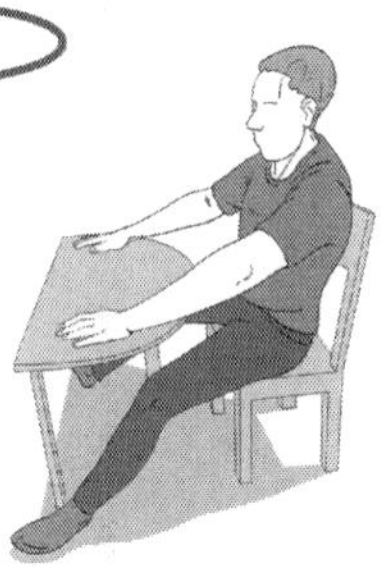

SP

1

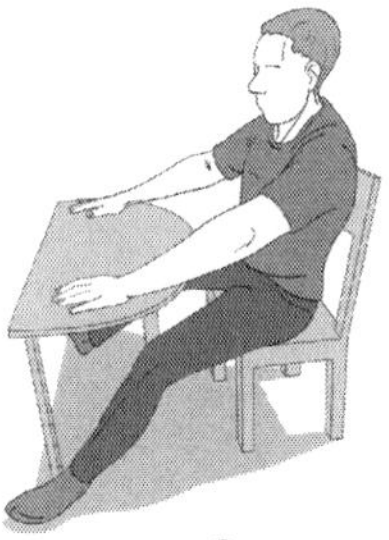

2

Starting position: Sit at a table. Place your palms on the table, with your arms and legs extended.

1. Lean down onto the table, simultaneously bending **both** your arms and legs.
2. Lift up, and return to the starting position by stretching out your arms and legs.

Repeat the exercise 12 times.

9

STNR

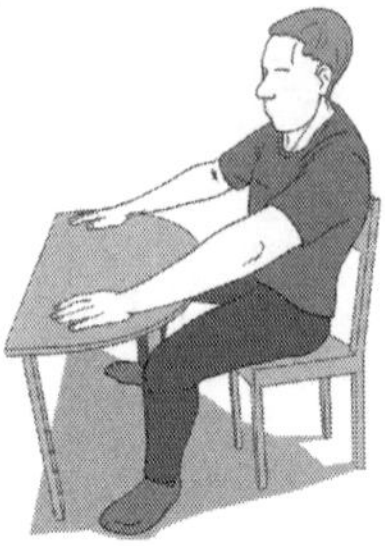

SP

1

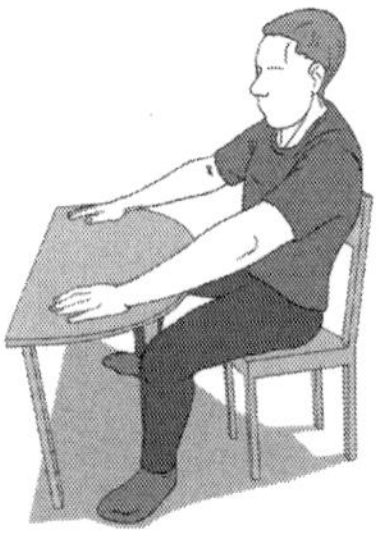

2

Starting position: Sit at a table. Place your palms on the table, with your **arms extended** and your **legs bent**.

1. Lean down onto the table, bending your arms and stretching your legs.
2. Lift up, and return to the starting position by stretching out your arms and bending your legs.

Repeat the exercise 12 times.

10

Make yourself comfortable in an armchair or on the bed. Massage your leg (calf muscle) from the heel (Achilles tendon) to the knee and back. Do the exercise back and forth 10–12 times on each leg.

CTGR

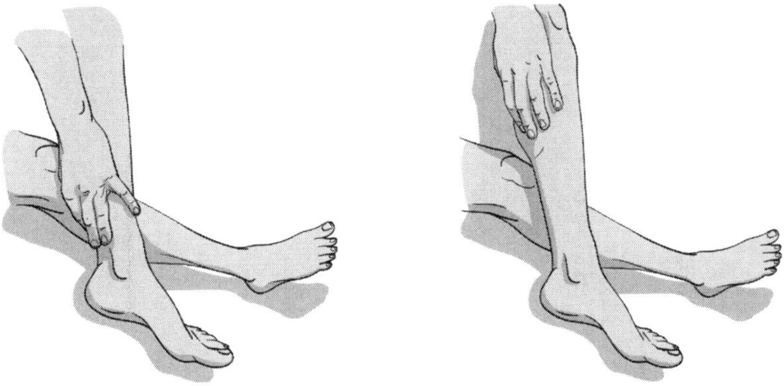

11

MORO

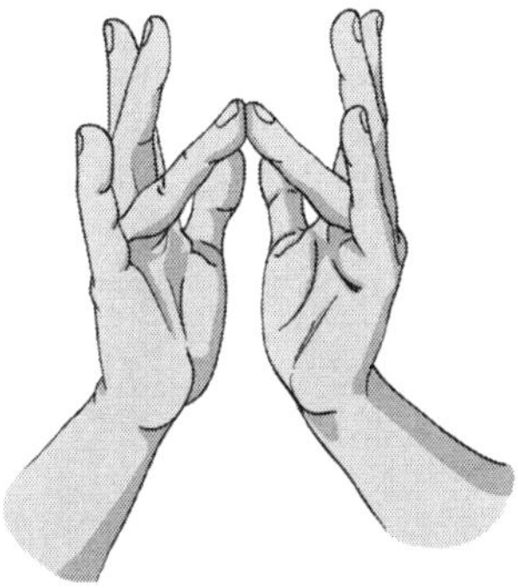

Push the ring fingers together for six seconds, then rest for a few seconds. Care must be taken not to touch the other fingers together during this exercise!
Repeat 6–8 times.

12

TLRB

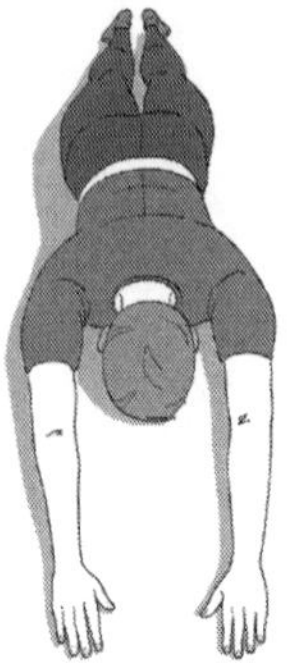

SP

1

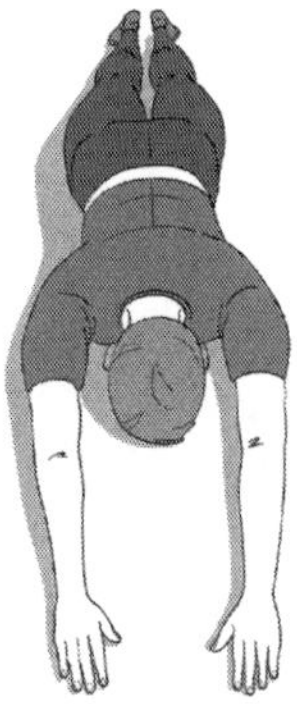

2

Starting position: Lie on your stomach, your arms fully extended forward.
1. Carefully lift your head and look forward. Keep your arms on the bed.
2. Lower your head back onto the bed.

Repeat 4–8 times.

Do this exercise slowly. If you have difficulty looking forward, lifting your head and looking down is sufficient.

ABOUT SENSORY ACTIVITIES

In the sixth chapter of this book, I wrote about the importance of sensorimotor integration. From the moment they are born, babies use their senses to explore and try to make sense of the world around them.

We are able to remember events many years later, and we remember information best when several senses are "exposed to" a subject simultaneously and the nervous system synthesizes the experiences from different directions.

I was maybe two or three years old, walking with my grandfather on a city road one November day. It was chilly and foggy. My hands were cold. My grandfather bought me roasted chestnuts to warm me up a bit. To this day, I remember the smell of roasting chestnuts, their shiny surface, and how good it felt to hold the paper bag with the warmth of the chestnuts in my hands. My grandfather used his giant fingers to peel the chestnuts, which tasted heavenly. Many sensory stimuli at once: sight, smell, touch, taste. It is common for our favorite memories to be linked to one or more of our senses. When we hear a voice, smell an odor, or experience other sensory stimuli associated with an old story, person, or event, our brain goes to work and recalls the memories.

Giving children the opportunity to actively use their senses is key to brain development. As they explore the world through touch, smell, sight, hearing, and other sensory functions, millions of connections are made between neurons in their brains. This enables children to perform more complex cognitive tasks, learn, process information, and understand new things quickly and economically. In this way, they develop their language, problem-solving, thinking, and social skills.

The activities and games in this chapter stimulate sensory activity and experience. They encourage children to use their senses to make new neural connections. As a result, their sensory integration is improved, and sensory experiences shape their behavior and their relationship with the world and themselves.

Children whose primitive reflexes have not integrated in time, for whatever reason, need to expand their sensory experiences because they did not have sufficient quality or quantity of these experiences at the beginning of their lives.

The following activities:

- Help build new connections in the brain so the child can perform more complex learning tasks
- Support language development, cognitive processes, fine and gross motor movements, problem-solving thinking, and social interactions
- Develop attention and memory
- Include various activities designed to calm a frustrated, anxious child
- Teach children about sensory attributes—slippery, sour, dry, quiet, etc.
- Are entertaining, and designed to bring fun into everyday life.

Choose those games and activities you or your child would like to do. And **have fun**!

Listen!

- Avoid having the radio or television continuously on at home
- Have your child listen to recordings of "white noise," splashing (or get an indoor fountain), or the sound of rain or the sea's roar
- Use simple, concise sentences when the parent or teacher asks or gives instructions
- Play tapping or clapping games with the child. For example, www.youtube.com/watch?v=_lAHDZhmytQ
- Read nursery rhymes or rhythmic poems to the child
- Play rhythm games: imitate simple rhythms, tapping, or drumming
- Play sound identification games. Stand behind the child or blindfold them and ask them to say what sound they heard.
    - Easy version: close, far, loud, soft, high, low
    - Medium difficulty: animal sounds. For example: https://www.youtube.com/watch?v=z-BqdY3zzDU
    - Difficult: various musical instruments
- In a safe environment, blindfold the child and give them instructions on how to find the "treasure" you hid

- Sharpen the child's hearing while at home, on the street, in the park, or in the garden. Sit down together and listen. Try to name as many sounds and noises as possible.
- Listen to music, focusing on the melody. Try to guess which instrument is playing.
- The child should learn to play an instrument. Choose one appropriate for their age and capability.
- Walk in the forest, and listen to the sounds of nature.
- Create sound-imitating tools together with the child, such as a rain stick: www.youtube.com/watch?v=k0C-K0VxMMk
- Throw/spread different things on the table, e.g., key rings, pebbles, dry leaves, sand, gravel, etc. Without looking, the child should try to guess what they are.
- Make noises with different parts of the body. Drum with the feet, tap the fingers, clap the hands, pop the lips and cheeks, click the tongues or fingers, tap your thighs, make "brr" and "bzz" noises with your mouth, rub your palms together, etc.
- Accompany the child in making different sounds. For example, animal noises, wind blowing, sirens, clapping, hissing, and musical instruments.
- Play a metronome at different frequencies and ask the child to distinguish between faster and slower. Metronome apps can be downloaded.
- With closed eyes or blindfolded, the child should guess what they hear. For example, stepping on paper, grinding coffee, popping corn, pouring water into a cup, stirring water or tea with a spoon, and closing a door.
- Ask the child to repeat words whispered in the ear or spoken when standing with your back to the child
- After listening to words and pronouncing them together, break them down into syllables and individual sounds, e.g., ANIMAL A-N-I-M-A-L
- Build up words from sounds, e.g., C-A-T CAT
- Wordchain: say a word using the final sound of a word heard, e.g., FOOD - DOG - GREEN - ...

Taste it!

- Blow bubbles
- If the child is old enough and sure not to swallow, chew gum
- Paint with bubbles: www.youtube.com/watch?v=m-n12RkV1zo

- The child should hold a thicker straw in their hand, blow into it, and try to keep a feather in the air
- Drink a thick smoothie through a straw
- Blow a whistle and try to imitate rhythms
- Blow on a harmonica or recorder
- Lift small light objects using a straw and move them from one container to another. Choose objects too big to fit through the straw, for example, a ping pong ball, or rolled-up scrap of paper.
- Eat crunchy foods like carrots, kohlrabi, and apples
- Try "sticky" foods like marshmallows, jellies, and honey
- Try foods and drinks that are different from what the child is used to: fizzy, slightly spicy, slightly bitter, slightly sour, etc.
- Blow up a balloon
- Blow out candles
- Use an electric toothbrush
- Whistle, hum, and make buzzing noises
- The child should try to draw or paint by holding the brush or pencil in their mouth (not suitable for very young children)
- Eat ice cream
- Blow a paper windmill. www.youtube.com/watch?v=AZrP2vSqhQ4
- Alternate between soft, medium, and hard toothbrushes
- Play the "What does this taste like?" game. With eyes closed or blindfolded, taste different flavors and guess what they are, e.g., chocolate, apple, carrot, bread, yogurt, jam, honey, lemon.

Grab it!

- Massage the fingers on each hand while telling a rhyme. Example:
  - *This little piggy went to market* – massage the thumb
  - *This little piggy stayed at home* – massage the index finger
  - *This little piggy ate roast beef* – massage the middle finger
  - *This little piggy had none* – massage the ring finger
  - *And this little pig cried wee-wee-wee all the way home* – massage the little finger
- Dough baking game. The child is the "dough."
  - While we say that we knead the dough, we massage the child's back.
  - While kneading, we can "add" different ingredients: sugar, flour, eggs, etc.

  - We can use our hands to pretend to sprinkle it on the child's back, smooth out the "sugar," crack the "egg," etc. When we have "kneaded" it well, we "stretch" it. At this point, we pull our forearm along the child's back a few times. Then we "put it in the oven," rolling the child slightly away from us. We "take it out of the oven," i.e., roll the child towards us. We "slice the cake"—using the edge of the palm of your hand to draw stripes lengthwise and widthwise across the child's back. Finally, "salt" or "sugar" it and "eat" it. You can say "num-num-num" and pretend to eat the child. (My own kids loved this game—they were all over each other.)
- Assemble a "bag of secrets." Put all sorts of small objects in the bag, things that the child can't accidentally hurt themselves with. It is best if they do not know what is in the bag. The child should reach in, try to name what they feel, then take it out and see if they were right. Variation: tell the child what to search for in the bag. The game should be played with each hand.
- Draw simple diagrams (or letters or numbers for school-age children) on the child's back or on the back of their hands (without them seeing). They guess what you drew.
- When bathing, spray shaving cream on the wall of the bathtub. Ask the child to draw with their fingers in the foam.
- Play with modeling clay (also known as putty or plasticine). You can make this at home too.
- Recipe for salt and flour modeling clay:
  - 250g salt (9oz)
  - 250g plain flour (9oz)
  - 1dL water (7 tablespoons)
  - 2 tablespoons of sunflower oil
  - This can also be allowed to dry on its own in warm sunshine and the child can paint it, or you can bake it in the oven at a low temperature for 40–60 minutes.
- Make pasta/noodles at home together with your child
- Play with "kinetic sand." Kinetic sand can be bought, but we can also make it home: www.youtube.com/watch?v=i7nd2_eUoxw
- Walk on a "barefoot path." If you have a garden, you can make it there. If not, you need a few trays. Fill the path or trays with differently textured materials and the child should walk barefoot on it. For example, sand, gravel, chestnut or acorns, dry beans, and cotton wool.

- Walk barefoot on the grass or possibly on the carpet, but it is more fun on the grass
- Jump into leaves in autumn, into snow in winter. This should only be done where you know there are no dangerous objects under the leaves or snow.
- Carve objects from clay with a wooden or plastic knife
- Play with the sticky substance known as "slime." You can buy this but children love to make it themselves from recipes on the internet.
- Visit a jacuzzi with your child
- Wade barefoot in the mud
- Paint on the bathtub while bathing. Special paints are available for this purpose.
- Make sensory cards for children. These can be kept in a box and the child can play with them under your supervision: www.youtube.com/watch?v=_8nt3sPbP6g
- Play with balls with different surface textures and hardnesses
- Play in the sandpit
- Fill balloons with different things: rice, sand, pearls, flour, etc., and let the child play with them
- Play with building toys: building blocks, Duplo, Lego, etc. The size of the blocks of course depends on age and development level.
- Mix different types of grain, rice, etc., together and the child should separate them out
- Touch different surfaces when out in nature. For example, bark, moss, soil, leaves, flower petals, pebbles, and stones.
- Play in the water
- Comb the child's hair regularly (even if it is short!)
- When bathing, name the child's body parts; when the child has learned them, ask which part of the body they are currently washing.

Smell it!

- Smelling different scented substances that are soluble in water
- Blow scented bubbles and drip various essential oils into soapy water
- Make a scented bath (chamomile, lavender, etc.) Allergy sufferers beware!
- Make scented paint. Mix different essential oils into tempera paint.
- Make scented salt and flour modeling clay

- Experience unpleasant smells—for example, vinegar, rotten vegetables, and decaying fruit
- Notice different smells while out walking. In the city, for example, a bakery, a pastry shop, a restaurant, and cars. But it is much better to do this in the forest.
- Burn scented candles, but only under parental supervision!
- Pair the image and smell of food
- With eyes closed or blindfolded, guess what smell you smelled
- If not in risk of being swallowed by the child, chew flavored chewing gum.

Note: Strong scents such as peppermint, pine, and clove are "activating"; softer scents such as lavender, chamomile, and lemongrass are "relaxing."

Look!

- Create a good weekly and/or daily timetable for your child
- Play "*starts with the letter...*" Glue or draw pictures beginning with different letters on a large sheet of paper. Tell your child, "*Find the pictures starting with the letter B...*", for example. They have to point to the book, the ball, the beetle, etc. This game can also be played by finding the objects around you that begin with a chosen letter—in the bedroom, kitchen, street, park, etc.
- Try to keep your child's room tidy. The toys that they play with most often should be out front.
- Solve mazes, play "*escape from the labyrinth.*" You can draw mazes on paper, but you can also build one out of boxes, for example.
- Make "shadow puppet shows" on the wall using the shadows of your and your child's hands
- Make figures and drawings using circles, squares, triangles, etc. In this game, the child must extend the starting shape to create an object or animal. For example, from a circle, the child could create a ball, sun, balloon, pig, spider, etc.
- Do jigsaw puzzles
- Group together objects and creatures of the same color
- Use coloring pages where the child has to distinguish between the figure and the background: www.pinterest.com/mtklra/alak-háttér
- Mix colors and paints

- Play "*Find the difference!*" The child should find the differences between two similar pictures that differ only in small details.
- Draw a simple shape on the wall with a flashlight. The child has to guess what simple shape you have drawn.
- If you can get a prism, observe how it breaks white light into colors
- Look through a kaleidoscope
- Shoot at a target with a water pistol
- Look at different objects and creatures with a hand-held magnifying glass
- Look into the distance with binoculars
- Draw with colored chalk on concrete
- Copy simple patterns. It is advisable to use square grid paper.
- Put four or five things on the table, cover them up, and ask the child to try to remember what was on the table. This visual memory exercise can be played in several ways. For example, put 10—12 objects on the table and then remove two while the child is looking away. The child should say what is missing.
- Show the child how to cut folded paper to make "paper snowflakes" (Kirigami technique)
- Hang up pictures made from scraps of paper, grains, pasta, pebbles, shells, etc.
- Project a slide film on the wall.

Spin and turn!

- Let your child play with different playground equipment as much as possible
- Play games that involve moving in a circle, e.g., turn in a circle together with your child, holding hands, and also with arms crossed. It is important to move in both directions!
- Tumble head over heels forward and backward, with assistance if necessary. Make sure the head is tucked in and body weight is not placed on the top of the head.
- Climb on a playground "spider's web" or climbing wall
- Crawl
- Jump on two legs and hop on one leg
- Leap down (at first with assistance) from a low height (the equivalent of 1–2 steps high)
- Trampoline

- Bicycle or tricycle
- Run in a circle and zig-zag left and right
- Run in a spiral, inwards and then outwards. You can draw a spiral line on the ground.
- Walk along a line drawn on the ground, facing both forwards and backwards
- Skip with a rope
- Balance on a balance board or a balance disc
- Roller skate
- Skate, roller blade, or ice-skate
- Ski
- Dance of any kind
- Spin in a swivel chair or "swivel egg"
- Spin and wobble in a "Bilibo"
- Bounce on a "fitball," with assistance
- Swing on rings. Older children can try hanging upside down with parental supervision.
- Handstand
- Climb on various obstacle courses
- Roll on the ground
- Roll the child into a blanket and let them roll over wrapped in it
- Swing in a hammock
- Do the Hokey-Pokey! www.youtube.com/watch?v=iZinb6rVozc

PRIMITIVE REFLEXES: SYMPTOM CHECKLISTS AND TEST EXERCISES

The following symptoms may occur as a result of undeveloped primitive reflexes. If one-fifth or more of the symptoms listed for a specific reflex are displayed by the child or adult, the reflex is either unintegrated or only partially integrated. In this case, it is recommended to start or continue with the relevant exercises.

Reflexes can also be physically tested. The necessary test is provided for each reflex, except for the FPR (fear paralysis reflex), for which the checklist can be used.

Exercise Videos

A set of videos are available that demonstrate how to perform tests for the existence of persistent primitive reflexes. Use the following QR code to go directly to the test video package, or visit https://drsarlos.com/videos where you can find more information, including my other videos which contain exercises designed to inhibit specific primitive reflexes.

Scan for video!

Moro

Symptom checklist

- Difficulty adapting to changing circumstances
- Anxiety
- Screaming
- Hitting, biting, scratching
- Does not like surprises
- Insecurity, mistrust
- Tires easily
- Sensitive to certain sounds, clothing, stroking, touching
- Occasionally has breathing problems
- Unnecessary nasal congestion
- Does not like to look others in the eye, avoids eye contact
- Does not like to try new activities
- Does not like to try new foods
- Negative thinking (e.g., "I can't do it", "I give up")
- Tantrums, hysteria
- Can't move and think at the same time
- Extreme fear of death
- Hypersensitivity
- Poor ball-handling skills
- Frequent blinking
- Panic reaction
- Fluctuating moods
- Red-faced when angry
- Aggressive outbursts
- Frequent earache or sore throat
- Inability to focus on details
- Sensitivity to background noise
- Digestive problems
- Sensitivity to food additives
- Strong cravings for sweet foods
- Picky eater
- Dizziness
- Frequent nausea

TEST FOR THE MORO REFLEX

Starting position: Stand behind the subject. Support the subject's head with one hand and their back with the other.

Task: Ask the subject to lean back against their palms and relax completely. You should let go for just a moment, but keep your hands in the starting position so you can safely catch the subject.

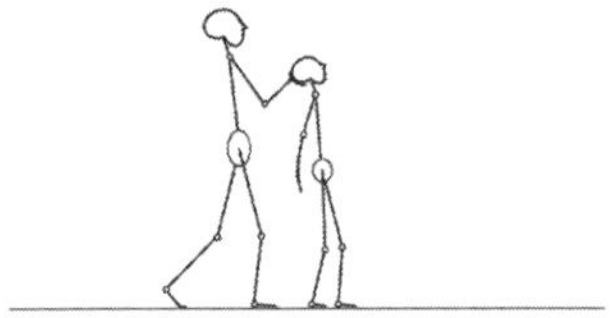

OK: If the arms do not swing out but remain hanging by the body, or the arms move backward in an attempt to prevent falling, as shown in the diagram above.

Reflex can be triggered: If the arms swing out to the side or forward, even if only one arm swings.

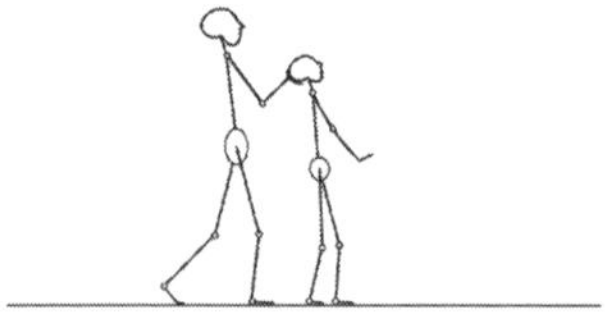

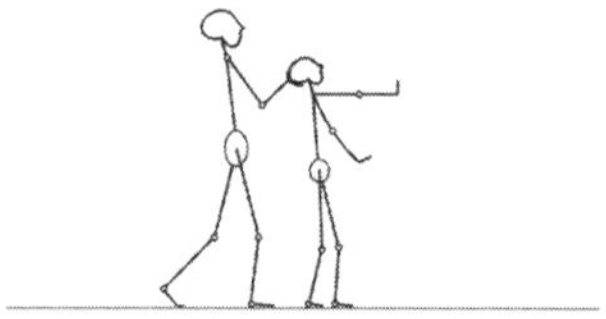

Tonic labyrinthine reflexes

Symptom checklist

- Poor sense of balance (especially static)
- Over-tight muscles (hypertonia)
- Over loose, relaxed muscles (hypotonia)
- Movement coordination problems
- Poor reading ability
- Slow or poor writing
- Problems with spelling
- Hypersensitive hearing
- Speech impediments
- “Squinting” when tired
- Problems with binocular vision
- Difficulty with visual perception
- Difficulty with auditory perception
- Walking on tip-toes
- Bedwetting
- Constipation
- Unusually liquid and frequent stools
- Reflux
- Gait and motor coordination problems
- Poor sense of time
- Poor sense of rhythm
- Reading difficulties
- Problems with copying
- Poor eye–hand coordination
- Inability to make decisions
- Problems with spatial vision
- Problems paying attention
- Shyness
- Easily influenced
- Fear of heights, depths
- Difficulty in developing a self-identity
- Feeling tired when sitting still (resting head)

TEST FOR TLR FORWARD

Starting position: The subject should lie on their back on the floor. Their arms should be stretched out on the floor next to their body, about 15–20 cm (6–8 inches) out from the body. Their palms should face upwards.

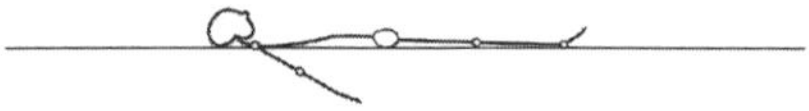

Task: The subject should lift their head forward. You can say to them, "Look at your feet."

OK: If they can lift their head with their arms fully extended and their shoulders are not pulled up into their neck.

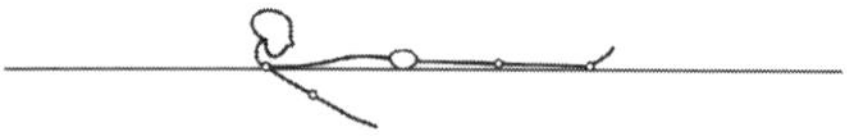

Reflex can be triggered: If one or both arms bend, or (if the exercise is challenging for them) the arms bend sideways, or the shoulders are pulled up into the neck.

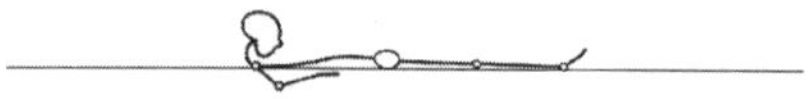

TEST FOR TLR BACKWARD

Starting position: The subject should lie face-down on the floor, arms bent alongside the body, palms facing up.

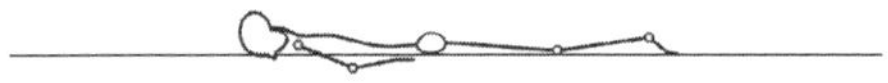

Task: The subject should raise their head, with eyes looking forward or slightly upwards.

OK: If the arms remain bent.

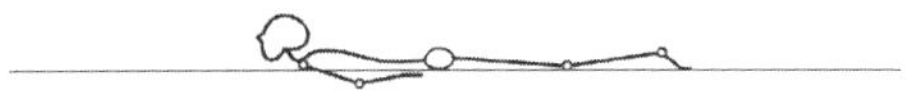

Reflex can be triggered: If the arms extend (straighten out) or if the subject reaches forward.

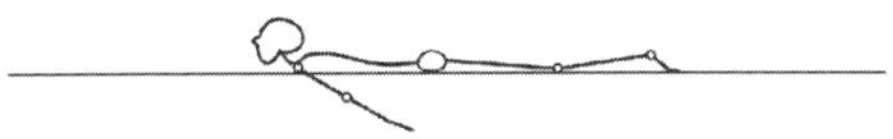

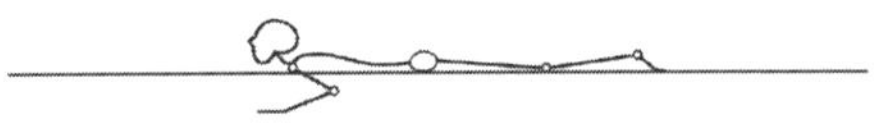

ATNR

SYMPTOM CHECKLIST

- Poor handwriting
- Poor drawing skills
- Problems with fine motor skills
- Problems with eye movement
- Unable to squint
- Cross-dominance
- Alternate dominance (ambidexterity)
- Hand cramps when writing
- Unable to follow the lines of text when reading
- Skips letters and words when reading
- Cannot judge distances
- Difficulty in oral and written expression
- Impulsivity
- Writes numbers and letters backward and in the wrong order
- Poor ball sense (especially handling)
- Poor eye–hand coordination
- Difficulty in learning certain sports

TEST FOR ATNR

Starting position: The subject should face the wall, arms extended a shoulder-width apart, with palms on the wall and fingers turned upwards.

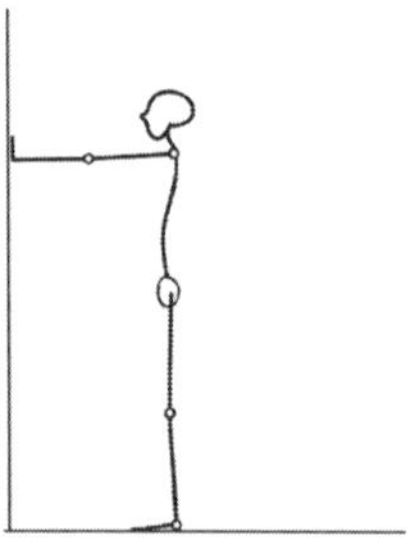

Task: The subject should turn their head to the left. The test is most accurate when you stand behind the subject and turn their head.

OK: If both arms and legs remain extended, the palms on the wall do not move, and the fingers remain facing up.

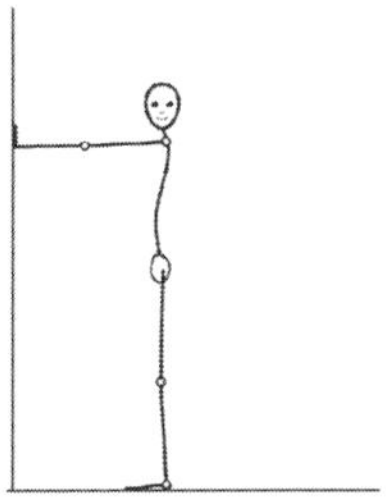

Reflex can be triggered: If the arm bends on the opposite side of the direction in which the head turns. (For example, if the head is turned to the left, the right arm bends.)

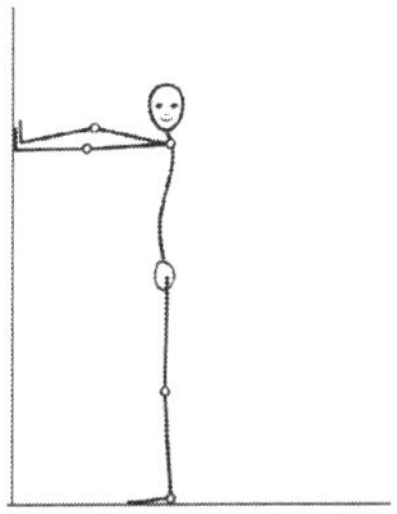

This test must be performed in both directions. A reflex is considered integrated only when it cannot be triggered on either side.

Spinal Galant reflex

Symptom checklist

- Bedwetting
- Constipation or loose stools
- Unable to sit still; squirming
- Poor attention span
- Poor short-term memory
- Constant fidgeting with the hands
- Repetitive movements (e.g., foot tapping)
- Hyperactivity
- Difficulty understanding what is heard
- Constantly causing a ruckus
- Dislikes tight pants or clothes around the waist
- Uncoordinated movement
- Frequent falls
- Unusual gait
- Desire to play sports
- Leaning to one side when standing
- Scoliosis

Test for the Galant reflex

Starting position: The subject should kneel on all fours.

Task: Draw the middle "knuckle" of your index finger, or a pencil, along the subject's spine, across the waist, to the hip-lumbar area, and back. Repeat 3–4 times.

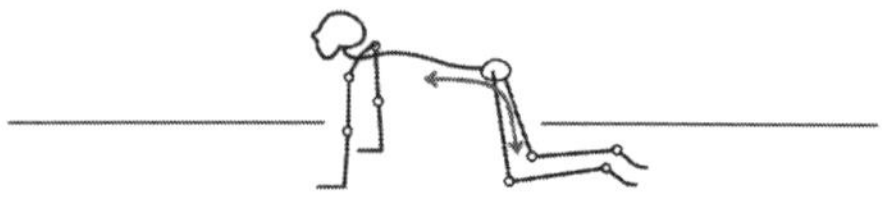

OK: If the spine and hips don't move, and the subject does not complain about being ticklish.

Reflex can be triggered: If the spine or hips move away from the original position or the subject feels ticklish in the stimulated area.

Grasping and sucking reflexes

SYMPTOM CHECKLIST

- Poor handwriting
- Inaccurate coloring ability
- Poor drawing skills
- Speech comprehension problems
- Speech perception problems
- Speech disorders
- Difficulties holding a pencil
- Urge to touch or rub things (e.g., fabrics)
- Repetitive hand motions (e.g., tapping, rubbing)
- Pencil chewing
- Nail biting
- Thumb sucking
- Urge to chew/suck things (e.g., gum, pen, clothes)
- Stuttering
- Swallowing problems
- Chewing problems
- Involuntary tongue movements when using fingers or hands (e.g., when drawing)
- Unable to eat with mouth closed
- Licking around the mouth
- Drooling
- Messy eating
- Leaning into the plate when eating

TEST FOR THE SUCKING REFLEX

Test the sucking reflex through the Babkin response.

Place a small ball in the subject's hand, and ask them to rotate the ball with their fingers using just that hand. If the subject is a small child, place the ball in the palm of your own hand and ask the child to turn it with one hand as if they were trying to open a tap.

Meanwhile, watch their mouth! If the lips or tongue move, the sucking reflex can be triggered.

TEST FOR THE GRASPING REFLEX

Starting position: The subject should extend their fingers loosely (it's not necessary to strain) and hold their palm facing upwards.

Task: Draw a pencil 3–4 times across the palm of the test person's hand, both crosswise and lengthwise. The test should be performed on both palms.

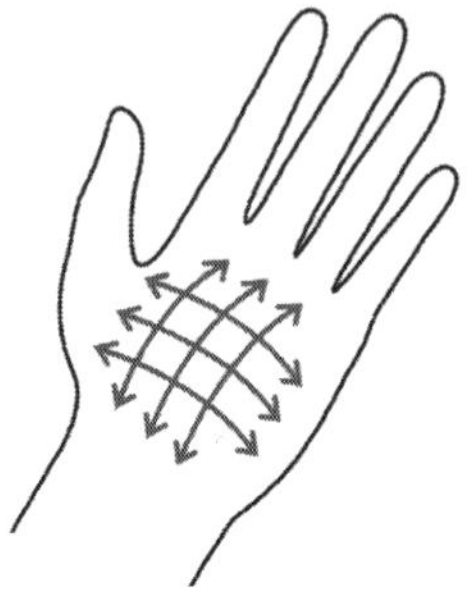

OK: If the fingers do not bend and the palm does not feel ticklish.
Reflex can be triggered: If the fingers bend or the palm feels ticklish.

TEST FOR THE ROOTING REFLEX

Task: Draw a pencil in a semicircular arc 3–4 times around the subject's mouth, starting from the top and working downwards.

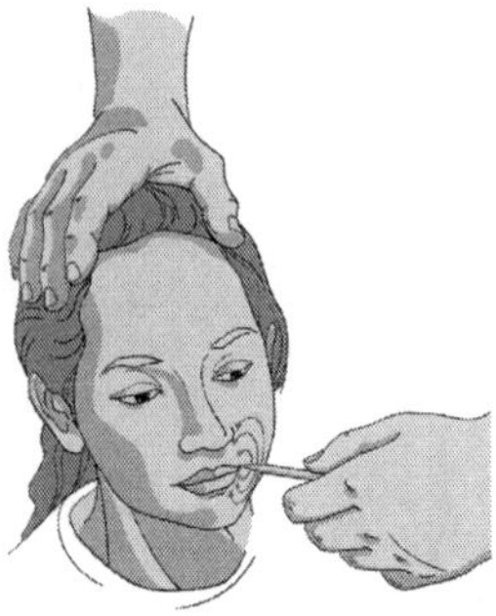

OK: If the mouth does not move and is not ticklish.
Reflex can be triggered: If the corner of the mouth moves in or it feels ticklish on the stimulated side.

STNR

Symptom checklist

- Frequent headaches from neck muscle strain
- Difficulties reading and writing
- Difficulty sitting patiently in school
- Vision problems
- Slowness
- Awkward, clumsy movement
- Frequent falls
- Poor, stooped posture
- The child skips crawling and directly starts to stand and walk
- "W-sitting," knees out front with feet on either side of the hips
- "Bear-walking," walking on all four feet
- Difficulty copying from the blackboard

Test

Starting position: The subject should kneel on all fours, arms extended, palms on the floor a shoulder-width apart and fingers extended, with feet on the ground.

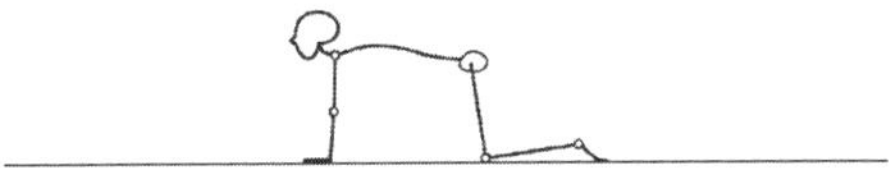

Task: Ask the subject to bend their head back and look upwards, then bend their head down and look back between their two arms towards their feet.

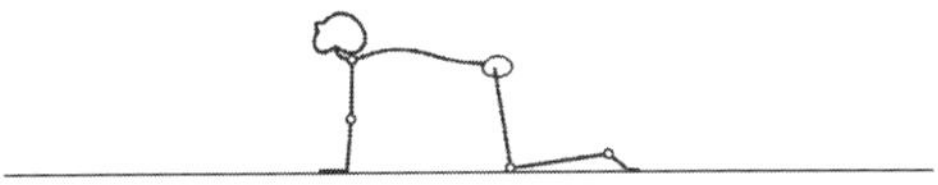

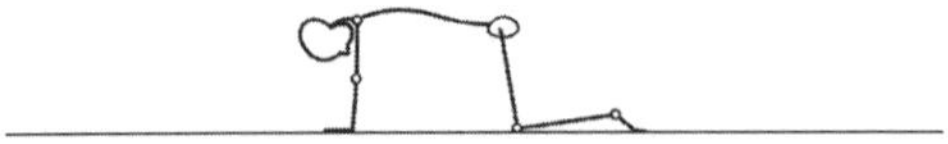

OK: If the arms remain extended throughout, the body does not move forward or backward, the subject's spine does not drop when the head is raised, and does not arch when looking back between the arms.

Reflex can be triggered: If the body moves forwards or backward, the arms bend, the body sits back on the legs, or the back arches.

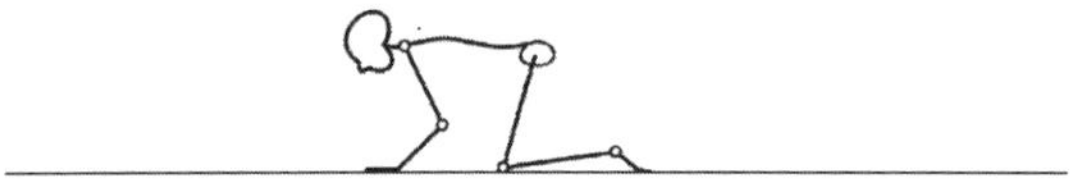

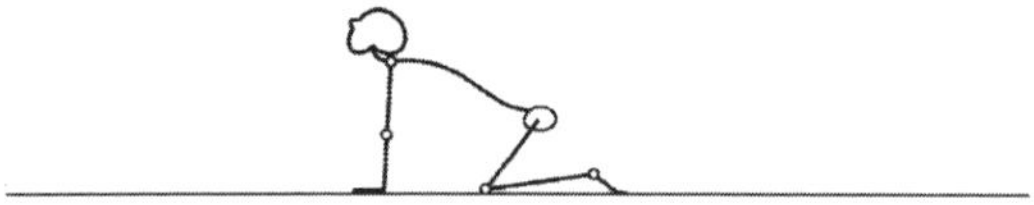

FPR

SYMPTOM CHECKLIST

- Low tolerance to stress
- Anxiety that appears to be unrelated to reality
- Hypersensitivity to touch, sound, specific frequencies of sound, and visual stimuli
- Dislikes change and surprise
- Hard to adapt to new situations and people
- Fatigue
- Selective mutism—unwillingness to talk in certain situations
- Holds their breath or often feels "short of breath"
- Fear of social interactions, especially in situations perceived as uncomfortable
- Does not feel safe
- Lack of confidence
- Social isolation
- Overly attached to certain people or, conversely, unable to accept or show affection easily
- Avoids nursery, school, and communities
- Compulsive behavior
- Pessimistic, negative attitude
- Difficulty trying new activities, or never tries
- Avoids situations where it is necessary to compete against others
- Frequent depression
- Tantrums
- Likes to control others
- Resistant behavior, especially in the home environment
- "Paralyzed" by stress—cannot think and move simultaneously
- Hypotonic muscles in many cases
- Nutritional disorders
- Constant need for attention
- Aggressive behavior due to frustration and confusion
- Poor sense of balance

CTGR

SYMPTOM CHECKLIST

- Rigid posture
- Poor sense of balance
- Foot and leg cramps
- Lower back pain
- Poor coordination of movements
- Difficulty walking and running
- Walking on tiptoe
- Delayed speech development and/or speech disorder
- Fear or anxiety, stress
- Getting excessively absorbed in a task
- May appear to "switch off" at times, not listening when spoken to
- Excessive shyness
- Hyperactivity
- Frequent freezing-up when faced with a challenge or in competitive sports

TEST FOR CTGR

Starting position: The subject should sit on the floor with legs outstretched. They can support themselves with their arms. Their feet should be bare.

Task: Draw a pencil from the area under the subject's big toe towards the heel 3–4 times.

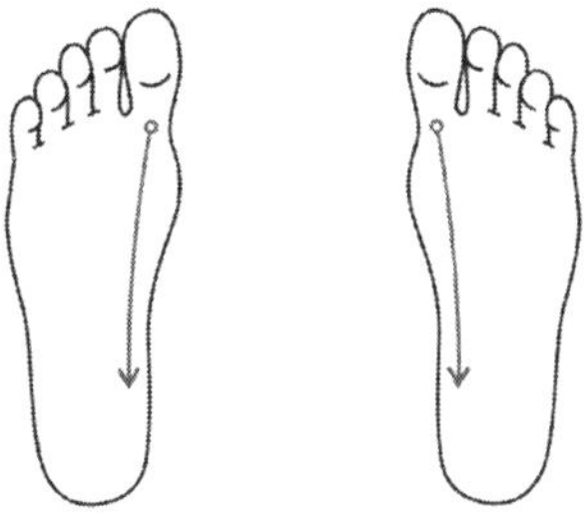

OK: If the foot does not move, or pulls back towards the body.

Reflex can be triggered: If the foot extends toward the stimulus (the pencil).

ACKNOWLEDGMENTS

While writing this acknowledgment, I realized how many people, directly or indirectly, were involved in publishing this book. Firstly, I would like to express my gratitude to Professor István Nahalka, who supervised one of the topics in my doctoral dissertation and accompanied me throughout the entire research process. In addition to his assistance, he provided critiques, asked questions, and, during one of our consultations, he raised the idea of writing a book on the subject. The professor not only deserves my gratitude but also that of the book's users, as I would not have thought of it myself.

My eternal gratitude goes to Professor György Bárdos, who undertook the professional review of the book. I will never forget my first meeting with the professor at the Fővám Square tram stop in Budapest. I asked him to take on the task, and we began a long walk around Corvinus University. He asked many different questions to which I tried to provide answers, and by the time we returned to the zebra crossing in front of the market hall he said he would take on the task. I was overjoyed. I looked forward to his critiques and comments on every occasion, even when I had to rewrite entire chapters.

I will never forget Professor Iván Falus, who helped me apply for my doctoral studies, supported me both personally and professionally—even when it was "a little difficult"—and on whom I could always rely.

I thank my large family for their support and encouragement. A special thanks to my husband, Patrick, for playing a major role in creating the English-language edition of this book, and for his infinite patience. He heard the phrase "Just wait a minute, I'll write two more sentences" many times during the writing of this book, which turned into either two sentences or five pages. Since I relied mostly on English-language literature, research results, and articles, whenever I didn't quite understand something, I turned to him for help to explain the exact meaning of a term. In addition to his invaluable contribution to the processing of my research results, endless editing of Excel spreadsheets, and rewriting my English translations, he cooked, washed, and cleaned, relieving me of such tasks. This book would not have been possible without him.

I thank my granddaughter, Kátya, for doing gymnastics with me, and contributing to the illustrations of the chapter for young children. I thank my parents, over 80 years of age, for "testing" the exercises for the elderly, and for asking every week if the book was finished yet.

I would like to thank Zsolt Kecseti, the illustrator, for his expertise, precise work, and for being able to fully realize what I envisioned. If my request was not clear, he adjusted the graphics until they took on their final form. When I couldn't find a drawing or illustration amid the chaos on my computer, Zsolt patiently sent them again—sometimes for the third time. I am grateful to Edina Virág for her participation in the creation of the illustrations. I thank Péter Hári for the book layout, and Selena Class for copy editing.

I cannot thank enough Bea Gutman and Péter Hasenfracz, who published the original Hungarian edition of the book. I greatly appreciate their enthusiastic work, their patience with me, and their flexibility. It was very easy to work with them. Although we never talked about it, throughout the entire process, I felt that this book was important to them because it will undoubtedly help children and adults.

I thank the educators who participated, with almost 800 children, in my doctoral research, which showed that sensorimotor maturity is closely related to the level of auditory and visual abilities required for learning. Their work is just as much a part of this book as the parents who honored me with their trust, brought their children to me for examination, and went through the program I prescribed for them. In addition to sharing their children's problems with me, I was in constant contact with many of them. We celebrated together when children were able to get rid of a "medical diagnosis" or when those who hated reading began to devour books. It was equally satisfying when someone became permanently toilet-trained, learned to swim, started talking, or was able to produce a bowel movement on a daily basis—the list goes on.

Hats off to every parent who is able to deal with their child day in and day out, even when it doesn't feel like a victory march. In writing this book, I often drew strength from the energy of the moms and dads, their attitude toward their children, and their daily struggles. I am grateful to everyone who taught me, who contributed to my understanding of the subject, and who helped me acquire new knowledge through their research, discoveries, and expertise. There are hundreds of them. From the domestic and international ranks, I would like to highlight two people: Professor Ferenc Katona and Marianne Berényi. Their work, their respect for life, and their willingness to help are exemplary. The literature published by them is still on my desk.

GLOSSARY

Autonomic nervous system: The part of the nervous system that functions independently of our will and regulates the functioning of the internal organs.

Axon: a long, thin, hollow, cylindrical extension of a neuron that normally carries a nerve impulse away from the cell body.

Bilateral coordination: using both sides of the body together to perform an activity.

Brainstem: the central trunk of the mammalian brain, consisting of the medulla oblongata, pons, and midbrain, and continuing downwards to form the spinal cord.

Central nervous system (CNS): the entire complex of neurons, axons, and supporting tissue that constitute the brain and spinal cord. The CNS is primarily involved in mental activities and in coordinating and integrating incoming sensory messages and outgoing motor messages.

Cerebral cortex and subcortical areas: in humans, the cortex is where many of the higher-level functions take place (e.g., decision-making and language). "Subcortex" means "beneath the cortex." The subcortex is where we process more primitive functions (e.g., emotions are processed in the amygdala).

Classical conditioning theory: this states that behaviors are learned by connecting a neutral stimulus with a positive one, such as the dogs in Pavlov's experiments hearing a bell (neutral) and expecting food (positive). The learned behavior is called a conditioned response.

Cognitive: based on cognition. Cognitive skills include perception, reasoning, attention, memory, and imagination.

Constructivism: a learning theory based on the idea that learners build on their existing foundation to learn new information.

Cortical inhibition: a neurophysiological process in which gamma-aminobutyric acid (GABA) inhibitory interneurons selectively reduce the activity of other neurons (e.g., pyramidal neurons) in the cortex.

Dyscalculia: an impaired ability to perform simple arithmetic operations, resulting from a congenital deficit.

Dysgraphia: a neurological disorder and learning disability that affects the ability to write.

Dyslexia: a condition of neurodevelopmental origin that mainly affects the ease with which a person reads, writes, and spells, typically recognized as a specific learning disorder in children.

Epistemology: the theory of knowledge, especially with regard to its methods, validity, and scope, and the distinction between justified belief and opinion.

Executive function: a set of mental skills that include working memory, flexible thinking, and self-control. We use these skills every day to learn, work, and manage daily life. Problems with executive function can make it difficult to focus, follow directions, and handle emotions, among other things.

Hippocampus: an ancient cortical structure that is indirectly connected to all sensory and associative areas of the cerebral cortex.

Hyperkinetic: characterized by increased and excessive muscular movements that are sometimes involuntary.

Hypertonic: a state of abnormally high muscle tone.

Hypoglycemia: low blood sugar level.

Hypotonic: a state of abnormally low muscle tone or strength.

Kinesthesia: awareness of the position and movement of the parts of the body by means of sensory organs (proprioceptors) in the muscles and joints.

Kyphosis: a spinal disorder in which an excessive curve of the spine results in an abnormal rounding of the upper back.

Laterality: the preferential use of one side of the body for certain functions, such as eating, writing, and kicking.

Locomotor movements skills: those in which the body is moved in one direction, or a combination of directions, from one point to another. Activities such as walking, moving forwards or backwards, skipping, running, jumping and hopping are considered fundamental locomotion movements.

Lordosis: excessive lumbar curvature of the spinal column.

Mechanoreceptors: cells that are sensitive to mechanical stimuli (e.g., pressure or vibration)

Motoneurons: motor nerve cells.

Motor coordination: the ability to use multiple body parts for a particular action. For example, dribbling a basketball means using your arms and hands to bounce the ball while your feet and legs move you around the court.

Musculoskeletal system: this includes your bones, cartilage, ligaments, tendons, and connective tissues. Your skeleton provides a framework for your muscles and other soft tissues. Together, they support your body's weight, maintain your posture, and help you move.

Myelination: the formation of an insulating layer around the long projections of nerve cells, called axons, which allows the nerves to conduct stimuli more rapidly and in a more targeted manner.

Myotatic unit: a unit of nerve cells and muscle fibers necessary to maintain normal muscle tone.

Neocortex: a part of the cerebral cortex concerned with sight and hearing in mammals, regarded as the most recently evolved part of the cortex.

Nervous system: the organized network of nerve tissue in the body. It includes the central nervous system (the brain and spinal cord), the peripheral nervous system (nerves that extend from the spinal cord to the rest of the body), and other nerve tissue.

Neural function: neurons are the key building blocks of the nervous system and responsible for receiving, processing, and transmitting information from sensory organs to other parts of the body to establish essential functions such as movement, sensation, perception, and cognition.

Neuro-endocrine system: the combined name for the nervous system and endocrine gland system.

Neurogenesis: the production of new neurons during early nervous system development and throughout one's lifespan. The failure or interruption of neurogenesis is implicated in neurological diseases such as Alzheimer's and Parkinson's, as well as in psychiatric disorders such as depression, bipolar disorder, and schizophrenia.

Neuroplasticity: neuroplasticity or brain plasticity is defined as the ability of the nervous system to change its activity in response to intrinsic or extrinsic stimuli by reorganizing its structure, functions, or connections. A fundamental property of neurons is their ability to modify the strength and efficacy of synaptic transmission through a diverse number of activity-dependent mechanisms, typically referred to as synaptic plasticity.

Neurons: the basic cellular unit of the nervous system.

Olfactory epithelium: the olfactory epithelium is membranous tissue located inside the nasal cavity.

Ontogenetic development: this can be conceptualized as the portion of physical, cognitive, emotional, and social development that can be attributed to experiences with the environment and the individuals within the environment.

Ontogeny: individual developmental of an organism within its own lifetime.

Pathological: abnormal.

Periosteum: a dense layer of vascular connective tissue enveloping the bones except at the surfaces of the joints.

Pervasive: comprehensive, affecting the whole personality.

Postural reactions: the postural reactions and locomotor movements are present in the elementary movement patterns. The harmony between the two prepares for the development of locomotion, the movement that relies on a stable posture for changing the body position.

Prefrontal lobe: the anterior part of the frontal lobe of the brain.

Primitive reflexes (infant reflexes): Involuntary motor responses originating in the brainstem that are present at birth and after birth in the early development of the child and that facilitate survival and the experience of stimuli from the external and internal environment. They become inhibited by the maturation of the brain around 4–6 months of age and should no longer be triggered at 2–2.5 years of age.

Procedural learning: learning to ride a bicycle, drive a car, tie a shoelace, or perform any other sequence of actions, where practice is needed to memorize the sequence of actions.

Proprioception: perception or awareness of the position and movement of the body, resulting from stimulation of proprioceptors located in the muscles, tendons, and joints and of vestibular receptors in the labyrinth of the inner ear. Proprioception enables the body to determine its spatial orientation without visual clues and to maintain postural stability.

Proprioceptive integration: proprioceptive signals are transmitted to the central nervous system, where they are integrated with information from other sensory systems, such as the visual system and the vestibular system, to create an overall representation of body position, movement, and acceleration.

Regression: falling back, going back to a previous level, a previous state.

Scoliosis: a sideways curve of the spine. Everyone has normal curves in the spine when viewed from the side, and normally, when looked at from behind, the spine appears straight.

Selective mutism: those who are able to speak freely in some situations but not in others.

Sensorimotor: describing activity, behavior, or brain processes that involve both sensory (afferent) and motor (efferent) functions.

Sensorimotor integration: the relationship between the sensory and motor systems (muscles) and the process by which these two systems communicate with each other. Sensorimotor integration is most intense from birth to age 7. The process is in three parts: (1) a sensory stimulus; (2) the nerves carry the information to the brain, where the information is interpreted; and (3) the brain then determines what response to make and transmits its instructions to the appropriate group of muscle fibers to carry out that response. The sensory and motor systems work in diametrical harmony.

Sensory: relating to the senses.

Sensory integration: the process that enables us to take in, interpret, organize, and respond appropriately to information from the external and internal environment. "Sensory integration is a neural process that makes stimuli from the body and the environment perceived and interpreted in a unified way, thereby ensuring an effective body response to stimuli. During integration, the incoming signals are not only added together, but the nervous system also differentiates and differentiates" (Katona, 2001).

Spatial perception: the ability to be aware of your relationships with the environment around you (exteroceptive processes) and within yourself (interoceptive processes).

Spinal cord: the spinal cord is a cylindrical structure containing tissues, fluids and nerve cells. It connects your brain to your lower back. Your spinal cord carries nerve signals from your brain to your body and vice versa. These nerve signals help you feel sensations and move your body.

Sympathetic nervous system: this mobilizes the body's energy, for example preparing it to repel an attack or to obtain food. Sympathetic action causes pupil dilation, constriction of the skin and digestive tract, reduced urine output, and increased myocardial contractions.

Synapse: the specialized junction through which neural signals are transmitted from one neuron (the presynaptic neuron) to another (the postsynaptic neuron).

Synaptogenesis: refers to the formation of synapses, the points of contact where information is transmitted between neurons.

Temporal sequence: how one thing follows another; succession.

Thalamus: a group of cells deep in the brain that functions as a "switchboard" for nerve signals coming from and going to the cerebral cortex, integrating the nerve pathways that pass through it. All sensory information except for smell is received in the thalamus and transmitted to other brain areas. It is also involved in the control of movement in the opposite direction. The thalamus is therefore like a huge, tangled junction where a lot of neural information is collected and connected to the rest of the central nervous system. In addition to its mediating role, it is also responsible for the regulation of consciousness, sleep, and wakefulness.

Vestibular system: a system in the body that is responsible for maintaining balance, posture, and the body's orientation in space, which plays an important role in regulating locomotion and other movements. It consists of the vestibular apparatus in the inner ear, the vestibular nerve, and the various cortical regions associated with the processing of vestibular (balance) information.

Visceroreception: the perception and processing of interoceptive signals arising from inner organs. Importantly, visceroception is not fully captured by visceral sensitivity alone, which primarily reflects sensory-discriminative aspects of perception.

Visceral perception: see Visceroreception.

BIBLIOGRAPHY

This bibliography includes all the sources I referenced in the text. In addition, it also contains several other relevant and important sources that I relied on during the writing of the book, including foreign-language sources that I have included for completeness. Therefore, interested readers are encouraged to browse this list as they may come across many useful sources of information.

Abdelkarim, O., Ammar, A., Chtourou, H., Wagner, M., Knisel, E., Hökelmann, A. & Bös, K. (2017). Relationship between motor and cognitive learning abilities among primary school-aged children. *Alexandria Journal of Medicine, 53*(4), 325–331. https://doi.org/10.1016/j.ajme.2016.12.004

About Kids GI (n.d.). *Soiling and functional fecal retention.* Retrieved April 30, 2022, from https://aboutkidsgi.org/lower-gi/childhood-defecation-disorders/soiling-and-functional-fecal-retention

Adkins, D. A. L., Boychuk, J., Remple, M. S. & Kleim, J. A. (2006). Motor training induces experience-specific patterns of plasticity across motor cortex and spinal cord. *Journal of Applied Physiology, 101*(6), 1776–1782. https://doi.org/10.1152/japplphysiol.00515.2006

Agostino, A., Johnson, J. & Pascual-Leone, J. (2010). Executive functions underlying multiplicative reasoning: Problem type matters. *Journal of Experimental Child Psychology, 105*(4), 286–305. https://doi.org/10.1016/j.jecp.2009.09.006

Alfano, C. A., Beidel, D. C., Turner, S. M. & Lewin, D. S. (2006). Preliminary evidence for sleep complaints among children referred for anxiety. *Sleep Medicine, 7*(6), 467–473. https://doi.org/10.1016/j.sleep.2006.05.002

American Psychiatric Association (1994). *Diagnostic and Statistical Manual of Mental Disorders* (4th edition). APA, Washington, DC.

Andermann, A. A. (1997). Hughlings Jackson's deductive science of the nervous system: A product of his thought collective and formative years. *Neurology*, *48*(2), 471–481. https://doi.org/10.1212/wnl.48.2.471

Anderson, M. (1992). *Intelligence and Development: A Cognitive Theory.* Blackwell, Oxford.

Arnheim, R. (2015). *Visual Thinking.* University of California Press, Berkeley.

Ashraf, F. & Najam, N. (2020). An epidemiological study of prevalence and comorbidity of non-clinical dyslexia, dysgraphia and dyscalculia symptoms in public and private schools of Pakistan. *Pakistan Journal of Medical Sciences*, *36*(7), 1659–1663. https://doi.org/10.12669/pjms.36.7.2486

Association for Children with Learning Disabilities (1986). *ACLD Description: Specific Learning Disabilities.* ACLD Newsbriefs, 15–16.

Ayres, J. (1979). *Sensory Integration and the Child.* Western Psychological Services, Los Angeles.

Babkin, P. S. (1960). The establishment of reflex activity in early postnatal life. In: Macy, J., Jr. (Ed.), *The Central Nervous System and Behavior*. Public Health Service, Washington, DC, 24–31.

Baillieux, H., De Smet, H. J., Paquier, P. F., De Deyn, P. P. & Marien, P. (2008). Cerebellar neurocognition: insights into the bottom of the brain. *Clinical Neurology and Neurosurgery*, *110*(8), 763–773. https://doi.org/10.1016/j.clineuro.2008.05.013

Bárány R. (1906). Über die vom Ohrlabyrinth ausgelöste Gegenrollung der Augen bei Normalhörenden, Ohrenkranken und Taubstummen. *Archiv Für Ohrenheilkunde*, *68*(1–2), 1–30. https://doi.org/10.1007/bf01834666

Bárdos Gy. (2003). *Pszichovegetatív Kölcsönhatások.* Scolar Kiadó, Budapest.

Bateman, B. (1965). An educational view of a diagnostic approach to learning disorders. In: J. Hellmuth (Ed.), *Learning Disorders* (Volume 1). Special Child Publications, Seattle, 219–239.

Becker A. (2010, May 6). "A többség határeset" – Dr. Donauer Nándor Klinikai szakpszichológus, neuropszichológus. *Magyar Narancs.* Retrieved July 11, 2023, from https://magyarnarancs.hu/lelek/a_tobbseg_hatareset_-_dr_donauer_nandor_klinikai_szakpszichologus_neuropszichologus-73702

Berényi M. & Katona F. (2014). *Fejlődésneurológia: Az öntudat, a kommunikáció és a mozgás kialakulása.* Medicina, Budapest.

Berquin, P. C., Giedd, J. N., Jacobsen, L. K., Hamburger, S. D., Krain, A. L., Rapoport, J. L. & Castellanos, F. X. (1998). Cerebellum in attention-deficit hyper activity disorder: a morphometric MRI study. *Neurology, 50*(4), 1087–1093. https://doi.org/10.1212/wnl.50.4.1087

Bilbilaj, S., Gjipali , A. & Shkurti, F. (2017). Measuring Primitive Reflexes in Children with Learning Disorders. *European Journal of Multidisciplinary Studies, 2*(5), 176–189. https://doi.org/10.26417/ejms.v5i1.p285-298

Birch, L. L., Gunder, L., Grimm-Thomas, K. & Laing, D. G. (1998). Infants' consumption of a new food enhances acceptance of similar foods. *Appetite, 30*(3), 283–295. https://doi.org/10.1006/appe.1997.0146

Blomberg, H. & Dempsey, M. (2008). *Movements That Heal: Rhythmic Movement Training and Primitive Reflex Integration.* Beyond the Sea Squirt, East Melbourne, Vic.

Blythe, P. (1992). *A Physical Approach to Resolving Learning Difficulties.* Institute for Neuro-Physiological Psychology, Chester.

Bob, P., Konicarova, J. & Raboch, J. (2013). Persisting primitive reflexes in medication-naïve girls with attention-deficit and hyperactivity disorder. *Neuropsychiatric Disease and Treatment, 9*, 1457–1481. https://doi.org/10.2147/ndt.s49343

Bobath, K. & Bobath, B. (1967). The Neuro-Developmental Treatment of Cerebral Palsy. *Physical Therapy, 47*(11), 1039–1043. https://doi.org/10.1093/ptj/47.11.1039

Boyd, S. C. (January, 2022). *The tendon guard reflex - understanding our protective reflex.* Highpoint Mind & Movement. Retrieved July 14, 2023, from www.highpointaz.com/christinas-blog/the-tendon-guard-reflex-our-protective-reflex

Bremner, J. G., Slater, A. M., & Johnson, S. P. (2014). Perception of object persistence: The origins of object permanence in infancy. *Child Development Perspectives*, *9*(1), 7-13. https://doi.org/10.1111/cdep.12098

Brown, L. L., Schneider, J. S. & Lidsky, T. I. (1997). Sensory and cognitive functions of the basal ganglia. *Current Opinion in Neurobiology*, *7*(2), 157–163. https://doi.org/10.1016/s0959-4388(97)80003-7

Brown, R. D. (2018). *Neuroscience of Mathematical Cognitive Development: From Infancy Through Emerging Adulthood.* Springer, Cham.

Buderath, P., Gärtner, K., Frings, M., Christiansen, H., Schoch, B., Konczak, J., Gizewski, E. R., Hebebrand, J. & Timmann, D. (2009). Postural and gait performance in children with attention deficit/hyperactivity disorder. *Gait & Posture*, *29*(2), 249–254. https://doi.org/10.1016/j.gaitpost.2008.08.016

Bushnell, E. & Boudreau, J. (1993). Motor development and the mind: The potential role of motor abilities as a determinant of aspects of perceptual development. *Child Development, 63*(4), 1005–1021. https://doi.org/10.1111/j.1467-8624.1993.tb04184.x

Büttner, G. & Hasselhorn, M. (2011). Learning disabilities: Debates on definitions, causes, subtypes, and responses. *International Journal of Disability, Development and Education, 58*(1), 75–87. https://doi.org/10.1080/1034912x.2011.548476

Cantell, M. H., Smyth, M. M. & Ahonen, T. P. (1994). Clumsiness in Adolescence: Educational, Motor, and Social Outcomes of Motor Delay Detected at 5 Years. *Adapted Physical Activity Quarterly, 11*(2), 115–129. https://doi.org/10.1123/apaq.11.2.115

Capute, A. J. & Accardo, P. J. (1991). *Developmental Disabilities in Infancy and Childhood.* Paul Brooks, Baltimore.

Capute, A. J., Palmer, F. B., Shupiro, B. K., Wuchtel, R. C., Ross, A. & Accurdo, P. J. (1984). Primitive Reflex Profile: A Quantitation of Primitive Reflexes in Infancy. *Developmental Medicine & Child Neurology, 26*(3), 375–383. https://doi.org/10.1111/j.1469-8749.1984.tb04456.x

Capute, A. J., Wachtel, R. C., Palmer, F. B., Shapiro, B. K. & Accardo, P. J. (1982). A Prospective Study of Three Postural Reactions. *Developmental Medicine & Child Neurology, 24*(4), 314–320. https://doi.org/10.1111/j.1469-8749.1982.tb13623.x

Carleton, S. C. & Carpenter, M. B. (1983). Afferent and efferent connections of the medial, inferior and lateral vestibular nuclei in the cat and monkey. *Brain Research, 278*(1–2), 29–51. https://doi.org/10.1016/0006-8993(83)90223-8

Cashdan, E. (1998). Adaptiveness of food learning and food aversions in children. *Social Science Information, 37*(4), 613–632. https://doi.org/10.1177/053901898037004003

Castelli, D. M., Hillman, C. H., Buck S. M. & Erwin, H. E. (2007). Physical fitness and academic achievement in third- and fifth-grade students. *Journal of Sport and Exercise Psychology, 29*(2), 239–252. https://doi.org/10.1123/jsep.29.2.239

Cattell, P. (1940). *The Measurement of Intelligence of Infants and Young Children.* Psychological Corporation, New York.

Chaddock, L., Hillman, C. H., Pontifex, M. B., Johnson, C. R., Raine, L. B. & Kramer, A. F. (2012). Childhood aerobic fitness predicts cognitive performance one year later. *Journal of Sports Sciences, 30*(5), 421–430. https://doi.org/10.1080/02640414.2011.647706

Chaddock-Heyman, L., Erickson, K. I., Kienzler, C., King, M., Pontifex, M. B., Raine, L. B., Hillman, C. H. & Kramer, A. F. (2015). Correction: The role of aerobic fitness in cortical thickness and mathematics achievement in Preadolescent Children. *PLoS ONE, 10*(9), e0138166. https://doi.org/10.1371/journal.pone.0138166

Chandradasa, M. & Rathnayake, L. (2019). Retained primitive reflexes in children, clinical implications and targeted home-based interventions.

Nursing Children and Young People, 32(1), 37–42. https://doi.org/10.7748/ncyp.2019.e1132

Cheatum, B.A. & Hammond, A.A. (2000). *Physical Activities for Improving Children's Learning and Behavior*. Human Kinetics, Champaign.

Chinello, A., Di Gangi, V. & Valenza, E. (2018). Persistent primary reflexes affect motor acts: Potential implications for autism spectrum disorder. *Research in Developmental Disabilities, 83*, 287–295. https://doi.org/10.1016/j.ridd.2016.07.010

Cicchetti, D., Toth, S. L. & Maughan, A. (2000). An ecological-transactional model of child maltreatment. In: A. J. Sameroff, M. Lewis & S. M. Miller (Eds.), *Handbook of Developmental Psychopathology*. Kluwer Academic/Plenum Publishers, New York.

Clarac, F. (2005). The History of Reflexes Part 1: From Descartes to Pavlov. *IBRO History of Neuroscience*. Retrieved July 15, 2023, from http://ibro.org/wp-content/uploads/2018/07/The-History-of-Reflexes-Part-1.pdf

Clarac, F. (2005). The History of Reflexes Part 2: From Sherrington to 2004. *IBRO History of Neuroscience*. Retrieved July 15, 2023, from http://ibro.org/wp-content/uploads/2018/07/The-History-of-Reflexes-Part-2.pdf

Cleveland Clinic. (n.d.). *Bedwetting (nocturnal enuresis): Diagnosis, tests, management and treatment*. Retrieved April 30, 2022, from https://my.clevelandclinic.org/health/diseases/15075-bedwetting

Csapó Á. (1991). A részleges érési zavar (MCD) szűrése és kivizsgálása ötéves korban. *Magyar Pediáter, 25*, 24–26.

Csépe V., Győri M. & Ragó A. (2007–2008). *Általános pszichológia*. Osiris, Budapest.

Csiszár O. (2011). *A nyelvi zavarok megjelenési formáinak és következményeinek vizsgálata* (dissertation). ELTE, Budapest.

Cumming, G. (2014). The New Statistics: Why and How. *Psychological Science, 25*(1), 7–29. https://doi.org/10.1177/0956797613504966

Damasceno, A., Delicio, A. M., Mazo, D. F. C., Zullo, J. F. D., Scherer, P., Ng, R. T. Y. & Damasceno, B. P. (2005). Primitive reflexes and cognitive function. *Arquivos De Neuro-Psiquiatria, 63*(3a), 577–582. https://doi.org/10.1590/s0004-282x2005000400004

Davis, E. E., Pitchford, N. J., Jaspan, T., McArthur, D. & Walker, D. (2010). Development of cognitive and motor function following cerebellar tumour injury sustained in early childhood. *Cortex, 46*(7), 919–932. https://doi.org/10.1016/j.cortex.2009.10.001

De Jager, M. (2009). *Mind Moves: Removing Barriers to Learning.* Metz Press, Cape Town.

de Quirds [sic], J. B. (1986). Diagnosis of Vestibular Disorders in the Learning Disabled. *Journal of Learning Disabilities, 9*(1), 39–47. https://doi.org/10.1177/002221947600900108

de Quirós, J. B. (1976). Significance of Some Therapies on Posture and Learning. *Academic Therapy, 11*(3), 261–270. https://doi.org/10.1177/105345127601100301

Di Paolo, E. & Thompson, E. (2014). The enactive approach. In: L. Shapiro (Ed.), *The Routledge Handbook of Embodied Cognition.* Routledge/Taylor & Francis Group, Abingdon, 68–78.

Diamond, A. (2000). Close interrelation of motor development and cognitive development and of the cerebellum and prefrontal cortex. *Child Development, 71*(1), 44–56. https://doi.org/10.1111/1467-8624.00117

Diamond, A. (2013). Executive functions. *Annual Review of Psychology, 64*(1), 135–168. https://doi.org/10.1146/annurev-psych-113011-143750

Diamond, A., Barnett, W. S., Thomas, J. & Munro, S. (2007). Preschool program improves cognitive control. *Science, 318*(5855), 1387–1388. https://doi.org/10.1126/science.1151148

Ditmar, M. F. (2011). Behavior and Development. In: R. A. Polin & M. F. Ditmar (Eds.), *Pediatric Secrets* (7th edition). Elsevier, Philadelphia, 43–80.

Dobbing, J. & Sands, J. (1973). Quantitative growth and development of human brain. *Archives of Disease in Childhood, 48*(10), 757–767. https://doi.org/10.1136%2Fadc.48.10.757

Doidge, N. (2010). *The Brain That Changes Itself: Stories of Personal Triumph from the Frontiers of Brain Science.* Scribe Publications, Brunswick, Vic.

Donáth T. (2008). *Anatómia-élettan.* Medicina Könyvkiadó, Budapest.

Dordel, S. & Breithecker, D. (2003). Bewegte Schule als Chance einer Förderung der Lern- und Leistungsfähigkeit. *Haltunk und Bewegung,* 23(2), 5–15. Retrieved April 26, 2023, from https://www.ssids.de/files/download/Bewegte_Schule-Dordel_Breithecker.pdf

Đorđić, V., Tubić, T. & Jakšić, D. (2016). The relationship between physical, motor, and intellectual development of preschool children. *Procedia - Social and Behavioral Sciences, 233,* 3–7. https://doi.org/10.1016/j.sbspro.2016.10.114

Dr. Kocsisné Kálló Veronika Györgyi, T. G. A. (n.d.). 2. A beszéd- és nyelvfejlődési zavarok okai | Nyelvfejlődési zavarok kognitív alapjai. Retrieved April 22, 2022, from www.jgypk.hu/mentorhalo/tananyag/Nyelvfejldsi_zavarok/2_a_beszds_nyelvfejldsi_zavarok_okai.html

Dwyer, T., Sallis, J. F., Blizzard, L., Lazarus, R. & Dean, K. (2001). Relation of Academic Performance to Physical Activity and Fitness in Children. *Pediatric Exercise Science, 13*(3), 225–237. https://doi.org/10.1123/pes.13.3.225

Eagleman, D. (2016). *The Brain: The Story of You.* Canongate Books, Edinburgh.

Eckhardt-Henn, A., Breuer, P., Thomalske, C., Hoffmann, S. & Hopf, H. (2003). Anxiety disorders and other psychiatric subgroups in patients complaining of dizziness. *Journal of Anxiety Disorders, 17*(4), 369–388. https://doi.org/10.1016/s0887-6185(02)00226-8

Ellenberger, H. F. (1970). *The Discovery of the Unconscious.* Basil Books, New York.

Elliott, J. G. & Gibbs, S. (2008). Does dyslexia exist? *Journal of Philosophy of Education, 42*(3–4), 475–491. https://doi.org/10.1111/j.1467-9752.2008.00653.x

Etnier, J., Salazar, W., Landers, D., Petruzzello, S., Han, M. & Nowell, P. (1997). The influence of physical fitness and exercise upon cognitive functioning: A meta-analysis. *Journal of Sport and Exercise Psychology, 19*(3), 249–277. https://doi.org/10.1123/jsep.19.3.249

European Commission (2018). *Country Report. Non Discrimination. Hungary 2018.* Retrieved July 15, 2023 from www.equalitylaw.eu/downloads/4749-hungary-country-report-non-discrimination-2018-pdf-2-60-mb

Fagiolini, M., Jensen, C. L. & Champagne, F. A. (2009). Epigenetic influences on brain development and plasticity. *Current Opinion in Neurobiology, 19*(2), 207–212. https://doi.org/10.1016%2Fj.conb.2009.05.009

Farmosi I. (1999). *Mozgásfejlődés.* Dialóg Campus, Budapest/Pécs.

Fearing, F. (1970). *Reflex Action: A Study in the History of Physiological Psychology* (2nd edition). MIT Press, Cambridge, MA.

Fetter, M. (2007). Vestibulo-Ocular Reflex. In: A. Straube & U. Büttner (Eds.), *Neuro-Ophthalmology: Neuronal Control of Eye Movements.* Karger Medical and Scientific Publishers, Basel, 35–51.

Fields, T., Diego, M. & Sanders, C. (2001). Exercise is positively related to adolescents' relationships and academics. *Adolescence, 36*(141), 105–110. PMID: 11407627

Fiorentino, M. (1981). *A Basis for Sensorimotor Development – Normal and Abnormal: The Influence of Primitive, Postural Reflexes on the Development and Distribution of Tone.* Springfield, IL: Charles C. Thomas Publisher.

Fletcher, J. M., Morris, R. D. & Lyon, G. R. (2006). Classification and definition of learning disabilities: An integrative perspective. In: H. L. Swanson, K. R. Harris & S. Graham (Eds.), *Handbook of Learning Disabilities.* Guilford Press, New York, 30–56.

Fogel, A. & Biederer, T. (2009). SynCAMs. In: L. R. Squire (Ed.), *Encyclopedia of Neuroscience.* Elsevier, Amsterdam, 823–828.

Fonyó A. (2011). *Az orvosi élettan tankönyve*. Medicina Könyvkiadó Zrt., Budapest.

Foster, M. & Sherringon, C. S. (1897). *A Text Book of Physiology*. Macmillan, London.

Franz, E. A. & Gillett, G. (2011). John Hughlings Jackson's evolutionary neurology: a unifying framework for cognitive neuroscience. *Brain, 134*(10), 3114–3120. https://doi.org/10.1093/brain/awr218

Freund T. (2005). *Lassú frekvenciájú agyhullámok és zajszűrés a hippocampusban*. Magyar Tudomány, 2005/1. Retrieved July 15, 2023 from www.matud.iif.hu/05jan/02.html

Fuchs, D. & Fuchs, L. (2006). Introduction to response to intervention: What, why, and how valid is it? *Reading Research Quarterly, 41*(1), 93–99. https://doi.org/10.1598/RRQ.41.1.4

Galant, S. (1917). *Der Rückgratreflex: Ein neuer Reflex im Säuglingsalter mit besonderer Berücksichtigung der anderen Reflexvorgänge bei den Säuglingen*. (Master's thesis, Basel, 1917). University of Basel, Basel.

Geers (n.d) Az emberi hallóképesség más élőlényekhez viszonyítva. Retrieved July 15, 2023, from www.geers.hu/blog/hallas-es-siketseg/az-emberi-hallokepesseg-mas-elolenyekhez-viszonyitva

Gesell, A. (1938). The tonic neck reflex in the human infant: morphogenetic and clinical significance. *The Journal of Pediatrics*, 13(4), 455–464. https://doi.org/10.1016/S0022-3476(38)80169-4

Ghanizadeh, A. (2011). Predictors of postural stability in children with ADHD. *Journal of Attention Disorders, 15*(7), 604–610. https://doi.org/10.1177/1087054710370936

Gieysztor, E. Z., Choińska, A. M. & Paprocka-Borowicz, M. (2018). Persistence of primitive reflexes and associated motor problems in healthy preschool children. *Archives of Medical Science, 14*(1), 167–173. https://doi.org/10.5114/aoms.2016.60503

Goddard, S. (2009). *Attention, Balance and Coordination: The A.B.C. of Learning Success*. Hoboken: John Wiley & Sons.

Goddard, S. (2015). *Reflexek, tanulás és viselkedés. Betekintés a gyermeki elmébe: A tanulási és magatartási problémák nem-invazív megoldása*. Medicina Könyvkiadó Zrt, Budapest.

Goddard, S., Duncombe, R., Preedy, P. & Gorely, T. (2021). Neuromotor readiness for school: the primitive reflex status of young children at the start and end of their first year at school in the United Kingdom. *Education 3-13*, 50(5), 654–667. https://doi.org/10.1080/03004279.2021.1895276

Gósy M. (1999). A beszédészlelés fejlődése. In: *Fejlesztő Pedagógia*. Különszám. Mentor-Szanator, Budapest, 54–62.

Gregory, S., Parker, B. & Thompson, P. (2012). Physical activity, cognitive function, and brain health: What is the role of exercise training in the prevention of dementia? *Brain Sciences*, *2*(4), 684–708. https://doi.org/10.3390/brainsci2040684

Grigg, T. (2018). *The influences of a primitive reflex integration programme within the classroom : teacher/parent perspectives and student results*. Thesis. University of Canterbury, Christchurch, New Zealand.

Grover, J. (2017, May 31). *How a retained primitive reflex in a child can be mistaken for ADHD or anxiety disorder*. In-tuned®. Retrieved April 30, 2022, from www.in-tunedchild.com/blog/2017/5/31/primitive-reflex-mistaken-for-adhd-or-anxiety-disorder

Grzywniak, C. (2017). Integration exercise programme for children with learning difficulties who have preserved vestigial primitive reflexes. *Acta Neuropsychologica*, *15*(3), 241–256. DOI:10.5604/01.3001.0010.5491

Guilford, J. P. (1971). *Nature of Human Intelligence*. McGraw-Hill, London.

Gyarmathy É. (1998). Tanulási zavarok szindróma a szakirodalomban. *Új Pedagógiai Szemle*, *43*(10), 59–68. Retrieved July 15, 2023, from https://epa.oszk.hu/00000/00035/00020/1998-10-lk-Gyarmathy-Tanulasi.html

Haapala, E. (2013). Cardiorespiratory fitness and motor skills in relation to cognition and academic performance in children – a review. *Journal of Human Kinetics, 36*, 55–68. https://doi.org/10.2478/hukin-2013-0006

Hamilton, S. (2002). Evaluation of clumsiness in children. *American Family Physician, 66*(8), 1435–1441. PMID: 12408418

Hammil, D. D. (1990). On Defining Learning Disabilities. *Journal of Learning Disabilities, 23*(2), 74–84. https://doi.org/10.1177/002221949002300201

Hámori, J. (1975). Az idegrendszer fejlődése és a mozgásszerveződés kölcsönhatása 6-18 éves korúaknál. In: *Tanulmányok az ifjúság testi neveléséről.* Sport, Budapest.

Head, H. [In conjunction with Rivers, W. H. R., Holmes, G., Sherren, J., Thompson, T. & Riddoch, G.] (1920). *Studies in Neurology.* Henry Frowde, Hodder and Stoughton, London.

Hickey, J. & Feldhacker, D. R. (2022). Primitive reflex retention and attention among preschool children. *Journal of Occupational Therapy, Schools, & Early Intervention, 15*(1), 1–13. https://doi.org/10.1080/19411243.2021.1910606

Hill, E. L. (2001). Non-specific nature of specific language impairment: a review of the literature with regard to concomitant motor impairments. *International Journal of Language and Communication Disorders, 36*(2), 149–171. DOI:10.1080/13682820010019874

Hillman, C. H., Erickson, K. I. & Kramer, A. F. (2008). Be smart, exercise your heart: Exercise effects on brain and cognition. *Nature Reviews Neuroscience, 9*(1), 58–65. https://doi.org/10.1038/nrn2298

Horváth Á. (2019). Propriocepció. In: *Tanulmányok az interocepcióról.* ELTE Eötvös Kiadó, Budapest, 103–122.

Hoskyn, M. & Swanson, H. L. (2000). Cognitive Processing of Low Achievers and Children with Reading Disabilities: A Selective Meta-Analytic Review of the Published Literature. *School Psychology Review, 29*(1), 102–119. https://doi.org/10.1080/02796015.2000.12086000

Huettig, C., Pyfer, J. & Auxter, D. (2001). *Gross Motor Activities for Young Children With Special Needs.* McGraw-Hill, Boston, MA.

Hutchins, J. B. & Barger, S. W. (1998). Why neurons die: Cell death in the nervous system. *The Anatomical Record, 253*(3), 79–90. https://doi.org/10.1002/(Sici)1097-0185(199806)253:3<79::Aid-Ar4>3.0.Co;2-9

Hyde, T. M., Goldberg, T. E., Egan, M. F., Lener, M. C. & Weinberger, D. R. (2007). Frontal release signs and cognition in people with schizophrenia, their siblings and healthy controls. *British Journal of Psychiatry, 191*(2), 120–125. https://doi.org/10.1192/bjp.bp.106.026773

Illingworth, R. S. (1987). *The Development of the Infant and Young Child: Normal and Abnormal.* Churchill Livingstone, London.

Interagency Committee on Learning Disabilities (1987). *Learning Disabilities: A Report to the U.S. Congress.* National Institutes of Health, Bethesda, MD.

International Dyslexia Association (2015, October 25). *Understanding dysgraphia.* Retrieved April 30, 2022, from https://dyslexiaida.org/understanding-dysgraphia

Iverson, J. (2010). Developing language in a developing body: The relationship between motor development and language development. *Journal of Child Language, 37*(2), 229–261. https://doi.org/10.1017%2FS0305000909990432

Jackson, H. (1884). Croonian Lectures: On the Evolution and Dissolution of the Nervous System. *The Lancet, 123*(3161), 555–558. https://doi.org/10.1016/s0140-6736(02)22511-8

Jacyna, L. S. (2011). Process and progress: John Hughlings Jackson's philosophy of science. *Brain, 134*(10), 3121–3126. https://doi.org/10.1093/brain/awr236

Jaiswal, M. & Morankar, R. (2017). Understanding Primitive Reflexes and Their Role In Growth And Development: A Review. *International Healthcare Research Journal, 1*(8), 243–247. https://doi.org/10.26440/ihrj/01_08/123

Joó J. G. (2012). A központi idegrendszer megismerésének fontosabb állomásai [The scientific history of the research of the human central nervous system]. *Orvosi Hetilap, 153*(6), 235–239. https://doi.org/10.1556/oh.2012.ho2386

Juhász, Á. (2007). *Logopédiai vizsgálatok kézikönyve.* Logopédia, Budapest.

Néma, J. (2016, September 23). Megsüketült testek – A propriocepció "wittgensteini" állapota. *Tétékás Nyúz, 53*(2) (online). Retrieved July 16, 2023, from http://nyuz.elte.hu/?p=1677

Katona, F. (2001). *"Az öntudat újraébredése": a humán idegrendszer ontogenesise.* Medicina, Budapest.

Katz, J., Stecker, N. A. & Henderson, D. (1992). *Central Auditory Processing: A Transdisciplinary View.* Mosby Year Book, St. Louis.

Kavale, K. A. & Forness, S. R. (2006). Learning disability as a discipline. In: H. L. Swanson, K. R. Harris & S. Graham (Eds.), *Handbook of Learning Disabilities.* Guilford Press, New York.

Kayani, S., Kiyani, T., Wang, J., Zagalaz Sanches, M. L. & Qurban, H. (2018). Physical Activity and Academic Performance: The Mediating Effect of Self-Esteem and Depression. *Sustainability, 10*(10), 3633. https://doi.org/10.3390/su10103633

Keef, K. D. & Co, C. A. (2019). Control of motility in the internal anal sphincter. *Journal of Neurogastroenterology and Motility*, *25*(2), 189–204. https://doi.org/10.5056/jnm18172

Kim, E., Fujita, T., Uno, H., Imashioya, H. & Iwaki, N. (2005). Error-Related Negativity in Children: Effect of an Observer. *Developmental Neuropsychology, 28*(3), 871–883. https://doi.org/10.1207/s15326942dn2803_7

Király T. & Szakály Z. (2011). *Mozgásfejlődés és a motorikus képességek fejlesztése gyermekkorban.* Dialóg Campus Kiadó, Budapest.

Kirk, S. A. (1962). *Educating Exceptional Children.* Boston, MA: Houghton Mifflin.

Kolb, B. & Gibb, R. (2011). Brain Plasticity and Behaviour in the Developing Brain. *Journal Of the Canadian Academy of Child and Adolescent Psychiatry, 20*(4), 265–276. PMID: 22114608

N. Kollár, K. & Szabó, É. (2004). *Pszichológia pedagógusoknak.* Osiris Kiadó, Budapest.

Konicarova, J. & Bob, P. (2013). Principle of Dissolution and Primitive Reflexes in ADHD. *Activitas Nervosa Superior, 55*(1–2), 74–78. https://doi.org/10.1007/bf03379598

Köteles, F. (2019). Interocepció és tudatosság. In: *Tanulmányok az interocepcióról.* ELTE Eötvös Kiadó, Budapest, 181–191.

Köteles, F. & Ferentzi, E. (2019). Interocepcio – a receptoroktól az agyig és vissza. Viszcerocepcio. In: *Tanulmányok az interocepcióról.* ELTE Eötvös Kiadó, Budapest, 19–91.

Kramer, A. F. & Erickson, K. I. (2007). Capitalizing on cortical plasticity: influence of physical activity on cognition and brain function. *Trends in Cognitive Sciences, 11*(8), 342–348. https://doi.org/10.1016/j.tics.2007.06.009

Kranowitz, C. S. & Miller, L. J. (2012). *Zűr-zavaros gyermek: Az érzékelési rendellenesség felismerése és kezelése.* Studio Nagy BT, Dunakeszi.

Kutzsche, S. (2020). Ernst Moro (1874–1951) was much more than the reflex that was named after him. *Acta Paediatrica, 110*(2), 400–403. https://doi.org/10.1111/apa.15504

Landau, A. (1923). Über Einen Tonischen Lagereflex Beim Älteren Säugling. *Klinische Wochenschrift, 2,* 1253–1255. https://doi.org/10.1007/BF01709671

László, Á.M. & Kóbor, Gy. (2009). *Beszédértés.* Ton-Ton, Budapest.

Lipkin, P. H. (2009). Motor Development and Dysfunction. In: W. B. Carey, A. C. Crocker, W. L. Coleman, E. Roy Elias & H. M. Feldman (Eds.), *Developmental-Behavioral Pediatrics* (4th edition). Saunders, Philadelphia, 643–652.

Luisier, A., Petitpierre, G., Ferdenzi, C., Clerc Bérod, A., Giboreau, A., Rouby, C. & Bensafi, M. (2015). Odor Perception in Children with Autism Spectrum Disorder and its Relationship to Food Neophobia. *Frontiers in Psychology, 6.* https://doi.org/10.3389/fpsyg.2015.01830

Máčaj, M. & Žovinec, E. (2013). Az agy fejlődését befolyásoló tényezők és a beszéd fejlődése. *Módszertani közlemények, SZTE Egyetemi Kiadványok, 53*(2), 1–5.

Magnus, R. (1924). *Korperstellung.* Springer, Berlin.

Malina, R. M., Bouchard, C. & Bar-Or, O. (2004). *Growth, Maturation and Physical Activity* (2nd edition). Human Kinetics, Champaign.

Mann, M. D. (2021). The nervous system in action. Retrieved July 15, 2023, from http://michaeldmann.net/The%20Nervous%20System%20In%20Action.html

Markham, C. H. (1987). Vestibular control of muscular tone and posture. *Canadian Journal of Neurological Sciences/Journal Canadien Des Sciences Neurologiques, 14*(S3), 493–496. https://doi.org/10.1017/s0317167100037975

Martin, R., Tigera, C., Denckla, M. B. & Mahone, E. M. (2010). Factor structure of paediatric timed motor examination and its relationship with IQ. *Developmental Medicine & Child Neurology, 52*(8), e188–e194. https://doi.org/10.1111%2Fj.1469-8749.2010.03670.x

Mather, D. S. (2003). Dyslexia and Dysgraphia: More Than Written Language Difficulties in Common. *Journal of Learning Disabilities, 36*(4), 307–317. https://doi.org/10.1177/00222194030360040301

McDonnell, M. N., Buckley, J. D., Opie, G. M., Ridding, M. C. & Semmler, J. G. (2013). A single bout of aerobic exercise promotes motor cortical neuroplasticity. *Journal of Applied Physiology, 114*(9), 1174–1182. https://doi.org/10.1152/japplphysiol.01378.2012

McEvoy, M. (1970). *The role of persistent primitive reflexes in learning difficulties: An evaluation of a new causal theory of dyslexia.* Dissertation. Trinity College, Dublin. Retrieved July 16, 2023, from www.tara.tcd.ie/handle/2262/79670

McGann, M. & Torrance, S. (2005). Doing it and meaning it: and the relationship between the two. In: R. D. Ellis & N. Newton (Eds.), *Consciousness & Emotion: Agency, Conscious Choice, and Selective Perception*. John Benjamins Publishing Company, Amsterdam, 181–195.

McPhillips, M., Hepper, P. G. & Mulhern, G. (2000). Effects of replicating primary-reflex movements on specific reading difficulties in children: a randomised, double-blind, controlled trial. *The Lancet, 12*(355), 537–541. https://doi.org/10.1016/S0140-6736(99)02179-0

McPhillips, M. & Jordan-Black, J. A. (2007). Primary reflex persistence in children with reading difficulties (dyslexia): A cross-sectional study. *Neuropsychologia, 45*(4), 748–754. https://doi.org/10.1016/j.neuropsychologia.2006.08.005

Meares, R. (1999). The Contribution of Hughlings Jackson to an Understanding of Dissociation. *American Journal of Psychiatry, 156* (12), 1850–1855. https://doi.org/10.1176/ajp.156.12.1850

Meggyesné Hosszu T. & Nagyné Hegedűs A. (2013). A tanulásban akadályozottak pedagógiájának komplex megközelítése. Retrieved July 16, 2023, from www.jgypk.hu/mentorhalo/tananyag/A_tanulasban_akadalyozottak

Melillo, R. (2011). Primitive Reflexes and Their Relationship to Delayed Cortical Maturation, Under Connectivity and Functional Disconnection in Childhood Neurobehavioral Disorders. *Functional Neurology, Rehabilitation, and Ergonomics, 1*(2), 279–314.

Melillo, R. (2015). *Disconnected Kids: The Groundbreaking Brain Balance Program for Children With Autism, ADHD, Dyslexia, and Other Neurological Disorders*. Perigee, New York.

Mesterházi, Zs. (1998). *A nehezen tanuló gyermekek iskolai nevelése*. Bárczi Gusztáv Gyógypedagógiai Tanárképző Főiskola, Budapest.

Mesterházi, Zs. (2019). A tanulási nehézségek típusai. In: Zs. Mesterházi & Á. Szekeres (Eds.), *A nehezen tanuló gyermekek iskolai nevelése: Egyetemi tankönyv a Gyógypedagógia szak Tanulásban akadályozottak pedagógiája szakirány számára*. ELTE Bárczi Gusztáv Gyógypedagógiai Kar, Budapest, 63–68, 88–92.

Mestre, T. & Lang, A. E. (2010). The grasp reflex: A symptom in need of treatment. *Movement Disorders, 25*(15), 2479–2485. https://doi.org/10.1002/mds.23059

Mohai K. (2013). *Szempontok Az Olvasási Zavarok Azonosításához És Differenciáldiagnosztikájához.* Dissertation. ELTE, Budapest.

Molnár, Z. (2004). Thomas Willis (1621–1675), the founder of clinical neuroscience. *Nature Reviews Neuroscience,* 5(4), 329–335. https://doi.org/10.1038/nrn1369

Montagu, A. (1986). *Touching: The Human Significance of the Skin.* Harper & Row, New York.

Moser, M. (2015, February 23). Időskori táplálkozás – tanácsok 65 év felettieknek [Nutrition for the elderly – advice for people over 65]. Semmelweis University. Retrieved July 15, 2023, from https://semmelweis.hu/mediasarok/2015/02/23/idoskori-taplalkozas-ovatosan-a-soval-es-a-cukorral

Nagy, E. (2021). *A baba első könyve: Vizuális élmény a babák látásfejlődéséhez.* Szalay Könyvek, Budapest.

Nahalka, I. (2002). *Hogyan alakul ki a tudás a gyerekekben: Konstruk tivizmus és pedagógia.* Nemzeti Tankönyvkiadó, Budapest, 84.

National Advisory Committee on Handicapped Children (1968). *Special Education for Handicapped Children* (First Annual Report). Department of Health, Education, & Welfare, Washington, DC.

National Institute of Mental Health (n.d.). *Autism spectrum disorder.* Retrieved April 30, 2022, from www.nimh.nih.gov/health/topics/autism-spectrum-disorders-asd

National Joint Committee for Learning Disabilities. (1981). *Learning Disabilities: Issues on Definition.* Unpublished manuscript. Available from Drake Duane, NJCLD Chairperson, c/o The Orton Dyslexia Society, 8415 Bellona Lane, Towson, Maryland 21204.

Nicolson, S. E., Chabon, B., Larsen, K. A., Kelly, S. E., Potter, A. W. & Stern, T. A. (2011). Primitive Reflexes Associated with Delirium: A Prospective Trial. *Psychosomatics*, *52*(6), 507–512. https://doi.org/10.1016/j.psym.2011.06.008

Niklasson, M. (2012). Could Motor Development Be an Emergent Property of Vestibular Stimulation and Primary Reflex Inhibition? A Tentative Approach to Sensorimotor Therapy. In: Shittiprapaporn, W. (Ed.), *Learning Disabilities*. InTech, Rijeka, 241–274.

Niklasson, M. (2013). The relation between postural movement and bilateral motor integration: Comment on Lin, et al. (2012). *Perceptual and Motor Skills*, *117*(2), 647–650. https://doi.org/10.2466/15.10.pms.117x23z9

Niklasson, M., Niklasson, I. & Norlander, T. (2010). Sensorimotor therapy: Physical and psychological regressions contribute to an improved kinesthetic and vestibular capacity in children and adolescents with motor difficulties and concentration problems. *Social Behavior and Personality: An International Journal*, *38*(3), 327–346. https://doi.org/10.2224/sbp.2010.38.3.327

Niskar, A. S., Kieszak, S. M., Holmes, A., Esteban, E., Rubin, C. & Brody, D. J. (1998). Prevalence of Hearing Loss Among Children 6 to 19 Years of Age. *JAMA*, *279*(14), 1071–1075. https://doi.org/10.1001/jama.279.14.1071

O'Connor Leppert, M. L., Shank, T. P., Shapiro, B. K. & Capute, A. J. (1998). The Capute scales: Cat/CLAMS—A pediatric assessment tool for the early detection of mental retardation and communicative disorders. *Mental Retardation and Developmental Disabilities Research Reviews*, *4*(1), 14–19. https://doi.org/10.1002/(SICI)1098-2779(1998)4:1<14::AID-MRDD4>3.0.CO;2-X

O'Halloran, C. J., Kinsella, G. J. & Storey, E. (2012). The cerebellum and neuropsychological functioning: a critical review. *Journal of Clinical and Experimental Neuropsychology*, *34*(1), 35–56. https://doi.org/10.1080/13803395.2011.614599

O'Regan, J. K. (2009). Sensorimotor approach to (phenomenal) consciousness. In: T. Baynes, A. Cleeremans & P. Wilken (Eds), *Oxford Companion to Consciousness*. Oxford University Press, Oxford, 588–593.

Ochsner, K. N. & Kosslyn, S. (Eds.). (2013). *The Oxford Handbook of Cognitive Neuroscience.* Volume 1. Oxford University Press, Oxford.

Odent, M. (2001). *The Scientification of Love.* Free Association Books, London.

Oláh. A. (2006). *Pszichológiai alapismeretek.* Bölcsész Konzorcium, Budapest.

Orbach, C. E. (1960). The Central Nervous System and Behavior: Translations from the Russian Medical Literature. *American Journal of Public Health and the Nations Health, 50*(12), 1963–1964. https://doi.org/10.2105/AJPH.50.12.1963-b

Ormainé Huba, J. & Erdélyi, P. (1984). Minimális agyi dysfunctió – mítosz vagy valóság. *Gyógypedagógiai Szemle, 12*(2), 86–91.

Pecuch, A., Gieysztor, E., Telenga, M., Wolańska, E., Kowal, M. & Paprocka-Borowicz, M. (2020). Primitive reflex activity in relation to the sensory profile in healthy preschool children. *International Journal of Environmental Research and Public Health, 17*(21), 8210. https://doi.org/10.3390/ijerph17218210

Pecuch, A., Gieysztor, E., Wolańska, E., Telenga, M. & Paprocka-Borowicz, M. (2021). Primitive reflex activity in relation to motor skills in healthy preschool children. *Brain Sciences, 11*(8), 967. https://doi.org/10.3390%2Fbrainsci11080967

Piaget, J. & Mérei, F. (1978). *Szimbólumképzés a gyermekkorban.* Gondolat, Budapest.

Pinczésné Palásthy, I. (2007). A kognitív funkciók zavarai. *Módszertani Közlemények, 47*(2), 49–50.

Pléh, Cs. (1999). Dennett "hozzáállásai" mint lehetséges rendezőelvek a pszichológiatörténetben. Presentation at the symposium "Dennett's Mind," March 23, 1999. JPTE, Pécs. Retrieved July 15, 2023, from www.c3.hu/scripta/scripta0/replika/36/06pleh.htm

Pléh, Cs. (2010). *A lélektan története.* Osiris, Budapest.

Pontifex, M. B., Raine, L. B., Johnson, C. R., Chaddock, L., Voss, M. W., Cohen, N. J., Kramer, A. F. & Hillman, C. H. (2011). Cardiorespiratory fitness and the flexible modulation of cognitive control in Preadolescent Children. *Journal of Cognitive Neuroscience, 23*(6), 1332–1345. https://doi.org/10.1162/jocn.2010.21528

Porkolábné Balogh, K. (1990). *Módszerek a tanulási zavarok csoportos szűrésére és korrekciójára.* Iskolapszichológia 17. ELTE, Budapest.

Porkolábné Balogh, K., Balázsné Szűcs, J., Szaitzné Gregorits, A. & Páli, J. (1996). *Komplex prevenciós óvodai program: kudarc nélkül az iskolában: óvodai fejlesztőprogram a tanulási zavarok megelőzésére.* Országos Közoktatási Intézet, Budapest.

Preston, J., Frost, S., Mencl, W., Fulbright, R., Landi, N., Grigorenko, E. & Pugh, K. (2010). Early and late talkers: School-age language, literacy and neurolinguistic differences. *Brain, 133*(8), 2185–2195. https://doi.org/10.1093/brain/awq163

Preyer, W. (1923). *Die Seele des Kindes [The Soul of the Child].* Th. Griebens Verlag, Leipzig.

Preyer, W. (2007). *The Mind of the Child, Part II.* [EBook, originally printed 1895. D. Appleton and Company, New York]. Retrieved July 16, 2023, from www.gutenberg.org/files/19549/19549-h/19549-h.htm#toc_47b

Prochaska, A., Clarac F., Loeb, G. E., Rothwell, J. C. & Wolpaw, J. R. (2000). What do reflex and voluntary mean? Modern views on an ancient debate. *Experimental Brain Research, 130*(4), 417–432. https://doi.org/10.1007/s002219900250

Prochaska, J. (1784). *De functionibus systematis nervosi: Commentatio.* W. Gerle, Prague.

Protevi, J. (2006). *A Dictionary of Continental Philosophy.* Yale University Press, New Haven, CT.

Purves, D., Augustine, G. J., Fitzpatrick, D., Hall, W. C., LaMantia, A.-S., McNamara, J. O. & Williams, S. M. (2008). *Neuroscience.* Sinauer, Sunderland, MA.

Pyfer, J. & Johnson, R. (1983). Factors affecting motor delays. In: R. L. Eason, T. L. Smith & F. Caron (Eds.), *Adapted Physical Activity*. Human Kinetics Publishers, Champaign, IL, 618–620.

Rašić Canevska, O. (2019). Persistence of primitive reflexes and associated problems in children. Годишен Зборник На Филозофскиот Факултет/ *The Annual of the Faculty of Philosophy in Skopje*, *72*, 513–522. https://doi.org/10.37510/godzbo1972513rc

Ratey, J. J. & Loehr, J. E. (2011). The positive impact of physical activity on cognition during adulthood: A review of underlying mechanisms, evidence and recommendations. *Reviews in the Neurosciences*, *22*(2), 171–185 https://doi.org/10.1515/rns.2011.017

Rentschler, M. (2008). The Masgutova Method of Neuro-Sensory-Motor and Reflex Integration: Key to Health, Development and Learning. In: S. Wenberg & M. Rentschler (Eds.), *Masgutova*. Retrieved July 16, 2023, from http://ekladata.com/bAsITI2Fy9Zarlub6yDSm1Oj4M8/article_Masgutova_Method.pdf

Reschly, D. J. (2005). Learning disabilities identification: Primary intervention, secondary intervention, and then what? *Journal of Learning Disabilities*, *38*(6), 510–515. https://doi.org/10.1177/00222194050380060601

Roberts, C., Freed, B. & McCarthy, W. (2010). Low aerobic fitness and obesity are associated with lower standardized test scores in children. *The Journal of Pediatrics*, *156*(5), 711–718.e1. https://doi.org/10.1016/j.jpeds.2009.11.039

Rókusfalvi P. (1972). *Általános lélektan*. Tankönyvkiadó, Budapest.

Rózsa, S., Nagybányai, O. & Oláh, A. (2006). *A pszichológiai mérés alapjai elmélet, módszer és gyakorlati alkalmazás*. Bölcsész Konzorcium, Budapest.

Sarlós, E. (2017). A szenzomotoros felmérésre épülő Fókuszált Szenzomotoros Tréning hatása a gyermekek tanulási képességeire a nagycsoportos óvodások körében. *VI. Interdiszciplináris Doktorandusz Konferencia 2017 Tanulmánykötet*. Pécsi Tudományegyetem Doktorandusz Önkormányzat, Pécs, 473–489.

Sarlós, E. (2018). Influence of sensorimotor exercises on learning abilities. *ICERI2018 Proceedings*, 10511–10518. https://doi.org/10.21125/iceri.2018.0983

Sarlós E. (2018). *Konferencia 2018/Conference 2018.* II. Nemzetközi Neuropedagógiai Konferencia, Budapest, 2021/International Conference on Neuroeducation II, Budapest, 2021. Retrieved September 26, 2021, from http://hatorszag.hu/conference_2018/

Sarlós, E. (2019). A szenzomotoros fejlesztés hatása a 4-8 éves gyerekek szenzomotoros fejlődésére, illetve az 5-8 éves gyermekek tanulási részképességeire. *A 16 éves PEME XIX. PhD - Konferenciájának előadásai.* Professzorok az Európai Magyarországért Egyesület, Budapest, 287–298.

Sarlós, E. (2019). The frequency of persistent baby reflexes which influence learning skills among children aged 4 to 8. *EDULEARN19 Proceedings*, 1217–1223. https://doi.org/10.21125/edulearn.2019.0377

Sarlós, E. (2020). The effect of sensorimotor training on the sensorimotor development of children aged 4-8 and on the learning abilities of children aged 5-8. *INTED2020 Proceedings*, 8047–8053. https://doi.org/10.21125/inted.2020.2189

Sarlós E. (2021). A szenzomotoros érettség és az auditív, vizuális részképességek közötti összefüggés az 5-8 éves gyerekek esetében. In: I. Koncz & I. Szova (Eds.), *Tizennyolc éve az európai Magyarország tudományos megújulása és a fiatal kutatók szolgálatában* (pp. 193–202).

Sarlós, E. (2021). Investigating the Association Between Retained Primitive Reflexes and Partial Visual Abilities in Children Aged 4–8 Years. In: *Proceedings of The 4th International Conference on Advanced Research in Education,* November 26–28, 2021, Oxford, UK, pp. 187–196. Retrieved July 16, 2023, from www.dpublication.com/wp-content/uploads/2021/11/080-739.pdf

Sarlós, E. (2021). To Investigate the Association between Vestibular Maturity and Partial Auditory Abilities in Children Aged 4-8 Years. In: *Proceedings of The 2nd Global Conference on Education and Teaching,* December 3–5, 2021, Athens, Greece, pp. 26–33. Retrieved July 16, 2023, from www.dpublication.com/wp-content/uploads/2021/11/02-756.pdf

Sečenov, I. M. & Koštoânc, H. S. (1954). *Az agy reflexei: kísérlet a pszichikai folyamatok fiziológiai magyarázatára*. Akadémiai, Budapest.

Sechenov, I. M. (1965) [originally published in 1863]. *Reflexes of the Brain*. MIT Press, Cambridge, MA.

Shaywitz, S. E., Shaywitz, J. E. & Shaywitz, B. A. (2021). Dyslexia in the 21st Century. *Current Opinion in Psychiatry, 34*(2), 80–86. https://doi.org/10.1097/yco.0000000000000670

Sherrington, C. S. (1906). *The Integrative Action of the Nervous System*. Yale University Press, New Haven, CT.

Sigafoos, J., Roche, L., O'Reilly, M. F. & Lancioni, G. E. (2021). Persistence of primitive reflexes in developmental disorders. *Current Developmental Disorders Reports, 8*, 98–105. https://doi.org/10.1007/s40474-021-00232-2

Sigmundsson, H. (2005). Disorders of motor development (clumsy child syndrome). In: W. W. Fleischhacker (Author), *Neurodevelopmental Disorders*. Springer, Vienna.

Sohn, M., Ahn, Y. & Lee, S. (2011). Assessment of Primitive Reflexes in High-risk Newborns. *Journal of Clinical Medicine Research, 3*(6), 285–290. https://doi.org/10.4021%2Fjocmr706w

Solve Learning Disabilities (n.d.). The Unlock Brilliance Way. Retrieved July 16, 2023, from www.solvelearningdisabilities.com/unlock-brilliance

Somisetty, S. & Das, J. M. Neuroanatomy, Vestibulo-ocular Reflex. [Updated 2022 Jul 25]. In: StatPearls [Internet]. Treasure Island (FL): StatPearls Publishing; 2023 Jan-. Retrieved July 16, 2023, from www.ncbi.nlm.nih.gov/books/NBK545297

Stanford Medicine Children's Health (n.d.). Age-Appropriate Speech and Language Milestones. Retrieved July 15, 2023, from www.stanfordchildrens.org/en/topic/default?id=age-appropriate-speech-and-language-milestones-90-P02170

Stuebing, K. K., Fletcher, J. M., LeDoux, J. M., Lyon, G. R., Shaywitz, S. E. & Shaywitz, B. A. (2002). Validity of IQ-Discrepancy Classifications of

Reading Disabilities: A Meta-Analysis. *American Educational Research Journal, 39*(2), 469–518. https://doi.org/10.3102/00028312039002469

Szántó, A. (2016). *Beszédfeldolgozási folyamatok változásai a fejlesztés függvényében.* Thesis. ELTE, Budapest, 65

Szecsenov, I. M. (1954). *Az agy reflexei.* Akadémia Kiadó, Budapest, 29–30.

Taylor, M., Houghton, S. & Chapman, E. (2004). Primitive reflexes and attention deficit/hyperactivity disorder: Developmental origins of classroom dysfunction. *International Journal of Special Education, 19*(1), 23–37.

Teicher, M. H., Samson, J. A., Tomoda, A., Ashy, M. & Andersen, S. L. (2006). Neurobiological and Behavioral Consequences of Exposure to Childhood Traumatic Stress. In: B. B. Arnetz & R. Ekman (Eds.), *Stress in Health and Disease*, WILEY-VCH Verlag GmbH & Co. KGaA, Weinheim, 180–195.

Tihanyi, B. (2019). Simogatás és bizsergés. In: *Tanulmányok az interocepcióról.* ELTE Eötvös Kiadó, Budapest, 133–150.

Tools To Grow. (2016, November 1). *Primitive motor reflexes & their impact on a child's function.* Retrieved July 16, 2023, from www.toolstogrowot.com/blog/2016/01/11/primitive-motor-reflexes-their-impact-on-a-childs-function

Touwen, B. C. L. (1984). Primitive reflexes - conceptional or semantic problem? In: H. F. R Prechtl (Ed.), *Continuity of Neural Functions From Prenatal to Postnatal Life.* J.B. Lippincott Co.

Trevo, R. (2009). Red Flags and Rules of Thumb: Sorting Out Developmental Delay. *A Pediatric Perspective, 18*(2), 1–5.

United States Office of Education (1976). *Education of Handicapped Children.* Federal Register, 41:52405. Government Printing Office, Washington, DC.

Vaughn, S., Linan-Thompson, S. & Hickman, P. (2003). Response to instruction as a means of identifying students with reading/learning disabilities. *Exceptional Children, 69*(4), 391–409. https://doi.org/10.1177/001440290306900401

Vellutino, F. R., Scanlon, D. M., Small, S. & Fanuele, D. P. (2006). Response to intervention as a vehicle for distinguishing between children with and without reading disabilities: Evidence for the role of kindergarten and first-grade interventions. *Journal of Learning Disabilities, 39*(2), 157–169. https://doi.org/10.1177/00222194060390020401

Voelcker-Rehage, C., Niemann, C., Hübner, L., Godde, B. & Winneke, A. H. (2016). Benefits of physical activity and fitness for lifelong cognitive and motor development—brain and behavior. In: M. Raab, P. Wylleman, R. Seiler, A.-M. Elbe & A. Hatzigeorgiadis (Eds.), *Sport and Exercise Psychology Research: From Theory to Practice*. Academic Press, London, 43–73.

Von Hofsten, C. & Rosander, K. (2018). The development of sensorimotor intelligence in infants. *Advances in Child Development and Behavior, 55*, 73–106. https://doi.org/10.1016/bs.acdb.2018.04.003

Wallace, B. & Lifshitz, J. (2016). Traumatic brain injury and vestibulo-ocular function: current challenges and future prospects. *Eye and Brain, 8*, 153–164. https://doi.org/10.2147/eb.s82670

Wang, S., Liu, H.-Y., Cheng, Y.-C. & Su, C.-H. (2021). Exercise dosage in reducing the risk of dementia development: Mode, duration, and intensity – A narrative review. *International Journal of Environmental Research and Public Health, 18*(24), 13331. https://doi.org/10.3390/ijerph182413331

Wassenberg, R., Feron, F. J., Kessels, A. G., Hendriksen, J. G., Kalff, A. C., Kroes, M., Hurks, P. P., Beeren, M., Jolles, J. & Vles, J. S. (2005). Relation between cognitive and motor performance in 5- to 6-year-old children: Results from a large-scale cross-sectional study. *Child Development, 76*(5), 1092–1103. https://doi.org/10.1111/j.1467-8624.2005.00899.x

Wepman, J., Cruickshank, W., Deutsch, C., Morency, A. & Strother, C. (1975). Learning disabilities. In N. Hobbs (Ed.), *Issues in the Classification of Children*. Volume 1. Jossey-Bass, San Francisco, 300–317.

Westendorp, M., Hartman, E., Houwen, S., Smith, J. & Visscher, C. (2011). The relationship between Gross Motor Skills and academic achievement in children with learning disabilities. *Research in Developmental Disabilities, 32*(6), 2773–2779. https://doi.org/10.1016/j.ridd.2011.05.032

Wiener-Vacher, S. R., Hamilton, D. A. & Wiener, S. I. (2013). Vestibular activity and cognitive development in children: Perspectives. *Frontiers in Integrative Neuroscience*, 7, 92. https://doi.org/10.3389/fnint.2013.00092

Yewchuk, C. & Lupart, J. (2000). Inclusive Education for Gifted Students with Disabilities. In: K. A. Heller, F. J. Mönks, R. Subotnik & Robert J. Sternberg (Eds.), *International Handbook of Giftedness and Talent*. 2nd edition. Pergamon, Oxford, 659–670.

Zafeiriou, D. I. (2004). Primitive reflexes and postural reactions in the neurodevelopmental examination. *Pediatric Neurology*, *31*(1), 1–8. https://doi.org/10.1016/j.pediatrneurol.2004.01.012

Zipfel, J. & Levitt, M. A. (2019). A patient with severe functional constipation, fecal impaction, and soiling. In: O. Nash, J. Choueiki & M. Levitt (Eds.), *Fecal Incontinence and Constipation in Children*. CRC Press, Boca Raton, 102–107.

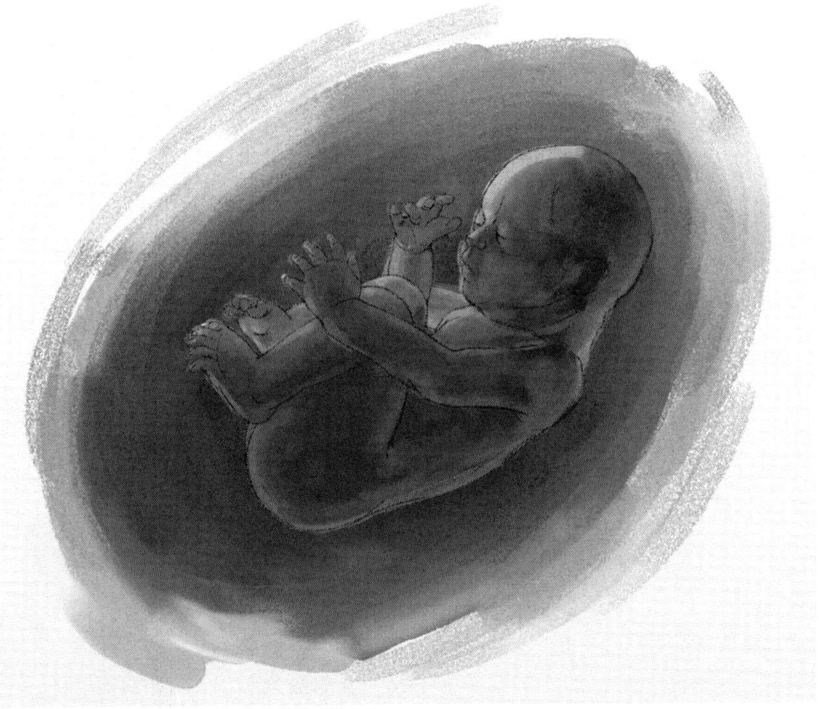

Printed in Great Britain
by Amazon

33677860R00231